THE
HANDY
TEXAS
ANSWER
BOOK

James L. Haley

Also from Visible Ink Press

The Handy Islam Answer Book
by John Renard, Ph.D.
ISBN: 978-1-57859-510-5

The Handy Law Answer Book
by David L. Hudson, Jr., J.D.
ISBN: 978-1-57859-217-3

The Handy Literature Answer Book
By Daniel S. Burt and Deborah G. Felder
ISBN: 978-1-57859-635-5

The Handy Math Answer Book, 2nd edition
by Patricia Barnes-Svarney and Thomas E.
  Svarney
ISBN: 978-1-57859-373-6

The Handy Military History Answer Book
by Samuel Willard Crompton
ISBN: 978-1-57859-509-9

The Handy Mythology Answer Book
by David A. Leeming, Ph.D.
ISBN: 978-1-57859-475-7

The Handy New York City Answer Book
by Chris Barsanti
ISBN: 978-1-57859-586-0

The Handy Nutrition Answer Book
by Patricia Barnes-Svarney and Thomas E.
  Svarney
ISBN: 978-1-57859-484-9

The Handy Ocean Answer Book
by Patricia Barnes-Svarney and Thomas E.
  Svarney
ISBN: 978-1-57859-063-6

The Handy Pennsylvania Answer Book
by Lawrence W. Baker
ISBN: 978-1-57859-610-2

The Handy Personal Finance Answer Book
by Paul A. Tucci
ISBN: 978-1-57859-322-4

The Handy Philosophy Answer Book
by Naomi Zack, Ph.D.
ISBN: 978-1-57859-226-5

The Handy Physics Answer Book,
  2nd edition
By Paul W. Zitzewitz, Ph.D.
ISBN: 978-1-57859-305-7

The Handy Presidents Answer Book,
  2nd edition
by David L. Hudson
ISB N: 978-1-57859-317-0

The Handy Psychology Answer Book,
  2nd edition
by Lisa J. Cohen, Ph.D.
ISBN: 978-1-57859-508-2

The Handy Religion Answer Book,
  2nd edition
by John Renard, Ph.D.
ISBN: 978-1-57859-379-8

The Handy Science Answer Book,
  th edition
by The Carnegie Library of Pittsburgh
ISBN: 978-1-57859-321-7

The Handy State-by-State Answer Book:
  Faces, Places, and Famous Dates for All
  Fifty States
by Samuel Willard Crompton
ISBN: 978-1-57859-565-5

The Handy Supreme Court Answer Book
by David L Hudson, Jr.
ISBN: 978-1-57859-196-1

The Handy Technology Answer Book
by Naomi E. Balaban and James Bobick
ISBN: 978-1-57859-563-1

The Handy Texas Answer Book
by James L. Haley
ISBN: 978-1-57859-634-8

The Handy Weather Answer Book,
  2nd edition
by Kevin S. Hile
ISBN: 978-1-57859-221-0

PLEASE VISIT THE "HANDY ANSWERS" SERIES
WEBSITE AT WWW.HANDYANSWERS.COM.

THE HANDY TEXAS ANSWER BOOK

Visible Ink Press®
43311 Joy Rd., #414
Canton, MI 48187–2075
Visible Ink Press is a registered trademark of Visible Ink Press LLC.

Most Visible Ink Press books are available at special quantity discounts when purchased in bulk by corporations, organizations, or groups. Customized printings, special imprints, messages, and excerpts can be produced to meet your needs. For more information, contact Special Markets Director, Visible Ink Press, www.visibleink.com, or 734–667–3211.

Managing Editor: Kevin S. Hile
Art Director: Mary Claire Krzewinski
Typesetting: Marco Divita
Proofreaders: Larry Baker and Shoshana Hurwitz
Indexer: Shoshana Hurwitz

Front cover images: Sam Houston (University of Texas at Austin Portrait Gallery), Dallas Cowboys football team (Billy Bob Bain), Texas flag and long horn steer (Shutterstock).

Back cover images: Shutterstock.

Library of Congress Cataloging–in–Publication Data

Names: Haley, James L., author.
Title: The handy Texas answer book / by James L. Haley.
Description: Canton, MI : Visible Ink Press, 2019. | Series: Handy answers | Identifiers: LCCN 2018041342 (print) | LCCN 2018042143 (ebook) | ISBN 9781578596829 (ebook) | ISBN 9781578596348 (pbk. : alk. paper)
Subjects: LCSH: Texas—Juvenile literature.
Classification: LCC F386.3 (ebook) | LCC F386.3 .H346 2019 (print) | DDC 976.4—dc23
LC record available at https://lccn.loc.gov/2018041342

10 9 8 7 6 5 4 3 2 1

Printed in the United States of America.

THE
HANDY
TEXAS
ANSWER
BOOK

James L. Haley

VISIBLE
INK
PRESS

Detroit

About the Author

James L. Haley is one of Texas's most distinguished historians. His first book, *The Buffalo War*, remains the definitive history of the last Indian war on the South Plains and has been in print for forty years. His biography *Sam Houston* won nine different awards, including the Tullis Prize of the Texas State Historical Association, the Spur Award of the Western Writers of America, and the Book Award of the Philosophical Society of Texas. His 650-page compendium of Texas history, *Passionate Nation*, won the T. R. Fehrenbach Book Award of the Texas Historical Commission. Most recently, after ghost writing the memoirs of famous Texas Ranger Joaquin Jackson, he completed a history of the Texas Supreme Court for the University of Texas Press, and his latest books are in the "Bliven Putnam Naval Adventure Series" for G. P. Putnam's Sons: *The Shores of Tripoli* (2016), *A Darker Sea* (2017), and the upcoming *The Devil in Paradise*.

Haley grew up in Fort Worth, graduated summa cum laude from the University of Texas at Arlington, and attended the UT School of Law in Austin. He resides in Austin, Texas.

Contents

Photo Sources

American Institute of Architects. Committee on the Environment, Top Ten Program: p. 165.

Chuck Andersen: 278.

Michael Barera: pp. 311, 340.

Bytor (Wikicommons): p. 61.

Walt Cisco, *Dallas Morning News,* p. 143.

Cmeide (Wikicommons): p. 21.

Coral Records: p. 336.

Ddal (Wikicommons): p. 222.

DTobias (Wikicommons): p. 17.

Federal Bureau of Investigation: p. 149.

Jay Godwin: p. 206.

Gail Hampshire: p. 224.

H. L. Hunt Press: p. 346.

Jason Helle: p. 288.

Independence National Historical Park Collection (Philadelphia, PA): p. 30.

Jillabus (Wikicommons): p. 12.

Jipwiki (Wikicommons): p. 188.

Jpo tx113 (Wikicommons: p. 23.

Elliot Landy: p. 146.

Library of Congress: pp. 85, 89, 98, 118, 123, 125, 128, 231, 268, 276, 296, 352.

Joe Mabel: p. 251.

Álvaro Montoro: p. 318.

Larry D. Moore: pp. 43, 287, 325.

Metro-Goldwyn-Mayer Studios: p. 332.

National Archives and Records Administration: pp. 16, 100, 211.

Paramount Pictures: p. 329.

Portal to Texas History: p. 109.

Andreas Praefcke: p. 253.

Clinton and Charles Robertson: p. 167.

Ed Schipul: p. 63.

Shutterstock: pp. 2, 7, 34, 104, 112, 137, 147, 154, 155, 158, 160, 162, 169, 172, 174, 175, 181, 186, 190, 192, 197, 204, 217, 219, 226, 228, 236, 238, 240, 243, 245, 247, 249, 256, 259, 262, 263, 265, 266, 274, 280, 285, 289, 293, 294, 302, 305, 308, 312, 313, 316, 332 (inset), 337, 342.

Kelly Teague: p. 179.

Texas State Library and Archives Commission: pp. 41, 93, 257.

John Trost: p. 119.

University of Houston: p. 140.

University of Oklahoma Press: p. 344.

U.S. Air Force: p. 326.

U.S. Army: p. 136.

U.S. Farm Security Administration: p. 81.

U.S. National Oceanic and Atmospheric Administration: pp. 131, 215.

U.S. Navy: p. 134.

Vami IV (Wikicommons): p. 303.

W. M. Vanderweyde: p. 322.

Steven Watson: 270.

Timeline

Year	Event
c. 14,000 B.C.E.	Proto-Indian flint quarries define Paleolithic Texas culture
1519 C.E.	Alonso de Piñeda maps Texas coast
November 6, 1528	Alvar Nuñex Cabeza de Vaca cast ashore on or near Galveston Island with eighty others; first Europeans to set foot in Texas.
April 22, 1540	Francisco Vázquez de Coronado mounts expedition that brings him through the Texas panhandle
May 21, 1542	Luís Moscoso de Alvarado enters Texas from the northeast, tortures Caddo Indians for information and directions; they steer him into central Texas to get rid of him.
April 29, 1554	Three Spanish treasure galleons carrying more than one million ducats in gold and silver sink in a storm off Padre Island
April 30, 1598	Juan de Oñate proclaims feast of Thanksgiving for having crossed the Chihuahuan Desert and reached the Paso del Norte; predates Massachusetts pilgrims by 23 years
February 18, 1685	René Robert Cavelier, Sieur de la Salle, lands French colonists near Matagorda Bay, staking a French claim to Texa
1685–1689	Spanish mount eleven different expeditions to discover whereabouts of rumored French incursion
April 22, 1689	Alonso de León discovers ruins of Fort St. Louis and bodies of its last French casualties, killed by Karankawa Indians
May 24, 1690	First mass said at first Spanish mission to Texas Indians, Mission San Francisco de los Tejas, near later site of Nacogdoches.
January 23, 1691	Domingo Terán de los Rios appointed first Governor of Coahuila y Tejas

Year	Event
July 18, 1714	French trader Louis Juchereau de St. Denis arrives at Mission San Juan Bautista
1718	Founding of first of San Antonio missions, later the city of San Antonio
March 9, 1731	Colonists from the Canary Islanders arrive at the San Antonio de Valero mission complex. They organize the Villa San Fernando de Béxar, the first civil government in Texas
May 15, 1755	City of Laredo founded
March 16, 1758	2,000 Comanche and other Indians attack Mission Santa Cruz de San Sabá, killing eight
October 7, 1759	Comanches and allies defeat Spanish under Diego Ortiz Parilla
March 21, 1801	Filibuster Philip Nolan killed in central Texas
August 8, 1812	Rebel Gutierrez-Magee Expedition enters Texas to liberate it from Spain in the Green Flag Rebellion
August 18, 1813	Battle of the Medina, royalist army under Joaquín de Arredondo decimates republican army and restores crown rule
1818	Pirate Jean Lafitte establishes buccaneer haven at Galveston, operates slave-running scam with Jim Bowie of Louisiana
1820	Moses Austin of Missouri seeks Spanish permission to establish American colonists in Texas
1821	Stephen F. Austin brings first American colonists into Mexican Texas
October 21, 1822	Banco Nacional de Tejas, first chartered bank west of the Mississippi, established, issues paper notes for military payroll
January 3, 1823	Austin succeeds in winning Mexican approval for his colony
December 16, 1826	Fredonian Rebellion breaks out in Nacogdoches
February 8, 1830	Last Texas missions secularized, ending 140 years of Franciscan mission work
April 6, 1830	Law of April 6 prohibits further immigration from the U.S.
June 26, 1832	Battle of Velasco almost starts Texas Revolution prematurely
1832	Convention of 1832
1833	Convention of 1833 sends Austin to Mexico City to petition for Mexican statehood for Texas separate from Coahuila
October 2, 1835	Texas Revolution opens with Battle of Gonzales
December 11, 1835	Mexican General Martín Perfecto de Cos surrenders San Antonio to Texas forces
December 27, 1835	First Masonic lodge meeting in Texas
March 2, 1836	Texas Declaration of Independence agreed to, signed the next day

Year	Event
March 6, 1836	Fall of the Alamo
March 27, 1836	Goliad Massacre, 400 Texas prisoners executed on Santa Anna's order
April 21, 1836	Battle of San Jacinto secures Texas independence
April 22, 1836	Capture of Mexican President Santa Anna near San Jacinto battlefield
October 22, 1836	Sam Houston inaugurated as first elected president of the Republic of Texas
August 19, 1837	Littleton Fowler, first Methodist missionary in Texas, arrives
December 5, 1837	Philosophical Society of Texas organizes in Houston, now the state's oldest learned society
May 6, 1838	Missionary Baptist Church organized near Nacogdoches, now Texas's oldest
July 16, 1839	Battle of the Neches drives Texas Cherokees out of the state
August 12, 1840	Texas Rangers, volunteers, and Tonkawa scouts defeat huge war party of Comanches at Battle of Plum Creek
June 1841	Santa Fé Expedition
February 11, 1842	Mutiny in Republic of Texas Navy
March 5, 1842	Mexican army invades Texas, briefly occupies San Antonio before retiring
March 25, 1842	Black Bean Episode
September 11, 1842	Mexican army invades Texas again, this time taking numerous hostages from San Antonio
September 3, 1844	Alsatian colonists under Henri Castro reach site of Castroville
July 4, 1845	Annexation Convention meets in Austin to consider the United States' offer to join the Union
December 29, 1845	U.S. Congress accepts Texas as the 28th state
February 00, 1846	Executive authority passes from the Republic of Texas to the United States
1850	Texas assumes its present shape under the Compromise of 1850
May 27, 1852	Invention of glass plate photography in Houston by J. H. Stephen Stanley
December 24, 1852	First Texas railroad goes into service, the Buffalo Bayou, Brazos & Colorado
January 5, 1854	Texas's first telegraph company chartered; office in Marshall connected to New Orleans and Natchez
1856	Capitol building, Governor's Mansion, and a General Land Office building all constructed in Austin, using settlement money

Year	Event
September 29, 1856	First Polish church in U.S. consecrated at Panna Maria
September 15, 1858	Butterfield Overland Mail stagecoach company begins service in Texas
December 28, 1859	Congregation Beth Israel established in Houston, now the oldest Jewish temple in Texas
September 13, 1860	Methodist minister Anthony Bewley of Burleson lynched in Fort Worth for suspected Unionist sympathies
February 1, 1861	Texas secedes from the Union and joins the Confederacy
July 24, 1861	2nd Texas mounted rifles capture Mesilla, adding Arizona to the Confederacy (briefly)
May 5, 1862	Mexican forces under Ignacio Zaragoza defeat French at Puebla; date becomes major Texas holiday
January 1, 1863	Confederate forces liberate Galveston from federal control
March 28, 1864	Guerrilla William Quantrill arrested in Bonham after terrorizing north Texas, escapes and flees into Indian Territory
January 8, 1865	Battle of Dove Creek makes hostiles of previously peaceful Kickapoo Indians
May 13, 1865	Battle of Palmito Ranch in South Texas is the last land battle of the Civil War. The fight is won by Texans under Ranger John Salmon "Rip" Ford.
May 17, 1865	Last Union POWs in Texas repatriated
June 19, 1865	Arrival of Union Gen. Gordon Granger, who proclaims freedom for Texas slaves, still celebrated as "Juneteenth."
September 20, 1865	Flight of spring-powered airship of Jacob Brodbeck of Luckenbach
March 22, 1866	First Texas convention for African American freedmen
August 20, 1866	Civil War officially ends with presidential declaration of peace between the U.S. and Texas
May 18, 1871	Warren Wagontrain Massacre
December 25, 1871	Railroad reaches Austin
1873	Wiley College established in Marshall, now the oldest black college west of the Mississippi
June 27, 1874	Hundreds of Plains Indians attack settlement of buffalo hunters at Adobe Walls, starting the Red River War
October 4, 1876	Opening of Texas A&M University, the first state college
July 19, 1878	Train robber Sam Bass mortally wounded in failed bank heist in Round Rock
July 29, 1878	National astronomers gather in Fort Worth to record total solar eclipse
February 6, 1879	First issue of first Czech-language newspaper in Texas

Year	Event
February 1, 1882	Construction begins on new state Capitol, the nation's largest
July 15, 1882	Texas Bar Association organized
August 2, 1882	Judge Roy Bean appointed justice of the peace in Pecos County
March 31, 1883	Cowboy labor strike in the panhandle
September 15, 1883	University of Texas opens
December 1, 1885	Debut of Dr. Pepper soft drink in Waco
July 22, 1887	First issue of Panhandle Herald newspaper, now the oldest in the panhandle
September 6, 1888	Jaybird-Woodpecker War, major Texas feud, erupts in Fort Bend County
October 5, 1889	Waco fundamentalists burn down Freethinkers Hall
March 10, 1890	Texas's first nursing school opens in Galveston
October 10, 1890	First gathering of Cowboy Camp Meeting, annual religious revival, near Fort Davis
October 14, 1890	Dwight D. Eisenhower born in Denison
November 3, 1891	Engineering marvel high bridge over the Pecos River opens
January 9, 1892	Texas Academy of Science founded at University of Texas
September 3, 1895	William Carrol Crawford, last surviving signer of the Texas Declaration of Independence, dies in Erath County, aged 90
February 21, 1896	Judge Roy Bean of Langtry dodges state and federal authorities to stage prize fight
May 25, 1896	First Texas meeting of the United Daughters of the Confederacy
1896	Texas Ranger Captain Bill McDonald arrives in Dallas to stop an illegal prize fight; origin of "One Riot, One Ranger" motto
June 17, 1897	First meeting of Texas State Historical Association
May 16, 1898	Lieutenant Colonel Theodore Roosevelt arrives in San Antonio to command 1st U.S. Volunteer Cavalry, the "Rough Riders," recruited among Texas cowboys
1900	Prohibitionist Carry Nation begins busting up saloons with her hatchet, including some in Texas
September 8, 1900	Hurricane destroys Galveston, killing 6,000 to 8,000 people, the worst natural disaster in U.S. history
January 10, 1901	Spindletop oil gusher
May 12, 1903	"The Eyes of Texas" first sung on University of Texas campus
1904	Inaccurate translating work results in Gregorio Cortez being falsely accused of theft, Cortez kills a sheriff defending himself
August 13, 1906	Brownsville melee blamed on black soldiers of 25th Infantry
November 12, 1906	Texas's first county agricultural agent hired in Tyler

Year	Event
December 29, 1909	Texas Folklore Society organized in Dallas
February 18, 1910	First airplane flight in Texas, in Houston
May 19, 1910	500-pound meteorite lands in northeast Texas during passage of Halley's Comet
April 17, 1911	U.S.S. *Texas* is launched, most powerful battleship yet built
April 24, 1911	Magnolia Petroleum Company established, later Mobil Oil
September 14, 1911	First Mexican-American civil rights conference, in Laredo
April 7, 1913	Sam Rayburn of Bonham enters U.S. House of Representatives, becomes Speaker 1940, dies in office 1961
September 22, 1913	Death of William P. Zuber, last survivor of the Battle of San Jacinto
December 8, 1914	Southwest Athletic Conference organized
October 11, 1915	Texas Woman's Fair opens in Houston
October 16, 1916	Pan American Round Table established in San Antonio
1917	Governor James E. Ferguson impeached, resigns
1918	Texas women permitted to vote in party primaries, two years before national suffrage.
July 11, 1919	Longview Race Riot
October 19, 1919	Texas League of Women Voters founded in San Antonio
June 30, 1922	First commercial country music recording, by Texas fiddler Eck Robertson
September 25, 1922	First radio broadcast in south Texas, WOAI in San Antonio
January 4, 1923	First country music radio show in the U.S. airs on WBAP in Fort Worth
January 1, 1925	Governor Pat Neff appoints a special term of the Texas Supreme Court, composed entirely of women
December 23, 1927	"Santa Claus" bank robbery in Cisco
December 4, 1928	Carl G. Cromwell strikes oil at 8,525 feet on U.T. oil land, world's deepest well at that time
January 17, 1929	National debut of Popeye, the Sailor Man, comic strip in *Victoria Advocate*
February 17, 1929	Founding of League of United Latin American Citizens (LULAC) in Corpus Christi
October 3, 1930	East Texas oil blows in with Daisy Bradford #3 well
October 26, 1930	First Cotton Bowl football game in Dallas; SMU beat Indiana 27–0
June 23, 1931	Texas aviator Wiley Post begins circumnavigation of the globe
September 22, 1931	Texas law limits acreage planted in cotton
April 14, 1933	Panhandle-Plains Museum opens in Canyon, first state museum in Texas

Year	Event
February 22, 1935	Transport of "hot" (unregulated) oil prohibited
March 9, 1936	Power line near Bartlett switched on, possibly the first power delivered by the Rural Electrification Administration
June 6, 1936	Texas Centennial Exposition opens in Dallas
November 9, 1936	Institute of Texas Letters organizes in Dallas
March 18, 1937	New London School explodes, killing 298, mostly children
1937	University of Texas completes a new main building, a thirty-story tower topped with a carillon and observation deck
May 29, 1939	Texas Soil Conservation Board formed to combat the "Dust Bowl"
September 1940	First performance by Kilgore Rangerettes
August 14, 1943	"Big Inch" pipeline completed, surging Texas oil to East coast refineries and avoiding German U-boats in the Gulf
January 26, 1945	Audie Murphy of Farmersville, most decorated soldier of World War II with thirty-three decorations, wins Medal of Honor
August 28, 1945	Medal of Honor posthumously awarded to Commander Samuel Dealey, most decorated sailor of World War II
September 27, 1948	First Texas television broadcast, WBAP in Fort Worth
July 11, 1949	Beauford T. Jester, only Texas governor to die in office, expires on a train in the arms of his mistress. Train is stopped, and she is thrown off.
October 24, 1952	Huston-Tillotson College founded in Austin by merging two previous, long-lived black colleges
November 14, 1954	Land fraud scandal breaks involving Texas Veterans Land Board
August 30, 1956	People and city of Mansfield defy federal court order to integrate schools
November 2, 1957	Hundreds of Texans in an around Levelland are alarmed at the sight of glowing blue UFOs
March 27, 1960	Discovery of Natural Bridge Caverns, largest in Texas
August 5, 1961	Amusement park Six Flags Over Texas opens in Arlington
September 11, 1961	Hurricane Carla flattens Corpus Christi, maintains its tropical characteristics north through Texas and into Oklahoma
November 1, 1961	Manned Spacecraft Center opens in Houston
June 28, 1962	Texas humorist John Henry Faulk wins libel suit over blacklisting
November 22, 1963	President John F. Kennedy is assassinated in Dallas
November 23, 1964	First successful coronary bypass surgery performed by Dr. Michael DeBakey in Houston
April 9, 1965	Astrodome opens in Houston, world's first enclosed, air-conditioned sports stadium

Year	Event
August 1, 1966	University of Texas Tower mass shooting kills 15 and wounds 31
April 6, 1968	HemisFair opens in San Antonio
April 8, 1968	Padre Island National Seashore dedicated
May 22, 1971	Dedication of LBJ Library in Austin, Texas's first presidential archive
June 18, 1971	First flight of Southwest Airlines
August 22, 1971	Racially integrated contemporary art exhibition opens in Houston
May 9, 1972	Garment workers in El Paso strike Farah, Inc., for right to unionize; action last twenty-two months until they win
June 1, 1972	First Kerrville Folk Festival
September 30, 1972	Guadalupe Mountains National Park established
June 3, 1973	Texas begins requiring bilingual education in primary schools
October 11, 1974	Big Thicket National Biological Preserve established
February 26, 1977	Texas farm workers march from Rio Grande to Austin for right to union representation
May 1, 1980	NBA awards franchise for the Dallas Mavericks
October 12, 1980	Texas songwriter Mickey Newbury inducted into Nashville Hall of Fame
April 19, 1983	Seventy-nine Branch Davidians are immolated in a fire at their compound at Mount Carmel near Waco
May 23, 1984	Mexican American Legal Defense Fund (MALDEF) files suit alleging that Texas school financing is discriminatory; they win
October 30, 1984	Five east Texas wilderness areas protected after lobbying free-for-all
February 19, 1988	Installation of first African-American Catholic bishop in Texas
August 27, 1990	Death of blues legend Stevie Ray Vaughan of Austin in a helicopter crash
March 31, 1995	Latina singing star Selena Quintanilla Perez murdered in Corpus Christi by her fan club's president
2009	Citizens in Andrews County, in the western panhandle, sitting atop the massive Ogallala Aquifer, vote 642–639 to use $75 million in bonds to construct low-level nuclear waste dump
February 2, 2013	Decorated Navy SEAL and sniper Chris Kyle is killed by a troubled veteran at a gun range in Erath County
April 2017	Proposal to add spent nuclear fuel to waste dump in Andrews County is suspended, owing to owner's financial straits

Introduction

Each of the fifty American states has its unique aspects, but seen from an international perspective no state is more recognizable, or brings its cultural associations so instantly to mind, than Texas. Even when reduced to parody, Texans, with their drawling accents, braggadocio, cattle ranchers and cowboys, tasteless *nouveau riche* produced by oil wealth, and conniving politicians and social climbers, have long been stereotyped, and not always humorously so. Such images barely scratch the surface of a state beneath which throbs a cultural and economic dynamo of staggering richness and diversity.

No other state can surpass Texas's geographical and biological diversity. From its stifling, alligator-infested swamps to its parched, trackless desert, and from a seacoast with the world's longest barrier island to its majestic high plains, its landscape provides unmatched biological and botanical variety; no other state embraces more than five thousand different species of wildflowers.

Texas maintained itself as an independent nation for ten years by force of arms and by diplomatic wiles. Within its borders lives an extravagant diversity of people: from native Indians and Spanish settlers who came in the wake of armored conquistadores to a frontier populated by English, Irish, French, Alsatians, Czechs, Poles, Swedes, and perhaps fifty thousand Germans. Because of its Spanish legal heritage, Texas was far ahead of other states in the rights of women, who could own land, operate businesses, and leave marriages with community property, which was unthinkable in older states established under the English Common Law.

Texas was the only state where the Old South met the Old West, where cotton farmers had to keep lookout against Indian attack. Its vast expanses of land contributed to its cultural legacy, including the cattle drives up the Chisolm Trail and the railroads and telegraph wires that snaked their way west and finally united its far-flung corners in time to join the rest of the country in the twentieth century.

Such a raw-boned, hard-bitten heritage gave Texas a unique presence in the modern United States. Texans have never backed down from a fight. No other state boasts a state police force to rival the Texas Rangers' history of being willing to "charge hell with a bucket of water." It was no accident that Teddy Roosevelt set up headquarters in San Antonio to recruit his Rough Riders from among Texas cowboys. Texas contributed more volunteers per capita in two world wars than any other state, including Audie Murphy, the most decorated soldier of World War II.

With their long history of tinkering and devising and making do, it is no surprise that Texans have contributed significant products and inventions to the American scene. From the ten-gallon hat to Fritos corn chips, and from Dr. Pepper to the electric typewriter and the silicon computer chip, such innovation has helped make the United States what it is today. From business empires to football dynasties, from actors to musicians to writers, Texans have left their bootprint on every aspect of American culture.

When introducing Texas in such a book as this—a rolling kaleidoscope of facts, figures, people, history, economy, quirks, and foibles—the object is to have fun. Encyclopedic completeness is not the goal. No people are quicker to take up for their own than Texans, and I can already foresee some small-town civic leader giving me grief for including the Sweetwater Rattlesnake Roundup while ignoring, say, his town's annual okra festival. (Well, rattlesnakes are rather more sexy as a topic than okra). One of the many sources I used, the *Handbook of Texas*, comprises six volumes, each of which is about twice the size of a classic *Encyclopedia Britannica*. The *Handbook* is a triumph of scholarship, but it cannot be enjoyed on a beach or in an airplane, and that was my job here.

People will also note that I did not dwell on negatives. I could have written about social injustice, school shootings, and the crooks, land shills, and ignoramuses in the gerrymandered legislature. They exist, and they are part of our daily reality, but they are not my subject here. Likewise, I have written Texana for more than forty years, which is long enough to know that one person's "fact" is often another person's "error," and it likely comes down to a difference of opinion as to what source is used or how data is measured.

Bottom line is that *The Handy Texas Answer Book* in intended as a broad introduction to the Lone Star State, a fun and informative look into a culturally and historically unique slice of the United States of America.

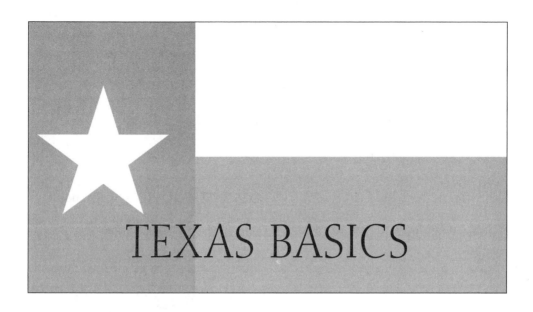

TEXAS BASICS

Where in the United States is Texas?

Texas dominates the south-central portion of the lower forty-eight states of the United States. It is bounded on the southwest by the Republic of Mexico, on the west by New Mexico, on the northwest by just a touch of Colorado, on the north by Oklahoma, on the northeast by just a bit of Arkansas, on the east by Louisiana, and on the south by the Gulf of Mexico.

What are its latitude and longitude?

Texas extends from longitude 93°31' west to 106°38' west; and from latitude 25°50' north to 36°30' north.

What are Texas's dimensions?

Texas's extreme dimensions are, north to south (from Dallam County in the upper northwest corner of the Panhandle to Cameron County and Brownsville in the south), 790 miles (1,271 kilometers). From east to west (from El Paso in the west to Newton County on the Louisiana border), it stretches 773 miles (1,244 kilometers).

Just how big is Texas?

From 1845 until 1959, Texas was by far the largest state in the Union. When Alaska was admitted, Texans had to endure a good deal of teasing for no longer being the biggest— which left Texans to counter that, at least, Texas was not frozen nine months of the year. Texas covers 268,581 square miles (432,239 square kilometers). Compared to other American states, it is about the same size as the sixteen smallest states combined. Or, looking west, it is larger than Washington, Oregon, and Idaho combined (with Maryland left over). On an international scale, it is about twice the size of Germany. As nations go, if it were independent again, it would rank fortieth in size, after Chile (292,258 square miles [470,344 square kilometers]) and Zambia (290,584 square miles [467,650 square kilometers]), and ahead of Myanmar (formerly Burma, 261,228 square miles [420,406 square kilometers]), Afghanistan (251,830 square miles [405,281 square kilometers]), and Somalia (246,199 square miles [396,219 square kilometers]).

Has Texas always been this size?

No. At the end of the Texas Revolution, Mexican president Antonio López de Santa Anna signed the Treaties of Velasco, recognizing Texas independence with the Rio Grande River as the boundary between them "from mouth to source." Although Mexico repudiated this treaty almost immediately, it gave Texas the claim to former Mexican territory east

Located in the south, central part of the United States, Texas borders Mexico and has a long shoreline along the Caribbean Ocean. It is surrounded by New Mexico, Oklahoma, Missouri, Arkansas, and Louisiana.

of the Rio Grande, which included much of the eastern area of the later states of New Mexico and Colorado and extended as far north as the Wind River Range of Wyoming.

What then accounts for Texas's odd shape?

When Texas joined the Union, its economy was based on cotton, which needed the labor of slaves, and slavery in the United States was already an extremely divisive political issue. Once statehood was effected, Texas commissioners traveled west and organized El Paso as a Texas county, which it still is. However, an American army had occupied Santa Fe in New Mexico during the Mexican–American War. Popular sentiment in Santa Fe was against Texas and slavery, and the army refused to allow its incorporation as a Texas county. Texas governor George P. Wood was furious and threatened to pull Texas right back out of the Union. The matter was settled as one element of the Compromise of 1850: Texas was allowed to keep El Paso, and it accepted ten million dollars to pay off its national debt in exchange for New Mexico and its claims further north. The northern boundary of the Panhandle was fixed at 36°30" north, the exact same latitude that U.S. law had long since fixed as the northern limit of slavery.

Where is Texas's geographical center?

The very center of the state is in McCulloch County, about 15 miles (24 kilometers) northwest of the town of Brady; 437 miles (703 kilometers) west to the Rio Grande beyond El Paso; 412 miles (663 kilometers) northwest to the corner of the Panhandle; 401 miles (645 kilometers) south to the Gulf of Mexico at Brownsville; and 341 miles (549 kilometers) east to the farthest bend of the Sabine River. The point was reckoned not by equal mileage to the state's extremities, but by dividing the state into equal areas, and the spot is noted by a marker on U.S. Highway 377, 2 miles (3 kilometers) south of Farm-to-Market Road 502.

How diverse is Texas's geography?

Because of Texas's size, it embraces an astonishing variety of landscapes. Extensive coastal beaches include Padre Island, at 113 miles (182 kilometers) the longest barrier island in the world. Inland from them, broad, coastal marshes provide critical habitat for species ranging from shrimp to game birds. The thick Piney Woods of East Texas are an extension of the vast Southern Woodlands and include a relict forest of the last Ice Age called the Big Thicket. The Rio Grande Jungle is the northern limit of the Central American rain forest, and the Trans-Pecos contains thousands of square miles of the Chihuahuan Desert. The state's highest point, Guadalupe Peak at 8,751 feet (2,667 meters), is in the Guadalupe Mountains, which is the southernmost spur of the Rockies. In the north, the table-flat Staked Plains and the Rolling Plains are the southern limit of the U.S. Great Plains. In the heart of the state lie 40,000 square miles (64,374 square kilometers) of limestone karst dotted with caverns and gigantic springs and occasional volcanic intrusions that include Enchanted Rock, the second-largest batholith in the United States. Its diversity is truly stunning.

When did Texas become a state?

As with many things about Texas, the answer is not simple. After nine years of effort and frustration, Texas finally won an offer from the U.S. Congress to join the Union in the spring of 1845. However, Texas was given only until the end of the year to draw up a state constitution, hold a popular referendum, and get word of the people's agreement to Washington. This Texas did with two days to spare, and on December 29, 1845, Congress accepted Texas as the twenty-eighth state—the broadly agreed date. However, executive powers did not formally transfer and the flag of the Republic was not lowered, until February 16, 1846. Either date is acceptable.

How many counties does Texas have?

There are 254 counties in Texas, more than in any other state. They range in population from about 4.6 million in Harris County, which contains most of the city of Houston, down to 113 souls in Loving County, in the west Texas oil patch. The smallest in area is Rockwall County, near Dallas, at 127 square miles (204 square kilometers); the largest is Brewster County in the Trans-Pecos, whose 6,192 square miles (9,965 square kilometers) is larger than Connecticut.

What is the origin of the state's famous "Lone Star" nickname?

The imagery of Texas as the Lone Star took hold during the Texas Revolution for independence from Mexico in 1836, but no one knows for certain how it originated. There are a number of possibilities. One of the stronger contenders is this one: When Santa Anna canceled the Mexican Constitution and assumed dictatorial powers, rebellions broke out in as many as eleven states. One of the most dangerous threats to him was the dual state of Coahuila y Tejas, and he sent an army to the state capital at Mónclova and broke up the legislature. Many Mexican federalists fled to Texas to continue the fight. The state's flag had been the Mexican tricolor featuring two stars in the central stripe and one each for its two components, Coahuila and Texas. After Coahuila fell, the Texas star was the only one left holding out the hope of a democratic government.

Has Texas always had the same state flag?

No. During the revolution, different volunteer groups fought under a variety of different flags. In the early days of the Republic, the Texas flag designed by President Sam Houston (1793–1863) was a gold Lone Star on a field of azure. He was succeeded by his hated rival Mirabeau Lamar (1798–1859), who opened his campaign to remove Houston's imprint on the government by redesigning it to its present white Lone Star on a red, white, and blue tricolor.

Why was this particular design of flag chosen?

Most likely, it was not just because Lamar wanted to erase Houston's impact on Texas, but here again, there are a number of possible reasons. One was that this design, seen from a distance, was almost identical to the flag of Chile (which had been adopted in 1817), and

Mexican warships still hostile to Texas would be reluctant to fire on vessels that might belong to a neutral country. And, of course, red, white, and blue were also the colors of the U.S. flag.

How did "Friendship" become the Texas motto?

Texans are famous for their hospitality, an ethic that became entrenched during frontier days, when traveling strangers often spent the night at roadside homes and were not usually allowed to offer payment. That fits the motto, but it is not the origin. In 1690, the first Spanish mission was established near the later site of Nacogdoches among the Tejas Indians, a name that meant "friend" or "ally." So, Texas actually does mean friend.

Does Texas have a state flower?

The legislature named the Texas bluebonnet as the state flower in 1901. *Lupinus texensis* is endemic to Texas, widely distributed, and became a cultural icon

The original Texas flag, which is known as the "Burnet flag" after interim President David Burnet, was the national flag from 1836 to 1839 (top; in color, it is a yellow star on azure). It was replaced in 1939 by what is now the state flag (bottom; in color, it has a white bar on top, red on bottom, and a white star on an azure background).

through the landscape paintings of Julian Onderdonk a century ago. Grayish-purple in dry years but an electric violet-blue with good rainfall, vast acreages of central Texas are carpeted with them in spring, usually peaking in mid-April, interspersed with scarlet spikes of Indian Paintbrush and the pale wash of Pink Evening Primrose. The sight of whole vistas of them is unforgettable. Since the 1960s, the Texas Highway Department has planted long stretches of right-of-way in bluebonnets, and their associated species both for their beauty and their effectiveness in erosion control.

Is "The Eyes of Texas" the state song?

No, it is the alma mater of the University of Texas, but so many people believe it is the state song that it has acquired a kind of informal standing. The actual state song is "Texas, Our Texas," which won three different competitions for the honor and was recognized by the legislature in 1929. The lyricist was Gladys Yoakum Wright (1891–1956), and the composer was William J. Marsh (1880–1971) of Fort Worth, who was a music professor at Texas Christian University, and who served as an organist and choir director at different congregations in the city. He was English, a naturalized U.S. citizen, and recycled the tune from a patriotic march he had written during World War I. He was a devout Catholic, and many of his other compositions were sacred in nature; "Texas, Our

5

Texas" bears an unnerving similarity to "God of Our Fathers," but John Philip Sousa, the "March King," praised it as the best state song he had ever heard.

TEXAS, OUR TEXAS

Texas, Our Texas! all hail the mighty State!
Texas, Our Texas! so wonderful, so great!
Boldest and grandest, withstanding ev'ry test
O Empire wide and glorious, you stand supremely blest.
(*Chorus*)

God bless you Texas! And keep you brave and strong,
That you may grow in power and worth, throughout the ages long.
God bless you Texas! And keep you brave and strong,
That you may grow in power and worth, throughout the ages long.
Texas, O Texas! Your freeborn single star,
Sends out its radiance to nations near and far,
Emblem of Freedom! it sets our hearts aglow,
With thoughts of San Jacinto and glorious Alamo.
(*Chorus*)

Texas, dear Texas! from tyrant grip now free,
Shines forth in splendor, your star of destiny!
Mother of heroes, we come your children true,
Proclaiming our allegiance, our faith, our love for you.
(*Chorus*)

What are other state symbols?

The pecan became the Texas State tree in 1919; the majestic trees, over 100 feet (30.5 meters) tall, can live for centuries, and Texas has long led the nation in production of native pecans, now augmented with bred varieties. The mockingbird, noted both for its peerless singing and for its fierce defense of its nest, was named the Texas State bird in 1927. That same year, the nine-banded armadillo became the state mammal.

In more recent years, various lobbying groups and industrial councils have leaned on the legislature to proclaim a silly number of additional state "symbols": a state stone and state gem (petrified palmwood and Texas blue topaz, both in 1969), a state dish (chili con carne, 1977), a state fish (Guadalupe bass, 1989), a state folk dance (square dance, 1991), a state reptile (horny toad, 1993), a state fruit (Texas ruby red grapefruit, 1993), a state insect (monarch butterfly, 1995), and a state plant (as opposed to tree or flower, prickly pear cactus, 1995). Also in 1995, the armadillo was particularized to the state small mammal to make way for the state large mammal, the Texas longhorn, and the state flying mammal, the Mexican free-tailed bat. Then came a state vegetable (sweet onion, 1997), a state snack (chips and salsa, 2003), a state dog breed (blue lacy, 2005), and a state cobbler (peach, 2013), not to be confused with a state pie (pecan, 2013).

Enjoy some of the official Texas state delicacies when you visit, including (clockwise from top left): chili con carne, salsa and chips, pecan pie, and peach cobbler!

POPULATION & DEMOGRAPHICS

What is Texas's population?

According to the Texas Department of Health and Human Services, Texas's estimated population in 2017 was 28,797,290, which ranks it behind California (39,506,094) to be the second most populous state in the United States and ahead of Florida (20,979,964), which recently overtook New York to become third.

What portion of the U.S. population is that?

Texas contains approximately 8.69 percent of the total U.S. population—as compared to California's 12.14 percent and Florida's 6.44 percent.

What is Texas's ethnic composition?

Anglo-Americans are no longer the majority race in Texas. There are 11,779,132 Anglos, which is 40.90 percent of the total; 11,804,795 people, or 40.99 percent of the total, identify themselves as Hispanic and 3,289,228 people, or 11.42 percent of the total, identify themselves as African American. "Other," which includes Asians of various nationalities, Native American Indians, etc., total 1,924,135 people, or 6.68 percent.

How accurate are these estimates?

The algorithms used to estimate population growth since the last census are quite sophisticated, but by definition, persons who are "undocumented" cannot be counted. As the United States continues to struggle to tighten its borders against illegal immigration, certainly several hundred thousand "indocumentados," at least, are already living off the books in Texas.

What is the population breakdown of urban vs. rural in Texas?

For many decades, Texas was preponderantly rural, and its economy was dominated by agriculture. Today, however, 25,566,822 Texans, or 88.78 percent, live within metropolitan areas, and only 3,230,468, or 11.22 percent, live in the country or in small towns.

What are Texas's major cities?

Twenty-six cities in Texas are large enough to have created Standard Metropolitan Statistical Areas. In descending order of metro population, they are:

Major Cities Ranked by Population

City	Population
Dallas–Fort Worth*	7,424,256
Houston	6,928,233
San Antonio	2,479, 874
Austin	2,112,172
McAllen	931,010
El Paso	908,421
Temple	474,838
Brownsville	466,790
Corpus Christi	457,971
Beaumont	423,300
Lubbock	315,568
Laredo	295,933
Amarillo	276,020
Waco	267,631
College Station	261,901
Longview	235,359
Tyler	232,478
Abilene	172,728

City	Population
Midland	157,536
Wichita Falls	153,706
Odessa	152,715
Sherman	129,680
San Angelo	115,222
Victoria	99,155
Texarkana	94,325

*Dallas Division = 4,942,676; Fort Worth Division = 2,481,580.

Populations within city limits are smaller than this, are they not?

Yes, but Texas still boasts of three cities among the ten largest in the United States. Giving city population estimates only (not metro), they are: Houston is fourth at 2,303,482, San Antonio is seventh at 1,492,510, and Dallas is ninth at 1,317,929. In addition, there are three more Texas cities in the top twenty: Austin is eleventh at 947,890, Fort Worth is sixteenth at 854,113, and El Paso is twentieth at 683,080. (California, by comparison, places four cities in the top twenty nationwide; other states have only one each).

EARLY TEXAS

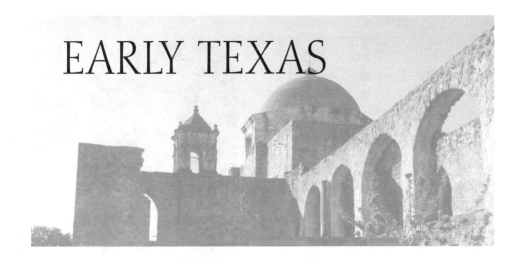

TEXAS'S NATIVE INDIANS

How long have native Indians lived in the area that became Texas?

Flint deposits along the Canadian River in the Texas Panhandle, now known as the Alibates Flint Quarries, have been exploited for weapons and tools since at least 11,000 BCE. For many years, the calibration of human habitation in North America was the Clovis culture, named for stone tools quarried near present-day Clovis, New Mexico, west of the Alibates site.

What is the Gault site?

Starting in 1929, a huge number of stone artifacts were dug willy-nilly from the farm of Henry Gault along Buttermilk Creek, near the town of Florence, some 40 miles (64 kilometers) north of Austin. He made extra money by turning it into a tourist pay-to-dig establishment. In 1998, professional archeologists took over the site and discovered that the Clovis artifacts lay atop layers of older artifacts. These discoveries pushed the estimated period of human occupation back at least another two thousand years and is still in flux. Proto-Indians are now believed to have lived in Texas for perhaps as long as twenty thousand years.

How many Indian tribes lived in the area that became Texas?

Altogether, the Spanish *conquistadores* named at least six hundred different groups of Indians in the land that became Texas. However, no one knows exactly how many tribes there were because those early explorers sometimes encountered the same groups but called them by different names, while others encountered different groups but called them by the same name. Later, many of the smaller groups were taken in by larger ones. Some tribes, such as the Jumano, simply disappeared, leaving scholars to wonder just who they were, while others who became well-known, such as the Comanche, arrived long after the Spanish. At the time of the Anglo-American arrival, the general boundaries between the major native groups had been set and were much more simplified.

Did any unbiased accounts survive of the native cultures?

Oddly enough, the very first European to find himself among Texas Indians, Álvar Núñez Cabeza de Vaca (1490–1559), who was shipwrecked in 1528, wrote a book in which his observations of native life, while colored by his own religious viewpoint, were surprisingly even-handed. He and his companions, who were eventually reduced to three in number, escaped from the Karankawa and spent years making their way back to New Spain and civilization. One tribe with whom they sojourned were

Located about 40 miles north of Austin, the Gault archeological site contains evidence of human habitation dating back sixteen thousand years.

functionally homosexual: warriors formed conjugal relationships with eunuchs, and they captured women and children from other bands to increase their number. Instead of dwelling on his shock and disgust, Cabeza de Vaca wrote that the eunuchs became very strong from their camp chores and "were capable of lifting heavy burdens." Today, his book is seldom read in detail, but in it, he bitterly denounced Spanish authorities and soldiers for brutalizing the natives in the name of Christianity.

Were any of the Texas Indians cannibals?

Scholars today typically de-emphasize, soft-peddle, or avoid this issue altogether. If cannibalism is acknowledged, it is usually framed in terms of its ritual or spiritual significance. The practice did have a ritual aspect but not in any polite sense of a communion wafer. Among a few tribes, there were orgiastic feasts upon the bodies of defeated enemies, while other tribes were horrified by such a thing. Early French traders from Louisiana witnessed Tejas Indians devouring the bodies of Hasinai (Caddo) enemies they had captured and tortured to death. As late as 1840, Texas Rangers were nonplussed at the sight of several Tonkawa who had scouted for them, roasting and eating several Comanche killed in the Battle of Plum Creek.

What were the main tribes with whom Americans first interacted?

By the time Anglo-American settlers came to Texas in 1821, the map of native Indian populations had become more simplified. The Woodland tribes in the southeast, who

Texas's iconic Indian tribes—Comanche and Apache—are so well known, is there any place to learn about the earlier Woodland cultures?

The Caddo people, which were an extensive nation of related tribes in the Piney Woods at the time of the Spanish arrival and lived as far west as Fort Worth in historic times, can be studied at the burial mounds and exhibits of the Caddo Mounds State Historic Site near Alto, just west of Nacogdoches.

were the recipients of the first mission, had been reduced to two, the Alabama and the Coushatta; others had moved away or been absorbed into the Cherokee, who were a recent arrival from the American southeast. The Caddo lived north of them. Along the coast, the Karankawa Indians were still a threat to American settlement, but they were defeated by 1840 and were absorbed into Coahuiltecan tribes further south. The Brazos Valley was occupied by a number of semisedentary plains tribes: the Waco, Keechi, Anadarko, Tawakoni, and Delaware, who were later immigrants. The Tonkawa generally lived northwest of them, buffering the Brazos Indian hunting grounds from the Comanche of the plains. Those two tribes avoided each other: the Tonkawa feared the Comanche because they were the fiercest warriors on the plains, and the Comanche were demoralized by the prospect of being eaten if they were killed or captured by the Tonkawa.

How did the Comanche come to dominate the plains?

The Comanche were an Uto-Aztecan tribe who had immigrated from the North Plains of the later Dakotas, having been defeated in fierce fighting with the Sioux, who were expanding out of Canada. Once in this new territory, they acquired the mastery of Spanish horses, which transformed them into a ferocious force of warriors, even more so after they acquired firearms. Americans came to call them the Lords of the South Plains.

Where did the Apache go after the Comanche drove them away?

The Apache were a large tribe, so far-flung that its eastern and western groups were only dimly aware of each other's existence. The Lipan Apache of the limestone hills west of San Antonio moved farther west into the eastern reaches of the Chihuahuan Desert. North of them, the Mescalero Apache vacated the plains and removed to the desert mountains of the Trans-Pecos and New Mexico. They eventually became the last Texan Indians to be militarily defeated by Americans.

Were the Comanche all of one tribe?

Yes, but they came to claim such a huge territory, from the Texas Hill Country north to the Staked Plains and east covering the Texas Rolling Plains and all of western Okla-

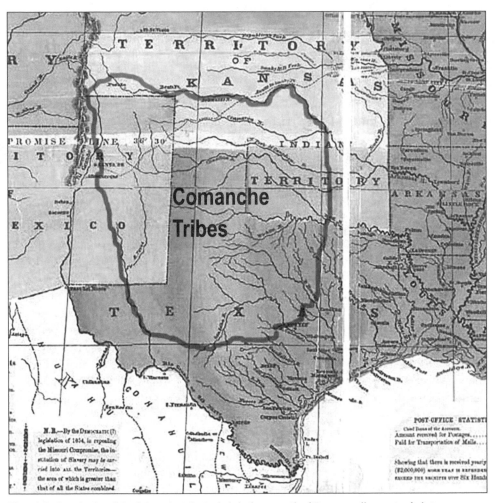

The original territories of the Comanche tribe included a large swath of Texas as well as parts of what are now the states of Colorado, Kansas, New Mexico, and Oklahoma.

homa, that several distinct bands evolved. Most familiar to the Spanish and then the Americans were the Penateka ("Honey Eaters") in the hills north and west of San Antonio. The fiercest and most aloof were the Quahadi ("Antelope") band of the Staked Plains. Of later importance to history were the Nokoni ("Wanderers") band because one of them, Quanah Parker (c. 1845–1911), became recognized as principal chief of all the Comanche bands and successfully transitioned from the frontier into the modern era.

Who were the other Plains tribes?

For many years, the Comanche fought another, smaller, tribe—the Kiowa—for access to the herds of buffalo upon which they both subsisted. That tribe had also been driven down from the north by the Sioux. In 1805, the Comanche and Kiowa made peace and confederated once they realized that there were plenty of buffalo for everybody. They became close allies and later shared a reservation. Those two continued to fight two other offshoots of Northern tribes who had been driven south—the Cheyenne and the Arapaho. In 1840 they all ceased fighting with each other for the same reason: there was no need to compete for buffalo when there were more than enough for all.

The Indians only killed what they could eat, didn't they?

That is rather a myth. They were not as wasteful as Anglo hide hunters, but the Indians cared more for efficiency than conservation. Riding alongside and firing arrows at running buffalo was dangerous. If they could maneuver a herd to a point where it could be stampeded over a cliff, called a "buffalo jump," they would do so. They would preserve as much meat and harvest as much hide and bone and sinew as they could carry away, but there was still considerable waste.

Since they spoke different languages, how did they communicate?

Plains Indians developed a sign language that became close to universally understood among the tribes. The sign for "Comanche," for instance, was to wiggle the hand while drawing it across the body—a snake going backward. After the American arrival, the language barrier was significant, and translators became indispensable in communicating with Indians. During the Republic, Jesse Chisholm (1806–1868), a nephew of Sam Houston's Cherokee wife, Diana Rogers, made a good living as a trader and interpreter because he spoke perhaps a dozen Indian languages.

How important were the buffalo to the Plains Indians?

Historians have noted how radically the Plains Indian culture changed after they acquired Spanish horses and even more, and more rapidly, after they acquired firearms from the Americans. Neither element was endemic to them, and once horses and guns led them to specialize in hunting buffalo during the nineteenth century, their very survival became tied to the survival, or destruction, of bison. An important Kiowa chief, Eagle Who Strikes with His Talons (c. 1835–1875), tried to explain to an Indian agent their importance to the Indians and also their resentment at the activity of American professional buffalo hunters: "The buffalo is our money. It is our only resource with which to buy what we need and do not receive from the government. The robes we can prepare and trade. We love them just as the white man does his money. Just as it makes a white man feel to have his money carried away, so it makes us feel to see others killing and stealing our buffaloes . . . which provide us meat to eat and means to get things to wear."

Why isn't this chief more well known?

He is better known by his more familiar name, Kicking Bird. Because of the ambiguities of translating from sign language, further muddied by the American penchant to give Indians unflattering names, their true meanings are sometimes not well known. Indian names could be powerfully evocative, but they were often lost in poor or even mocking translation. Kicking Bird's actual name, Tene-angop'te, meant Talons of the Striking Eagle. Another Kiowa chief became known in history books as Stumbling Bear when actually his name, Set-Imkia, meant Pushing, or Attacking, Bear. Another chief, a Comanche, became known as Gray Leggings when his true name, Asa-to-ya-teh, was Striding through the Dusk. Bowdlerization also played a role, as native names could be earthy and quite shocking to American sensibilities. An important Comanche medicine man of the 1870s, Isä-tai, was variously translated as Little Wolf, White Feather, and other names when in fact it meant Wolf Shit.

Chief Tene-angop'te (Talons of the Striking Eagle), known to white people as Chief Kicking Bird, was a leader of the Kiowa tribe. A great warrior, he was also noted for his peace efforts and as an advocate of education.

Why aren't there any Indian reservations in Texas?

There are, but they are quite small. During the ten years (1836–1845) of the Republic of Texas and during the period of frontier statehood, Anglo hostility to native Indians was such that all the tribes who had fought them—the Comanche, Kiowa, and Apache—were driven from within the boundaries to live with others of their tribes elsewhere. Also evicted were the Texas Cherokee, who despite decades of accommodation to the whites and despite the Anglos promising them secure land title if they would not side with Mexico in the revolution were driven out in the Cherokee War of 1839 because Anglo settlers were determined to take their land. Today, there are only two reservations in Texas, one at the Tigua Indian pueblo near El Paso and one at the Alabama-Coushatta Reservation north of Houston. The Alabama-Coushatta were always inoffensive, and their welfare enjoyed a measure of intercession from Sam Houston.

Who are the only Pueblo-dwelling Indians in Texas?

Traditionally associated with the large pueblos of New Mexico, the Tigua Indians migrated south from New Mexico after 1682 and established themselves south of the Paso del Norte. As a result of cultural dilution and their land being taken by whites, many assumed that the Tigua had passed into extinction, but they had not. They were finally recognized as a tribe in 1968 and their remaining lands declared a reservation—one of only two in Texas. Native history of the El Paso area is interpreted at the El Paso Museum of Archeology and its transformation since that time is covered at the El Paso Museum of History and with the El Paso County Historical Society.

THE SPANISH *ENTRADAS*

Who was the first European to see Texas?

After the voyages of Columbus began in 1492, the Spanish undertook further exploration in the New World. The first European to lay eyes on what later became Texas was a Spaniard, Alonso Álvarez de Piñeda (ca. 1494–1520), in 1519. He mapped the whole curve of the Gulf of Mexico farther south to the enclave of the conquistador, Hernán Cortés, at Villa Rica. There is no record that he sent parties ashore to find food and water, but he may have done so, and if he did, they were the first to step Western foot onto Texas. He did prove that the shore was of one continuous continent, for some had believed that Florida was an island.

Who was the first Western explorer in Texas?

The first Spaniard known to land in Texas was Álvar Núñez Cabeza de Vaca (1490–1559), who was shipwrecked and washed ashore on November 6, 1528, with about eighty other survivors of the incompetently led expedition of Pánfilo de Narváez. At first they were welcomed—sheltered and fed by Karankawa Indians who lived about the lagoons and barrier islands near today's Galveston. As the natives began dying of Western diseases against which they had no immunity, the guests became captives as the Karankawa enslaved and abused them. It took seven years for Cabeza de Vaca and a dwindling number of survivors to escape and make their way to the settlements in Mexico.

Why didn't the Karankawa just kill the Spaniards?

They thought about it, but these Indians had a surprisingly sophisticated system of justice. To debate executing them, they called a council, called a *mitote*, and the Spaniards were assigned one warrior to act as their defense counsel. He argued that if these strangers were indeed casting spells to kill the Indians, as they were accused, they would have spared themselves from disease, but they had died in equal numbers and therefore could not be guilty of deliberately bringing the misfortune.

What triggered the Spanish craze to explore Texas?

When Cabeza de Vaca returned to Spain, he uttered the magic word—gold—claim-

A bust of Spanish explorer Álvar Núñez Cabeza de Vaca can be visited at Hermann Park in Houston.

ing that he had seen walled cities, glinting in the sunlit distance, in the interior of New Spain. What he really saw were pueblos, but he awakened ancient Iberian legends of the Seven Cities of Cíbola, New World cities supposedly founded by Christian bishops who escaped the Moors by sailing west. These cities were said to have become so vastly wealthy that their streets were paved in gold. Spanish court was crowded with young adventurers eager to emulate the conquests of Cortés and make fortunes for themselves.

How could the Spanish believe such things about golden treasures?

Cortés had already looted a staggering fortune in gold and silver from the Aztec. Spanish ships brought back wondrous foods never before imagined, such as chocolate, and exotic birds and animals. After experiencing such things, in a time as credulous as the early sixteenth century, it was not a great leap to imagine cities paved with gold.

What was the first organized exploration into Texas?

In February 1540, Francisco Vázquez de Coronado (1510–1554) led a huge expedition north into the pueblo country and then east through the later Texas Panhandle. With him were a thousand men, with attendant cooks, servants, and camp followers, with a full complement of stock—a thousand horses to ride, five hundred cattle, and five thousand sheep to eat. He was the first European to see pueblos up close, with their walls not of gold but of mud. He pillaged several, and to get rid of him, the Pueblo Indians assured him there was gold further east and gave him a Pawnee Indian captive as a guide. Coronado penetrated as far as central Oklahoma and perhaps Kansas, where his Pawnee guide admitted under torture that his job was to get them lost. Coronado had him garroted and went home.

Didn't they encounter wild Texas longhorn cattle and hunt those?

No, but they were the first Europeans to discover buffalo, and not having a special name for them, they called them cattle. In fact, Coronado and the conquistadors who followed him made a practice of releasing some of their stock into the wild to increase and provide food for those who might follow. The sheep did not last long among the cougars and prairie wolves of the wilderness, but the cattle—a big, tough, raw-boned Andalusian breed with wicked, spreading horns—thrived in this new country and reproduced abundantly. So, in point of fact, the Spanish introduced the first longhorns into Texas, and by the time Anglo-Americans arrived, there were hundreds of thousands of them.

Were there other *entradas*?

Yes, but their number declined, as it became clear that Coronado was correct in concluding there was no gold to be found. In 1542 Luís de Moscoso Alvarado (1505–1551) entered later Texas from the northeast. He led the survivors of Hernando de Soto's Florida expedition afoot for more than three years, and they decided after de Soto's death to try to reach Mexico by continuing west overland. Seeking directions from various Indians, then torturing and killing them for getting them lost, Moscoso's expedition pen-

> ## How could the Spanish government afford Coronado's expedition?
>
> It couldn't, at least not at first. Spain's King Carlos was a notorious miser, and he gave preference to explorers who could finance their own expeditions and pay the crown a royalty—generally 20 percent, or the "Royal Fifth"—of whatever gold, silver, jewels, spices, and other treasure they plundered from the natives. Coronado married into money and used his wife's fortune to help fund his massive exploration.

etrated as far as the later vicinity of Waco before returning to the Mississippi. Other notable explorers included Antonio de Espejo (c. 1540–1585), who entered Texas in 1582, and Juan de Oñate (1550–1626), who discovered the Paso Norte access to the upper Rio Grande, later site of El Paso, in 1598.

Wasn't there any concern for the Indians' welfare?

Yes, there was. Despite what he had suffered at the hands of natives during his seven-year odyssey, Cabeza de Vaca protested Spanish abuse of the Indians in Mexico. Coronado was tried for cruelty to the natives, and as the frontier of New Spain extended to the northeast, others were held to account: Luís de Carvajal (c. 1539–1591), who in 1579 obtained a land grant that sprawled far north of the Rio Grande, was imprisoned and died there for enslaving Indians. Eleven years later, Nuevo León vice governor Gaspar Castaño de Sosa (c. 1550-c. 1593), who was known to deal brutally with Indians, led a large but unauthorized foray northeast. Troops overtook him and shipped him home in chains for invading the domain of peaceable natives. The Indians suffered much from European contact, but incidents such as these prompted the government to engage the church in tightening control over relations with natives.

FRENCH INTERLOPERS

What prompted the French to compete with the Spanish in the New World?

The voyages of Columbus triggered the whole Age of Exploration, and none of the European powers—British, French, Dutch, Portuguese—could miss the Spanish treasure galleons creaking home loaded with their cargoes of gold, silver, and emeralds (little of it from Texas, of course). By late in the seventeenth century, France had colonized Canada, and one of their explorers, René-Robert Cavelier, Sieur de la Salle (1643–1687), gave them a strong claim to the Mississippi River. With France and Spain often at war, establishing a major French colony at the mouth of the Mississippi would split the Spanish dominions in the New World and expand the French empire at Spanish expense.

Who was La Salle?

Born in Rouen to a rich merchant family, La Salle emigrated to Canada at twenty-two and quickly gained importance as a fur trading concessionaire and explorer. He discovered the Ohio River and gave France a strong claim to the Mississippi River basin by exploring its entire length down to the Gulf of Mexico. He named the vast territory Louisiana, to curry favor with King Louis XIV. La Salle's intrepidity as an explorer was unquestioned, but he was also arrogant, vindictive, and a practitioner of court intrigue. However, naming a third of a continent after the king got him noticed, and he was granted a fleet of four ships to return and establish his colony on the Gulf of Mexico. He sailed from La Rochelle on July 24, 1684, with three hundred colonists.

French explorer René-Robert Cavelier, Sieur de la Salle ventured all over North America from Canada and the Great Lakes to the Gulf Coast and the Mississippi River Valley.

What went wrong with La Salle's expedition?

Almost from the start, things with the voyage went disastrously awry. The captain of their thirty-six-gun escort, *Le Joly*, quarreled with La Salle and sailed so far ahead of them that Spanish pirates captured the small ketch *St. François*. Many volunteer colonists learned to despise him and deserted, forcing him to replace them with recruits rounded up in Saint-Domingue (now Haiti). His 300-ton (272,155-kilogram) supply ship *L'Amiable* ran aground entering Matagorda Bay and later sank. After a couple of months, *Le Joly* returned to France, carrying more French who thought better of the whole scheme. Leaving the coast where Spanish ships might spy on them, La Salle erected Fort St. Louis on Garcitas Creek, about 50 miles (80 kilometers) from where they landed. Crops failed, Indians turned hostile, disease ran rampant, and La Salle began undertaking months-long expeditions to find the Mississippi and help.

How could La Salle actually miss the Mississippi River?

It is worth remembering that La Salle was the explorer who had previously paddled down the whole length of the Mississippi from Canada to the Gulf. If anybody knew where it was, he did. It was also he who prepared the map erroneously showing the Mississippi emptying into the Gulf right next to the Rio Grande. There was also a mysterious passenger on his voyage, a mining engineer named Jean-Baptiste Minet. Most likely, the scheme was to deliberately sail past the Mississippi and land within striking distance of the Spanish silver mines in Mexico which, La Salle wrote, the Spanish were "too weak and effeminate" to hold in the face of their manly French conquest. If he meant to over-shoot the Mississippi, he probably did not mean to do so by 400 miles (644 kilometers).

Why was La Salle assassinated by his own men?

Quite apart from stranding them in a hostile wilderness, La Salle gave his colonists plenty of reasons to loathe him. According to the engineer Minet, who returned to France on *Le Joly* with several others who could not abide him any longer, the colonists nearly starved while La Salle reserved a private stock of meat and wine for himself and his favorites, he insulted and abused the Indians who had previously shown a friendly attitude, and he forced himself on some of his younger and more handsome men.

What happened to those French left at Fort St. Louis?

The Spanish inevitably learned that there were French interlopers afoot somewhere in the east of New Spain and sent out no fewer than eleven expeditions to find them—five by sea, one of which found a French shipwreck in Matagorda Bay, and six by land. On April 16, 1689, a column led by Governor Alonso de León (1639–1691) of Coahuila dis-covered the ruins of Fort St. Louis and the bodies of the last French holdouts, killed by Karankawa Indians three months before. De León recovered a few French children from their Indian captors, learning from them that after the number of survivors was reduced to about twenty, the Karankawa gained entry to the fort with signs of friendship and then carried out a massacre.

Which of La Salle's ships was later excavated for a vast time capsule of artifacts?

Of La Salle's squadron of four ships with which he left France, the 40-ton (36,287-kilo-gram) barque-longue supply vessel, *La Belle*, was the smallest. Only 54 feet (16 meters) long, 15 feet (4.6 meters) in the beam, and drawing 8 feet (2.4 meters) in draught, *La*

One of La Salle's ships, *La Belle* was excavated in 1995, and the hull of the vessel is on exhibit at Bullock Texas State History Museum in Austin, along with numerous artifacts. The official artifacts repository for the ship, however, is located at the Corpus Christi Museum of Science and History.

Belle was the last of La Salle's ships available for his colonists' use until it sank during a storm in Matagorda Bay. Discovered 310 years later in 1995, *La Belle* yielded more than a million artifacts, from cooking utensils to hawk bells and ax heads for trading to Indians, from carpentry and smelting hardware to firearms. The hull itself was excavated, preserved by chemical soaking and freeze-drying, and is now reassembled in the Bullock Texas State History Museum in Austin.

Was *La Belle* La Salle's flagship?

Although often described today as the flagship, *La Belle* was a minor vessel built from a kit that was intended to be assembled after reaching North America, as it was probably unsafe for an ocean crossing. However, after the loss of the larger *L'Amiable*, its salvaged cargo was transferred to *La Belle*, accounting for the extraordinary number of artifacts later discovered on such a tiny ship.

SPANISH MISSIONS

What was the Spanish response to the French incursion?

With other European powers showing interest in their vast New World empire, the Spanish realized that the only way they could enforce their claim to the country was to begin to settle it. To do so, and to protect and civilize the Indians, they adopted the method of establishing missions.

How did the mission system work?

During the late sixteenth century, events in Mexico prompted the government to recruit the church to protect and civilize the Indians. Each mission was meant to be a self-sustaining, closed community of resident natives, who received religious instruction from priests, learned trades, performed agricultural labor to feed themselves, and otherwise made progress toward becoming part of the European culture. They were to be protected from marauding hostile Indians by soldiers stationed at *presidios*, which were walled fortresses located near the missions, but not too near, to insulate the natives from abuse at the hands of soldiers, of which there was already a long history. The soldiers, their wives and children, and the families of the civilian workers would form the nucleus of a frontier community. Eventually, civilian settlement at these locations would strengthen Spain's claim to the territory, and the missions could eventually be "secularized" as the Indians were judged suitably integrated.

Who ran the missions?

Throughout Mexico, parish priests might come from any religious order, but the Texas missions were the responsibility of the Franciscans, the order established by St. Francis of Assisi in 1206. They were known for their piety and willingness to face danger, even martyrdom, challenge the privileged, and advocate for the poor.

A somewhat inexact replica of the Mission San Francisco de los Tejas can be visited at Mission Tejas State Park, near Weches in Houston County.

Where was the first Texas mission established?

After his expedition that discovered the remains of the French colony, Governor Alonso de León returned in March 1690 with four priests led by Father Damián Massanet and sufficient soldiers to leave a protective garrison. Massanet had accompanied de León on his previous journey and had made friendly contact with a chief of the Tejas Indians. To send a signal to the French that Spain would not be intimidated by their ambition, they passed La Salle's Fort St. Louis and continued another 200 miles (322 kilometers) east into the Tejas domain on the Trinity River in present-day Houston County. The first mass was held, commemorating the Feast of Corpus Christi, on May 24, 1690, at the new Mission San Francisco de los Tejas, near the present site of Nacogdoches.

How well did the priests and soldiers get along?

Not well. Massanet called his garrison commander an "incapable and undeserving old man." Priests and soldiers were different kinds of people pursuing different goals, but they were chained together by regulations that placed Indians in care of the church but gave most control over the location and maintenance of missions to the military command. The first mission folded in three years, as the Tejas turned hostile after epidemics of disease began killing them off.

How many missions were there in Texas?

Not counting numerous installations along the Rio Grande, whose influence extended into Texas, and Los Adaes, which was quickly abandoned back to Louisiana, twenty-six missions were founded within the future boundaries of Texas. Not all were active at the same time, and several underwent various adjustments to their location, so there was greater presence and activity than that number would suggest.

Was La Salle the last they saw of the French?

They thought it would be, for a while. Then on July 18, 1714, Louis Juchereau de St. Denis (1676–1744) showed up at the Mission San Juan Bautista (near the Rio Grande, about 35 miles [56 kilometers] downstream from the later site of Eagle Pass) with a load of trade goods to sell. He had traveled the entire width of Texas from Louisiana, and the Spanish were shocked. They arrested him but then learned an interesting story. The founder of the San Juan Bautista mission was Father Francisco Hidalgo (1659–1726), who had served with Father Massanet at the first mission to the Tejas in 1690. He grew increasingly frustrated with the Spanish government's lack of energy in Christianizing the Indians, so he took it upon himself to write to the governor of Louisiana, the Sieur de Cadillac, to ask his aid in maintaining a Christian eye over the east Texas Indians. Believing relations between their two countries to be in a friendly phase, it was Cadillac who had sent St. Denis to open trade.

What happened to St. Denis?

St. Denis used this period of his internment to court and marry Manuela Sánchez, the granddaughter of San Juan Bautista's garrison commander. He entered Spanish service and guided Father Hidalgo with seven priests, about twenty soldiers, and some thirty civilian settlers to reestablish the Tejas mission and further missions at the later sites

What was the "Chicken War"?

Europe at this time was a free-for-all of wars among the various powers, and colonial governments in the Western Hemisphere were always late in receiving news. Administrations in Louisiana and New Spain hardly knew how to act toward each other, because word of a fresh war, or peace, could arrive at any time. France was already annoyed with Spain for setting up their "capital" at Los Adaes, well inside Louisiana. When France entered upon the War of the Quadruple Alliance against Spain in 1719, an expeditionary force of seven—Lieutenant Philippe Blondel and six soldiers—captured Los Adaes, which was held by one soldier and a Catholic lay brother. Blondel also seized the Spaniards' chickens, which he tied to his saddle, but their fluttering and squawking caused his horse to throw him. In the confusion, the lay brother escaped into the forest and reached the nearest garrison at San Augustine. They sent for reinforcements but none came, and the Spanish abandoned the entire region and withdrew to San Antonio de Béxar. The French, therefore, had effectively conquered East Texas with an army of seven men.

of San Augustine and Nacogdoches. They then crossed the Sabine River and established the Mission San Miguel de Linares de los Adaes in what had to be French territory. St. Denis remained a colorful figure on the French–Spanish frontier for another twenty years. Back in French service, he was commandant of their outpost at Natchitoches and continued his activities as trader in times of peace, or smuggler, when there happened to be a war, and sometimes outbidding the Spanish for Indian loyalty. When he died in 1744, the viceroy was heard to sigh, "Thank God."

How did the native Indians respond to the mission effort?

That was a hit-and-miss proposition. Some Indians were willing to trade their labor at mission agriculture in exchange for subsistence, friendly relations, and more importantly, protection from marauding tribes such as the Apache and, later, Comanche. Missionary efforts accounted for much of further exploration of Texas in the late sixteenth and throughout the seventeenth centuries.

Who was the "Lady in Blue"?

In July 1629, some fifty Jumano Indians from the Rio Grande Valley walked almost as far as Albuquerque to request that missionaries be sent among them. The Spanish were astonished that the natives already knew the basics of the Christian faith, and, when they were asked how this happened, the Jumano said they had been instructed by the Lady in Blue. Inquiries were passed from the church in Mexico back to Spain, where authorities already knew of a Franciscan nun, Maria de Jesús de Agreda (1602–1665), from the Convent of the Immaculate Conception of the Poor Clares, who were the companion order to the Franciscans. The brown and white habit of this order was surmounted by a blue cloak. Sister Maria de Jesús had entered hundreds of trances, in which she said she found herself preaching the gospel to primitive people whom she could not identify. When missionaries arrived among the Jumano, some two thousand of them were baptized.

How well did the Spanish civilians answer the call to colonize Texas?

Seven of the soldiers who accompanied St. Denis back east took their wives with them, and they were the first Spanish women to settle in Texas. Traffic back and forth between San Juan Bautista and Los Adaes blazed a well-marked trail, El Camino Real, across Texas. The authorities decided to establish a provincial capital about halfway between the two and thus founded the Mission San Antonio de Valero (known later as the Alamo), soon followed by four more missions nearby, guarded by a presidio, in a scenic area of limestone hills and fulsome freshwater springs. Texas, however, attracted few civilians. The isolation from their homes in the Mexican interior, and the threat of hostile Indians, were just insuperable.

What is the "Oldest Town in Texas"?

As with many Texas brags, the boast of "Oldest Town in Texas" depends on where you start counting from. The present city dates from 1779, but only because the Spanish crown ordered the previous town abandoned seven years earlier in a strategic contraction of the frontier. The Nacogdoches mission dated from 1716. Nacogdoches began collecting a civilian population years before in San Antonio did in 1731. Key to the city's claim to be Texas's oldest, however, is that Nacogdoches did receive official designation as a *pueblo*, which would indeed make it the oldest official "town" in Texas.

How did the Spanish finally attract more settlers to Texas?

The crown began looking for settlers from places other than Mexico and resorted to a little bit of deception. They turned to the Canary Islands, a Spanish colony off the west coast of Africa, and offered those settlers land and the station of *hidalgos*—gentlemen—if they would relocate to Texas. Fifty-six people comprising fifteen families of Canary Islanders arrived at the San Antonio missions on March 9, 1731. Separately from missions or presidios, they organized the *villa* of San Fernando de Béxar, the first civil settlement in Texas. It became known as Béxar for short, and, eventually, San Antonio. The *Isleños* were shocked to discover that the hard frontier life was not what they were led to expect. They fell into bitter conflicts and filed Texas's first lawsuits against each other.

What was the most successful mission?

Mission San José y San Miguel de Aguayo, founded February 23, 1720, as one of the San Antonio mission complexes, had living quarters for 350 Indians built into its stone perimeter wall, fields irrigated by *acequias*, and a beautiful rose window illuminating the sacristy, all of which led it to be called the Queen of the Missions.

What mission failed over a sex scandal?

In July 1749, after much prompting by Central Texas Indians such as the Tonkawa, the church opened the Mission San Francisco Xavier de Nájera and two satellites on the San Gabriel River, more than 100 miles (161 kilometers) northeast of any oversight from San Antonio. The fifty-soldier garrison protected the installation from hostiles, but the priests were hard-put to protect the Indians from the presidio commander, Captain Felipe de Rábago y Teran (died c. 1769). He not only allowed his troops to have native women at will, he himself consorted with his tailor's wife, and upon being remonstrated with, tied his tailor to a cot and forced him to watch as Rábago ravished her. When the padres excommunicated the entire garrison in February 1751, most repented, but the mission was relocated when both the cuckolded husband and a priest who sheltered him were murdered. Rábago blamed the Indians, who fled in fear of reprisal, but his own guilt was all but certain. Mission activity was pulled back as far as the San Marcos River, which was closer to San Antonio's protective umbrella, and Rábago was reassigned and eventually cleared to command elsewhere.

Designated a World Heritage Site in 2015, Mission San José y San Miguel de Aguayo in San Antonio was the most successful of the Spanish missions in Texas.

How did Spanish Texans feel about the missionary efforts?

Spanish settlers about San Antonio complained bitterly that the padres favored the Indians by assigning them the most fertile land and best pasturage. For the most part, the government sided with the settlers and threw up obstacles to mission success. Texas's increasing number of wild cattle, for instance, were declared crown property, with a price of four *reales* to kill and butcher one—a cost enforced against mission padres, whose oath swore them to poverty. One governor, Carlos Benites Franquis de Lugo (1691–?), who took office in 1736, undermined the missions with such vindictiveness that the church managed to get him recalled the next year. In 1766 King Carlos III dispatched a fact finder, the Marqués de Rubí, who largely sided with the government and even charged that what little success the Texas missions attained owed to their importing tame Indians from the Mexican interior.

What was the San Sabá Massacre?

After some years of alliance with the Apache in fighting the Comanche, the Spanish learned that the Apache had been playing them for suckers. Four Apache chiefs came into San Antonio in August 1749 and requested that a mission be established in their home range on the San Sabá River, more than 100 miles (161 kilometers) northwest. The padres agreed;

27

the military was suspicious but, moved by hopes of finding gold and silver in that region, went along. It also helped that a silver magnate offered to fund the mission for three years if his cousin, Father Alonso Giraldo de Terreros (1699–1758), would lead it. Terreros held the post of guardian at the College of Querétaro and was a man whose zeal was a long time thorn in the viceroyal administration. What the Apache chiefs did not mention was that the Comanche had already driven them out of the San Sabá Valley. Furthermore, the Apache raided Comanche villages, leaving behind enough Spanish trade goods for the Comanche to know who was supplying them. On the morning of March 16, 1758, a shrieking horde of some two thousand Comanche with allies from many other tribes swarmed the Mission Santa Cruz de San Sabá. Father Terreros, three other priests, and five soldiers were killed as clerics barricaded themselves in an office. The Indians knew better than to try to storm the presidio, whose soldiers ventured out after the horde pounded away.

What was the worst defeat that the Spanish suffered at the hands of Indians?

Captain Diego Ortiz Parrilla (c. 1715–c. 1775), who had commanded the presidio at the San Sabá mission, undertook a large punitive expedition, doubly motivated after a second attack on his fort that killed twenty men, not with arrows but with French-supplied munitions. Late in summer 1759, he marched north with five hundred men, including (as they were not yet aware of the role the Apache played in the massacre) 130 Lipan. Early in October, he chased a small band of hostiles into the Red River bottoms, only to find he had ridden into an ambush—a favorite Indian tactic. The Indians had built a fort on the north bank of the river, flying a French flag, no less, and they cost Ortiz Parrilla fifty-two casualties. It was the worst defeat of the Spanish by Indians in Texas. Later, when the Spanish learned of the Apache' trickery, they fashioned an alliance with the Comanches and opened hostilities against the Apaches, a stance that lasted until the end of the frontier.

AMERICANS ARRIVE IN MEXICAN TEXAS

How successful were the Spanish at colonizing Texas?

The royal administration under Texas governor Domingo Cabello (c. 1725–?) conducted a census in 1783, after Spain had controlled the territory for a quarter of a millennium. They counted 2,819 people; 668 lived in and about the settlement of La Bahía near the coast (which later evolved into Victoria), while 349 lived in and about the eastern outpost of Nacogdoches. The greatest number clustered about the four missions of San Antonio de Béxar: 331 men, 311 women, 321 boys, and 284 girls, plus clergy. It was not a lot to show for 250 years of effort.

Why didn't more people move up from the Mexican interior?

Conditions in Texas had not substantially changed for centuries: it was still hundreds of miles from people's homes in Mexico, and in Texas, a lonely death from disease, accident, or hostile natives was a daily threat. Most people just were not interested.

What was the only ethnically Mexican land grant in Mexican Texas?

In the mad scramble by Anglo-American impresarios to obtain land grants from the new Mexican government, there was, ironically, only one Mexican citizen who joined the fray, Martín De León (1765–1833). Well connected and vastly wealthy, De León used his influence to win more generous terms than were offered to Anglo impresarios, including a lax definition of his colonial boundaries, and then preferential treatment in his disputes with neighboring colonies because he was a Mexican citizen and they were not. He dominated town councils with his extensive family of sons and sons-in-law and incurred Anglo hatred in other ways. De León died before the revolution broke out, but under the Republic, his family lost most of their Texas holdings despite their open opposition to Santa Anna. Nevertheless, his capital, Victoria (named for Mexico's first president, Guadalupe Victoria), survived and thrived. As one of Texas's oldest cities, there are eighty properties on a self-guided driving tour available from the Victoria Visitor Information Center.

What was the "Neutral Ground Agreement"?

The United States' purchase of Louisiana in 1803 altered the complexion of affairs on the Southwestern frontier. That always fuzzy line between New Spain and Louisiana now had to be settled but was sharply disputed. The United States claimed the Sabine River as the boundary, but the Spanish claimed it was the Arroyo Hondo, which was a third of the distance to the Mississippi. Spain sent troops under Simón de Herrera (1754–1813); the United States sent troops under General James Wilkinson (1757–1825), who was a shady character implicated in various schemes to pry Texas away from Spain but was now back in uniform. Facing each other in the middle of nowhere, they did something extraordinary: they agreed not to fight. "The subject of our test," Wilkinson wrote Herrera, "is scarcely worth the blood of one brave man." Wilkinson offered to pull his forces back to Natchitoches, if Herrera withdrew to Nacogdoches, to await a political settlement. Herrera answered Wilkinson that he was moved by "the peace-

Who were the filibusters?

As the United States grew in power and prestige, New Spain learned to keep a wary eye on its northeastern border. American adventurers began scheming to wrest Texas away from Spain and either add it to the United States or set up their own tin-horn republics. Collectively, they were known as filibusters. One of the most troublesome was Philip Nolan (1771–1801), who entered Texas four times starting in 1791 supposedly on "mustanging" expeditions to catch wild horses to sell in Louisiana but more likely to explore and map the country to facilitate a later invasion. He was killed by Spanish troops at a fort he and his men built, probably near the site of Hillsboro, on March 21, 1801.

ful ideas that possess you," and the two armies marched away from each other. Amazingly, both governments accepted the arrangement until the Sabine River was made the boundary as one provision of the Adams–Onís Treaty of 1819.

How did the Mexican Revolution take place in Texas?

The educated class in Latin America followed the American Revolution with the keenest interest, and ambition grew to establish republics independent of the Spanish crown. Insurrections started breaking out in 1810, from Argentina north to Mexico, where the *grito de Dolores* (cry of the city of Dolores) of Father Miguel Hidalgo y Costilla (1753–1811), in which he demanded justice for the poor, took place on September 16, 1810. On January 22, 1811,

A man of great disrepute, General James Wilkinson switched his loyalties a couple of times from America to Spain to Mexico.

Spanish governor Manuel María de Salcedo (1776–1813) was captured by a militia rebellion but was quickly restored in a countercoup.

What was the Green Flag Rebellion?

As this first phase of the revolution flickered out in Mexico (Hidalgo was executed on July 30, 1811), his confederate Bernardo Gutiérrez de Lara (1774–1841) continued the struggle in Texas, where it was known as the Green Flag Rebellion. He obtained some money and aid in Washington before recruiting a force of American volunteers and disaffected Spanish and invaded Texas from Louisiana on August 7, 1812. Under the green flag they adopted, by spring, they had captured Nacogdoches, La Bahía, and San Antonio and issued a Declaration of Independence (for Texas, under Republic of Mexico sovereignty) on April 6, 1813. Gutiérrez de Lara was quickly overthrown by his confederate, José Álvarez de Toledo y Dubois (1779–1858), who was more warmly embraced by their American advisers. Their republic was doomed by the failure of the broader Mexican Revolution.

What was the bloodiest battle ever fought on Texas soil?

To stamp out the last vestige of the 1810 revolution, the viceroy sent Joaquín de Arredondo (1768–1837), a field marshal and one of Spain's ablest commanders, to suppress the insurrection in Texas. He encamped his army of 1,830 men a few miles from San Antonio, and to spare the city the ravages of battle, Álvarez de Toledo marched south to meet him with 1,400 men. The Battle of Medina on August 18, 1813, resulted in fifty-five of Arredondo's soldiers dead, against more than a thousand of the rebels, although most of the principals escaped back to the United States to resume plotting against Spain. Arredondo proceeded to execute hundreds of persons he suspected of participating, or sympathizing, in the republican insurrection.

What makes James and Jane Long important to Texas?

Under the Adams–Onís Treaty, the United States was given Florida in exchange for giving up its specious claim to Texas. This outraged American expansionists, who undertook a new round of filibustering plots to conquer Texas on their own. Among them was the ever-busy General Wilkinson, who helped supply his niece's husband, James Long (1793–1822), with a ragtag army. They sortied from Point Bolivar opposite Galveston Island on September 19, 1821, and shortly captured La Bahía but were forced to surrender and were taken as prisoners to Mexico City. There, Long was murdered on April 8, 1822. He had left behind on Galveston Island his pregnant wife, Jane Wilkinson Long (1798–1880), with her slave, Kiamatia, to fend for themselves during the unusually cold winter of 1821–1822, constantly threatened by the Karankawa. On December 21, 1821, she gave birth to Mary James Long, for many years celebrated as the first American baby born in Texas. That was erroneous, but Jane Long's pluck, and her later return as a colonist, gave her fame as the "Mother of Texas."

How did American immigration into Texas get started?

Although the Spanish had claimed Texas for more than two hundred years, they never succeeded in convincing many of their people to move hundreds of miles from home to a land roamed by hostile Indians. Yet, they needed to strengthen their claim to the area to keep other imperial powers from taking it. In 1820, a bankrupt American businessman from Connecticut named Moses Austin (1761–1821) showed up in San Antonio with an offer to manage a colony of American settlers in Texas, who would all be Catholic and swear loyalty to Spain, in exchange for a suitable land grant for himself. The governor, now Antonio María Martínez (?–1823), ordered him out of town. After a more formal application, however, the royal government saw this as an efficient way to populate the area, make it productive, and also establish a barrier between themselves and Texas Indians.

What cadet in Arredondo's army later became infamous?

Nineteen-year-old cadet Antonio López de Santa Anna (1794–1876) was cited for bravery at the Battle of Medina. He scrutinized the effectiveness of Arredondo's mass summary executions, and adopted the same method to stamp out opposition to his own dictatorship twenty years later.

EUROPEAN IMMIGRATION INTO TEXAS

Who was the first German settler in Texas?

Johann Friedrich Ernst (1796–1848) arrived in Austin's colony in 1831, received a land grant, and founded the town of Industry in present-day Austin County. That was his assumed name, for he was really Christian Friedrich Dirks, who was on the run after embezzling ten years of receipts from the Duke of Oldenburg, whom he had served as postmaster. He struggled at first with the Texan notion of subsistence farming, but when he noticed that everyone used tobacco but no one grew it, his fortune was made. Further German immigrants sought him out for advice and assistance.

How did the massive German immigration get started?

Ernst wrote a letter home to family and friends, describing Texas almost literally as a land flowing with milk and honey and political freedom. In Germany this letter was widely published; it caused a sensation and opened a clamor for emigration to Texas. August Hoffmann von Fallersleben who later wrote the German national anthem, "Das Lied der Deutschen," penned a paean to this new beacon of hope and freedom, "The Star of Texas," which cost him his professorship and a ten–years' exile. Some of the more progressive German nobility, however, recognized an opportunity in all this discontent. Adolf, Duke

The Warhenberger House in Austin is a reminder of German immigration in Texas. The building served as a boarding school for the German-American Ladies College and also as a boys school for German immigrant families.

of Nassau, convened a conference of twenty other princes and dukes to meet at his palace in Wiesbaden. They agreed that if they sponsored an organized emigration program, the liberals, students, and radicals could be gotten out of the country and with leadership they would not disperse into the New World but would remain a distinct German community. Functionally then, if not in sovereignty, the German states would have one asset that they lacked, which England and France had long enjoyed: a colony, providing a market for German manufactured goods, and an abundant supply of agricultural products. Overpopulation, discontent, and imperial envy would all be solved at once.

Who was the Baron de Bastrop?

The "Baron" de Bastrop, for whom the city of Bastrop was named, was actually an alias of Felipe Enrique Nerí (1759–1827), which was the further alias of his real name, Bögel (pronounced "burgle"), which was singularly appropriate. He was a crooked Dutch tax collector on the lam with embezzled money from Guiana, remaking himself in Texas. A smooth con man, he had insinuated himself into San Antonio society and enjoyed the confidence of the best people. In perhaps the wildest coincidence in Texas history, he was also a past acquaintance of Moses Austin, whom he encountered wandering the plaza in dejection after Martínez rejected him. Bastrop used his influence, and his ability to draft an appropriately obsequious petition, to win approval for Austin's scheme and a future for himself as his land commissioner.

Where is Texas's oldest continuously operating dance hall?

The early German settlement of Gruene (which is pronounced "green," owing to Anglos' lack of facility with the German umlaut), is now a suburb of New Braunfels. Its Gruene Hall opened in 1878 and has never gone out of business. Unlike their impossibly (and often hypocritically) religious Anglo-American neighbors, the Germans happily brewed beer, pressed wine, and sought the good life. (In fact, the area's motto became

Where in Texas can one find a living history farm reflecting the German way of life?

Adjacent to the LBJ Ranch unit of the National Historic Park is a state park of the same name. A major part of it preserves the Sauer-Beckmann Living History Farm, named after the first two families (both German) who owned the farm and were neighbors of the Johnsons. There are three adjoining houses that were built as the families grew, and the farming continues by paid staff according to German traditions. Germans introduced sauerkraut to the Texas diet, which is made the traditional way and demonstrated to tourists, and inside, the houses feature German cultural elements such as "hair flowers," woven of locks of hair from deceased ancestors to keep their memory alive.

Gruene Hall in New Braunfels is the oldest operating dance hall in Texas.

In Neu Braunfels ist das Leben schön ("In New Braunfels, life is beautiful.") Apart from dancing, a big part of Gruene's current economy is outfitting, catering to canoers and tubers who float down the Guadalupe River from Canyon Dam.

What was the *Adelsverein*?

The princes subscribed a large sum of money to found the *Verein zum Schutze der Deutsche Einwanderer in Texas*, the Society for the Protection of German Immigrants in Texas, or, in short, the *Adelsverein*, the Society of Nobles. They bought Fisher's land grant; Carl Emich III, prince of Leiningen and half brother of Britain's Queen Victoria, was made president; and the operational director to lead the exodus was Prince Carl of Solms-Braunfels. Seven thousand Germans came in the first wave, settling mostly on their huge empresario grant in the Hill Country west of Austin—a number that grew to about fifty thousand during the following years.

Why would Prince Carl give up his vast castle and move to Texas?

It has not become part of the traditional Texas history narrative, but Carl, while he was a prince of Solms-Braunfels, was not *the* prince of Solms-Braunfels. In fact, he was a third son with no prospects, who had made a morganatic marriage and had three children with his commoner wife. The principality itself was also on the skids, having lost most of its sovereign powers in the consolidation of tiny German states that took place in 1806. After Carl's father drank himself to death in despair, it was Carl's formidable mother, Princess Frederica of Mecklenburg-Strelitz, who was a niece of Britain's Queen Charlotte, who set about rescuing the family. She remarried, to the Duke of Cumberland, knowing that she would become Queen of Hanover. The two of them forced Carl to abandon his morganatic wife and become engaged to Princess Sophie of Salm-Salm. Carl came to Texas partly to escape the family tyranny but also in hopes of establishing a cadet branch of the house of Solms with a new kingdom in the New World.

How did Texans react to this large, new foreign presence?

American travelers entering Texas from the east were barraged with stories of the Germans being lazy, venal, dishonest, and dirty. Only when they reached the German settlements did they discover that while the Americans seemed content in their log cabins, the Germans had built snug homes from the prevalent white limestone. The Americans warmed themselves and cooked at smoking fireplaces; the Germans had brought or made efficient stoves. The Americans consumed a daily diet of fried pork and cornbread; the Germans had dairies, orchards, smokehouses, and vegetable gardens. Within a few years, the hard-working Germans totally outstripped the American Texans in standard of living, and what was unforgivable, they did it without slaves. Hardly any self-respecting German who came to Texas seeking freedom for himself and his family would countenance owning another human being. Texans who had come from the South felt challenged, threatened, even a little ashamed, and they reacted with loathing.

How did the Germans maintain their identity and resist assimilation?

One large factor was their education. To American Texans, school meant reading, writing, and arithmetic learned in a one-room schoolhouse. The Germans came from a tradition of liberal education and included history, philosophy, music, rhetoric, even physical conditioning. They continued to enjoy their favorite sports, such as gymnastics and rolling ninepins, that did not appeal to Americans. Starting German-language newspa-

Is there really such a place as Luckenbach, Texas?

Although made famous only in the Waylon Jennings country-western song, the German settlement of Luckenbach really is at least as old as Fredericksburg, 13 miles (21 kilometers) to the west. The name is German for "Gap Creek," which runs nearby, but which is mistranslated as "Grape Creek." During the Civil War, it was home to schoolteacher Jacob Brodbeck (1821–1910), who sold stock in his flying machine company and actually got a contraption off the ground in 1865. (It is not counted as a successful heavier-than-air flight because it crashed.) Luckenbach is reached by taking FM 1376 south from US 290, but the turn-off is easy to miss because tourists keep stealing the sign with the town's name on it.

pers made it less urgent to learn English, and Germans led Texas in various areas of cultural advancement, including the first symphony orchestras and *Singverein*, or choral societies. Their physical isolation in the Hill Country also helped preserve their traditions.

What is the best museum to see the German experience in Texas?

Before Prince Carl of Solms-Braunfels led the first influx of Germans to Texas, his ambitious mother forced him to divorce his commoner wife and become engaged to a princess of his own rank, Sophie of Salm-Salm. For her, Carl hoped to establish the German nobility in Texas, and he planned a mighty fortress name for her called the Sophienburg in New Braunfels. Sophie, however, refused to leave Germany, and Carl had to return to marry her. That site now houses the Sophienburg Museum and Archives, with one of the best exhibits of social history in Texas, that displays German life right down to a fully stocked mercantile. Conservation Plaza preserves various historic homes built in *fachwerk* (grid of panels), as well as a music studio, a cabinet shop, and the Church Hill School, all of which evince the Germans' different approach to life from the Americans.

How did New Braunfels get its start?

By the time the first wave of several hundred German immigrants arrived in Texas late in 1844, the finances of their supervising *Mainzer Adelsverein at Biebrich am Rhein* (Society for the Protection of German Immigrants in Texas) were in disarray. Prince Carl of Solms-Braunfels was not a good manager, and the society's funds were spent as the Germans started their trek inland to their land grant. Exhausted and starving, hundreds of them died along the trail inland. To give the immigrants a chance to rest and

How much of the old German culture still continues in the old colonial Texas capital?

Once named best small town in Texas in a survey by *Texas Monthly*, Fredericksburg is devoted to maintaining its street atmosphere of *Gemütlichkeit*, a festive friendliness that well serves its dependence on the tourist industry. The area's history is presented in the Pioneer Library, and the Pioneer Museum includes an 1847 house and, notably, bathhouse, showcasing one large difference between life among the early Germans and the Anglo-Americans. One prevalent aspect of early life was the custom of the "Sunday House." Farmers from the outlying hills would maintain small cottages so that they could come into town on Saturday, take care of their marketing and business, visit friends, and stay over for church on Sunday before returning home. Many of these Sunday houses still stand. Fredericksburg's visitors center is housed in the Vereins Kirche, a reconstruction of the octagonal church that was the center of nineteenth-century community life.

plant crops, Carl purchased 1,100 acres (4.5 square kilometers), including Comal Springs, about 30 miles (48 kilometers) northeast of San Antonio. He named the settlement New Braunfels after his home state in western Germany. The first arrivals came in March 1845 and began building homes and planting.

Why on earth was a Texas settlement called "Nederland"?

Nederland is not nearly as old as the colonial, Republic, or antebellum-era towns in southeast Texas. In fact, it was not settled until 1897. When the Kansas City Southern Railroad constructed its line from Kansas City to the Gulf at Sabine Pass, it was done largely with Dutch financing. Arthur Stilwell, who built the line, gave Dutch names to new towns that he fostered along the route, and "Nederland" is the Dutch name for the Netherlands. Part of the payment scheme to repay this financing was to provide Dutch immigrants a place to live in lowlands that would remind them of home. There remains a strong Dutch influence in Nederland today and, Holland being famous for its windmills, their culture can be enjoyed at the Dutch Windmill Museum.

Where did Danish immigrants settle in Texas?

While the Germans were the most numerous, the allure of Texas spread throughout Europe, and people of many countries packed up and came looking for a better life. The town of Danevang (the name meant "Danish Fields") hosted many of those from Denmark. That history is displayed in the Danish Heritage Preservation Society museum complex.

In addition to immigrants from the American South and abroad, were there not also a number of French descendants from southern Louisiana?

Yes, a number of French Acadians came from Louisiana, but most of them did not come far and, like the Dutch, they remained in a country that reminded them of home, in the marshes and cypress bayous just across the Sabine River. Nederland, in the southeast corner of the state, preserves their history in the La Maison des Acadiens Museum.

What is the oldest permanent Polish settlement in the United States?

As word spread through the various German states (there was no unified Germany yet) that people were organizing to leave for a new life in Texas, Polish priest Leopold Moczygemba (1824–1891) began recruiting colonists in Upper Silesia, which was ethnically Polish but politically part of Prussia. His settlers arrived on the Texas coast in December 1854; there was no transportation to take them inland, so they walked to their land grant in Karnes County, 55 miles (89 kilometers) southeast of San Antonio. They named their settlement Panna Maria (Polish for "Virgin Mary") and did not assimilate into the dominant culture. They were Unionists and banded together as protection against rebel vigilantes and had a strong religious network, with Polish priests and their own schools taught by Polish nuns. Most importantly, the railroad passed them by. However, as the colony came close to foundering, Father Moczygemba left under pressure, re-

> ## Who are Alsatians, and where is their best-preserved settlement in the United States?
>
> **A**lsace-Lorraine lies on the border between France and Germany, a distinct cultural region that has changed hands with successive wars. In 1842, colonial impresario Henri Castro (1786–1865) obtained a land grant on which he settled Alsatians in the Hill Country—485 families and 457 single men—on the Medina River west of San Antonio. Today, Castroville has the highest percentage of registered nineteenth-century buildings in the United States. The Castroville Inn raked in customers for its claim that it was the last chance to get a hot bath between there and Laredo. The bathhouse had two stories: the lower one for the fire, the upper one for a large, communal hot tub—although now that it is a bed-and-breakfast run by the Texas Historical Commission, both chambers are guest rooms.

locating to Michigan; he died in 1891 but was reinterred in Panna Maria in 1974. Much of the community's history is preserved in the St. Joseph School Museum, the 1875 Pilarczyk Store, and the Panna Maria Visitors' Center. (It was a Silesian immigrant, Joseph Hannig, who became the fifth and final husband of Alamo survivor Susanna Dickinson.)

Where did Czech immigrants into Texas settle?

Immigration into Texas from central Europe started quite early; since there was no Czechoslovakia yet, Czech meant people from Bohemia, Moravia, and the southern portion of Silesia. Frederick Lemsky played the fife at the Battle of San Jacinto. During the Republic, there came to be at least some Czech presence all over the Republic, but Fayette County was their center. Today, the prevalence of bumper stickers in central Texas asking "Jak se más?" ("How are you?") attests to their continuing cohesion. Much of that story is told in the Texas Czech Heritage and Cultural Center in La Grange.

What Texas town has the most eclectic collection of early residents?

That is probably a tough competition, but one top contender would be Paris, in northeast Texas. Its gallery of prominent, old-time Texans includes cattle king John Chisum, Frank James (who was a store clerk here when he was not robbing banks with his more famous brother, Jesse); outlaw Belle Starr, before her violent days ended in Oklahoma; and most prominently, Sam Bell Maxey, a Confederate general whose elegant Queen Anne house is one of Paris's historic sites. It was built in 1868, shortly after Maxey was pardoned and before he began his two terms in the U.S. Senate.

How did the Comanche feel about this invasion of their hunting grounds?

The Hill Country Comanche had been engaging in war to the knife with Texans after the Council House fight, but John O. Meusebach (1812–1897), who took over the *Adelsverein* after Prince Carl returned home to marry Princess Sophie, surprised them. Against the most strident advice, he entered their territory with only a small escort, invited the chiefs into his new town of Fredericksburg, and there distributed gifts and concluded a detailed treaty of amity and mutual engagement. The American Texans were furious, and not without reason. The advent of repeating pistols had begun to give them the upper hand in Indian fighting. The Comanche were ready to bargain for peace after a couple of devastating defeats when in swept the Germans, who reaped the benefit. Nevertheless, the Meusebach-Comanche Treaty remains the only agreement ever reached between Anglos and native Indians that was never broken.

AUSTIN

After their experience with filibusters, why did the Spanish let Austin in?

Although left mostly to fend for themselves, the Spanish government in the New World was faithful to the Constitution of 1807. That document provided that persons who had previously been loyal Spanish subjects and moved away who wished to return must be allowed to do so. In earlier years, Austin had successfully managed a lead mine in Missouri during the brief period when Louisiana belonged to Spain. Realizing that Austin fell under this provision of the Constitution, Governor Martínez and the military commander, Arredondo, approved Austin's plan for an American colony.

What happened to Austin?

Moses Austin was triumphant with his success, but on his way back to the United States, he was bushwhacked, robbed, and left for dead. He managed to walk all the way back to Natchitoches in the freezing weather of January 1821. He began rounding up colonists, but his health continued to fail, and he died on June 10, 1821. Famously, with his dying words, he importuned his older son, Stephen Fuller Austin (1793–1836), to undertake the venture in his stead.

How many colonists did Austin recruit?

Austin's contract called for him to settle three hundred families on his land grant. The eventual total of 297 families, some of whom were households headed by women

Moses Austin, the father of Stephen Austin, was an American businessman and early settler of Texas.

and some even constructive families of unrelated men, have been collectively known as the Old Three Hundred and comprise a rootstock of Texas heritage.

Why would women come to Texas?

Under the Spanish law in Texas, women enjoyed a much better position than they did in the United States, which used English common law. In the United States, women ordinarily could not own property, go into business, enter into contracts, or exercise other rights that men took for granted. In New Spain, women could do all those things. One example was Rosa María Hinojosa de Ballí (1752–1803), who owned and operated a ranch of more than 1 million acres (4,047 square kilometers) in south Texas. Independent-minded American women came to Texas to make better lives for themselves, just like the men did. One of the most successful was Obedience Fort Smith (1771–1847), the widow of a Revolutionary War veteran with eleven grown children. Her land grant, luckily, was located on what later became downtown Houston.

How did the Mexican Revolution affect Austin's colony?

The effect was drastic, but it was a trial that demonstrated Austin's character and mettle. Moses Austin made his contract with the viceroyal government of New Spain. By the time Stephen F. Austin returned, met at the border accompanied by a deputation of San Antonio's leading citizens with his colonists en route, that government was no more. Martínez was making way for the first Mexican governor, and he advised Austin to go to Mexico City and rescue his contract as best he could. Barely financed for the journey, Austin learned Spanish on the road to the capital. He and his party were robbed and fleeced by Indians, and once in Mexico City, he was appalled to see presidents, strongmen, congresses, and even an emperor rise and fall one after the other. It took a year and a half of patient, diplomatic labor to win a new, binding contract for his venture.

Brazoria County is in the heart of the original Austin colony; does any local museum preserve that history?

Angleton is now the county seat, and the Brazoria County Historical Museum in the 1897 former courthouse contains many exhibits of the Austin colony. Just west of the city lies the Austin-Munson Historical Park, which has a visitor center and hosts reenactments and living history demonstrations throughout the year. It is located on Austin's own personal grant of land, which he later conveyed to his colonist, Henry William Munson, whose family donated the land for the park. Dominating the landscape is a somewhat pharaonic 76-foot (23-meter) statue of Austin by David Adickes, who also created the colossal Sam Houston at Huntsville.

What were the terms for Americans settling in Texas?

What most caught Americans' eyes was that each head of a family would be given a league and a labor of land, an almost unimaginable empire for an American farmer. A league was a Spanish measure equaling 4,428 acres (18 square kilometers). This was dry land for stock raising. They would also get the labor, a further 177 acres (0.7 square kilometers), of arable land for farming. They would have to settle on it, and eventually pay Austin a fee for surveying and providing for defense, but it was sufficient inducement to bring colonists streaming.

COLONIAL LIFE

What kind of people came to Texas?

Under the terms of his contract, Stephen Austin was held accountable for the good character and industrious habits of the immigrants he brought. However, people who made an ample living and had a good life in the United States had little incentive to leave. Therefore, many who immigrated had suffered financial reverses, were escaping romantic entanglements, were seeking some shortcut to riches, or otherwise were less than the cream of society. Austin offered huge tracts of extra land to wealthy Americans to pull up stakes and bring their financial means with them.

How did the Texans manage an economy when there was almost no money or infrastructure?

With almost no roads except for the Camino Real, Austin cleverly allotted his grants in long, narrow parcels that backed up to a stream. Riverboat captains published handbills publicizing the dates when they would be in each vicinity, and settlers would have their produce—cotton, corn, cow-hides, and rendered tallow, waiting on the riverbanks to trade for the supplies and consumer goods brought by the boats. Cash was in very short supply, so barter was the principal medium of exchange.

How did people get by in the absence of consumer goods?

Virtually all manufactured hardware had to be imported and was ferociously expensive, so Texas pioneers became masters of innovation. When metal door hinges were unobtainable, they crafted their own from

Stephen Austin, the "Father of Texas," succeeded where his father could not by establishing a successful settlement of Americans in Texas in 1825.

41

> ## What was a dogtrot?
>
> American settlers in Texas came to favor a style of house that was admirable for its innovation. It began with a single log-pen cabin that could shelter a family temporarily. Later, a second cabin was built next to it with an open breezeway—the dogtrot—between them. Still later, this was closed in for a third room. A covered porch or veranda could be added across the width of the front, and the roof lowered in back for the addition of shed rooms. Then, if the ceilings were high enough, loft rooms were added in the eaves, reached by steep stairs. Thus, a single-room cabin could be expanded bit by bit into an ample dwelling.

rawhide. In the absence of door handles, they made do with latch strings. According to one memoir, wheat flour was so expensive at ten dollars per barrel that children were born and grew up having tasted only cornbread. One of the most precious commodities was tallow for candles, and home made candlesticks screwed up from the bottom so not a drop would be wasted. Coffee and tobacco were considered indispensable, of course, and had to be bought or traded for.

Why were kitchens built separately?

Kitchens were the likeliest place in a household where a fire could get out of control; better for just the kitchen to burn down than the whole house.

What did people do for fun?

Much of the men's recreation also served a useful purpose. They could hunt, fish, and chop down bee trees for honey. Austin forbade gambling, except on horse races, which he regarded as a means to improve the stock. They argued and sometimes fought over politics. Between domestic chores and child-rearing, women generally had fewer opportunities for fun outside the home. When they could gather, it was often for communal activity such as quilting. There was a reason people said that Texas was heaven for men and dogs but hell for women and oxen. A dance was considered a major social occasion, and women would unpack the best dresses they had brought from the United States. A dirt-floored cabin might be laid with a new puncheon floor, and the success of the dance was measured in how many floor-boards were broken.

How did the Texas Rangers get started?

Stephen F. Austin is almost universally credited with starting the Texas Rangers. However, he was still in Mexico trying to rescue his colonial enterprise when his militia captain, Moses Morrison (born c. 1793), mustered the first ten volunteers in May 1823, mounted and equipped at their own expense, to be ready to make hostile pursuit after Karankawa raiders. As soon as Austin returned, he approved of Morrison's act and wrote

The Texas Rangers Hall of Fame and Museum is located in Waco.

to Mexican Texas's governor, José Felix Trespalacios (?–1835), seeking to recruit more men to "act as rangers for the common defence." Nothing more happened immediately, but Trespalacios had previously commanded a similar unit in Mexico, which were called *compania volante*, or flying company. His instructions to Austin on their disposition and tactics give him large credit for starting the Texas Rangers, although they were not given that official name for many years.

Was Austin's the only American colony?

Hardly. Noting the success that Stephen Austin made of his colonial venture, the legislature of Coahuila was inundated with applications to set up further colonies, including three more, over time, from Austin himself. Within a few years, Texas was divided up into a patch-quilt of about two dozen grants to colonial empresarios. Within a decade, Texas was home to at least twenty thousand Anglo Americans—a stunning success at finally populating that empty place but a success that carried its own seeds at destroying their relationship with Mexico.

Was populating Texas the Mexican legislature's only goal?

No. The state legislature of Coahuila y Tejas was dominated by federalists, politicians who wanted a government on the U.S. model of authority divided between the national and

43

state governments. The fees (and probable bribes) they collected from colonial empresarios helped to finance their opposition to the various centralist strongmen who dominated the national regimes.

Why was slavery allowed in Texas when it was illegal in Mexico?

Most American settlers were agriculturalists from the American South, and it was accepted that the Texas economy would depend on cotton, which could not be profitable without using slave labor. There again, the legislature of Coahuila y Tejas was working different interests from the federal government in Mexico City, and they worked out creative accommodations with the Americans to get an economy going in Texas. Slaves, for instance, were deemed to be indentured servants instead.

How did the requirement for settlers to convert to Catholicism work out?

Because the Catholic Church was allied with the royalist side in the Mexican Revolution, the new national government was strictly secular. No priest was even assigned to administer the necessary sacraments in Texas for nearly a decade. The colonists, for their part, were willing to become Catholic in order to get land, largely because most of them took no religion seriously. Quite the opposite, religion played very little part in colonists' lives for years after the American arrival.

How did things start to go wrong in Austin?

Austin made a good start on settling his colony with educated and industrious yeomen. One traveler was astonished to hear one settler reciting a Latin lesson while slopping his hogs. As word spread in the United States of the thriving colonies in Texas, however, a stream of derelicts and have-nots turned into a flood of illegal immigrants who squatted on the ample unclaimed land. Austin lost control over who could come, and other less particular empresarios who were anxious to fill their immigration quotas (on pain of losing their contracts) did not look too carefully at who filled their roles. These "leatherstockings," as Austin contemptuously called them, felt no loyalty to him, did not share his loyalty to Mexico, and many actively desired to separate Texas from Mexico and add it to the United States.

Why did General Manuel de Mier y Terán's inspection tour have such devastating consequences?

In response to unrest in Texas, the Mexican government sent one of its most capable military figures, General Manuel de Mier y Terán (1789–1832), to make a thorough inspection of Texas. His entourage included scientists to evaluate natural resources and surveyors to run a boundary line between Texas and the United States, but his most important commission was to evaluate political conditions. He worked for well over a year, and his report, detailed and articulate, landed on the government like a bombshell. He frankly admitted that most American settlers were honest and grateful to Mexico for

What was the "Fredonian Rebellion"?

Haden Edwards (1771–1849) was a wealthy American planter who was in Mexico City to lobby for a colonial land grant at the same time Stephen Austin was there and, in fact, lent Austin the money to continue his effort. After being awarded a contract to settle eight hundred families in the vicinity of Nacogdoches, Edwards and his brother rode roughshod over the settlers already there, many of them Hispanic whose history there dated to the region's early settlement. After giving land preference to his own settlers and winning a local election that was overturned by the governor for its irregularities, Edwards and his followers declared the independence of the Republic of Fredonia on December 21, 1826. This was the first attempt by American newcomers to secede Texas from Mexico. Austin was appalled at Edwards ignoring his pleas to stand down, so he formed a hundred of his own settlers into a militia that marched with government forces to restore order in the area. It was a clear signal to Mexico that all was not well in their ever-vexsome Texas.

the chance at a better life. He also allowed that "ignorant and venal" Hispanic officials made a practice of cheating the settlers, denying them justice in local courts, and there was no appeal closer than Saltillo, 700 miles (1,127 kilometers) away. The Americans, however, "carry their constitutions in their pockets" and knew their rights, and by sheer weight of numbers they "could throw the entire nation into revolution" if the government did not act decisively.

What was the Law of April 6?

In response to Terán's alarming but accurate report, the government issued the *Ley* (law) of April 6, 1830, which closed the loopholes in the laws prohibiting slavery and, most alarmingly, prohibited any further immigration from the United States. Terán himself had doubts about the wisdom of its more draconian features, and Austin eventually won repeal of the ban on further immigrants, but trust between the two sides was permanently fractured.

What were the "Anahuac disturbances"?

Austin's original settlement contract called for national taxes not to be imposed for a period of seven years. The expiration of that period coincided with efforts to enforce provisions of the Law of April 6. The government sent a Virginia adventurer in Mexican service, "Juan" Davis Bradburn (1787–1842), to install a customs house at Anahuac. His corruption and imperious methods aroused local fury, which coalesced around an Alabama hothead not yet twenty-four years old, William Barret Travis (1809–1836). When Bradburn had him arrested, a mob seized the town of Anahuac on June 10, 1832. The

Nacogdoches commandant marched to Bradburn's relief but instead met the rebels' demand that Bradburn be dismissed and Travis and others released. The colonists were able to talk their way out of further trouble by claiming in the "Turtle Bayou Resolutions" that they were acting in support of a rising strongman, Antonio López de Santa Anna, whom Bradburn and the central government opposed, thus winning protection from an advancing army led by a Santanista general. It was now clear to many observers that a revolution in Texas was inevitable.

THE REPUBLIC OF TEXAS

THE TEXAS REVOLUTION

What caused the Texas Revolution?

There were many reasons that the Anglo colonists rebelled against Mexico. A large cause was slavery, which was illegal in Mexico, but which the state government in Coahuila informally overlooked because the Texas economy depended upon cotton. As tensions increased between the state and federal governments, the Texas slavery question was caught in the middle. Another cause was freedom of religion. Americans coming to Texas were required to convert to Catholicism, which they knew before they came. The Mexican government, however, was strictly secular and did not assign a priest to administer the sacraments in Texas for ten years. Most of the Americans came from Protestant families, and the 1830s was the height of a fervent revivalist movement in the United States. Most Texans were not religiously observant but still felt it wrong for any government to tell people how to worship. A third cause was the lack of a judicial system. As Terán reported in 1828, Americans were often dealt with unfairly in local courts and there was no closer appeal than the state capital hundreds of miles away, and even then they were not confident of a fair hearing. There were other irritants as well.

How did Santa Anna complicate the picture?

After the Anahuac disturbances, Texas firebrands declared their support for Santa Anna, who became president in 1833, having run as a federalist. Once in power, however, he abolished the constitution and ruled as a centralist autocrat. To many Mexicans, loyalty to Mexico meant loyalty to the nation, whatever government was in power; to the Texans, loyalty was to the constitution, and once that was gone, the obligation ceased. The Texas Revolution did not take place in a vacuum. When Santa Anna abolished the constitution, eleven different rebellions broke out, of which Texas was only one—but the only successful one.

What was the spark that started the revolution?

In 1832, the military authorities in San Antonio had lent a small cannon to the town of Gonzales, about 50 miles (80 kilometers) east of there, for purposes of Indian defense. It was a sorry little gun with a damaged touch hole, but with trouble brewing, the colonel in San Antonio sent a hundred dragoons under Lieutenant Francisco de Castañeda to Gonzales to reclaim it. Volunteers buried the cannon and sent out calls to neighboring colonies for reinforcements. Naomi DeWitt, daughter of the local empresario, donated her wedding dress to make a flag depicting the cannon above the legend "Come and Take It." The volunteers dug up and repaired the gun, crossed the Guadalupe River early in the morning of October 2, 1835, and fired it as they drove off the dragoons.

What was the aftermath of the Battle of Gonzales?

Well before the trouble at Gonzales, Santa Anna had vowed to teach the Texans a lesson. He sent an army under his brother-in-law, General Martín Perfecto de Cos, to occupy San Antonio and then root out the colonial government at San Felipe de Austin. As he passed through Goliad, 50 miles (80 kilometers) south of Gonzales, he disarmed the local citizens and forced them to labor for his army—taste enough for the locals of what a Mexican occupation would be like. A week after Gonzales, Texas volunteers overwhelmed

Who was Launcelot Smither?

This figure of the early period of the revolution has remained uncelebrated, perhaps because his experience impeaches some of his heroic motives. Acting as a doctor to the Mexican garrison in San Antonio, Launcelot Smither (1800–1842) believed he could mediate the two sides' differences and was sent to the dragoons at Gonzales. After conferring with Castañeda, Smither approached the Americans to arrange discussions, for Castañeda's orders were to avoid violence. The volunteers agreed to talk, but when Castañeda withdrew to camp, they feared he was awaiting reinforcements, so they crossed the river and attacked. Castañeda was furious, took Smither's money and horses, and confined him until he sent him across to the Americans to learn why they attacked. Suspicious of his friendliness with the Mexicans, they arrested him again and confined him at the rear. Such was the fate of a would-be peacemaker when the locals' blood was up. One month later, still in Gonzales, Smither was beaten nearly to death by American looters posing as "volunteers" to sack the town. Later, he was one of the couriers who bore Colonel Travis's famous letter "To All Americans in the World" from the Alamo and was later killed during one of the Mexican reinvasions in 1842.

the garrison that Cos had left behind to guard his supplies. They went on to evict Mexican troops from Fort Lipantitlán and the Mission Concepción near San Antonio. On December 5, under nominal command of Austin but led by Ben Milam, Texans attacked San Antonio, and afterward, house-to-house fighting forced Cos to surrender and leave Texas under parole not to return.

How did Texas organize politically during the revolution?

During the weeks of early fighting, a gathering called the Consultation formulated a provisional government for Texas, but its muddled purpose and divided authority

A mural at the Gonzales Memorial Museum depicts Texan soldiers.

proved so unsatisfactory that a convention was called to meet on March 1, 1836. One accomplishment of the Consultation was to appoint command of Texas forces to Sam Houston of Tennessee, which was an enormously controversial step.

Who wrote the Texas Declaration of Independence?

When the convention met in Washington, Texas, on March 1, 1836, a committee to write a declaration of independence was appointed immediately. The chairman was George Childress of Tennessee, thirty-two, a protégé of President Andrew Jackson and the brother-in-law of future U.S. president James K. Polk, who had only been in Texas for ten weeks. It is likely that Childress came with a draft already in his pocket, for it was presented to the convention the next day.

Is it true that Sam Houston had them hold up signing the Declaration so that it could be done on his birthday, March 2, 1836?

No, that is a legend. In fact, when the document was presented on March 2, it was found to be so full of errors that it was sent back to be corrected. The document was then

Who was the first casualty of the Texas Revolution?

Samuel McCulloch was a free person of color from South Carolina, whose right shoulder was shattered by a musket ball while storming the Mexican officers' quarters at Goliad, two days before his twenty-fifth birthday. The wound left him a partial invalid for life. The first fatality was Richard "Big Dick" Anderson, killed at Concepción.

signed on March 3, although the March 2 date (which was indeed Houston's birthday) was kept on it. Delegates continued signing it as they arrived at the convention until the last one, Sam Maverick, signed it on March 10.

Why was Sam Houston such a polarizing figure?

At the time he arrived in Texas on December 2, 1832, Houston was already one of the most famous—and controversial—men in America. Back in Tennessee, he rose as a protégé of Andrew Jackson, which made him a focus of anti-Jackson hatred. In addition, Houston had left Tennessee under a scandal. He had been the governor, running for reelection, when his new wife left him after only ten weeks of marriage. He resigned his office and removed to life with the Cherokee in the Indian Territory for three years. In truth, she left him, he didn't leave her, but Jackson's enemies made the most of it to portray him

Sam Houston was twice president of Texas before serving as a U.S. senator and then governor of Texas when it became part of the Union. He was the only Southern governor to oppose secession before the U.S. Civil War.

as a rogue and cad. Moreover, Houston was an alcoholic in an era when that was considered a moral weakness and not a disease. Worse, in a time when nearly all Anglos favored Indian extermination or at least removal, Houston made no secret of his affection for them, and he tried to treat them fairly. Worst of all, although he was a Southerner and owned a few slaves, he disliked the institution, opposed its spread, and opposed reopening the African slave trade, so wealthy people regarded him as a traitor to his class.

Why is Independence an important stop for Sam Houston buffs?

Located on a state farm-to-market road that carries traffic between Brenham and College Station, Independence is an important site for Sam Houston history. In antebellum Texas, it was one of the wealthiest towns in the state and noted for its excellent Baptist schools, including the beginnings of both Baylor University and the University of Mary Hardin–Baylor. Sam and Margaret Houston moved here so their children could get a good education; their farm was west of the town and south of the school their daughters attended, whose ruins still exist. The Texas Baptist Historical Center preserves the pew in which Houston carved his initials and also the bell to which Margaret's mother donated her family silver "to sweeten its tone." The tall, severe Greek Revival house where Margaret lived out her brief widowhood still stands on the hill to the west of the

Where is the best place in Texas to study the life of Sam Houston?

Although there are significant collections of Sam Houston's papers and artifacts in Austin and at the San Jacinto Museum of History in La Porte near Houston, by far the richest trove of Sam Houston materials is in Huntsville, where the Houston family lived for most of the last fifteen years of his life. Preservation of the family residence that Sam Houston himself designed and called "Woodland" was the project of history students at the neighboring college, then the Sam Houston Normal Institute (now Sam Houston State University). The students bought a few acres of the original Houston farm and moved Woodland and Houston's log cabin law office back to their original locations in 1911. The museum was begun in 1927 and expanded in 1936 as Huntsville's centennial project. Also in 1936, the "Steamboat" house in which Houston died in 1863 was moved onto the property from several blocks away. Today, the collection of Houston family artifacts is unmatched, and the much-expanded grounds offer a broad array of exhibits and education programs on life in east Texas in the nineteenth century.

church, and she and her mother are both buried in the small family cemetery. Rocky Creek, where Sam Houston was finally baptized after Margaret's fourteen-year effort, still receives converts about 1.5 miles (2.4 kilometers) south of the town.

Why then was he given command of the Texas Army?

Houston was legitimately a war hero, whose wounds received in the War of 1812 had never healed. Afterward, he had risen to the position of major general of the Tennessee state militia, he was a student of military history, and he had demonstrated during his tenure in the U.S. Army a gift for command. Plus, as Texas lay on the fringe of the American West, Jackson had more friends than enemies, and Houston was well connected among the faction at the convention that declared independence from Mexico.

Did Travis really draw a line in the sand with his sword before the Battle of the Alamo?

This is a famous link in the Texan revolutionary heritage, that Lieutenant Colonel William Barret Travis, the fort's twenty-six-year-old commander, announced to the garrison that their position was hopeless, drew a line in the sand, and invited those who would stay and die with him to step across, which all did save one. Most historians now doubt this. However, the only source for the story was that one, Louis "Moses" Rose, an old Napoleonic who was let out a window that night and escaped. He sought refuge for a while with the family of William P. Zuber, who became the first written source for the story. While Zuber's literary exaggerations and purple prose damage his credibility, he may well have been relating what Rose told his family, and certainly, such a theatrical gesture was the very kind of thing that Travis might have made.

The 1903 painting *The Fall of the Alamo* by Robert Jenkins Onderdonk shows Davy Crockett heroically wielding his rifle as a club after running out of bullets. How Crockett died, however, is not exactly known. He might have died fighting, or he might have been captured and executed.

How did Davy Crockett really die?

There are eyewitness accounts on both the Texan and Mexican sides that have Crockett falling in furious combat. There are eyewitness accounts on both the Texan and Mexican sides that place Crockett among a small group that surrendered and were summarily executed. Susanna Dickinson, the only adult Anglo to survive the battle, said when she was led out of the chapel, she saw his body and "his peculiar cap by his side." The true circumstances of his death will never be known with certainty, but that does not matter. The whole garrison knew that if they stayed and fought, their lives would be forfeited. Sam Houston ordered the Alamo abandoned and blown up, and their decision to defend the fortress to the last was not the most intelligent, but nothing can dim the heroism of that choice.

Why didn't Houston turn and fight instead of retreating across the whole width of Texas?

After the Alamo fell, Houston had fewer than four hundred men at Gonzales. When he invaded, Santa Anna split his army into several forces to sweep across as broad a front as possible. If Houston had tried to fight with his untrained volunteers, he would not only have had to fight and defeat Santa Anna, who was chasing him with his army, but also General Joaquín Ramírez y Sesma close after him with eight hundred, General An-

Can you still visit the site of the filming of John Wayne's *The Alamo*?

Few viewers of Wayne's classic 1960 film are aware of the headaches he had trying to raise money to make *The Alamo*. After many frustrating years trying to get the project underway at Republic Pictures, Wayne formed his own production company. The original Alamo was unsuitable for filming both because of the need to protect the historic structure but also because it lies in the heart of downtown San Antonio, and most of the large complex no longer exists. Wayne contracted with Brackettville local Happy Shahan to build a set outside of Brackettville, which Wayne thought a suitable location despite its more arid landscape. When the project ran out of funds, Shahan offered to complete the set if Wayne would make good on it later, which saved the film. For many years after, "Alamo Village" was a popular tourist destination with restaurants and a museum, but business faded with awareness of the movie. It closed to tourists in 2010 but remained available for shooting films, such as parts of *Lonesome Dove* in 1988. The 2004 Alamo film was shot elsewhere; plans are put forward periodically to reopen the Brackettville site.

tonio Gaona to his north with a thousand more, General José de Urrea with two thousand somewhere to the south, and General Juan Jose Andrade behind in San Antonio with fifteen hundred more. There was no conceivable way Houston could have succeeded. If he had caved in to the demands of the hotheaded amateurs in his army, the revolution would have ended in the same kind of bloodbath as the Alamo.

What was the Goliad Massacre?

In the confused opening of the revolution, the Texan forces were not concentrated in one place. As Houston retreated east from Gonzales, a second army under Colonel James Walker Fannin was in Goliad, 50 miles (80 kilometers) south. Houston sent orders for Fannin to join him, but Fannin delayed until he was overtaken by General Urrea, who defeated him in the Battle of Coleto Creek. Urrea confined them at the Goliad mission, treating them as prisoners of war. Santa Anna angrily rebuked him for this and ordered the Texans' summary execution. On Palm Sunday, March 27, 1836, about four hundred prisoners were marched a few miles from town, lined up, and shot (a few escaped), while Fannin and his officers were executed in the chapel courtyard. Houston kept news of this from his army until the threat of mutiny became so great that he informed them they were the only army in Texas, and the outcome of the revolution depended upon the first battle they had.

What was Houston's strategy?

For many years, Houston admirers wrote that by retreating to the east, Houston was cleverly stretching Santa Anna's supply lines to the point that any mistake the dictator made would be fatal. More modern revisionists have claimed that Houston instead was an ineffectual drunk, disrespected by his own troops who forced him to turn and fight at San Jacinto. Neither view is true. It is now known that Houston had worked out a deal with U.S. president Andrew Jackson that if Houston could lure Santa Anna into crossing the Neches River, which the United States claimed as the boundary with Mexico, Jackson would conveniently have an army assembled in western Louisiana that would pounce across the border and finish the fight. Houston in fact was in regular contact with that American force's commander, General Edmund Pendleton Gaines. Santa Anna took the bait and followed but then turned to try to capture the rebel Texan government as they fled for the coast. Houston was obliged to turn south as well, and despite advice from Gaines's camp—"do not be goaded into a battle"—Houston shattered the Mexican Army and captured the dictator at San Jacinto.

How did the Battle of San Jacinto transpire?

Houston's six weeks of retreat, known in Texas lore as the Run away Scrape, and his refusal to discuss his reasons, almost caused a mutiny in the Texas army. When captured dispatches revealed that Santa Anna was nearby and vulnerable, Houston took cover in timber near the mouth of the San Jacinto River, placing his two cannons in open prairie in front of the tree line where Santa Anna could not miss them. After a skirmish on April 20, the Mexicans were prepared for an attack on the morning of April 21. When it did not come in the morning or midday, they let down their guard—many were having their *siesta*—and Houston attacked furiously at about 3 P.M., with stoked and near-rabid volunteers shouting "Remember the Alamo!" The battle took only eighteen minutes, but the killing continued for hours as Mexican soldiers tried to wade to safety through a marsh. Eight Texans were killed; six hundred Mexicans died, and seven hundred were captured.

Who really was "The Yellow Rose of Texas"?

Today yellow roses are an informal Texan icon, but they are a metaphor for an actual event in the history of the revolution. Emily West was a free woman of color from Connecticut who came to Texas indentured to work for planter James Morgan, who lived near the town of New Washington. (She was known for many years as Emily Morgan, from the assumption that she was his slave, which she was not.) Near the end of his eastward sweep, Santa Anna burned New Washington, capturing several women whom he turned over to his soldiers to have their pleasure with. Santa Anna, of course, claimed first choice of the most beautiful, and Emily West was a light-skinned mulatto, known at the time as "high yellow." At the time of Sam Houston's attack, Santa Anna was said to have been in his tent with her and was caught literally with his pants down. Houston later told a British travel writer that he had planted her there. He was joking, but the probability is that Emily West was diverting the dictator's attention, assuring a quick and total victory for the Texans. A minstrel song first published in 1858 celebrated "The Yellow Rose of Texas" for her beauty but omitted her historical significance.

How was Santa Anna captured?

The day after the battle, Texan scouts combed the countryside and looked for stragglers. Santa Anna was found hiding in tall grass, disguised in either a private's blouse or civilian clothing but given away by his diamond studs and the other Mexican prisoners' gasps of "El Presidente!" After the butchery at the Alamo and Goliad, the Texan soldiers clamored to hang him, but Houston refused to begin Texas nationhood with such an act. The dictator was handed over to the civilian government to sign the Treaties of Velasco, recognizing Texas independence.

A portrait of Mexican general Antonio López de Santa Anna is on display at the Mexico City Museum.

LAW AND POLITICS

Why did the capital of Texas keep moving around?

Santa Anna's invasion of Texas had two purposes. The first was to enforce his boundary claims against the United States, while the second was to root out the Americans and their rebel government. Today, we would call this "ethnic cleansing." During the Runaway Scrape, whole towns were burned, either by retreating Texans to keep them out of Mexican hands, such as Gonzales and San Felipe, or by Santa Anna, as at New Washington, which was the closest town to San Jacinto. He bypassed Columbia (now West Columbia), and the government located there for a year, despite an almost total lack of facilities. In 1837, developer brothers Augustus C. and John Allen offered the government a free capitol building if they would relocate to their new town of Houston. President Houston was enchanted to have a capital named after himself and agreed. When Mirabeau Lamar replaced him, he moved the capital in 1839 to a raw frontier village built for the purpose, 80 miles (129 kilometers) northeast of San Antonio, named Austin. When Mexico invaded again in 1842 and occupied San Antonio, Houston (back in power) moved the capital to Washington-on-the-Brazos. Government returned to Austin in 1845; it was named the state capital, confirmed by an election in 1850.

Whatever happened to Stephen F. Austin's colonial capital of San Felipe?

The town was burned during the Runaway Scrape of 1836 to prevent the buildings from falling into the hands of the advancing Mexican Army and rebuilt only slowly. With the Texas capital moved to Washington and then ignored by the railroads, the town barely ever regained its prerevolutionary population of about six hundred until the twenty-

55

first century. Although central to Texas history, with the original buildings destroyed, the site remained mostly undeveloped. A new museum and interpretive center finished in 2018, with a slate of lectures and educational programs, promises to restore San Felipe to the position that its historical importance deserves.

For some years, Washington was the capital of the Republic of Texas—how did it manage to die off so completely?

Faced with the prospect of paying off a railroad to run the line through their town, Washington's leaders chose instead to bet their future on the fortunes of two Brazos riverboats. They guessed wrong.

Why was Austin finally selected for the capital?

Officially, Lamar wished to have a capital located inland, where he envisioned that east-west trade routes would intersect with north-south travel. Unofficially, he would not countenance governing from a capital named for his hated rival. His commissioners selected a site 80 miles (129 kilometers) northeast of San Antonio, along the Colorado River, on the edge of the well-wooded and -watered Balcones Escarpment. Laid out in 1839, Austin was at the very edge of settlement, and Comanche Indians picked off unwary citizens for years.

What was the governmental structure of the Republic of Texas?

The Constitution, adopted two weeks after the Declaration of Independence, was drafted in the haste of the Mexican approach and was bare-bones in its brevity. It was modeled on the U.S. Constitution, with co-equal legislative, executive, and judicial branches, but with greater restrictions on governmental powers. Reflecting Jacksonian populism, rep-

THE REPUBLIC OF TEXAS

resentatives were elected for only one year and the president for two years in the first election, with three-year terms thereafter. There were twenty-two counties, organized into four judicial districts whose chief judges, when meeting en banc with a chief justice, would comprise the supreme court. In a referendum of September 1836, Texans voted 3,277 to 91 to join the United States, and thereafter, statutes and constitutional amendments were drafted to be consistent with American law to ease the transition.

What Texas museum combines outstanding exhibits on the social history of the Republic with a living history farm?

Much of the original town site of Washington, about 100 miles (161 kilometers) east of Austin, is as heavily wooded as it was when delegates to the Convention of 1836 knocked their shins against tree stumps on what were generously called "streets." Only a few hundred yards from a reconstruction of Independence Hall, the Star of the Republic Museum houses displays of what it was like to be a doctor, surveyor, or practitioner of other professions in that day. Their crown jewel is the only surviving Lone Star flag that is known to have flown over the Republic of Texas. Only a short walk away lies Barrington, the plantation home of Dr. Anson Jones, last president of the Republic. It is now a living history farm, which is run faithfully to the practices of the mid-nineteenth century, even hand plowing their demonstration cotton patch behind two gigantic oxen—a skill at which tourists are welcome to try their hand—and keeping heritage breeds of chickens authentic to the 1840s, when they laid green and blue eggs.

In what Texas town did citizens leave rather than become citizens of the United States?

Laredo is one of the oldest settlements in Texas, dating back to 1755, almost exclusively Hispanic with little Anglo influence from then through the period of the Republic. After losing the Mexican–American War, Mexico was forced to recognize Texas as an Ameri-

---

What was the Republic of the Rio Grande?

During the Texas Revolution, notable Mexican federalists who opposed Santa Anna's dictatorship, such as Lorenzo de Zavala, joined the Texas cause. Others laid low within Mexico; emboldened by Texas's success, representatives from several interior Mexican states met in Laredo on January 17, 1840, and declared the Republic of the Rio Grande, with territory in both Mexico and Texas. Their military force under Antonio Canales Rosillo was virtually destroyed in a battle with a centralist army, and in November the breakaway attempt was ended with Canales accepting a post in the centralist army. The building in which independence was declared is now one of Laredo's oldest, and it houses the Republic of the Rio Grande Museum.

can state. Despite their distaste for Mexican centralism, the citizens of Laredo held a referendum and voted to remain part of Mexico. When the U.S. Army rejected their petition, seventeen families abandoned their homes and relocated across the river, even carrying with them the bodies of family members disinterred from the cemetery. They founded the city of Nuevo Laredo.

What was the "Archives War"?

During the presidential election of 1841, it was widely alleged that Sam Houston would move the capital from Austin back to Houston if he won. Although he hated its isolation, he did not do so; in fact, he took a buggy ride up scenic Mount Bonnell and pronounced that this must have been the high place where the devil tempted Jesus with the riches of the world. With the Mexican invasion of 1842, however, Houston determined to move the government for safety to Washington (now Washington-on-the-Brazos), 90 miles (145 kilometers) to the east. It was difficult for the government to function without its papers, which had been buried into the Land Office, and twice (October and December), Houston sent armed Rangers to recover them. Austin citizens were alert to this possibility and foiled the first attempt before it began. In the wee hours of December 30, more Rangers began loading the papers onto three wagons. Austin's prominent boardinghouse proprietress, Angelina Peyton Eberly (1798–1860), spied the activity and fired a nearby cannon that was kept primed and loaded for Indian defense. A mob gathered, and as grapeshot raked the building, the Rangers fled with what they had been able to gather. After a gunfight on Brushy Creek (in which no one was hurt), Austinites recaptured the papers and returned with them. While the government continued in Washington, the archives remained in Austin, secured in Eberly's cellar.

Why did Texas keep using Spanish law after the Revolution?

After Santa Anna's atrocities in Texas, anti-Hispanic feeling ran so high that many people wanted to throw off every vestige of Spanish heritage, including the law. However, the chief justice of the Supreme Court, John Hemphill, was an expert in Spanish law, and he recognized that there were huge benefits to keeping certain aspects of the Spanish legal system. His decisions, frequently reached by strong-arming agreement from the other judges and enforced over the dismay of Texas's lawyers who were trained in the United States and who were facile with using the common law, maintained Spain's simplified legal procedures, provided continuity to thousands of marriages, contracts, and land sales made under Spain and Mexico, and preserved the legal protections for women and debtors that would have disappeared under the American common law.

What were the political issues under the Republic?

Texas never developed political parties during the Republic, and factions formed around the principal antagonists, Sam Houston and Mirabeau Lamar. Houston labored for annexation to the United States, while Lamar envisioned Texas as the third great power in North America, along with the United States and Mexico. Houston sought fair treatment

> ## How did Texas become a haven for American debtors?
>
> The United States, descending from English common law, was harsh in its treatment of debtors, even still maintaining debtors' prisons in some areas. Spanish law was far more lenient. Throughout the colonial period and Republic, many immigrants were Americans who were escaping creditors at home. Texas found it good policy, in building up the population, to give people a fresh start. This sentiment increased after the United States began rejecting Texas's attempts to join the Union. U.S. debts were not allowed to be collected from immigrants who came to Texas; even marriages valid in the United States were not recognized as supporting a charge of bigamy if one remarried in Texas.

and secure land titles for Texas's native Indian tribes, especially the Cherokee, as a reward for their remaining neutral in the revolution; Lamar was shrill in demanding that Texas Indians be exterminated or driven away. Houston came to represent the small holders and common people, while Lamar and his faction were supported by the planter elite. Until he married in 1840, Houston was an alcoholic and was tolerant of others' foibles; Lamar was a tight-vested moralist. These were the natural fault lines in Texas society as it developed, so it is not surprising that each demographic group found its champion.

What was the Cherokee War?

East Texas was the most thickly settled region of the country, and Anglo settlers there coveted lands on which Cherokee Indians had settled only a few years before Americans began arriving. With Houston out of power and indeed out of the country, and with the discovery of documents showing that Mexico intended to try to ally with the Cherokee to renew hostilities in Texas, Lamar sought the expulsion of the Cherokee. In July 1839, five hundred Texas troops drove the Cherokee northward to the Indian Territory in a series of bloody firefights that killed about a hundred Indians, including their eighty-four-year-old chief, Bowl. His body was scalped and a razor strop cut from his back; his three-cornered hat was sent to Houston as a pointed insult.

What happened at the Council House Fight?

Simultaneously with moving against the Cherokee, Lamar also opened hostilities against the powerful Comanche, a conflict that had no hope of final success. Initial attacks managed only to set off a spate of Comanche raids. However, the band that lived nearest San Antonio, the Penateka, were also the least warlike, and they asked to come into the city and talk peace. A delegation of chiefs and warriors entered San Antonio on March 19, 1840, with a number of women and children to show their peaceable intentions. They brought with them only one white captive, a girl named Matilda Lockhart, instead of all the captives they had agreed to. Lockhart's condition sparked outrage; she had been

59

hideously abused and tortured, her nose burned entirely off (a claim now challenged by revisionist historians, who are more politically correct than factual). Lockhart told the Texan commissioners that the intention of the Comanche was to bring in captives one at a time to negotiate the maximum ransom. When informed that they would be held hostage until the rest of their prisoners would be brought in, the Comanche drew knives and strung bows, and the Texans started shooting. Nearly all the Indians were killed or captured. When Comanche outside the city learned of it, they tortured and killed the remaining captives, and hostilities continued more furiously than ever.

Why did Mexico invade Texas in 1842?

Mexico had never abandoned its claim to Texas, so the forays of March and September were meant to maintain its claim. More immediately, Lamar during his presidency repeatedly provoked Mexico by renting out the Republic of Texas Navy to Mexican rebels in Yucatan to harass Mexican shipping and by mounting an extravagant trade caravan to Santa Fe, whose purpose Mexico quickly discovered was to invite New Mexico to secede and join itself to Texas. Houston succeeded Lamar in December 1841, but by then Mexico had already decided it was time to assert itself. The March sortie lasted barely a week, but a second strike in September was more substantial. San Antonio was occupied, and hostages, including an entire court of judges, jury, and witnesses, were spirited back to Mexico.

What was the "Black Bean" episode?

Back in office, Houston was keenly aware that Texas was not strong enough to carry a war into Mexico, but the temper of the country made inaction impossible. He ordered an army of 750 under Alexander Somervell to the Rio Grande, where they occupied Laredo, but finding the invading army long gone, Somervell ordered them to return home. Two mutinous officers who also harbored anti-Houston ambitions, William S. Fisher and Thomas Jefferson Green, led 350 men into further pillaging until they were overwhelmed and captured by a Mexican army under Pedro de Ampudia. When the prisoners attempted an escape, Santa Anna ordered a decimation. A total of 159 white beans were placed in a jar with seventeen black ones. Texan prisoners were forced to draw beans from the jar, and the unlucky seventeen were shot. It was gory and protracted, as many prisoners had to be shot several times before they were killed. The incident further inflamed anti-Mexican feeling in Texas.

FRONTIER ECONOMY

After independence, how did Texans manage to start an economy from scratch?

Independence removed the legal impediment to slavery, and like the American South, cotton production and export took hold in a big way. Customs duties levied at Texas ports

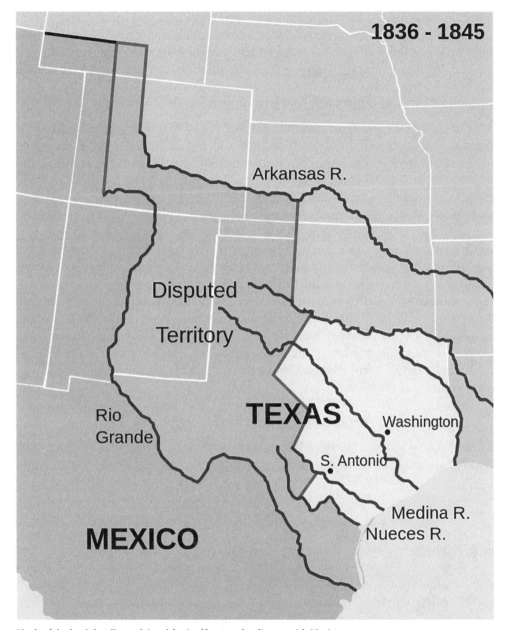

1836 - 1845

Arkansas R.

Disputed

Territory

Rio
Grande

TEXAS

Washington

S. Antonio

Medina R.
Nueces R.

MEXICO

Much of the land that Texas claimed for itself was under dispute with Mexico.

were the largest source of governmental income. The Republic of Texas never issued coinage; the first issue of paper currency was promissory notes, which President Houston instructed the commercial agent in New Orleans to float only gradually so as not to depreciate their value. Most of the money in circulation came from the United States with immigrants, and the American dollar became the measure of the Texas dollar. Lamar

61

was far more profligate than Houston, financing Indian wars and antagonizing Mexico with repeated issues of unsupported paper money, until it was finally worth only a few cents on the American dollar. For most Texans, life had to be as self-sufficient as possible, and that meant growing their own corn, slaughtering their own hogs, and hunting.

How much land did settlers receive for coming to Texas?

After independence, the Texas government sought to build up the population as fast as it could, so it continued the Mexican practice of giving land away to those who would live on it and work it. The 1836 Constitution provided that all heads of white families who resided in Texas as of the time of independence would receive the previous Mexican measure of a league and a labor of land, or 4,605 acres (19 square kilometers). Single men would receive a third of a league, or 1,476 acres (6 square kilometers). As time passed, the terms became less generous. Families who came after the Declaration of Independence and before October 1, 1837, could receive two sections of land, or 1,280 acres (5 square kilometers), and single men half that; these were called second-class headrights. Families who came after this but before January 1, 1840, received one section, and single men half a section; these were third-class headrights. Such grants became more conditional after this, but the Republic still gave away nearly 37 million acres (149,734 square kilometers) in headright grants and a few million more acres in bounty and donation grants to military veterans. Such land was important not just as freeholds for citizens, but they also became a medium of exchange, especially in payment of large debts.

What were the most popular professions in early Texas?

Given that land was most people's principal resource, Texas attracted immigrants who revolved around that. Many were, or became, surveyors. Although Texas law in several

Why was newspaper publishing such a large concern?

No matter how isolated people were in Texas, they still desired to know current events. Moreover, the chronic dearth of reading material through the country meant that newspapers filled that need. Thus, papers did not print just news but also poetry, humor, short fiction, inspirational vignettes, and other reading for diversion. Of equal importance to the editors was advertising revenue. A disproportionate number of ads sought to recover runaway slaves; in fact, the first woodcuts used to illustrate Texas newspapers depicted runaway blacks slinking away with their belongings tied in a handkerchief at the end of a pole. Some advertisers displayed good wit. Two law partners who found the competition too great decided to become barbers instead, a profession from which, they announced, they would "continue to clip the public."

In the early days of Texas cattle ranching, the animals were mostly feral or semiferal longhorns, which were hunted down instead of domestically raised.

respects continued to follow Spanish civil law, which complicated practice for American attorneys who came to Texas, land law thrived. In fact, when Baltimore attorney J. Wilmer Dallam went to Texas in 1839, he made his fortune by collecting and publishing the decisions of the Texas Supreme Court—which was standard practice in the United States, but no one had yet thought to do that in Texas. Virtually every attorney in Texas needed to have a copy, not so much for the Court decisions but more because Dallam also explained Texas's byzantine Spanish land law. A doctor in the community was always highly prized, and many educated men, including Dallam, sought to edit and publish newspapers.

Was cattle ranching a big business in early Texas?

It seems surprising today, but no. The great cattle drives to northern markets still lay decades in the future. Cattle, which at this time still meant feral or semiferal longhorns, were herded and managed only distantly, and slaughtering meant as much hunting as anything else. Hides and tallow were still considered valuable media of exchange, especially tallow, for candles remained so precious that boarding schools charged extra tuition to students who could not bring their own. As far as actual stock raising went, however, a visiting Methodist minister was surprised to find that in most people's estimation, "a man who is weak handed, can, nevertheless, raise stock." Small cattle drives were not unknown, but they headed east to market in New Orleans, not north.

How well did preachers do in early Texas?

The Texas Revolution took place during the height of the Second Great Awakening in the United States, a religious movement that began in the northeast. It was highly emotional, highly Pentecostal, and suspicious of bookish education. From the upper Appalachians, the fervor came down the Ohio and Mississippi rivers and reached Texas just about the same time as independence. Protestants had been driven from Texas under Mexico, but now it was a ripe field for the harvest of souls. The Baptists and the Methodists entered into a hard competition with each other, and while Texas's crusty settlers sometimes blustered that preachers were not welcome, ministers who stood up for themselves generally managed to make a living. That was the experience of Robert Alexander (1811–1882). He preached once in Washington, in the billiard hall in the attic above Hatfield's saloon (which doubled as the Senate chamber when the government was in session). Affecting not to hear the jeers and protests as he laid his Bible on the billiard table, by the time he finished, the patrons shook his hand and took up a collection for him.

What professions were open to women?

Texas was the first real manifestation of the society that became identified with the "Wild West." For many years, men far outnumbered women, saloons outnumbered churches, and schools were a rarity. Refined women who came to Texas as teachers, such as Frances Trask (1806–1892) of Massachusetts, commanded great respect in the community. President Houston escorted her to the first San Jacinto Ball in April 1837, and the girls' finishing school that she ran was well attended. Even she, however, also relied on the security of inheriting her brother's headright grant. It was far more common for women to support themselves by running hotels or boarding-houses, as did several of Texas's leading female personalities, including Jane Long, Angelina Eberly, and Pamela Mann. Mortality being what it was, many women were widowed and left to run the family farm by themselves, and Texas women were renowned for being as tough, shrewd, self-reliant, and foul-mouthed as any man.

How did slavery figure into the Texas economy?

Cotton production would have been impossible without slave labor, so from that standpoint the Texas economy would have crumbled without it. There were other subtler as-

---

How did sawmills become important?

Stephen F. Austin's early colonists typically built log dog-trot cabins for themselves, but as the social classes began to pull apart, the well-to-do desired the distinction of living in houses of sawn lumber. The whole broad eastern belt of Texas was heavily forested in old-growth pine, and millers with timber and water power made a very good living.

pects as well, though. A few slave owners, such as Sam Houston, allowed their slaves to seek outside employment on their own time and keep the money they earned, so they participated in the economy on their own. It was more common for masters to hire out their slaves and keep the money, which was how the former provisional president, David G. Burnet, supported himself in his old age. A few hundred free persons of color also lived in Texas, and some of them gained importance to their local economy. One such was William Ashworth (1793–?), who operated a ferry across Lake Sabine. The local Anglo community found the goods and services provided by Ashworth and his large extended family so necessary that they successfully petitioned the Texas Congress to exempt the Ashworths from an 1840 law that gave free blacks two years to leave the country.

INTERNATIONAL RELATIONS

What was Texas's standing with the world's other countries?

While Texans would have preferred annexation to the United States, the final act of Andrew Jackson's administration was to recognize the Republic of Texas. The British and French were quick to see the development of Texas cotton as a potential relief from their dependence upon American cotton, and each recognized the Republic after it maintained itself against Mexican hostility for a believable length of time. Various German states saw the potential for trade and a destination for their own quasi-colonial emigrant exodus. Even countries that did not have a direct interest in Texas sent tokens of their friendly regard. During Houston's second term, the Empress of China gifted him with a dazzling porcelain tea service. The Ottoman Sultan sent him a suit of embroidered red silk, complete from fez down to billowing pantaloons and curled-toe, Arabian-night booties in yellow leather—an ensemble that caused Houston's chronically depressed wife, Margaret, to shriek in laughter when he tried them on.

What kind of representatives did other countries send to Texas?

Texas was not important enough for other countries to send representatives of ambassadorial rank. The United States, Britain, and France all sent chargés d'affaires, a rank below an ambassador, and they worked out of legations rather than

Sir Charles Elliot, a former governor of Bermuda and administrator of Hong Kong, later served as a British diplomat to the Republic of Texas.

embassies. Texas was rather a backwater in world affairs, and it was a diplomatic posting where inexperienced or problematic foreign service officers might not get in too much trouble. Among the more interesting were British captain Sir Charles Elliot (1801–1875), the recent administrator of Hong Kong, who was demoted and sent to Texas after being accused of showing too much conscience for the Chinese during the Opium War. The French sent Alphonse Dubois, Comte de Saligny (1809–1888), the secretary of the French delegation to the United States and a journeyman whose watchfulness for French dignity outweighed his diplomatic skills. The United States made the clearest statement of its interests, sending Joseph Eve of Kentucky (1784–1843), who was an ardent backer of annexation.

How did international representatives get along with each other in Texas?

In a more established and prosperous country, the different countries' legations need not have had much contact with each other. When the Texas capital was in Washington, there was only one boarding-house, and the British and American chargés sometimes got into shouting matches over their respective country's positions when they had to eat at the same table.

What was the Pig War?

None of the foreign diplomatic corps was more put off by Texas's rude frontier conditions than the French Comte de Saligny. He arrived in Austin with his chef, Eugene Pluyette; he was shocked at seeing pigs of uncertain ownership foraging in the streets. While his legation was being built, Dubois resided at the Bullock House Hotel at Congress Avenue and Pecan Street; when one of the semiferal hogs broke into his room and ate some diplomatic dispatches, Dubois had Pluyette kill the animal and cook it. The pig turned out to have been Bullock's. When Dubois moved out, he accused Bullock of padding his bill and refused to pay it, an incident culminating with Bullock socking the chargé in the nose. Dubois demanded legal redress and was not satisfied with Bullock being charged with assault when the insulted dignity of France required something far more draconian. When this was not forthcoming, he packed up and moved to New Orleans to guffaws of local laughter. The Texans may have made up jokes about the "No-Account de Saligny," but the joke was really on them. Texas desperately needed a loan of money from a friendly foreign power, but it turned out that the French finance minister was none other than Dubois de Saligny's brother-in-law, so that ambition went nowhere.

How did Texas become so friendly with the German states?

After the Republic of Texas was recognized by England and France, relations naturally followed from some of the many German states (German unification still lay a generation into the future). Henry Fisher (1805–1867), whom Texas sent as consul to the Hanseatic League, was himself a native of Hesse and owned an interest in a vast empresario grant in the Hill Country west of Austin. Finding Germany in political and social turmoil, he sold his interest in the land grant (with perhaps a few material misrepresentations as to its location and convenience to commerce) to a consortium of nobles who were looking to sponsor German emigration to Texas.

ANNEXATION TRICKERY

Why didn't the United States want Texas?

Although Texas was populated almost entirely by Americans, nearly all of whom wanted their new country to join the United States, the U.S. Senate twice rejected treaties of annexation. First, while Texas independence was widely recognized by the major powers, Mexico still claimed it, and annexing Texas would probably mean war, which would be difficult, expensive, and uncertain. The second big issue was slavery. The United States was already straining over sectional differences, and slave states and free states had held an equal number of senate seats following the Missouri Compromise of 1820. To admit Texas as a slave state would have upset that balance, to which the North was adamantly opposed.

How did Texas manage to get into the Union?

The one possibility that alarmed the United States more than admitting Texas as a state was Texas becoming a client state of Great Britain. The British already held the Pacific Northwest, Canada, and numerous islands in the West Indies. If Texas sought affiliation as a British protectorate, the United States would have been surrounded by what Andrew Jackson called an "iron hoop" that America could never have broken through. During his second term as Texas president, Sam Houston played this to the hilt. He continually slighted the U.S. representatives in favor of the British, he held up trade on the Santa Fe Trail between the United States and Mexico where it crossed the Texas national boundary, and he even secretly authored newspaper articles attacking the idea of annexing Texas to the United States.

What was the Snively Expedition?

The Treaties of Velasco conceded Texas sovereign territory to lie east of the Rio Grande "from mouth to source," which extended even into present-day Wyoming. This meant that the profitable U.S.–Mexico trade carried on the Santa Fe Trail passed through the Republic of Texas. As one way of showing his aloofness to the United States, Sam Houston during the spring of 1843 sent one of his minions, Jacob Snively (1809–1971), to in-

The Santa Fe Expedition was intended to help Texas lay claim land to territories in the northwest, including the route of the Santa Fe Trail. This map shows the route of the expedition in 1841.

terdict that trade. Assembling a motley column of 150, Snively marched north. They fought a column of Mexican dragoons, killing seventeen while sustaining no casualties, after which U.S. troops asserted control over the route. They disarmed Snively's force and sent them home, which still played into Houston's hand by creating an unpleasant international incident that disguised his continued determination to get Texas into the Union.

How else did Houston manage to disguise his annexation gambit?

Houston let Captain Charles Elliott, the British chargé, know that Texas as a British sphere of interest would help them keep their hands on Oregon, which American expansionists were clamoring for. He also believed that Britain's real game was to keep Texas and Mexico at each other's throats but without a victory by either side so as to continue their trade with both, and Britain had been profitably selling arms to Mexico. Houston's friendly engagement with the British kept their attention away from discovering Houston's annexation effort.

Why was Texas annexed by Joint Resolution of the Congress and not by a treaty?

Andrew Jackson was retired and in failing health, but he remained vitally interested in getting Texas into the Union. Sam Houston was nearing the end of his own second term and decided the time was right to drop his European pretense. He sent his trusted private secretary, Wash Miller, to deliver a letter to Jackson, avowing his desire to see Texas annexed but indicating that time was running out. Jackson sent Miller and the letter on to Washington, D.C., and to Robert J. Walker of Mississippi, who was managing the annexation effort in the Senate. Under the U.S. Constitution, treaties must be ratified by a two-thirds majority of the Senate. That kind of support could never be found to accept

---

What was "Manifest Destiny"?

The Texas question was the single most important issue that was argued in the U.S. presidential election of 1844. James Knox Polk of Tennessee, who had risen to replace Houston as Jackson's most important protégé, was ardently in favor; the Whig Henry Clay of Kentucky was opposed with equal passion. During the campaign, a widely read newspaper piece argued that it was God's will for the United States to spread its civilization across the whole of North America, that it was America's "manifest destiny" to occupy Texas and eventually the far West. In fact, Polk's campaign slogan was "Fifty-four forty or fight," a pledge that if he were elected, he would seize all of the British Oregon country up to its northernmost latitude. Clay missed out on becoming president by a mere thirty-eight thousand votes, but Polk carried so many states—barely—that his electoral majority was impressive enough to convince the outgoing president, John Tyler of Virginia, to cooperate in the Texas effort.

Texas. However, nothing in the Constitution required annexation to be accomplished by treaty. A joint resolution of the Congress would have the same effect and require only a simple majority of both houses.

How did the other powers respond to the news of annexation?

Houston had been encouraging the French and British to continue negotiating with Mexico on Texas's behalf, and he withdrew the small Texas navy from the Gulf to demonstrate his peaceable bearing toward Mexico. When news of the U.S. annexation resolution broke, Santa Anna realized that he had been played, and he was furious, but France and England talked him down by reaching a deal with Texas. They would convene a delegation of "umpires" to sort out Texas–Mexico relations based on the premise that Mexico would recognize Texas independence if Texas would agree never to join the United States. Houston was succeeded as president by his secretary of state, Dr. Anson Jones, who won election without committing himself on the issue of annexation. Thus, it fell to Jones to manage the timing, to call an election of delegates, and lay before them the choice either to join the United States or to accept Mexico's word—and that meant Santa Anna's word—that he would finally recognize Texas as an equal nation.

What were the final terms on which Texas entered the Union?

As long as the U.S. government believed that Texas was serious about going British, that would have been a calamity for American interests. Thinking that this was their last chance, they offered far better terms than in the treaty they had just rejected. Texas could enter the Union directly as a state, even though the population was only about half what was otherwise needed for statehood. Texans could later split into as many as five states if they wished. Best of all, Texas could keep its vast public domain and use it to defray its mounting national debt, whereas with a territory the public land passed to the federal government. The deal was almost too good to be true. As Texas diplomat J. P. Henderson wrote, "Houston has played it off well."

Did Sam Houston ever explain his annexation strategy?

He did, once, after the joint resolution was safely passed. He had retired from office and had begun a triumphal progress through the South toward a last visit with Andrew Jackson. At the end of May 1845, he was called upon to speak at the Arcade in New Orleans. As set down by a reporter: "My friends, I have been accused of lending myself to England and France; but, I assure you, I have only been *coquetting* with them. . . . Supposing a charming lady has two suitors. One of them she is inclined to believe would make the better husband, but he is a little slow to make interesting propositions. Do you think if she was a skillful practitioner in Cupid's court she would pretend that she loved the other "feller" the best and be sure that her favorite would know it? [Laughter and applause.] If ladies are justified in making use of coquetry in securing their *annexation* to good and agreeable husbands, you must excuse me for making use of the same means to annex Texas to Uncle Sam. [Laughter and cheers.]"

NOTEWORTHY CHARACTERS
OF THE REPUBLIC

What Houston madam consorted with Sam Houston and was later sentenced to hang?

During the Runaway Scrape, in order to haul his cannons, Sam Houston borrowed two oxen from Pamela Mann (d. 1840) on the promise that the army would turn north toward Nacogdoches and her stock would be in no danger. When instead they turned south to fight at San Jacinto, Mann chased them down on her horse, cussed Houston up one side and down the other, cut her oxen free, and led them away. Later, she moved to Houston City and opened the Mansion House, an establishment that kept, according to one patron, a downstairs stocked with whiskey and an upstairs stocked with "fawn-necked damsels." She and Houston became convivial buddies while the capital was located in Houston, and he was best man at her son's wedding. Mann was accepted in Houston society despite her notorious living, although later she was tried and convicted of forgery, which was a capital offense. The jury, knowing what trouble madams sometimes had collecting fees from their patrons, recommended clemency, which President Lamar granted. While married to her fourth husband, she died of yellow fever on November 4, 1840. She left an estate of a remarkable $40,000.

What abolitionist traveled to Texas to start a demonstration colony of freed slaves?

Benjamin Lundy (1789–1839) was a Quaker who was born in New Jersey and lived in Ohio, but he was ubiquitous in his quest to see American slaves freed. He was as opposed to Northern discrimination against people of color as he was to Southern slavery, yet he also disfavored the prevalent movement to export freed slaves to the Pepper Coast (now Liberia) in West Africa. Building on visits to Canada and Haiti, he went to Texas in 1833 seeking land on which to relocate freed slaves to show that given a fresh start and equal footing, they could prosper as well as Anglos. Unknown to Lundy, abolitionists back in the North, such as his protégé, William Lloyd Garrison, opposed his plan for a demonstration

Benjamin Lundy was a Quaker, abolitionist, and founder of antislavery newspapers who opposed Texas joining the Union as a slave state.

colony because that suggested a way toward gradual, incremental freeing of slaves, whereas they demanded immediate emancipation of all slaves, regardless of its effect on the Southern economy. Unaware that his own people had cut off his support, Lundy went broke, served time in debtor's prison, and conceived that he was ruined by a conspiracy of the Southern planters who wished to extend their hegemony into Texas. Lundy wrote a fiery pamphlet, claiming that Texas's desired annexation to the United States was nothing more than a plot by Southern slave owners to add to their power in Congress. With help from former U.S. president John Quincy Adams, who shared his views, Lundy's pamphlet was distributed to every member of Congress. It was an indispensable part of the U.S. refusal to admit Texas for a decade, and some revisionist historians still accept the "Southern Conspiracy."

What was the Regulator-Moderator War?

Watt Moorman (1817–1850) was the single greatest influence over life in much of east Texas during the life of the Republic, though he was elected by no one and held no office. Born in Alabama and raised in Mississippi, he went to Texas with his parents fleeing the Panic of 1837. It was their bad luck to settle in Shelby County. Starting with the Neutral Ground Agreement of 1806, East Texas had been a lawless hell of squatters, fugitives, and petty tyrants. The local economy revolved around slave running and fraudulent land certificates that were avidly traded in despite everyone knowing that they were bogus. Over respective merits long since lost to history, two feuding factions coalesced, bushwhacking enemies and burning out homes, one the Moderators and the other the Regulators, of whom Moorman took control, evincing his psychopathy and announcing his arrival with bleats on a hunting horn. After the deaths of more than fifty, marshals of the Republic arrested ten from each side, including Moorman, arbitrated their differences, and the violence ceased as inexplicably as it began.

Why was Judge Robert Williamson called "Three-legged Willie"?

Robert McAlpin Williamson (1804?–1859), during his youth in Georgia, was attacked by an illness, perhaps polio, that left him bedridden for two years and bent his right leg back at the knee. Fitted with a wooden prosthesis, he became known as Three-legged Willie, which, upon arriving in Texas about 1828, did not prevent him from becoming one of the most celebrated dancers in the state. An editor of various frontier newspapers in which he proved himself an early and fiery advocate of independence from Mexico, he is sometimes accorded the honorific as the Patrick Henry of Texas. After independence, Williamson was named chief judge of the Third Judicial District, which included the dangerous purgatory of Shelby County. As he convened the first court session in that part of the country, one of the local feudists approached, thumped his Bowie knife into Williamson's bench, and declared, "This, sir, is the law of Shelby County!" Unfazed, Williamson leaned back, drew his pistol, and said, "Then this, sir, is the constitution that overrules your law." The case proceeded. Clever as well as brave, Williamson named one of his sons, born during the uncertainty of whether Texas would join the Union, Willie Annexus.

What became of Susanna Dickinson, who survived the Alamo?

Dickinson (1814–1883) was only twenty-two when her husband died in the Alamo, leaving her with their infant daughter, Angelina, to raise. After appeals to the Texas Congress for aid were turned down and needing a husband, she married John Williams late in 1837. He was a drunk who beat her and the baby, and she divorced him after four months. She wed again in 1838, then she was widowed again five years later. She supported herself for ten years (apparently living for a time in the Mansion House with her distant relative, Pamela Mann) before marrying for a fourth time, in 1847. That man divorced her ten years later, accusing her of adultery and prostitution, as sworn by witnesses. She had already left him, moved to Lockhart, opened a boardinghouse, and prospered due to her cooking. She then married Joseph Hannig, a Silesian immi-

Alamo survivor Susanna Dickinson suffered many tough years, including three failed marriages, until finally marrying a younger man who became successful in business, providing a comfortable home at last.

grant many years her junior. They moved to Austin, where he became a wealthy businessman. Susanna then lived in comfort, first in a solid stone house downtown at Pine and Neches (now a museum) and then on a scenic farm overlooking Waller Creek, north of the city, until her death in 1883. Her tumultuous life spanned the whole range of challenges that frontier women faced in Texas.

What white captive of the Comanche became the mother of their greatest chief?

As different sects of the Second Great Awakening in Texas developed ever more peculiar ideas of how to be saved, the Baptists particularly divided and subdivided into two-seeders, predestinarians, antimissionaries, and whatnot. One family clan of about thirty, headed by Elder John and Granny Parker, established their private fort near the later site of Groesbeck. On May 19, 1836, the Comanche approached under signs of friendship but upon being denied a cow killed five of the men, pinned Granny to the ground with a lance and raped her, and, as help arrived, escaped with two more women, a girl, and two boys. Most were eventually ransomed, but the girl, Cynthia Ann Parker (1825?–c. 1871), was traded to a distant band, became acculturated, and became the woman of the chief of the Nokoni Comanche band. She bore three children, of whom her son, Quanah ("Fragrance") Parker, left the Nokoni and lived on the Staked Plains with the feared Quahadi band. He became the last Comanche chief to surrender, and he led that nation through their transition to Anglo life. When "rescued" in 1860, Cynthia Ann Parker lived miserably and had to be watched to prevent her escape back to her adopted people.

What Texas Ranger finally gained the upper hand in Comanche warfare?

During Mirabeau Lamar's hotly prosecuted war against the Comanche, the Indians held the advantage in warfare, for in the time it took a Texas soldier to reload his musket or single-shot pistol, a warrior could advance and lose five or six arrows. One Texas Ranger, John Coffee Hays (1817–1883), became impressed with the potential of the new Colt pistols that could fire five shots from a revolving cylinder before needing to be reloaded. Acquiring some of these as surplus from the Texas Navy, Hays put them to the test in June 1844, when his Ranger company encountered a war party of Comanche near the Pedernales River. The Indians, typically, waited for a volley and attacked but were cut down by the repeating fire. One Ranger and at least two dozen Comanche were killed. The survivors were left to wonder how the white men had "as many shots as they had fingers." It was the beginning of the end for Comanche power.

TEXAS AS ANTEBELLUM STATE

OLD SOUTH MEETS OLD WEST

Who comprised the first state government?

J. Pinckney Henderson (1808–1858), who had served the Republic as minister to the courts of Europe, was elected first governor of Texas. At this time, when U.S. senators were chosen by the state legislatures, they selected Sam Houston and Thomas Jefferson Rusk. Texas sent two representatives to the Twenty-ninth Congress. Elected from the Eastern District was David Kaufman (1813–1851), a Pennsylvanian and Princeton graduate who arrived in Texas after the revolution. Despite his lack of roots, he was elected to three terms in the Texas Congress, the latter two serving as Speaker, then a year and a half as a senator before going to Washington as chargé d'affaires. The Western District elected the much older Timothy Pilsbury (1780–1858), a Massachusetts sailor who had commanded a privateer during the War of 1812. He had also served in both the House and Senate of the Republic.

Who was Texas's first First Lady?

Frances Cox Henderson (1820–1897) was a prodigiously talented woman and in many ways more interesting than her husband. She was born in Philadelphia, was educated in Paris, and met J. Pinckney Henderson when he was minister plenipotentiary to the Tuileries. They married in London, and once in Texas made their home in San Augustine, where her piano may have been the first heard in those parts. When he became governor, he was unwilling to expose his treasured Fanny to the frontier dangers of Austin, so she learned law and ran his office while he was out of town. A dedicated Episcopalian on a frontier where Baptists and Methodists were at war with each other, she obtained credentials, journeyed east, and obtained clergy to found Episcopal churches in Texas. Aside from also being a skilled mathematician, she was an astounding linguist: she edited a book, *Epitome of Modern European Literature*, with selections from nineteen languages—which she translated herself. She was also an early advocate of women's suffrage.

How did the Texas Supreme Court change from Republic to state?

Under the Republic, each judge of the four judicial districts was perforce a judge (not justice) of the Supreme Court, presided over by the chief judge, who had no district of his own. Under the state, the number of judges was reduced to three, now termed justices, in line with other American states. The first three were John Hemphill as chief justice, Royall Wheeler (1810–1864), and a new appointment, Abner Lipscomb (1789–1856). The latter two were no shrinking violets. Lipscomb read for the law in the office of John C. Cal-

Texas' first lady, Frances Cox Henderson, married the first state governor, J. Pinckney Henderson.

houn and served in the Alabama legislature before spending twelve years as chief justice of the Alabama Supreme Court. Wheeler was a paradox, a Vermont Yankee who studied law in Ohio, but who, as a lawyer in Arkansas and then Texas, became one of the slaveocracy's most virulent defenders.

Supreme Court justices were appointed, not elected?

Yes. This question was vividly thrashed out at the convention that prepared Texas's first state constitution. The United States had just elected a Jacksonian Democrat, James Knox Polk, as president, and Texas was prime country for those principles of the most local control of the democracy and trust in the simplest common man to safely guide the country. T. J. Rusk, who had been the Texas Court's second chief justice, railed against the idea of placing the judiciary in the hands of the voting mob, arguing that judges should be cut from more distinguished cloth and rise above party factions to give more reasoned decisions. Hemphill backed him and they won the day, but within a few years, the supporters of electing everybody had passed a constitutional amendment, and Texas soon began subjecting judges to popular scrutiny. It is an issue that Texas has struggled with ever since.

What became of Texas's last president, Anson Jones?

Jones (1798–1858) had always been sour, brittle, and irritable. He was a Massachusetts native and Pennsylvania resident before business failures led him to start over in Texas.

He always claimed bitterly that it was he and not Sam Houston who was the true architect of annexation; he desired to go to Washington as one of Texas's first senators, but when the legislature snubbed him without a single vote, he descended into mental illness. He edited his memoirs repeatedly with increasing venom, and on January 9, 1858, he committed suicide on the steps of the old capitol building in Houston.

How did the Mexican–American War affect Texas?

The advent of war with Mexico in 1846 caused deep division in the United States, but in Texas, the feeling was nearly unanimous in its favor. Texas, unlike the eastern part of the country, had been victimized since its inception by the incessant revolutions, coups, and juntas that came to power in Mexico and fell, often in the smoke of firing squads. This chaos created chronic unrest along the border, and in Texas the war was argued as a matter of border security, not territorial expansion.

Didn't the United States begin the Mexican–American War?

Today's revisionist historians argue so, but the issues are more complex than that. Despite his shocking brutality at the Alamo and Goliad and burning town after town to cleanse American settlers out of Texas, Santa Anna lost the campaign to keep Texas in Mexico. Wars have consequences, and he was compelled to sign the Treaties of Velasco, which awarded Texas the Rio Grande as the border between the two countries. Texas had maintained its independence by force of arms for ten years. One of the terms of annexation was that the United States would protect Texas from further Mexican aggression until the change was affected completely. As soon as he learned that annexation was imminent, Santa Anna declared war, which he termed "defensive war," and the United States moved troops into the Nueces Strip, which was the territory between the Nueces and the Rio Grande, which by the treaty (that Mexico had repudiated) was now

What two later U.S. presidents fought in a battle near Brownsville?

Before the commencement of the Mexican–American War, the United States moved troops into the "Nueces Strip" of largely vacant land north of Matamoros, Mexico, to stake the American claim to the Republic of Texas it had just annexed, which claimed the Rio Grande as the boundary under the Treaties of Velasco. Mexico considered this a challenge and moved an army across the Rio Grande to engage the Americans at the battles of Palo Alto on May 8, 1846, and Resaca de la Palma the following day. The result was a withering defeat of the Mexican force. The American general commanding was Zachary Taylor, president from 1849 to 1850; one lieutenant who fought under his command was Ulysses S. Grant, president from 1869 to 1877. Nearby is the site of the Battle of Palmito Ranch, the last land battle of the Civil War. All three sites are preserved and interpreted.

Texan. Modern historians consider this a hostile act, but not the Mexican Army's crossing the Rio Grande to attack them.

Having worked so hard to get into the Union, why did Texas threaten to leave again almost immediately?

The United States admitted Texas to the extent of its treaty boundaries, which included the Rio Grande "from mouth to source" and included territory as far north as Wyoming. However, Texas was a slave state, and the Missouri Compromise of 1820 had placed a northern limit on slavery of the 36°30' north parallel of latitude. After Texas commissioners organized El Paso as a Texas county, they continued north to Santa Fe. There, the American general at the terminus of the Santa Fe Trail drew upon both his own anti-slavery beliefs and the desire of Santa Fe residents not to be part of Texas to block the Texas commissioners from organizing Santa Fe as a Texas county. Texas officials were livid, claimed that this was a violation of the annexation agreement, and the governor even hinted that U.S. troops would come off second best in a contest with Texas Rangers.

What did Texas do with all that money?

After retiring the national debt, Texas used its boundary settlement funds to build a large, Greek revival governor's mansion and capitol. With land still being Texas's principal resource and those records being irreplaceable, they built a state-of-the-art, fireproof land office building with a stone staircase (replaced with cast iron when the weight of the stone began to pull the walls in) and whose stove flues were buried in the masonry.

How did relations with the Indians progress under statehood?

Even within its reduced boundaries, Texas was far larger than its population could occupy, and the line of settlement crept only slowly northwest into Comanche lands. Because Texas kept its public domain, the federal government had no land to set aside for Indian reservations. That suited most Texans, as they were still more interested in exterminating Indians than making peace. In 1854, however, they created two small reservations on the upper Brazos on which to place the Penateka Comanche, who had formerly troubled Austin and San Antonio, and the other for the central Texas tribes such as the Keechi and Waco. The Indians began farming and won the respect of their white neighbors, but hostile militia mobs caused so much violence that the natives were escorted to the Indian Territory in 1859. Their Texas agent, Robert Neighbors, was assassinated upon his return for his sympathy and fair dealing with them. The exile of the Penateka Comanche had one unintended consequence: when the Comanche bands of the Indian Territory, still powerful and free-roaming, got a good look at what trying to become white had done to the Penateka, they determined that they wanted nothing to do with that and resolved to continue to live by hunting and pillaging.

COTTON AND SLAVERY

Was slavery in Texas materially different from that of the American South?

If anything, the lot of slaves in Texas was harder than in the United States, first because the land had to be cleared before it could be cultivated, and second because most of the immigrants who came to Texas were not of the wealthy class. Those who had it made in Tennessee or Alabama stayed there. Texas's poor but ambitious settlers who owned only one or two slaves worked them hard. Third, Texas was isolated from the commodities and creature comforts available in the states, and slaves got the least of what little there was. And fourth, there was the danger of Indian attack, which was no longer the case in the United States.

Did owners feel differently about their slaves in Texas?

One journalist who traveled through the South and then Texas noticed one great difference. In the Deep South, the institution had existed for so long that it was ingrained in society and accepted as the natural order. The journalist wrote that in Texas—newer and rawer, with a history of subverting Mexican law against slavery owners seemed conscious of the "existence of a wrong relation" that made them more defensive and defiant.

How much did Texas cotton production increase after statehood?

Figures for the earliest years are inconsistent, but in 1849, Texas's fourth year as a state, the reported harvest was 58,073 bales, each weighing 500 pounds (227 kilograms). Ten years later, in 1859, this had ballooned to 431,645 bales, a staggering increase. It was the result of a flood of immigration from the United States onto free headrights granted by the state and the eviction of the Brazos Valley Indian tribes from central Texas, which was prime cotton land.

How much did slaves cost?

During this period, $800 was considered a fair price for a prime field hand, which is almost $25,000 in current value—an astronomical investment that few families could afford. Unskilled, general-purpose slaves might be obtained for about half that. No doubt, inheritance and natural increase accounted for a good deal of slave ownership.

Were slaves still being brought from Africa?

The African slave trade had been illegal in the United States since 1808, but there

Slaves were used to harvest Texas' considerable cotton crops.

79

were efforts to subvert the law and smuggle in new ones. One enterprising woman was caught trying to unload a cargo of captive Africans in Texas, thinking to mask their odor below decks with a cargo of live camels topside. She was able to get away, dumped the camels, and sold her Africans in Cuba instead.

What protections existed for slaves in antebellum Texas?

Slavery was horrific and morally indefensible, yet the antebellum social reality was that most owners were not gratuitously vicious to their slaves. Cruel "slave drivers" were not respected, and it was not unknown for people to buy slaves out from under them, which was, for instance, how Sam Houston acquired his long time personal attendant, Jeff Hamilton. One abolitionist journalist reporting from Texas was astonished to hear an owner proclaim that, of course, she took the best care of her people that she could because "eight hundred dollars is a great deal of money to lay out on a thing that might lie down the next day and die."

Did the Texas courts exercise any control over slavery?

Slaves had very few protections under the law, but in Texas, surprisingly, courts would often hear their grievances and sometimes even act in their favor. They were not allowed to testify against white people, but often a sympathetic citizen would appear in court as their "next friend" and give evidence on their behalf. Some surprising cases made their way up to the state Supreme Court. One of them upheld the conviction of a white man for assaulting a free person of color, another upheld the freedom of a slave woman freed in Ohio who sued the administrator of her late owner's estate when he tried to claim her when she returned to Texas soil, and still another upheld a manslaughter conviction of a white for killing a slave, in which the Court ruled that Texas law meant "to throw around the life of the slave the same protection which is guaranteed to a freeman." On the eve of the Civil War, the Texas Court ruled that in a charge of murder, the state must provide a black defendant with competent counsel if he could not afford his own—a stunningly modern decision.

Was it possible for slaves to win their freedom in Texas?

Surprisingly, yes. This was at least partly through the influence of the bachelor Chief Justice Hemphill, who had two daughters with his slave and long time companion, Sabina. He acknowledged his daughters and enrolled them in the newly opened Wilberforce University in Ohio. He could not marry Sabina because it was illegal, and he dared not free her because she would have been vulnerable to kidnapping and resale. Thus, he was sensitive to the legal impediments facing free persons of color, and he exercised his power in the case of a man named Adam Smith, who was similarly situated. Smith freed his slave Margaret and their daughter, but when he died his heir claimed they now belonged to him because her manumission document, which required five witnesses, only had one. The Court ruled that Smith's clear intention trumped any defect in the document. Margaret was declared free, and she got out of Texas while the going was good.

How could Chief Justice Hemphill defend the slaveocracy while sending his mixed-race daughters to college in Ohio so they would be free?

When Sam Houston retired from the Senate in 1859, the legislature selected Chief Justice Hemphill to replace him, a man who could be relied on to vindicate Southern interests, which Houston had declined to do. Undoubtedly, Hemphill was conflicted on the issue of slavery. On his way to Washington, he visited Ohio and told the president of Wilberforce University that his intention was to leave his entire estate to his daughters, Theodora and Henrietta. Sabina had died, and Hemphill was estranged from his birth family in South Carolina. Perhaps unwilling to face the social repercussions of such a step, Hemphill died without a will in 1862, and his South Carolina family stepped in to take everything. After the war, Texas courts backed Theodora (Henrietta had died) in squeezing a settlement out of them for $6,000—about $100,000 in present value. Hemphill was hardly alone in navigating this issue, for most of the student body at Wilberforce was comprised of mixed-race children of Southern planters.

Were free blacks allowed to sell themselves into slavery?

In Texas, this was not legal until January 1858. This had been occurring informally to some degree, and the legislature stepped in to require a process with protections to ensure that free persons of

A former slave shows off a horn in Marshall, Texas, that was once used to summon slaves.

color were not being railroaded into bondage. Before the law passed, a black man named Red Rolls, having been previously freed, sold himself back into slavery to his former master in Johnson County, near Fort Worth. He later ran away, not to freedom but to the nearby farm of a man who owned the mother of Red Rolls's children. They began to follow the new legal form, but the first owner arrived and retook him at gunpoint. After an acrimonious legal battle, Red Rolls was awarded to his new owner. If Red Rolls had known that selling himself to his first owner was not legally enforceable, then that was his good fortune. The first owner should have been at least as well informed, and the law would not intervene to help him.

Did the Underground Railroad operate in Texas?

Texas was too far removed from the Deep South for runaways to have much hope of reaching freedom in the North. Texas slaves made their way instead to Mexico, where slavery was still illegal and there was an active community of ex-slaves for support.

How did Texas churches respond to slavery?

The social schism that increasingly separated North from South affected the mainstream churches no less. Southern churches relied on biblical passages such as Ephesians 6:5–9, enjoining slaves to obey their earthly masters and owners to treat their slaves with forbearance as evidence that slavery was a divinely approved institution. Northern churches disagreed vigorously, and in 1845 the Baptist Mission Board declined to appoint a Georgia slave owner as a missionary. The Southern Baptist Convention was born out of this schism with a tighter hierarchy to enforce their orthodoxy than Baptists traditionally believed in. Northern Methodists hung on for a while longer, finally ceasing operation in Texas after the lynching of one of their ministers, Anthony Bewley, in Fort Worth for being a suspected Unionist. Nonevangelical churches endured similar fractures, such as the formation of the Southern General Assembly of Presbyterian Churches, after the main assembly based in Philadelphia endorsed the Union at the start of the war.

TEXAS DIVIDED OVER SECESSION

How did Texans feel about secession from the Union?

In the decades after the Confederacy lost the Civil War, Southern heritage groups and apologist historians fashioned the narrative of the Glorious Cause: it was not fought over slavery but states' rights, with support that was near-unanimous. That is understandable, for no group wants to believe it made horrific sacrifices in an evil cause. But, they did. On the eve of the war, three-quarters of Texas families owned not a single slave. Union sentiment was strong in north and west Texas and in Austin and San Antonio. Secession was popular in the cotton-planting counties of east Texas and among the very wealthy, who believed that their financial prospects would improve under a proslavery government.

What happened to the pro-Union Sam Houston?

Houston, who had represented Texas in the U.S. Senate since admission in 1846, spoke there repeatedly against disunion, without attacking slavery but berating the delusions of Southern Democrats, trying to prevent the oncoming Civil War. He so angered the Texas Legislature that they named his replacement in 1857, two years before the end of his term—an unprecedented insult. Without resigning his Senate seat, Houston returned to Texas, ran for governor, and was badly defeated. After being forced from the Senate in 1859, he ran again for governor. He was clear in his support for the Union, arguing that the South was better protected inside than out. Indeed, the North had protected slavery in the Compromise of 1850, the Kansas–Nebraska Act of 1854, the *Dred Scott* decision in 1857, and even in the campaign of Abraham Lincoln, who said that if he could hold the Union together by not freeing any slaves, he would do it. Houston was elected governor in 1859 by a wide margin.

How did Sam Houston prepare for the oncoming war?

Although in declining health, Houston undertook a speaking tour against secession. To a committee of the legislature, he stripped off his shirt to reveal his still seeping wounds from the War of 1812. "War is no plaything," he warned them. He also used the issue of frontier defense to increase recruitment in the Texas Rangers but appointed Jacob Kuechler, a pro-Union German immigrant, as recruiter so that if war came, he would have a reliable pro-Union cavalry at his disposal. That plan failed, however, as events overtook him.

What were the "Texas Troubles"?

While pro-Union feeling in Texas was strong enough to elect Houston governor, that support eroded in 1860. During the summer, there was a series of fires, the worst in downtown Dallas, but also in Denton, Waxahachie, and Kaufman. The likely culprit was a new brand of friction matches that were stocked in general stores that spontaneously combusted in the 110-degree heat. However, an equally combustible young newspaper editor, Charles Pryor of the *Dallas Herald*, published what today would be called a conspiracy theory, that abolitionists and the slaves they hoped to free were burning down the business districts as a prelude to a general slave rebellion. Some luckless slaves were tortured into confessing, and they and suspected Unionists alike were strung up until some unknown number, perhaps fifty, had been lynched and the panic subsided.

By what steps did Texas secede?

In December 1860, an associate justice of the state Supreme Court, Oran Milo Roberts (1815–1898), and other influential men called an election of delegates to a secession convention to meet in Austin. The election was held on January 8, 1861. This was illegal, for only the state legislature could call a convention, and Governor Houston waited until after this to call a special session of the legislature to derail the scheme. Instead, the legislature met and endorsed the convention, for most of the legislators had been elected to attend. The convention then became the *de facto* state government and scheduled a referendum, which took place on February 23. Meeting again on March 5, the convention voted to send delegates to the Confederate Congress, to which all state officers were compelled to swear an oath of loyalty. This Houston refused to do, and the convention removed him from office on March 16 and swore in the lieutenant governor, Ed Clark, as the new chief executive.

Why did so many Texans vote against seceding from the Union?

In Texas the Ordinance of Secession passed by a vote of 46,153 to 14,747, which seems like a landslide. Actually, it took courage to vote against pulling out of the Union. In at least some places, the right of voting by secret ballot was suspended, and armed secessionist poll watchers could see how

Justice of the Texas State Supreme Court Oran Milo Roberts was one of the main movers in a call to secede. Roberts later became chief justice and was seventeenth governor of Texas from 1879 to 1883.

people voted. Bright pink cardboard ballots preprinted FOR SECESSION were handed out at the polls, and one had to ask for a pen to strike out FOR and write in AGAINST in full public view. James Hall Bell, a justice on the Texas Supreme Court, did exactly that, and one poll watcher told him, "I am very sorry to see you do that. You're going to regret it." In the face of such intimidation, it is amazing that so many Texans did vote against secession.

How was support for the Southern cause enforced before the war?

In many places, firebrands for secession formed themselves into vigilante mobs, intimidating people who opposed leaving the Union. Pro-Union newspapers had their presses smashed or their offices burned down, and many suspected Northern sympathizers were lynched or else had their homes or businesses fired. In strongly pro-Union West Texas, most counties had "dead man's holes," caverns down which the bodies of murdered Unionists were cast. Undoubtedly, majority sentiment in Texas was for secession but not nearly by the margin claimed and then assumed by later heritage groups and apologist historians.

Wasn't Robert E. Lee on duty in Texas when the war began?

He was. Lee (1807–1870) was posted here on Indian defense from 1855 to 1857, when he took a leave of absence to put his late father-in-law's Virginia plantation in order, then he came back in 1859 to quell border mayhem caused by the bandit Juan Nepomuceno Cortina (1824–1894). In Austin, Lee paid a call on Governor Houston, whose wife, Margaret Lea Houston, was his distant cousin. Texas had long suffered from chaos along the Rio Grande, often a function of the approximately two dozen coups and revolutions Mexico had undergone since its own independence. The Unionist Houston, however, did not query Lee about his support. Houston had been nursing a scheme to extend an American protectorate over Mexico both to end the border bloodshed and give American factions a common enemy to unite against. He was curious whether Lee would accept an appointment as governor of Mexico. With his usual diplomacy, Lee did not commit himself.

How was the powerful Union force in Texas put out of the war so quickly?

At the time the conflict opened, there were about twenty-five hundred federal troops in Texas, which was about 10 percent of the prewar standing army. Their commander, General David E. Twiggs (1790–1862), was its second-ranking officer, whom Congress had awarded a jeweled sword for valor in the Mexican–American War. Twiggs was also a Georgia slave owner, caught between his conviction that states had the right to secede and his determination, as he expressed to Texas officials, that he would die before disgracing his troops by disarming them. Himself under arrest and his San Antonio troops surrounded by state militia, Twiggs agreed to a compromise, for federal troops in Texas to be marched to the coast and embarked and federal property in Texas, which was worth about $1.3 million, to be turned over to the state.

What did Abraham Lincoln do about Texas secession?

President Lincoln was keenly aware of Sam Houston's bitter struggle to hold Texas in the Union. As war broke out, Lincoln dispatched three different messengers to Houston with an offer of fifty thousand Union troops and the rank of major general if he would assume command of them to keep Texas out of the Confederacy. Houston was now sixty-seven, and for one of the few times in his life, he sought the advice of his friends. They voted four to one to refuse the offer, and Houston burned Lincoln's letter in the fireplace of the Governor's Mansion library. "I had resolved to take your advice in this matter," he told them, "but if I were ten years younger I would not."

General David E. Twiggs fought for the United States in the War of 1812, Black Hawk War, and Mexican–American War before siding with the Confederacy and leading Texan troops.

TEXAS IN THE CIVIL WAR

What happened on the frontier when so many of the men marched away to fight?

Comanche and Kiowa Indians watched in astonishment as so many white men left the frontier unguarded as they marched east to fight each other. During the course of the Civil War, the Plains Indians raided the frontier with such ferocity that they pushed the line of settlement back to the southeast, in some places more than 100 miles (161 kilometers). Settlers grouped together in "home forts" for protection, and the Confederate state government organized some mounted militia units—which young men were eager to join as a way to avoid being drafted into the rebel army—but during the war years, the balance of power on the frontier shifted back toward the natives.

If the war was so popular in Texas, why did so many men resort to draft dodging?

Despite their claims of wide popular support for the conflict, the rebel forces could not enlist enough volunteers to prosecute the war effectively. The Confederate government therefore passed a conscription act, predating the Union's, and thus was the first draft law in American history. This also proved insufficient, and the pool was enlarged, twice, to eventually include all men between the ages of eighteen and forty-five. As the war took bad turns, some thousands of Texans simply refused and disappeared. Many draft dodgers hid out in parts of Texas where Union sympathy had been strong before the war, such as the northern tier of counties along the Red River, where thick-bottom forest provided effective cover. There were so many that Department commander E. Kirby Smith employed the services of a brutal guerrilla raider from Missouri, William Clarke Quantrill, to flush them out. This was a step too far. It resulted in such a bloodbath that Smith was relieved of command and local forces drove Quantrill's Raiders back across the river.

How did Texas Germans react to the war?

The German community was divided by the war. Thousands of them had come to Texas to seek freedom for themselves and would not countenance owning another human

How did Corsicana become noted as a center for Civil War studies?

The Pearce Collections at Navarro College in Corsicana are a gift of local benefactors Charles and Peggy Pearce. One collection features Western art, while the other contains thousands of original documents dating from the Civil War—unique in its presentation from both the Union and Confederate points of view. Charles Pearce's first purchase was a letter written by Union brigadier general Joshua Lawrence Chamberlain, famous for his leadership at the Battle of Gettysburg, and grew to more than fifteen thousand documents, photographs, and artifacts.

being. In the 1860 census, in heavily German Gillespie County, only five families owned slaves. Further east, Germans were under greater pressure to adapt to their adopted land's way of life. Surrounded by Confederates, Germans around New Braunfels formed into volunteer companies and served in the war.

What was the Battle of the Nueces?

Texas Germans who lived in the Hill Country were further removed of rebel intimidation. Some, especially among the community of *Freidenker*—intellectuals and atheists who had a particular distaste for slavery—decided to try to reach Mexico, then California, where they could volunteer for Union service. About sixty-five of them set off in August 1862 but were ambushed on the west bank of the Nueces River in present-day Kinney County by about ninety rebels. Nineteen Germans were killed, and the nine wounded left in camp were executed; eight more were killed in a second fight closer to Mexico. After the war, their remains were gathered and buried beneath a white obelisk in the town of Comfort, still mourned by a thirty-six-star flag flying at half-staff.

How well did Texas units acquit themselves in the war?

Texas regiments acquired a reputation for peerless ferocity. At the Second Battle of Manassas, General John Bell Hood's Texas Brigade attacked a force of New York Zouaves and inflicted the highest casualty rate of the entire war. When, in turn, they were decimated in the cornfield at the Battle of Antietam, the Union commander praised them sadly that he had never seen men who needed so much evidence to convince them that they were beaten. When one journalist called Robert E. Lee's attention to the ragged condition of the Texas regiments' clothing, especially the seats of their pants, Lee remarked that it was no matter, for "the enemy never sees the backs of my Texans."

Didn't Texas Rangers play a big role in the conflict?

No. The Eighth Texas Cavalry regiment of the Confederate Army, under a Fort Bend County planter named Benjamin Franklin Terry, fought under the sobriquet of "Terry's Texas Rangers," but it was purely a nickname. Terry himself was killed in their first battle, at Woodsonville, Kentucky, on December 17, 1861.

How did Texas contribute to the Confederacy?

The South was jokingly famous for entering the Civil War without a single cannon foundry, but Texas did its best to supply the effort. The great stone Land Office in Austin, which was all but fireproof, was converted to manufacturing cartridges using gunpowder made in Waxahachie and Marshall. At the newly expanded factory in Tyler, two hundred workers pieced together Enfield and Austrian rifles, and in 1863 the Little Rock arsenal was relocated there to stay out of Union hands. The nearby towns of Rusk and Palestine, and another works in Bastrop, turned out some eight hundred firearms per month. The state foundry in Austin began casting heavy guns, as did a new installation in Galveston; seven different shops turned out two hundred wagons, one thousand har-

Why wasn't Texas ever invaded?

It wasn't for want of trying. The Union high command was keenly aware of Texas's economic importance—cotton that evaded the blockade by being floated across the Rio Grande, the quantities of materiel that streamed eastward. Indeed, invading Texas took on a high priority. A Union force occupied Brownsville in the fall of 1863 but discovered that the Rio Grande was too long and too isolated to keep cotton bales from being floated across to market or even loaded on camels that the federals abandoned when they evacuated. The Union occupied Galveston in October 1862 but kept it only three months before it fell again in a furious Texas assault. Two of the most remarkable battles of the Civil War, at Sabine Pass and at Red River, were fought to fend off Union invasions of Texas.

ness sets, and 350 saddles per month. Officials turned to the state penitentiary for textiles, which produced 300,000 yards (274 kilometers) of woolen clothes and 1.5 million yards (1,372 kilometers) of cotton. All this, plus shoes, cookware, and everything needed for the war effort, made Texas indispensable.

Where can one see where the Union invasion of Texas was defeated?

About 8 miles (13 kilometers) south of downtown Port Arthur, but still in the city limits, lies the site of the Second Battle of Sabine Pass, fought on September 8, 1863. In that fight, Lieutenant Dick Dowling and forty-six fellow Irish gunners manning four cannons defeated a Union invasion force of four gunboats, a dozen transports, and some five thousand federal soldiers. A bronze statue of Dowling stands over the site, which includes a pavilion where visitors can see a model and interpretive exhibit of the battle. Just north, there is saltwater fishing in the estuary of Sabine Lake and its Pleasure Island recreational district. South of Sabine Pass lie federal wildlife refuges and Sea Rim State Park. In Port Arthur proper, the Museum of the Gulf Coast displays both the natural and human history of the region, and house museums such as White Haven and the Pompeiian Villa document past lives of the well-to-do.

With Brownsville occupied, how loyal was the Hispanic community to rebel Texas?

Given the poor relationship between the Anglo and Latino communities in postrevolutionary Texas, it is not surprising that most Hispanics were lukewarm to the Confederacy. About twenty-five hundred did serve in the rebel army, but most were probably under some pressure. Emblematic of their experience was Adrián Vidal (1840–1865), son-in-law of riverboat captain and rancher Mifflin Kenedy. Assigned first to protect the mouth of the Rio Grande, Vidal was cited for bravery and promoted for leading the capture of a Union gunboat, but he grew so disgusted by his men's poor treatment and supply that he and his unit switched sides and were already fighting as partisan Union rangers when the North occupied Brownsville in November 1863. Discovering equal contempt and discrimination in the Northern service, they deserted to Mexico to fight for Benito Juárez, but Vidal was captured by imperial forces and quickly executed.

What was the importance of the Battle of Sabine Pass?

The fall of Vicksburg in July 1863 probably spelled the Confederacy's eventual doom, and it also made a full-scale Texas invasion more feasible. On September 7, four heavy Union gunboats, backed by eighteen transports carrying five thousand troops, were sighted at the bar of Sabine Pass. It was defended only by Fort Griffin, mounting six guns, only four of which could be brought to bear. In command was twenty-five-year-old Irish immigrant Lieutenant Richard W. Dowling (1838–1867) and forty-seven men of his company, grandly calling themselves the Jefferson Davis Guards, mostly Irish, mostly patrons of the saloons that Dowling owned. The attack had to be made up Sabine Pass's two channels, which the Irish gunners had staked with range markers. Within minutes of the action commencing, they sank one gunboat in each channel. Convinced that he was facing overwhelming force, the Union commander threw his stock overboard and fled. As a result of this humiliating defeat, Union bonds sank to their lowest value of the war. The medals struck to honor the Davis Guards are today the most valuable artifacts of the conflict.

What happened at the Battle of Red River?

More determined than ever after the failure of Sabine Pass, the Union sent one of its ablest admirals, David Dixon Porter, to attempt a new invasion, this one carried out by gunboats and transports sent up the Red River through Shreveport. The invasion was aborted when a fall in water levels made it impossible to proceed, giving Texans time to muster sufficient forces to block them. In land actions at Mansfield and Pleasant Hill in April 1864, the invasion was stymied. Trapped at Alexandria, Porter built crib dams across the Red River and waited for the water to back up as rebel troops lined artillery down both banks below the city. In mid-April, he ordered the dams opened, and the whole

Admiral David Dixon Porter commanded Union ships sailing up the Red River, but falling water levels forced him to retreat while harried by Texas troops in one of the worst chapters of his otherwise successful naval career.

After the Civil War, four regiments—the Twenty-fourth and Twenty-fifth infantries and the Ninth and Tenth cavalries—were composed of African American soldiers, who were often assigned to west and south Texas because it was considered the least desirable posting in the service. This scheme was maintained through the end of the frontier. The Ninth Cavalry's Troop D fought with distinction in Cuba during the Spanish–American War, and when it was posted to Ringgold after the war, the men chafed under the renewed racism and hostility from Rio Grande City's Anglo population. On the night of November 20, 1899, the post commander believed that they were under attack by a mob from town and ordered a Gatling gun to spray rounds in the direction of the town to deter the citizens, resulting in one injury. Townspeople were outraged, prompting Texas governor Joe Sayers to request that the Ninth Cavalry be replaced with a white regiment.

flotilla began careening downstream on the crest, pummeled by cannonfire. Five gunboats were sunk in one of the most spectacular retreats of the war.

How many casualties did Texas suffer in the Civil War?

Texas's Civil War governor, Frank Lubbock, asserted that ninety thousand Texas men served in the Confederate forces, but that number is surely too high, as it nearly equaled the state's total population of men eligible to serve (i.e., those between the ages of eighteen and forty-five). Total deaths are unknowable but probably on the order of fifteen to twenty thousand.

Where was the last land battle of the Civil War?

Lee surrendered to Grant at Appomattox on April 9, 1865, and eight days later, Joe Johnston surrendered to Sherman in North Carolina. Included in Johnston's command were Texas units who had fought through the entire war—indeed, some Texans slipped away home and were able to boast that they had never surrendered. Back in Texas under orders to take over civil administration, Union troops headed into coastal towns, including Lieutenant Colonel David Branson, who set off from a bivouac on Brazos Island with three hundred African American infantry to assume the administration of Brownsville. On May 13, 12 miles (19 kilometers) from the town, they were pounced on by a rebel force under Colonel John Salmon ("Rip") Ford (1815–1897), who inflicted thirty casualties and captured 113. The traditional story was that Ford and his men did not know that the war was over. However, they had known of the South's fall after seeing a New Orleans newspaper on May 1, and they had conferred with Union Major General Lewis Wallace about surrender terms. They just decided to keep fighting.

TEXAS CHARACTERS OF THE CIVIL WAR

How did Anthony Bewley's bones teach Confederate loyalty to children?

The Missouri Conference of the Methodist Episcopal Church was one of those that split over slavery. Many ministers who had been assigned to Texas opposed slavery; in fact, of the nearly forty thousand members of the church in Texas, more than 20 percent were black. One such pastor was fifty-six-year-old Anthony Bewley, shepherding a flock 16 miles (26 kilometers) south of Fort Worth in what became the town of Burleson. Stranded in hostile territory and learning of the beatings of two Methodist ministers in Dallas, Bewley started moving his large family north. A letter, probably forged, implicated him in the spurious "Texas Troubles." A posse tracked him all the way to Missouri and brought him back to Fort Worth, where he was lynched on September 13, 1860. He was buried for three weeks and then dug up, his bones stripped and placed atop Ephraim Daggett's storehouse, where little rebel children could play with them as an object lesson in what happens to those who oppose slavery. The Northern Methodists ceased operations in Texas after this.

What was the "Great Hanging" in Gainesville?

The northern tier of counties along the Red River had voted against secession and became a haven for draft dodgers to hide themselves in the thick forests. The job of rooting them out was given to Brigadier General William Hudson, who hit on an ingenious

In 1862, the "Great Hanging" in Gainesville occurred when forty-one men suspected of sympathizing with the Union were hanged.

method of separating friend from foe: he issued a call for volunteers to comb through the woods in search of fugitives—and then ordered the arrest of every man who did not volunteer! Hudson turned the dirty work over to Colonel James G. Bourland, who initially arrested 150, made certain that the juries were made of up slaveholders, and declared that convictions could be obtained by majority vote, not unanimous. Seven were condemned and hanged, fourteen more were lynched, and subsequently another nineteen were strung up after Bourland's trial assistant was assassinated. Ten more were hanged in Decatur and Sherman, and various others murdered, to enforce Confederate loyalty.

What Texan was the youngest spy hanged by the North?

Shortly before the war began, Andrew Marion Dodd of Victoria moved his wife, son, and two daughters to Little Rock, Arkansas. When fighting started, he and his son, David Owen Dodd, worked as sutlers in northern Louisiana. When the Union army captured Little Rock, the elder Dodd materialized in there to escort his wife and daughters back into rebel-held territory. The only way David could get a pass from Confederate authorities to go help was to agree to report back on Union troop strength. Young Dodd was nearly passed back through the lines, but his notes in Morse Code were discovered in the sole of one of his shoes. He was tried and condemned, but the presiding general offered to drop the charges if Dodd would identify the Union soldier who had helped him. Dodd refused and was hanged before a crowd of several thousand on January 8, 1864; at seventeen, he is believed to be the youngest rebel spy to be executed.

How was the pro-Union Sam Houston treated once the war started?

Forced into retirement after the Secession Convention declared his office vacant, Houston lived simply at his summer home at Cedar Point, earning money by selling firewood in Galveston and at a rented house in Huntsville. Confederate detectives questioned his friends, servants, and children to try to discover him in some disloyal opinion, but they failed. Houston complained bitterly of this treatment to Governor Frank Lubbock, who was an old friend, but he remained under observation. He spoke at patriotic rallies, and once, he donned his Republic of Texas uniform and inspected and drilled the company of recruits that his son, Sam Houston Jr., had joined. He died on July 23, 1863, in Huntsville, grieving that his personal belief that the South would end "in a sea of blood and ruin" was about to come true.

How was Sam Houston Jr. saved?

Sam Jr. was declared missing in action after Shiloh and presumed dead, his name deleted from the muster roll, which sent his mother into paroxysms of Victorian grief. Unknown to his parents, however, he was found and rescued in the field at Shiloh by a Union chaplain, who had been among those who had protested passage of the Kansas–Nebraska Act in 1854 and whom Sam Houston had defended on the Senate floor. Though grievously wounded in the groin (as his father had been in the War of 1812), the Bible that his mother had given him stopped the bullet that would have gone into his heart. He was repatriated, and his father lived to see him return.

What Texans suffered the greatest material loss in the war?

Thousands lost their husbands and sons, of course, which were losses beyond price. But the family that probably fell the furthest were the brothers David and Robert Mills of Brazoria. They had owned four plantations, worked by eight hundred slaves. They baled and exported their own cotton on their own steamboats and were worth an estimated $4 million. They lost it all.

Who was the last governor of Confederate Texas?

Frank Lubbock did not seek reelection but joined the rebel army as a staff colonel of President Jefferson Davis. He was succeeded by Pendleton Murrah, an Alabama orphan of uncertain age but young, handsome, winsome, and consumptive. Until he became governor, the most remarkable thing about him was his unconsummated marriage. He wed Sue Ellen Taylor of Marshall when she was fifteen. After the ceremony, he expected her to come downstairs to him, while she waited upstairs for him to come up. Neither gave in, and they were politely mad at each other for thirteen years. Once, when a fire broke out in the Governor's Mansion, he called her "dear" as he carried her to safety; she burst into tears because it was the first endearment she had ever heard from him. Murrah proved equally stubborn in dealing with the Confederate government, finding ways as the war went badly to avoid sending further Texas conscripts beyond the border of the state.

What happened to the Confederate high command in Texas at the end of the war?

Most of them, ironically, followed a generation of slaves and escaped to Mexico. The rebel commander in Texas, E. Kirby Smith, who may have been the South's last four-star general, and his number-two man, J. Bankhead "Prince John" Magruder, surrendered to Union general E. R. S. Canby at Galveston on June 2, 1865, before slipping away. Magruder entered the service of Emperor Maximilian, and before too long, Smith had made his way to Kentucky and sold insurance. Governor Murrah's consumption had worn him down; he put on a Confederate uniform and left Austin on June 12, and he died in Monterrey on August 4. As the Union occupation

Pendleton Murrah was governor of Texas during the last three years of the Civil War.

fanned out across the state, many local rebel officials followed suit in absconding to Mexico.

Is it true that the state treasury was robbed at the end of the war?

In a way, the Texas group who must have been the most brazen and daring were the forty thieves who cleaned out the state treasury on August 3, 1865. Confederate bonds and currency were now worthless, but the $5,000 in coins might have made the venture worth the risk.

How did Texas's pre war secession leaders fare?

However wrong headed Texas's vociferous secessionists were, many of them underwrote their rhetoric with their lives. Ben McCulloch, who took the surrender of Union forces in San Antonio at the start of the war, was killed at Pea Ridge in March of 1862, which was part of a scheme to capture Missouri that he had condemned as lunacy. William P. Rogers, for whom Sam Houston named his third son only to see Rogers change his mind and join the secessionists, was cut down by a hail of bullets as he carried the Second Texas Infantry colors at Corinth, Mississippi. Albert Sidney Johnston, at one time general of the Army of the Republic of Texas, rose to command the Army of the Mississippi and fell at Shiloh. Their cause was deplorable, but they kept their grit to the end—such as former Republic congressman William Read "Dirty Neck Bill" Scurry, who became a particular enemy of Houston's. Mortally wounded at Jenkins' Ferry in April 1864, he hung on to ask, "Have we whipped them?" Assured that they had, he ordered, "Now take me to a house where I can die easy." Not all died. Oran Roberts, who led the Secession Convention and deserted the Supreme Court for a field command, in later years reinvented himself in Texas as chief justice, two-term governor, and a founding professor of the University of Texas law school. After lying low during Reconstruction, for a generation thereafter, political advancement was tied to having worn the gray.

RECONSTRUCTION TO URBANIZATION

DEFYING THE OCCUPATION

What Texas holiday began as a result of the Civil War's end?

Most slaves in Texas had never learned of the Emancipation Proclamation. When General Gordon Granger landed in Galveston on June 19, 1865, with early units of the Union occupation, he published that "in accordance with the proclamation of the Executive, all slaves are now free." Ever since, African Americans in Texas have celebrated "Juneteenth" as the beginning of their freedom. Granger's declaration, however, was not as sympathetic as it now seems. In a latter passage no longer quoted, Granger added that free blacks in Texas "are advised to remain at their present homes, and work for wages. They are informed that they will not be allowed to collect at military posts; and that they will not be supported in idleness either there or elsewhere."

Why wasn't Texas readmitted to the Union in 1870 as was provided when the rebellion in Texas was proclaimed to be at an end?

If Abraham Lincoln had not been assassinated, he would have had an enormously difficult struggle with Congress over control of putting the country back together. Lincoln's doctrine of showing "malice toward none, with charity for all" crashed hard against the Republican radicals in Congress, who wanted the South to suffer maximum punishment. Lincoln's position was that secession had been illegal, therefore the states had never actually left the Union, which meant that reconstruction was his responsibility. The radicals' position was that the Southern states had actually left the Union and could only be readmitted by Congress, which gave them the power instead. Congressional radicals sidelined Lincoln's ineffective successor, Andrew Johnson, and Texas was just one of the states whose return on equal footing was postponed.

95

What were the "Black Codes"?

Like other Southern states, Texas was required to draw up a new state constitution that made no reference to slavery. The Texas Constitution of 1866 extended certain rights to freedmen: they could buy and sell land, enter into contracts, and were granted access to the courts. However, certain others of its provisions were so oppressive to free blacks that one would have thought Texas won the war: they could not vote. (As expressed by Oran Roberts, it was of paramount importance to "keep Sambo away from the polls.") They could not serve on juries or testify against white people. Worse, blacks arrested for vagrancy could be forcibly apprenticed to a trade, with their employers allowed to discipline them by withholding wages or administering beatings. All persons with one-eighth or more Negro blood were subject. In an important way, the truculence of the 1866 Constitution made Texas responsible for much of its own trouble during its extended reconstruction.

Who were the "Carpetbaggers"?

Northern opportunists who showed up in the defeated South to take advantage of the situation, either by political appointments in the gift of the occupation army or to snap up financial investments to be had on the cheap, often traveled with inexpensive luggage

What was the war between the Jaybirds and the Woodpeckers?

The end of the Civil War brought Union occupation and peace, of a sort, to Texas, but for decades thereafter, local feuds reflected the continuing bad blood between vindicated Unionists and defeated Confederates. Before the war, Fort Bend County had been heavily dependent upon the plantation economy, and thus after, the war had a black majority from the number of freed slaves—one of only six Texas counties with black majorities. After the lifting of the Iron clad Oath, the Republicans and freedmen were able to keep control of the county government in its seat at Richmond, and frustrated, ex-Confederate Democrats resorted to violence. The name of the feud was derived from the popular notion that bluejays (or jaybirds, in this case the Democrats) would typically fuss at and harass woodpeckers (entrenched freedmen and Republicans) until they drove them from their nest, which the jaybirds would then appropriate for themselves. Violence escalated until there was an open gun battle in front of the courthouse on August 16, 1889, resulting in the killing of several people, including the sheriff, which led to a Jaybird takeover of the county government. This they kept by means of a poll tax, whites-only primaries, and intimidation until the U.S. Supreme Court declared the whites-only primary unconstitutional in 1953. Although the existing courthouse dates from 1910 and did not witness the shootout, various historic structures are on display at Decker Park, and the Fort Bend Museum interprets all eras of the local history.

fashioned of carpet fabric, hence the name. This insult did not extend to Southern Unionists who were now ascendant; defeated rebels had their own epithet for them: scalawags.

What was the "Iron clad Oath"?

As government by military decree began to give way to a return to civilian democracy, the Reconstruction powers felt it imperative that the white Southern reactionary vote be kept at bay. Thus, the franchise was extended only to those white Texans who could swear an "iron clad oath" that they had never supported the rebel cause or acted in disloyalty. This, of course, disenfranchised tens of thousands of Confederate veterans and ensured the election of Unionist candidates.

How many African American Texans served in the state legislature during Reconstruction?

In all, forty-one black Texans served in the Reconstruction legislature, and eleven were delegates to a constitutional convention during Reconstruction. The most prominent black leader and organizer in post war Texas was not a legislator but George Thompson Ruby (1841–1882), New York native, Florida resident, and in white Texans' eyes, a paradigm carpetbagger. He organized schools for the Freedmen's Bureau, taught school for the returning Methodist Episcopal Church, and became the first state president of the Union Loyal League, which was the black and Unionist response to the Ku Klux Klan. After Ruby came Norris Wright Cuney (1846–1898). Although he was defeated in his own runs for various political offices, he became customs collector in Galveston and thus an important source of patronage, and he was a delegate to every Republican national convention for twenty years.

What was the Freedmen's Bureau?

Even before the war ended, Congress had created the Bureau of Refugees, Freedmen, and Abandoned Lands. Aid to white Southern Unionists who had fled the Confederacy was one of its aims, but its much more important work was to aid freed slaves in assimilating into mainstream society. The bureau in each state was entrusted to Union officers; in the case of Texas, that role belonged to Brigadier General Edgar M. Gregory of the Ninety-First Pennsylvania, a tried and true abolitionist. He had to overcome not just resident rebel hostility but also the apathy of Union occupation officers who did not view black advancement favorably.

What did the Freedmen's Bureau accomplish?

One of the most contentious programs of the Freedmen's Bureau was establishing schools, fifteen of which were functioning by the end of 1865, although rebel arsonists struck when they could get away with it. This became their most successful effort; by the time they closed in 1870, ten thousand free blacks were attending 150 schools. The bureau's Texas agents, who numbered forty to sixty at a given time, supervised black-white relations, cancelling sharecropper contracts whose terms they felt were abusive, and giving black tenants a legal lien on the crop until they were paid. They also monitored the cases of freedmen in state courts to make sure they received justice, and they tried to reunite black families whose members had been sold to different owners. Former rebels hated that bureau agents collected information on continuing disloyalty, and when they exceeded their authority, they were coddled by occupation military tribunals. Three agents were bushwhacked and some others beaten or run out, prompting the national administrator to pronounce Texas as his most intractable state.

How did the Ku Klux Klan come to Texas?

White former rebels in Texas seethed at what they perceived as endless insults and indignities heaped upon them by the Union occupation and were left ripe candidates for

A U.S. congressman and later senator from Texas, Roger Q. Mills also led the Ku Klux Klan in the Lone Star State.

clandestine organizations in which to vent their hatred and perhaps get some of their own back. The Klan was actually preceded in Texas by the Knights of the White Camelia, which began in New Orleans and attracted the better and more prominent layer of society, and also by the Knights of the Rising Sun. The Klan, which originated in Tennessee in 1866, reached Texas in the spring of 1868 and became the secret society of choice both for its penchant for direct and more violent action and for its bizarre rituals and costumes. Its state leader was Roger Q. Mills (1832–1911) of Corsicana, a lawyer and later congressman and U.S. senator. There was little leading to do, for local Klansmen already had in mind at the time they formed who was in, who was out, and who they wanted to go after. When an army examination showed that almost half of Texas's 939 post war murders were whites killing blacks, the military courts came down hard on the Klan. They suspended the right of habeas corpus for members of secret societies and convicted nearly thirty Klansmen, which caused their membership to dwindle and eventually go dormant until the next century.

What was the "Semicolon Case"?

With disloyal voters sidelined by the Iron clad Oath, the Union occupation finally allowed elections for state officers to be held in 1869. Elected governor was Edmund J. Davis (1827–1883), a Florida native but resident in Texas since 1848, prominent in law and politics in the Rio Grande Valley since then. When war came, he raised a regiment of Texas Union cavalry, which was regarded as the height of treason, and as governor replaced the Texas Rangers with the State Police Force, comprised largely of freedmen,

What was the "Exoduster Movement"?

New governor Richard Coke was a member of the Secession Convention and a wounded Confederate captain. All of his appointments to the reconstituted Supreme Court were Confederate veterans, with Oran Roberts as chief justice. The legislature passed a law barring freedmen from homestead lands, and blacks in Texas could see oppressive times returning. Word spread like wildfire that Kansas was going to offer homestead land to freedmen, and with the endorsement of black leaders such as George T. Ruby, there began a mass migration of "Exodusters" from Texas. In a remarkable irony, Kansas, which in 1854 the South had seen as a target for expanding slavery, now became a haven for more than ten thousand African American Texans who caught the "Kansas Fever" and trekked north. In an ever-richer irony, this exodus created a shortage of sharecroppers in Texas, forcing white landlords to give better terms to black tenants.

which made him more hated than ever. As governor, he appointed a new Supreme Court of like-minded jurists. Davis ran for reelection in 1873, but with the Ironclad Oath finally lifted, he was trounced more than two to one by the Democratic candidate, Richard Coke. Davis's partisans raised the objection that the polls had been open only one day when the Constitution mandated four days of voting. The Supreme Court, noting that two key clauses of the Constitution were separated by a semicolon and not a comma, invalidated the election, keeping Davis in power until a new election could be held. The shock and outrage at the "Semicolon Case" was sensational.

How and when did Reconstruction in Texas finally end?

E. J. Davis relied on the Semicolon decision to continue in office, but by now, resurgent Democrats were not having any of it. Armed militias supporting Coke converged on the Capitol grounds, forcing a political crisis. Barricaded on the second floor of the Capitol, Davis telegraphed President Ulysses Grant for troops to sustain him in office. Grant, formerly the commanding general of the Union armies, decided that ten years of punishing the South was enough and declined. Davis was forced to decamp, although when he left, he defiantly took the keys to his office with him. It was the only time in American history that an election result was overturned by a coup d'état.

THE INDIAN WARS

What Indians were left in Texas by the end of Reconstruction?

In east Texas, the Cherokee were long gone. Sam Houston used what little political capital he had to get the Alabama and Coushatta exempted from the Confederate draft, and they caused no trouble. West and northwest Texas was a different story. During the war, frontier raids pushed the line of settlement back at least 100 miles (161 kilometers) as the Comanche and Kiowa reclaimed old hunting grounds, and in the Trans-Pecos desert, the Lipan and Mescalero Apache were equally unbowed.

How did President Grant's "Peace Policy" affect the Texas frontier?

Virtually the entire West erupted in Indian wars in 1868, which suited popular Texas sentiment just fine. Grisly excesses, however, such as the Washita Massacre, gave impetus to a reform movement. President Grant was persuaded to withdraw troops and assign Indians' agencies to different religious denominations and to give food and agricultural training to natives who would swear to remain at peace. The Society of Friends, or Quakers, known for their pacifism, drew care of the Kiowa and Comanche, which caused considerable eye rolling in Texas. They were not entirely wrong in their opposition. The army established Fort Sill in 1869 just across the Red River in Indian Territory as an agency and feeding station for the Kiowa and Comanche. Several of the more warlike chiefs did indeed lead raids into Texas, then retreat into what the Texans called their "City of Refuge" at Fort Sill before they could be apprehended and butter up the Quaker agent with peace talk.

Why didn't the chain of frontier forts protect the Texas frontier from Indians?

When federal troops returned to the edge of settlement after the war, they established or reopened an impressive chain of forts: Clark, McKavett, Concho, Griffin, and Richardson. In reality, however, the frontier was so vast that these installations merely gave native raiders points to avoid. In just over two years from the end of the war, a detailed census could enumerate forty-three women and children taken captive and 162 Texans killed in Indian raids.

What top-ranking army general very nearly lost his scalp in Texas?

When Grant became president, William Tecumseh Sherman was advanced to commanding general of the army. Crusty and cynical where the clamor of citizens was concerned, Sherman suspected that cries for more troops to control Indians in Texas were really intended to increase federal spending on supply contracts. Traveling with a light escort on May 18, 1871, he made an inspection tour of the Texas fron-

Civil War hero William Tecumseh Sherman was named commanding general of the U.S. Army by President Ulysses Grant. Despite such experience, his troops suffered great losses by the Indians in Texas.

100

Who were the only Indian raiders arrested and tried for murder in a Texas court?

When Sherman reached Fort Sill, he and post commander Colonel Benjamin Grierson enlisted the aid of the Quaker agent in questioning the chiefs. The Kiowa, accustomed to the impunity of their agency, made no secret of the raid, and Sherman had three leaders arrested. Chief Satank (Sitting Bear) was killed attempting an escape. Satanta (White Bear) and Addo-etta (Big Tree) were taken to Jacksboro, Texas, near the scene of the massacre, tried, and condemned to hang for murder. Governor E. J. Davis, who was already unpopular, made himself more so by paroling them back to their people, believing that would buy peace on the frontier. He was wrong.

tier. Leaving Fort Griffin, the little column passed over the Salt Prairie, closely eyed by a war party of more than a hundred Kiowa concealed on an overlooking hill. Their medicine man, Skywalker, had told them not to molest the first party they saw on the road but wait for the second, which would be bigger. A short time later, the wagon train of army contractor Henry Warren passed the same spot and were annihilated. Sherman was awakened late that night as a survivor straggled into Fort Richardson; he still refused to believe his narrow escape until he read the post surgeon's report of seven men killed, mutilated, and scalped.

What caused the last Indian war on the Texas plains?

The Quaker Indian agents for the Kiowa and Comanche at Fort Sill, and for the Cheyenne and Arapaho at Darlington northwest of there, did their level best to feed and care for their charges. However, rations often failed to be delivered, sometimes owing to corruption higher up in the Indian Bureau. Also, authorities in Texas did nothing to prevent horse thieves from raiding the Indians' pony herds. Then, too, plains Indian culture was rooted in war and raiding, and chiefs who gained their status by it were unwilling to change. Still, the single greatest cause was the destruction by white commercial hunters of the buffalo herds upon which the tribes subsisted. With no buffalo and no rations, the Indians were facing starvation.

How did buffalo hunters go about their business?

Completion of the Transcontinental Railroad split the vast population of bison into two herds, whose migratory patterns diminished as hunting increased. From the beginning of the hide-hunting business, the buffalo in southern Kansas and the Indian Territory were wiped out in less than three years. From 1872 to 1874, the three railroads that served Dodge City carried away 4,373,730 buffalo hides. This left only one large herd, on the Staked Plains of the Texas Panhandle. Early in 1874, a large, well-armed expedition left Dodge City and established a village at Adobe Walls on the Canadian River. The hunters' favorite gun was the octagonal-barreled, .50-caliber Sharps "Big Fifty," which had an effective range of over 500 yards (457 meters). (During the war, hunter-turned-army-scout Billy Dixon shot an Indian off his horse at 1,538 yards [1,406 meters]—lucky but famous on the frontier as Dixon's "long shot.") A hunter would pick out and shoot the leader of a herd, leaving the rest milling about while he made his "stand," sometimes shooting more than a hundred before sending out his team of hired skinners. They also took the tongues and hams, for which there was a market, and smoked them; the rest was let to rot. According to one successful hunter, shooting more than one's skinners could handle in a day "would waste buffalo, which wasn't important, but it would also waste ammunition, which was."

Why was the Red River War significant?

It was the final resistance of the Comanche, Kiowa, Southern Cheyenne, and Southern Arapaho tribes to white domination. More fundamentally, the native Indians' most lethal enemy was neither the army that fought them nor the settlers who took over their lands. It was the buffalo hunters who destroyed their food supply; as long as there were buffalo, the Indians had an avenue of resistance. Yet in the entire history of the American West, this is the only time that the chiefs realized it. Quanah Parker intended a revenge raid against the Tonkawa in Texas, but it was two shrewd old brothers-in-law,

the chiefs White Wolf and Hears the Sunrise, who said, "You pretty good fighter, Quanah, but you not know everything. We think you take [war] pipe first against white buffalo killers. You kill white buffalo hunters, make your heart good." At dawn on June 27, 1874, perhaps five hundred warriors from all the tribes opened the war by attacking the buffalo hunters at Adobe Walls. The hiders, fortified in their buildings with lethal firepower, inflicted a terrible defeat on them.

How did the army respond to this Indian outbreak?

The strategy for prosecuting the Red River War began with Major General Philip Sheridan commanding the Division of the Missouri. His favorite field commander, Ranald Mackenzie of the Fourth Cavalry, had established in an 1872 sortie that when the tribes were under pressure, they

Colonel Ranald Mackenzie distinguished himself in the Civil War and later during the Indian Wars, defeating the Indians at the Battle of Palo Duro.

What hunter killed the only white buffalo in Texas?

J. Wright Mooar of Vermont, who with his brother had begun the business of hunting for hides, settled on a ranch near the later town site of Snyder in Scurry county. The great herds were gone, but southern buffalo still hung on in small groups. In brush near Deep Creek, Mooar was stunned to see an animal commonly supposed to exist only in Indian legend: a white buffalo, surrounded protectively by a few animals of normal color. He dropped her with his Sharps .44, and her skin hung for many years in the family ranch house. Later photographs reveal her to have been largely, though not purely, albino.

retreated into the canyons of the Caprock, and now, five different columns would converge there from the west, north, east, southeast, and south. Setting twenty-five hundred troops in motion, it was the largest force ever thrown against Indians up to that time.

What was the aftermath of the Red River War?

After many skirmishes across the entire theater of conflict, the Indians' bid for freedom was doomed by Colonel Ranald Mackenzie at the Battle of Palo Duro on September 28. He learned the location of a huge, secret encampment by torturing a *comanchero* (a trader in contraband such as arms and whiskey) into revealing it. The renegades were routed, and after capturing their pony herd, Mackenzie slaughtered over a thousand head of horses, leaving the warriors dismounted and virtually helpless. The last hostile bands surrendered at their agencies in summer of 1875. The reservations were later broken up into individual grants, and the natives looked to leaders such as Quanah Parker, who became a judge on the Indian court and rode in Theodore Roosevelt's inaugural parade, to help them adjust to the "white road."

What mocked and derided cavalry officer finally figured out how to defeat the Apache?

Soldiers universally considered the Southwestern deserts the worst duty in the army, so it was routinely assigned to African American regiments who began to be recruited during the Civil War. The white officers who commanded them then became the butt of jokes, especially Colonel Benjamin Grierson of the Tenth Cavalry "Buffalo Soldiers," a former music teacher. Nevertheless, it was Grierson who realized the futility of chasing Apache raiders. The Chiricahua chief Victorio made a foray into Texas in 1880, driven onto the warpath by circumstances similar to those in the Indian Territory. Instead of pursuing him, Grierson anticipated his movements and seized the waterholes on his route, repeatedly denying water to the hostile Apache. Victorio and his warriors were forced into Mexico and a fatal defeat by Mexican soldiers at Tres Castillos.

103

What was the "Great Panhandle Indian Scare"?

Although the Comanche and Kiowa had lived on their reservation since 1875, occasionally riding into the Texas Panhandle to work on the ranches, memories died hard of the gruesome torture and mutilation carried out in their raiding days. On January 29, 1891, cowboys on the Rocking Chair Ranch chased and shot a steer, which they intended to barbecue, but the fire got away from them. A ranch wife in the next valley heard the shots and whoops, saw the smoke, bundled up her children, and fled, spreading an Indian alarm. For three days, terror gripped the Panhandle. Hardware stores sold out of ammunition; families forted up together and kept watch until Captain Bill Macdonald arrived with a company of Texas Rangers and discovered the cause of the alarm. Most Texans thought this hilarious—except those who had ever lost family to raiders.

THE CATTLE EMPIRE

After Indian removal, how long did it take for northwest Texas to become ranch land?

Only about a year, and it was brought about by an accidental alignment of circumstances. The U.S. financial Panic of 1873 wounded the national economy, but by the time the Indians cleared the plains in 1875, the recovery was well underway. Beef prices in the settled parts of the country were rising, and railroads were making their way west across the Great Plains to provide transport to that market. All this set the stage for an explosion in the Texas cattle business. The first Panhandle lands were patented, and the first cattle were brought to the state in 1876.

When did barbed wire come on the scene?

Although barbed wire was invented in Illinois, where it was patented in 1874 by Joseph Glidden, the product made its most dramatic impact in Texas. One of Glidden's salesmen, John Warne Gates (1855–1911; he had not yet acquired his famous nickname, "Bet-a-Million," which was years later in the oil business), erected a barbed-wire enclosure in Alamo Plaza in the heart of San Antonio. In it, he confined a small herd of longhorns, who were well known to make short work of regular fencing. To the amazement of the townsfolk, the barbed wire held. Sales skyrocketed, and Texas ranching was fundamentally changed.

The simple invention of barbed-wire fencing changed the cattle ranching industry forever by making it easier to control and breed herds.

How did the invention of barbed wire change ranching life?

Barbed wire had a dramatic effect on Texas ranching. After a generation of harvesting the wild longhorns, effective fencing made it possible to control breeding and produce meatier cattle. Barbed wire also sharpened competition, as one rancher could claim and fence off the only source of water for miles and drive his neighbors out of business. It was also very expensive, which began the transformation of ranching from a matter of individual enterprise to one of corporate capital investment.

What was the first big ranch in the Panhandle?

Charles Goodnight (1836–1929) was already a frontier legend by the time, at age forty, he drove sixteen hundred longhorns from Denver to start a herd at his Home Ranch in Palo Duro Canyon. As a youth, he had supported his widowed mother ranching at the edge of the Comanche frontier, driving cattle to markets in New Mexico and Colorado as Texas endured the Civil War. He lost his partner, Oliver Loving, in a fight withthe Comanche, doggedly bringing his body home to bury it—an event recalled in the great Larry McMurtry western *Lonesome Dove*. Returning to Colorado just at the time when large capital became necessary to start a profitable ranch, he obtained a loan from John Adair, a Scots-Irish lord who had come to America to lend money at higher interest than he could get in Britain. Thus began the JA Ranch, with Goodnight hired to run it for $2,500 per year and a one-third share. Goodnight returned to the land with one hundred Durham bulls to develop an improved breed. At its height, the JA extended across 1.3 million acres (5,261 square kilometers) and returned a half-million-dollar profit.

Texas has many dude ranches for recreational riding, but is there any place where people can observe and appreciate cutting horses?

Cutting horses are those that are trained and participate in competitive events to demonstrate their skill and intuition at herding cattle. Mount and rider are required to cut two cows from a herd, one from the edge and one from the interior. After separating the animal from the others, the cowboy drops his reins and, only giving hints with leg pressure, allows the horse to use his own instincts to keep it from rejoining the herd. Such skills were treasured on the frontier, and today, frequent demonstrations of it are given at the Nueces Canyon Equestrian Center near Brenham.

Where is the largest museum dedicated to Texas ranching life?

Established in 1969 on the Texas Tech University campus, the National Ranching Heritage Center features an astonishing array of art and artifacts to commemorate that way of life. More than fifty historic structures have been relocated here to interpret the Texas ranch from the 1700s to the mid-1900s. There is also an important collection of windmills showing the evolution of their development.

What were cattle drives really like?

Until railroads eventually came to northwest Texas, cattle had to be driven to railheads in Kansas. This was not that far from the Panhandle ranches, but from those deeper in Texas, it might mean two months in the saddle. Fifteen hundred to three thousand cattle were typically moved in a herd, usually not more than 15 miles (24 kilometers) in a day to let them rest and graze, or they would lose weight. They were managed by ten cowboys, often very young, each with a remuda of three or four horses, and there was the trail boss and all-important cook who lorded over the operation from his chuckwagon. This was a cleverly arranged portable kitchen and medical dispensary, whose invention is credited to Goodnight.

Was being a cowboy as romantic as it is portrayed in the movies?

Not in the least. After the ranches came under corporate management, cowhands were commonly forbidden to drink, gamble, or fight. On trail drives, they were usually forbidden to carry firearms because a gun discharge could cause a deadly stampede. Once they reached their destination, however, and got paid, the cowboys cut loose with abandon—and cow towns throughout the West got their reputation for wide-open vice and violence. While cattle drives and cowboys have become an icon of the American West, their heyday really only lasted about twenty years before the arrival of railroads in west and northwest Texas made cattle drives unnecessary.

Why did the cowboys put up with such intrusive restrictions?

Traditionally, cowboys could take part of their pay in calves and were allowed to claim and brand unowned mavericks, which gave them hope that, in time, they could run their own spreads. Cowboys resented the limitations on their personal lives, foreign owners with hired managers who had no regard for Western culture, and the lack of respect and money they received for hard and dangerous work. Led by Tom Harris of the LS Ranch, cowboys there and several neighboring ranches struck for better wages. The walkout lasted two and a half months and involved more than three hundred cowboys. Labor actions were seen nationally as dangerous and un-American, and local newspapers printed wildly false stories about the cowboys' alleged goals. In time, they were just fired

Who was Old Blue?

Like most hoofed stock, cow herds have a leader, and sometimes, a rancher could groom this animal as a "bell steer," one that could be hung with a bell every morning. When he got up and started walking, the herd would follow, and it made drives much less work. Goodnight's lead steer, Old Blue, seemed to know how valued he was and he became quite spoiled, bedding down with the horses and eating with the hands at the chuckwagon.

and replaced, for the West was full of rootless young drifters looking for work. Once the strike was broken, however, many of the men were allowed to return to work by reporting themselves to the foreman and apologizing. Most people today are unaware that one of the first labor actions in the United States was not at an Appalachian coal mine or Midwestern railroad but was the Texas Cowboy Strike of 1883.

Didn't small-time ranchers also object to this corporatization?

The vast increase in capital necessary to begin a ranch is what began the demotion of cowboys from a cultural icon to, essentially, minimum-wage workers. Large and well-financed operations ran miles of barbed wire and fences across public roads, enclosing enormous acreages of public domain that they did not own. Mail delivery was cut off, and legally homesteaded farms found themselves enclosed with no way out. Farmers and lesser cattlemen who depended on the open range responded by cutting fences, which was a hugely expensive vandalism. The situation degenerated into an open range war that caused over $20 million in damaged fences. In 1884 a special session of the legislature made fence cutting a felony, but large ranchers were required to place gates in their fences every 3 miles (5 kilometers) and not cut off public roads. The biggest factor in restoring peace, though, was just a growing acceptance that the days of free open range were gone.

What was the cause of the conflict between cattle ranchers and sheep men?

To most cowmen, there were simply no lower forms of life than sheep and shepherds. To an extent, their antipathy was understandable. Sheep grazed grass right down to the roots, leaving nothing for cattle, and their sharp hooves cut up the dirt, leaving a dusty wasteland in their wake. Most of their contempt, however, was rooted in culture. Most sheep raisers were Latino or from central or southern Europe—different groups whom the Anglo majority lumped together as "greasers."

Was the Sheep War successful?

Far from it. People eventually realized that sheep could make use of range land that would not support cattle, and wool was as needful a product as ever. In 1870, there were about 1.25 million sheep in Texas; in 1880, there were about six million.

Weren't there racial minorities among the cowboys?

One would never guess it from watching Hollywood movies, but about one-third of all the cowboys on the Texas frontier were Latino or black. In fact, at the beginning of the Union occupation after the Civil War, when the army advised freed slaves to stay on their plantations and work for wages, many African Americans headed to the frontier for the greater freedom and pay of cowboys. In later years, this had the curious effect of making integration easier in west Texas, where respect was based on the work one could do more than on color.

Who was the most prominent black cattleman?

Daniel Webster Wallace (1860–1939) was born into slavery in south Texas. His mother was sold to a young, white mother named O'Daniel to wet nurse her children. After his mother's death, he and his siblings were raised by the O'Daniels. Wallace left home at seventeen and went west to be a cowboy, working for some of the leading ranchers such as C. C. Slaughter. He became widely known under the nickname of "80 John" Wallace, named after the brand of his long time employer, Clay Mann, who withheld some of Wallace's wages as a kind of savings plan. Establishing his own spread near Colorado City (between Abilene and San Angelo), Wallace grazed six hundred cattle on 8,000 acres (32 square kilometers), employed ten tenant families, and became a prominent member of the local stock raisers' association.

Why is Charles Goodnight so revered as a rancher?

Building on his exploits before he settled in the Panhandle, Goodnight proved himself supremely able and practical. He would make a deal with anyone if it helped the ranch, including the famous cattle thief Dutch Henry Borne, to keep his rustling off the JA. He did not share the widespread hatred of sheep and shepherds, indeed keeping sheep on rocky parts of the ranch where cattle could not graze. Concerned at the near-extinction of the buffalo, he raised them on the ranch, occasionally sacrificing one to visiting Indians, more for old times' sake than for subsistence, and he experimentally cross-bred them with his stock to create "cattalo." Goodnight was, however, also ruthless in his acquisition of ever more land, fencing in hundreds of thousands of acres of public domain to which he had no right, attempting to avoid grazing fees on public land, and cowing local juries with his stature to obtain favorable trial verdicts.

What was the largest ranch in Texas?

The vast XIT Ranch in the far northwest corner of the Panhandle was the ultimate corporate operation. The state capitol in Austin had long been deemed inadequate, but the legislature was unwilling to appropriate money to build a new one. Consequently, they cobbled together 3 million acres (12,141 square kilometers) of Texas's last remaining public domain, which stretched for some 220 miles (354 kilometers) along the New Mex-

A photo of cowboys at the XIT Ranch in 1891.

ico border. This was sold to a consortium of investors in Chicago at fifty cents an acre, plus allowing them an additional 50,000 acres (202 square kilometers) to pay for the survey. Ironically, the investors' motive was to break up the parcel and sell smaller ranches at a profit, but the state's new policy of selling off the remaining public domain as rapidly as possible ruined the market. They made preparations instead to raise cattle with $5 million more in development capital from British investors, such as the Earl of Aberdeen.

Where did the famous XIT brand come from?

The fact that the venture was shared by ten investors in Chicago gave rise to the story that "XIT" stood for "Ten in Texas," but that is not true. One of their contractors to deliver stock to start the operation was Ab Blocker (1856–1943), who devised the famous XIT brand. Cattle rustling was still a big business, and Blocker scratched different combinations in the dirt, trying to devise a brand that thieves could not alter. Branding irons came as blank slugs of straight bars and had to be forged to create the different designs, and he discovered that the letters XIT could not be changed to anything else.

How successful was the XIT?

Within a few years, the mammoth ranch was running an average of 150,000 head, surrounded and cross-fenced by 1,500 miles (2,414 square kilometers) of barbed wire. The

109

XIT employed about 150 cowboys who earned up to $30 per month, but as on Goodnight's JA Ranch, they were bound by strict codes of clean living. A hundred dams were built in draws to create waterholes, and more than three hundred wells were drilled. An average of thirty-five thousand calves were branded every year. Even with such a scale of operation, the expenses of running such a huge place (and a long history of graft and embezzlement) kept profits modest, and the British investors wanted their loan and interest paid off. As land prices recovered, operations decreased and parcels were sold off. The last XIT cattle were disposed of in 1912 and the last land sold in 1963.

Did ranches in north Texas take prominence from those in south Texas?

Because of the romantic image of cowboys on the plains, they have taken a larger place in American culture, but cattle ranches in south Texas remained important and productive. The largest was the King Ranch, founded by (of all people) a New York-born river boatman, Richard King (1824–1885). In partnership with Pennsylvanian Mifflin Kenedy (1818–1895), they built it into an empire of 1.25 million acres (5,059 square kilometers) at its height. Among the ranch's later contributions to Texas history were progress against the tick-borne Texas Fever and developing the Santa Gertrudis breed of heavy beef cattle.

TEXAS AS A PROGRESSIVE LEADER

How did the railroads hasten the end of the frontier?

Construction of railroads across the vastness of Texas altered life in a number of ways. For one, they ended the necessity of months long trail drives of cattle north to Kansas. Instead, cattle needed only to be herded to a local siding and transported to new stockyards in Fort Worth or other Texas towns. Travel times for passengers was drastically reduced, from weeks to a day or two, which made settling remote areas far more feasible. Even more attractive, the advent of mail order catalogs made it possible to have merchandise and modern conveniences delivered to the nearest rail station.

How did mail order work?

Settlement of the West, including Texas, was given a gigantic boost when Montgomery Ward of Chicago began offering sales by mail order in 1872, and they were soon given competition by Bloomingdale's and Sears, Roebuck & Co. Circulars and then whole catalogs were distributed. Small items could be delivered by mail at one cent per ounce to a maximum of 4 pounds (1.8 kilograms); larger wares were commonly paid cash on delivery ("c.o.d.") to the railroad agent. Aware that consumers were wary of paying in advance for goods not yet seen, the policy was set early on to guarantee satisfaction or refund the money. Bulk ordering was encouraged, so consumers shared in larger (and more economical) sizes of merchandise.

How much did mail order goods cost?

A selection of commonly ordered items from the 1875 Montgomery Ward Catalog: of dry goods, cotton prints sold for 7 cents per yard, gingham 9 cents, or 11 cents for the best quality. They offered five different quality denims in blue and brown from 10 to 23 cents per yard. Five different quality table napkins rose from 85 cents to $2.75 per dozen, as did both ladies, and gentlemen's handkerchiefs. Men's white dress shirts ran from $1.25 to $2.00. Ladies' fine shawls ran from $3.00 to $4.50; kids' gloves were a dollar. There was a selection of ladies' drawers, chemises, and night dresses from 75 cents to $1.00. For the house, lace curtains ran from $1.00 to $2.75; for amusement, a combination checkers and backgammon board and pieces cost $1.00. Twelve yards (11 meters) of 1-inch (2.5-centimeter) colored ribbon was 90 cents. Umbrellas cost 65 cents to $1.40. A complete men's toilet set cost $1.00. There were also luxuries, such as a ladies' genuine mink muff and boa for $22.00. Even in 1875, mail order catalogs offered every conceivable item for a person or household.

For the house, good silver-plated flatware cost $2.50 per dozen pieces, a 1-gallon brass kettle was $1.50, three-bladed pocket knives were fifty cents, and pocket watches cost from $6 to $25, depending on the quality. For travel, a buggy harness cost $16; a good travel trunk from $2 to $3, depending on its size, and although fancy, zinc-reinforced trunks topped $10. And these were early products; within a few years, the whole array of farm equipment, garden seeds, and hardware supplies were added—and soon, even houses themselves were shipped out in kits.

Why did Texans build such a gigantic capitol?

Texans were keenly aware of their place as the largest state, and their resurgent economy, and proud of their history both revolutionary and Confederate. Plans were already underway to replace the 1856 Capitol when it burned to the ground on November 9, 1881. The contest to design a new one was won by Elijah Myers of Chicago, who had already designed four state and territorial capitols. His grandiose vision stretched 200 yards (183 meters) wide, 100 yards (91 meters) long, containing 8 acres (32,375 square meters) of floor space, 392 rooms with 22-foot (6.7-meter) ceilings and much higher in the sky light House and Senate chambers, custom-cast brass door knobs and hinges, and chandeliers with the letters TEXAS in between the points of the stars. Depending on where it was measured from, the dome rose 309 feet (94 meters), just a shade taller than the federal Capitol in Washington, which may have expressed just a small post-Reconstruction statement of states' rights. Similarly, a legend sprang up that the goddess

It could be fairly said that the Texas Capitol Building in Austin is as grand and beautiful as the federal building in Washington, D.C.

on the dome faced south, and the great, four-story arch of the front entrance faced south to turn their back on the Yankees. That was not true; the Capitol was built to face the city, almost all of which lay south of it.

Why was the Capitol built of pink granite?

The original plan was to build the Capitol of white limestone, and the contractor delivered 60 tons (54,432 kilograms) of it from his quarry at Convict Hill, near Austin. However, it was discovered that the limestone contained tiny crystals of iron, which rusted and streaked red in the rain. That stone was used to finish out the basement and interior walls, while landowners near Marble Falls put it out that they would furnish building stone for the Capitol, free for the taking. The state therefore built a special railway to its otherwise-useless granite mountains and brought back hundreds of carloads. The new Capitol was dedicated on March 2, 1885.

How did Texas pay for its extravagant Capitol, and what does that have to do with Dalhart?

During Governor Oran Roberts's time in office (1879–1883), Texas embarked on a pay-as-you-go regimen of financial austerity, which involved selling or trading away the remainder of the state's public domain. It eased pressure on the budget, but divesting the state of its patrimony of land was controversial. To finance construction of the gargantuan Capitol, the state cobbled together the last large bloc of public land, 3 million acres

(12,141 square kilometers) in the far northwest of the Panhandle, which was sold to a consortium of businessmen from Chicago and managed as the XIT Ranch. The ranch was an ongoing business at the time Dalhart was established at a rail junction in 1901 near the XIT's northern headquarters at Buffalo Springs. After the last of the cattle and land were sold off and the XIT ceased to exist, Dalhart hosted the annual reunion and barbecue held for ranch employees. It now celebrates the history of the XIT generally, and the reunion is held every year in early August.

How did Texas politicians come into the stereotype of being fat, loudmouthed boors?

Probably because there was a succession of Texas politicians who were fat, loudmouthed boors. Richard Coke, the Confederate colonel who took office after the coup that brought down Reconstruction in Texas, weighed 300 pounds (136 kilograms). His successor, Richard Hubbard (1832–1901), weighed 350 pounds (159 kilograms), and when he entered polite society, he could not find gloves large enough to fit his beefsteak hands. (As U.S. minister to Japan, Hubbard registered his approval of the law that said a man had to house his mistress in a different part of the city from where his family lived.) And after them, but separated by the tenure of trim and erudite Oran Roberts, came the portly Big Jim Hogg (1851–1906), whose rowdy children reinforced the stereotype by sliding down the banister in the Governor's Mansion and keeping a menagerie on the grounds that included two ostriches. And still after them came the majestically corrupt Senator Joe Bailey, so that stereotype became well and truly rooted in American folklore.

How did Texas become a leader in the Progressive Era?

Throughout the United States, resistance to the concentration of power in corporate hands was based in the rural section of the economy. In Texas, owing to a whole new wave of immigration, the amount of acreage under cultivation more than tripled to 126 million acres (509,904 square kilometers). The Patrons of Husbandry, started in New York in 1867, spread like wildfire and enjoyed a large Texas membership. They advocated control of the railroads, but mostly, they helped farmers help themselves through forming consumer cooperatives. This was altogether too little for Texas farmers, who began forming Greenback Clubs in 1876, which soon became the Greenback Party and then the Southern Farmers' Alliance the following year. This home grown coalition was far more political and elected a dozen members of the legislature in 1878.

Weren't Governor Hogg's children named Ima and Ura?

Hogg's daughter Ima (1882–1975) was named for the heroine of an epic poem written by Hogg's brother. He insisted that he did not realize he was saddling the girl with a name that people would make fun of until it was too late. She had three brothers, Will, Mike, and Tom. To the unfailing chagrin of Texans raised on the story, there was no sibling named Ura and no cousins named Heza and Sheza.

Why would Texas come to the forefront in championing the cause of farmers and small businesses?

Because of the great distances in Texas, its people were more dependent than anyone else in the country upon the transportation and communication industries, which in a practical manner meant railroads and telegraph companies. Texans had a long tradition of not putting up with tyrannical behavior, so when those entities began abusing their position—as, for instance, when a railroad ran its competitors out of business, gained a monopoly in serving a given area, and jacked up its rates unreasonably—Texans found ways to fight them, as the number of railroad cases in Texas courts doubled between 1882 and 1884.

Why should the railroads have owed any duty to the public good when they were in business to make money?

The state of Texas had helped finance construction of railroads in the state by giving the companies vast amounts of land from the public domain, in many cases granting them sixteen sections of land (10.42 acres [42,168 square meters]) for every mile of track laid. Eventually, the state gave them more than 32 million acres (129,499 square kilometers) of land—rather a long arm in overseeing railroads' bearing on the public welfare.

With all this emphasis on rural economy, how did Texas cities fare in the late nineteenth century?

Texas population doubled during the 1870s to 1.6 million, owing to a combination of the influx of poor Southerners from the defeated Confederacy, Texas's continuing homestead generosity, and a new wave of foreign immigrants, who now included Swedes,

Is it true that Abilene began as a bribe?

One aspect of bribes is secrecy, but probably yes. By 1880, the seat of Taylor County was Buffalo Gap, with twelve hundred people, a newspaper, a saloon, a jail, a hotel, a Baptist church, and advanced plans for a Presbyterian college, and it was calling itself the "Athens of the West." Once it became known that the Texas and Pacific Railroad would come through the county, ranch owners in the county's northern reaches preferred that the railroad come to their area rather than the county seat. The story is that a deputation of them went to visit the railroad's surveyor with a suitcase full of cash. Once the new route was announced, more than three hundred town lots were sold on March 15–16, 1881, to the hundreds of people who were already camping at the site of "Abilene," named for the cattle railhead in Kansas. In an election two years later, they captured the county government as well, and Buffalo Gap began to wither.

Poles, and other nationalities. Galveston, which had been Texas's largest city, doubled between 1870 and 1890 to twenty-nine thousand people. All the other cities had ground to make up and more than tripled in size: San Antonio from twelve thousand to thirty-seven thousand, Austin from four thousand to fourteen thousand, Houston from nine thousand to twenty-seven thousand. Even more dramatically, cities on the Plains blossomed from almost nothing in the same twenty years: Fort Worth from five hundred to twenty-three thousand and Dallas from three thousand to thirty-eight thousand.

What Texas country boy changed Texas law forever by breaking his leg?

In the early 1880s, ten-year-old S. P. Simpson lived near Denton and was playing with friends in a field near his house. Then, as they often did, they crossed onto the property of the Houston and Texas Central Railway Company to play upon the ponderous turntable that rotated locomotives to head out in different directions of tracks. Suddenly it moved, young Simpson was trapped, and his leg was crushed. His parents sued the company for damages and won $3,500, which the railroad appealed. There was no state or federal law that forced property owners to protect the safety of trespassers, and there was no precedent in court cases. When the case reached the Texas Supreme Court, the justices ruled that, despite the lack of law or precedent, maintaining dangerous machinery on property that might attract the attention of children was to be liable for a nuisance. This was the foundation of the "doctrine of attractive nuisance" that changed Texas law forever.

How could a court just step in and create a law where there was none?

The idea that courts can only interpret law, and that they become "activist" if they go beyond it, has far more currency today, but that was not always the case and certainly not in Texas. In historical, traditional practice, courts have two jobs to perform: to interpret law and also to dispense justice in the case before them. Texas courts used to be far less hesitant than they are now to act in "equity jurisprudence" to craft a fair remedy in a case where none exists in the law. To that extent, modern, right-wing politics has perverted the traditional function of the courts.

How did the Texas Railroad Commission get started?

Progressives gained such momentum in Texas that they began fielding their own candidates for statewide office. In the election for governor in 1890, their choice finished an alarmingly close second behind the Democratic winner, James Stephen (Big Jim) Hogg, and finishing ahead of the Prohibitionist and far ahead of the Republican. Hogg realized the necessity of adopting enough of the Progressive program to lure many of them back to the Democrats, and the key element of their program was corporate regulation. The railroads lost a spirited battle to have the commission declared unconstitutional before the Texas Supreme Court, and thereafter, they were compelled to fight a vigorous rearguard action in the courts challenging specific issues and power. In general, they lost more than they won, and it was lucky for them that Governor Hogg was himself a shrewd businessman and did not use the Railroad Commission to the extent that he could have.

MODERN TEXAS

THE TWENTIETH CENTURY

What two epic events launched Texas into the new century?

Occurring barely four months apart, the Galveston hurricane that came ashore on September 8, 1900, and the Spindletop oil gusher that blew in on January 10, 1901, ushered Texas into the 1900s with unparalleled destruction followed by unmatched promise.

Where does the Galveston Storm rank among U.S. natural disasters?

Of the various kinds of natural disasters that strike North America—tornadoes, earthquakes, blizzards, floods—tropical storms have caused the most fatalities. Hurricane Katrina, which destroyed much of New Orleans in 2005, took 1,833 lives. The Okeechobee hurricane of 1928 drowned at least 2,500 people. The number of casualties of the Galveston Storm could never be determined, but there were a minimum of 6,000 dead, probably closer to 8,000 and perhaps as many as 12,000. That makes it by far the deadliest natural disaster in U.S. history.

Why wasn't Galveston better prepared?

Galveston had been struck by hurricanes in 1766, 1818, 1867, and 1875, so they should have been more alert. The Weather Bureau began issuing bulletins on a gulf storm on September 4, but people were lulled into a false sense of security by having lived twenty-five years without a direct hit. Forecasting was in its most primitive infancy, and by the time the bureau's Galveston observer, Isaac Cline, noted a tide rapidly rising against a strong, offshore wind, which he had never seen before, it was too late.

How much in relief funds was spent to help Galveston recover?

The Galveston Storm took place in a time before spending public funds to alleviate disasters was recognized as good public policy. Newspaperman William Randolph Hearst was the first to get a reporter into Galveston, and she covered both the disaster and the supplies that Hearst sent, so Hearst got to look charitable while selling millions of newspapers. The U.S. Army did supply tents to temporarily house those left homeless, and Texas governor Joe Sayers visited New York to encourage new investment in the city, which was rather a wasted errand.

What icon of American charity went to Galveston to help with relief?

Clara Barton (1821–1912), the founder of the American Red Cross, was seventy-eight when she journeyed to Galveston to oversee dispensing of aid. It was her last public service.

How did the nearby city of Houston respond to the Galveston Storm?

With communications cut off, individual people from Houston raced to Galveston almost immediately to help however they could, but the city of Houston itself took a different attitude. It had been competing economically with Galveston almost since Houston was founded in 1837. With news that Galveston had been all but wiped out, Houston began dredging a ship channel up Buffalo Bayou, advertising its own immunity from coastal devastation, to capture the lion's share of ocean-going traffic before Galveston could recover. At this, they succeeded.

What gigantic construction project allowed Galveston to rebuild?

The storm destroyed more than three thousand buildings in Galveston, most of which had been built only a few feet above sea level. Two years after the storm, the city began laying a concrete seawall some 17 feet (30.5 centimeters) high, footed with granite riprap on the ocean side. The first section, 3 miles (5 kilometers) long, was later extended to 10 miles (16 kilometers). Behind the wall, sand pumped from the floor of the Gulf raised the grade of the entire city by a similar height, and more than two thousand surviving buildings were raised and placed on new foundations. The effort was a success, for a storm of similar strength that struck in 1915 killed only fifty-three people in the city.

Damaging or destroying every house in Galveston and wreaking havoc from the Gulf to Canada, the 1900 Great Galveston Hurricane boasted 145 mile-per-hour (230 kilometer-per-hour) winds and flooded the island with 8 to 12 feet (2.5 to 3.5 meters) of water.

What happened at Spindletop that changed the U.S. economy forever?

The industrial revolution created the need for a fuel that was more efficient than coal, and the nation had turned to petroleum. National production, centered about Pennsylvania where it was first drilled, totaled 63 million barrels. An eccentric and self-taught petroleum engineer named Pattillo Higgins believed that oil underlay the geologic features known as salt domes near the Gulf Coast. Experts chuckled as Higgins formed a partnership with a like-minded Austrian, Anthony Lucas, raised money, and started drilling at Spindletop, a low hill near Beaumont that was the exposed top of a salt dome. On January 10, 1901, having drilled to a depth of about 1,100 feet, the roughnecks were surprised to see mud issuing from the hole. Then, the ground rumbled underfoot as lengths of drilling pipe shot out of the hole like javelins, ripping the crossbeams from the derrick, then came mud, a violent hiss of natural gas, and an eerie quiet. Then came the oil in a geyser that reached 150 feet high. The well was engulfed in a lake of oil in the nine days it took to cap it, after which that well—that single well—exceeded the production of all other oil wells in the United States put together, more than 100,000 barrels per day.

Was Spindletop the first oil discovered in Texas?

No. Spanish mariners learned early that they could dock at one upper Texas bay and caulk their vessels from a natural asphalt seep. In 1865, Lyne Barret (1832–1913), who was in the mercantile business in Nacogdoches, drilled for petroleum at a place with the promising name of Oil Springs and struck oil at a depth of 106 feet, and that well produced ten barrels per day. Despite the oil being graded as superior, the economics of Reconstruction interfered, and Barret was unable to attract enough investment. A much more commercial field was discovered while drilling for water near Corsicana in 1894. Still, Texas production was 863,000 barrels in 1900, about 1.4 percent of total U.S. oil.

What major American oil companies got their start at Spindletop?

Within a year of the Spindletop oil strike, more than five hundred corporations were chartered to cash in on the boom. Chief among them were Sun Oil; Magnolia, which later merged with another firm to become Mobil; the Texas Company, which became Texaco; Gulf, which was later merged into Chevron; and Humble Oil, which later became Exxon.

One of the gushers at Spindletop near Galveston, Texas, in 1901. The discovery of vast oil reservoirs in the state had a dramatic impact on world industries.

What is a "wildcatter"?

Within a short time of the discovery, most drilling was carried on by well-capitalized companies, but Texas oil has always provided a home for the independent, risk-taking entrepreneurs, flashy and high-rolling, playing their hunches, making and losing fortunes with horse-laughing equanimity. They were the proverbial wildcatters. Their domain was to chance sinking exploratory wells in land that experts thought marginal. When they succeeded, they made huge amounts of money; when they failed, which was often, they could lose everything.

What was the effect of the Spindletop strike?

With the sudden glut of supply, the price of oil plummeted. The power of John D. Rockefeller's Standard Oil monopoly was broken. Cheap gasoline to power internal combustion engines made mass ownership of automobiles possible. Development of Texas's own refining capacity transformed the state from an internal colony and supplier of raw resources into an economic dynamo.

Were there other oil strikes in Texas?

Lucas and Higgins were vindicated in their belief that there was oil in the salt domes, but everyone was surprised at how quickly they played out. The Spindletop field produced 17.5 million barrels of oil in 1902, then quickly slacked off. Equally dramatic strikes, however, blew in at Saratoga, Sour Lake, and Batson in southeast Texas, as well as further gushers near Corsicana. Between 1902 and 1904, a whole new source was discovered: oil fields in Henrietta, Petrolia, and Electra in the Pease River breaks, where the Comanche and Kiowa used to pounce on wagon trains and lone ranchers. Oil was now suddenly "Texas tea."

What form of mass transit was pioneered in Texas?

In 1900, the north Texas towns of Sherman and Denison were linked with an electric railroad. This "interurban" was a great advance over steam locomotives, making frequent stops to pick up commuters. Fort Worth and Dallas followed suit in 1902, and Texas soon had more than five hundred miles of interurban lines.

Why did interurbans fail?

Texas oil made possible cheap gasoline, and the advent of affordable, mass-produced automobiles gave Texans their taste for individual transportation that has prevailed ever since.

Why was Prohibition such a huge political issue in Texas?

Texas in earlier days was famous as a hard-drinking place. With the close of the frontier, however, influences such as increasing urbanization, the competition among evangelical, tee totaling churches, and women's unwillingness to suffer alcoholic husbands came together in the Women's Christian Temperance Movement, which became a major political force. A statewide election to prohibit alcohol was crushed by ninety thousand votes in 1887. Four years later, the "dry" forces won a constitutional amendment that allowed them to seek to ban alcohol not just in counties but in individual precincts of the counties. Ultimately, Prohibition in Texas became an issue more determined by effective local organization than it ever was widely supported.

When was the first airplane flight in Texas?

Although Texans had been tinkering with flight since the Civil War (and at least one contraption made it into the air but crashed), no successful heavier-than-air powered flight occurred over Texas until 1910. Ned Green, the railroad baron who had also introduced Texans to the automobile, shipped a Wright plane to Dallas (on a train) for fairgoers to see late in 1909, but there was no demonstration. Otto Brodie and his Curtiss model did give Dallas a taste of flight in February 1910 just as the "French birdman" Louis Paulhan got his Farman biplane into the air over Houston. There, local machinist L. L. "Shorty" Walker was already putting a Bleriot Model XI together in his garage, which also flew in Houston later in the year.

When did Texas military aviation begin?

The U.S. Army saw possibilities for flying machines in communication and observation, so it gave the Army Signal Corps the job of starting an air wing. The Wright Brothers assembled a Model A for the Army, but it crashed during its trials, nearly killing Orville Wright and taking the life of his observer. The army assigned Lieutenant Benjamin D. Foulois to go to San Antonio with a second plane, the SC No. 1 (SC for Signal Corps). Airplanes did not yet fly from place to place but were shipped by rail and assembled on-

Why is Corsicana important to Texas oil history?

Corsicana was home to the first oil refinery build in Texas in 1897—three years before Spindletop—and became a very important center not just for drilling but for supplying the industry after a large strike nearby in 1923.

site, the SC No. 1 filling seven large crates of components and spare parts. With almost an hour of flight training from the Wrights, Foulois, who was selected for his slight build that would not overload a plane, took to the air over San Antonio's Fort Sam Houston on March 2, 1910.

What invaluable advance did Foulois make to aviation?

After repeatedly crash-landing the SC No. 1, Foulois suggested to the Wrights that they replace its landing skis with wheels. After Foulois made some sixty flights, the Army purchased several more planes with a 1911 budget of $125,000, and aviation became an ongoing part of the military.

Who "put a little color" into Texas aviation?

For a couple of decades after the Wright Brothers' first flight, airplanes and fliers were great novelties throughout the country, and air shows that featured stunt flying (known as "barnstorming") were heavily attended. One such showman, a twenty-two-year-old showoff from Michigan named Charles Lindbergh, might have killed himself when he took off too slowly from a field in Camp Wood and took the corner off a local hardware store. Bessie Coleman (1892–1926), born into a large sharecropping family in Atlanta, Texas, and raised in Waxahachie, dreamed of flying, but the dream seemed hopeless, for she was black (and partly Cherokee) and a woman, either one of which would disqualify her for flight school. At twenty-four, she moved to Chicago, lived with her brothers, and earned her money as a manicurist with a second job in a chili parlor. With her savings, and with the backing of Chicago's black community newspaper, she caught a ship for France and trained for and received an international pilot's license from the Fédération Aéronautique Internationale. This earned her acclaim back in the United States, but even with a license, no one would give her advanced training. Undeterred, she sought out leading airplane designer Anthony Fokker, polished her skills in Germany, returned to the States, and became a sensational barnstormer, flying under the stage moniker of Queen Bess. When asked about her breaking ground as the nation's first black woman to be a pilot, she joked that it was about time "to put a little color" into aviation. Ironically, she was a passenger, looking over the terrain for a future parachute jump, when her Curtiss Jenny suddenly lurched into a dive, throwing her out. She fell 2,000 feet to her death as the plane, with a wrench jamming the controls, crashed and killed the pilot.

What famous cereal magnate spent millions on a social experiment to help poor Texas dirt farmers get ahead?

Absentee ranch investors gained a hard reputation for not caring about their employees. Charles Goodnight said that without his intervention, the JA cowboys would have beaten up their boss, John Adair, many times over. Charles William (C. W.) Post (1854–1914), however, harbored a soft spot for poor tenant farmers. To prove that they could prosper if given a fair shake, he purchased more than 200,000 acres in Garza County, astraddle the Caprock east of Lubbock. He divided it into quarter-section farms, each fully kitted with fences, house, barn, windmill, and well. He ran excursion trains out to his middle of nowhere, and those who bought a plot did not pay a fare. He established the town of Post as a marketing center, with running water, electricity, and a sewage system, boasting a hotel, cotton gin, and even a golf course. There, he sold $1,500 houses for $250 down and $25 per month, and he lived to see twelve hundred people living there.

So why did people think C. W. Post was crazy?

Stories of Post's eccentricity grew the more he tried to make it rain. He got it in his mind that during the Civil War, artillery battles were often followed by thunderstorms. Starting in June 1911, he began setting off charges of dynamite at

Charles William Post is remembered for pioneering the breakfast cereal; he also founded the town of Post, which was specifically created as a home to help tenant farmers improve their lives.

the top of the Caprock, and when that didn't work, he launched kites with 2-pound charges attached to them. His first "rain battle" used 168 pounds of dynamite, but it produced no rain. His second try soon after, however, was followed by ten days of showers—enough to keep him trying and trying.

Who saved the Alamo from being torn down?

Texans' dedication to their history dates largely from the early 1900s; before that, progress was the watchword, and many historic structures were demolished to make way for modern times. One partial exception was the Alamo, the essential shrine of Texas freedom, which downtown San Antonio had grown to surround. The state purchased the chapel in 1883 but then let it go to ruin, and the remainder of the complex was sold off or repurposed, including the convent that stretched northward from the chapel, which had become the warehouse of a wholesale grocer. Beautiful young Clara Driscoll (1881–1945), who was prominent in the recently formed Daughters of the Republic of Texas because both of her grandfathers had fought at San Jacinto and because her father had grown immensely wealthy in south Texas ranching, started a campaign to purchase and restore the property, which was even then in negotiations to be demolished. A $5,000 state appropriation passed the legislature, but the governor vetoed it. Clara announced that she would do whatever was necessary to save the Alamo, but she was only interested in saving the chapel. A second faction among the Daughters insisted on reclaiming as much of the original Alamo complex as they could, especially the convent/grocery warehouse. Their heroine of the "Second Battle of the Alamo" was Adina de Zavala (1861–1955), the 123

What was the best hotel on the Plains?

Arguably, it was Post's Algerita Hotel. Post was a millionaire from the Midwest and used to the good life. The town of Post was his experiment in *noblesse oblige*, and he wanted the hotel there to be finely appointed. He knew his market, though, instructing the cook to give his dishes simple names. "Don't try to make the cow-punchers think we are a bunch of frog-eating French," he ordered. And, ever the businessman, he made sure that in the dining room, covered dishes of Post Grape-Nuts were available on every table. The Algerita gained wide fame, but it was built on a rubble foundation and had to be demolished in 2014 as exterior walls came apart and threatened to crash onto the sidewalks.

diminutive, middle-aged granddaughter of the vice president of the Republic of Texas, Lorenzo de Zavala. When a demolition crew showed up with the blessing of the Driscoll faction, Miss de Zavala chased them off with a shotgun and barricaded herself inside. As much as they fought with each other, the two women won public sympathy, and with Driscoll's money, three acres of the complex became the shrine that is preserved today.

What did Texans do for leisure when they had spare time?

Most popular sports extended from frontier skills—rodeo events and trick shooting. Adolph "Ad" and Elizabeth Toepperwein became a national attraction as marksmen. Using her trusty .22, Elizabeth once hit 1,995 of 2,000 two-inch wooden blocks tossed in the air twenty feet away.

WORLD WAR I AND THE TWENTIES

Who was Gregorio Cortez?

Made famous by a border *corrido* (ballad) and then in a 1958 book by the folklorist Americo Paredes and a 1981 *American Playhouse* television production, Mexican tenant farmer Gregorio Cortez came to embody everything that could go wrong with Anglo–Latino relations. In June of 1901, a sheriff and an officious deputy who spoke too little Spanish to translate questioned him about a horse theft. After a series of momentous errors of language—"you can't arrest me for nothing" was rendered "no white man can arrest me"—Cortez killed the sheriff and then led a thousand "deputies" on a chase that ended thirty miles from the border and freedom. The pursuit, capture, and trial were all sensationally reported day by day. Cortez was sentenced to prison but later pardoned. Contrary to popular myth, the Texas Rangers were not involved in the pursuit of Cortez. After his capture, the Rangers did intervene to protect him from any reprisal by white local authorities.

What was the Plan of San Diego?

Although it originated in Monterey deep in the Mexican interior, this "irredentist" scheme to restore Texas and the Southwest to Mexican rule surfaced in the Duval County town of San Diego in January 1915. Black, Mexican, and Japanese residents of the valley would unite in a race war against Anglos, executing white males over the age of sixteen and forming a new government that could then seek readmission to the Mexican federation. Starting the following July, thirty raids from across the Rio Grande claimed twenty-one Anglos' lives and destroyed property. Discovery of the San Diego manifesto sent white Texans in the valley into a panic, and both the U.S. Army and Texas Rangers descended on the Rio Grande Valley at terrible cost to the Tejano community. Responsibility for the Plan of San Diego is not known with certainty, but the leading candidate was Venustiano Carranza, one of several contenders for power in Mexico, who many believed used the plan as a means of forcing U.S. recognition of his regime. This ultimately happened, after which raids greatly decreased.

What did Germany have to do with Rio Grande conflicts?

As events in Europe came closer to drawing the United States into World War I, Germany saw an opportunity to create trouble for the United States with an alliance with Mexico. In 1915, German naval intelligence gave former Mexican president Victoriano Huerta $12 million to harass U.S. interests, and German saboteurs working from Mexico damaged military installations in California and New York. Early in 1917, Germany feared that when it resumed unrestricted submarine attacks, the United States would declare war. German foreign minister Arthur Zimmermann sent a coded cable to the Mexican ambassador, offering "generous" financial assistance to Mexico for its participation and sweetening the deal with a promise to restore Texas, New Mexico, and Arizona to Mexico. British intelligence intercepted and decoded the cable and forwarded it to the United States, where it created a firestorm of anti-German sentiment. In Mexico, Venustiano Carranza's government studied its chances hopefully but concluded that German aid was unreliable and

that even if Germany won the war in Europe, Mexico had no hope of a southwestern *Reconquista* of territory that would be ungovernable even if taken. Along with other German provocations, the Zimmermann note helped the United States decide to declare war on Germany.

How did the thousands of German-descended Texans fare during World War I?

The "Great War" provided an opportunity for Anglo Texans to brutalize the German

Mexican President José Victoriano Huerta Márquez accepted $12 million from the Germans as payment to harass U.S. interests along the Rio Grande.

125

Texans one more time, but it was really just a new expression of the bad blood that American descendants had felt against the Germans since before the Civil War. The German language was criminalized, and universities ended German classes; a few people were even lynched when overheard speaking German. Germans could be reported if neighbors discovered nationalistic art on their walls, and bankers scrutinized Germans' bank accounts to see that they were buying war bonds.

What did Texans think of having a new battleship named after their state?

When it joined the fleet in 1914, the USS *Texas* was the largest and most powerful battleship in the world, mounting ten .45 caliber fourteen-inch rifles, which Texans thought suitable to bear their name. During a port of call in Galveston, citizens presented it with a magnificent chaised silver service for the officers' wardroom. At 35,000 tons, it was so big that it ran aground off Block Island when departing to join the British Grand Fleet for Atlantic operations. After the Battle of Jutland, the German fleet did not venture out again, so *Texas*'s big guns were never fired in anger. On January 30, 1918, it did direct five-inch rounds at a German periscope and heeled hard over to avoid a torpedo.

What Texan became an indispensable, political guru to President Woodrow Wilson?

Edward M. House, a banker and businessman from Houston, broadly educated in Virginia, New York, and England, guided the political ascent of four successive Texas governors: Jim Hogg, Charles Culberson, Joe Sayers, and Samuel Lanham. He was widely known as Colonel House, but that was a nickname given him by Governor Hogg; House had no military background. As Wilson's chief adviser, House turned down any cabinet position or public office, preferring to remain in the background. He remained powerful

---

What famous artist lost her job for her lack of patriotism?

Georgia O'Keeffe, born in Wisconsin and raised in Virginia, was new to Texas when she took up her duties as superintendent of penmanship and drawing for the Amarillo public schools. In the era of the hyperfeminized "Gibson Girl," O'Keeffe drew stares for the severity of her appearance: lean, swarthy, angular, plainly dressed, and given to expressing abrupt opinions. She left her job after refusing to adopt a state-approved textbook, and she went back east for further study. But she was drawn to Texas, a country of "terrible winds and a wonderful emptiness." She returned to teach at West Texas State Normal College (now known as West Texas A&M University) in Canyon, located one county south of Amarillo. When war was declared, she was virtually alone among the faculty in encouraging her male students to finish their studies before enlisting. "What," she demanded, "does patriotism have to do with seeing a thing as green when it is green and red when it is red?" That was the end of her time in Texas, which she left in June 1918.

Why did hamburgers lose their popularity in Texas during the Great War?

Because the name contained the word "Hamburg," Germany's principal port city. They were relabeled "liberty burgers." That was only one portion of Texas's de-Germanification effort. Sauerkraut was renamed "liberty cabbage." The German-sounding Texas town of Brandenburg, founded by German immigrants in 1903, became Old Glory to demonstrate its inhabitants' loyalty.

until late in Wilson's second term, when the president's declining health and judgment, and the animosity of the first lady, Edith Wilson, prompted him to vacate the scene.

Who was the only Texas governor to be impeached?

Taking office as governor early in 1915, James E. Ferguson was a banker and businessman from Temple. He was also ill-educated, a cornpone populist, and majestically corrupt. He came to power by promising land reform during the unrest of a national recession that caused wide misery among Texas tenant farmers. As governor, he incurred the wrath of University of Texas regents for demanding the hiring of certain faculty, and he vetoed the entire appropriation when they refused. At their instigation, investigators determined that Ferguson had received a $150,000 loan from Texas brewers, had deposited state money in banks of which he was part owner, and diverted part of another university's appropriation to pay a personal note—enough for him to be impeached and convicted. Ferguson did resign before his removal became official, which allowed him to claim that he was still eligible to run for public office again if he wished to do so. However, the Court of Impeachment ruled otherwise.

How did Pa and Ma Ferguson get their nicknames?

Until he was impeached, James Ferguson's sobriquet was "Farmer Jim." It was a bit of theater meant to help tenant farmers identify with him. Unable to run for governor again, Ferguson's wife, Miriam Amanda Ferguson, ran for the office in 1924. They made no secret of the fact that she was running as his proxy; in fact, their campaign slogans were "Two Governors for the Price of One" and "Me for Ma—And I Ain't Got a Durned Thing Against Pa." "Ma" was derived from the initials of her name, and "Pa" naturally followed as a bit of folksy electioneering. Once she took office, they worked at adjoining desks.

Why were Texas women allowed to vote before they could elsewhere in the United States?

Because of their long history of legal privileges under Hispanic law, Texas women were used to managing their own affairs when they had to. Plus, their support for William P. **127**

Hobby in impeaching Governor James Ferguson and winning the election in his own right came with a price tag: his support for women's suffrage, which he was probably inclined to do anyway. Republicans in Texas were so irrelevant to politics that voting in the Democratic primaries was tantamount to voting in the general election. When the legislature accorded women the right to participate, the Supreme Court ruled that primaries are private party functions, not governed by general election law, and it was perfectly constitutional if a statute allowed women to vote in them.

Miriam Amanda Wallace "Ma" Ferguson was the first female governor of Texas, a position she held twice from 1925 to 1927 and again from 1933 to 1935.

Was Ma Ferguson the first woman to be a governor in the United States?

No. She was the first woman to be elected governor, but two weeks before her inauguration, Nellie Tayloe Ross, the first lady of Wyoming, was suddenly widowed and was sworn in to finish her husband's term. Ironically, Ma Ferguson did not support female suffrage.

Were Texas suffragists active on the national scene?

With deep roots in Texas's Hispanic legal heritage and in earlier organizations, by 1915, the Texas Woman Suffrage Association boasted twenty-one chapters with twenty-five hundred members. Dynamo Minnie Fisher Cunningham was elected president, and three years later, there were nearly a hundred chapters and the TWSA had espoused Prohibition, which wrested support from "dry" conservatives who might otherwise have balked. There was good reason that national suffrage leader Carrie Catt referred to her Texas contingent as her "heavy artillery," for their effort at female voter registration—supervised by the aptly named Nellie "The Ramrod" Doom—netted nearly four hundred thousand women added to the rolls.

Who were the first women prominent in Texas politics?

The first woman to hold statewide office was Annie Webb Blanton, elected superintendent of Texas public instruction in 1918. After many years of lobbying for home and hearth issues, Jane Yelvington McCallum was appointed Texas secretary of state by the progressive Governor Dan Moody in 1927. She was retained by his successor, Ross Sterling, making hers the longest tenure in that office; she was dismissed by Ma Ferguson after her election to a second term in 1933. The first woman to serve in the state legislature was Edith E. T. Williams, who served from 1923 to 1925. She then unsuccessfully ran for governor and left politics. The first woman state senator, Carthage newspaper publisher Margie Neal, served four productive terms.

In what ways were the Fergusons so corrupt?

They were usually discreet enough not to demand cash. They published a political newsletter, the *Ferguson Forum*, in which competing highway contractors purchased advertising space. "Farmer Jim" did own a farm as a sideline, and another way to influence them was to buy stock from them at exorbitant prices. But they were most famous for selling pardons to escape state prison. Jane Y. McCallum, who served two anti-Ferguson Texas governors, tallied that in her first term, Ma had pardoned 33 rapists, 133 murderers, 124 robbers, and 127 bootleggers. She also wrecked the legendary Texas Rangers, who resigned in droves as she appointed hundreds of political cronies as "Special Rangers," who in some instances were bigger criminals than the ones they began shaking down. The story was prevalent in the Capitol that a man accidentally stepped on the governor's foot in an elevator and said, "Pardon me." Without hesitation, she said, "You'll have to talk to Pa."

How did the Texas Supreme Court come to be composed entirely of women?

The 1920s were the heyday of ambitious businessmen helping their careers by belonging to fraternal lodges and benefit associations. There was a mania for secret signs and societies, of which the Ku Klux Klan was a negative manifestation. Most had beneficent purposes. Texas Supreme Court justice William Ramsey, for instance, was a Mason, an Elk, a Knight of Pythias, and a Red Man of the Improved Order. He also belonged to the International Woodmen of the World, which provided, among other things, life insurance and burial services. (Their tree-trunk headstones are still seen in many cemeteries.) When a lawsuit involving the Woodmen was appealed to the Supreme Court in 1925, all the justices had to recuse themselves because they were members. Governor

What was the "Santa Claus Holdup"?

During the oil boom in Cisco, December 23, 1927, the Saint Nick who was greeting people on the street in front of the bank was joined by three accomplices, with whom he entered the bank and held it up. News of this raced through the business district so fast that before the robbery was finished, an armed mob surrounded the bank. Santa and his helpers took hostages and shot their way out. Eight people were killed or mortally wounded, plus one of the elves; Santa and the remaining bandits started to flee but could not start the car; they made good an escape when the pursuing mob recovered the money but were soon captured and convicted. After one of the elves was executed, another principal, Marshall Ratliff, began acting in a bizarre manner in order to establish an insanity defense. An attempted escape resulted in his being lynched from a power pole.

Pat Neff, claiming that he could not find any male judges or lawyers who were not also disqualified, appointed a special term of the Supreme Court selected from among Texas's two dozen female attorneys. In truth, Neff was a backer of women's legal and political advancement, and this was a way to promote the cause without paying too high a price. He could have found men if he had tried.

What were the repercussions of the Santa Claus Holdup?

The Texas Bankers Association was so outraged not just at this robbery, but the growing litany of bank heists, that it published a reward promising $5,000 for any dead bank robber but "not one cent for live ones." The result was dramatic but unintended. Corrupt politicos began arranging the murders of hapless vagrants, planting incriminating evidence on their bodies and collecting an easy five grand. It was Texas Ranger Captain Frank Hamer who broke the ring and brought the madness to an end over the irate opposition of the Bankers Association. When he was cautioned whether he really wanted to incur the wrath of such a powerful organization, Hamer was said to have replied, "When you go fishing, what kind of fish do you like to catch? Big ones or little ones?"

Who was Old Rip?

At the dedication of the Eastland County courthouse in 1897, a time capsule was sealed in the cornerstone, whose contents included Old Rip, a live Texas horned lizard, more colloquially known as a horny toad. When that courthouse was demolished in 1928, a horned lizard was produced, allegedly from the cornerstone, dehydrated but alive. The event attracted wide attention to the town, and the lizard went on a national tour, even meeting President Calvin Coolidge in Washington. It died eleven months later and was placed on display in the new courthouse. More than forty years later, the Old Rip story was revealed to be a hoax.

FROM DEPRESSION TO WAR

What was the effect of the Great Depression in Texas?

After the stock market collapsed on October 29, 1929, it took time for the full impact of economic calamity to settle in, but by 1932, four hundred thousand Texans had lost their jobs, and about a quarter of those had no resources to fall back on. Pig hunting became survival for many, as feral pigs became known as "Hoover hogs," and any given camp of hobos was a "Hooverville." Texas politicians, most deeply conservative, believed that charity was the domain of churches and the private sector, and they were slow to realize the depth of the emergency.

Shouldn't Texas's oil wealth have softened the hard times?

To be sure, discoveries of more new oil fields had turned Texas into one giant oil spigot. Columbus Marion Joiner (1860–1947), one of Texas's most flamboyant wildcatters, had

A dust storm approaches Stratford, Texas, in this 1935 photograph. The Dust Bowl hit Texans hard.

the idea that there was oil in Rusk County, in northeast Texas. Raising money on the strength of doctored geological reports, selling the same shares to different people, and using other shady means, Joiner kept drilling after abandoning two dry holes. On his third try, he punched into the East Texas Oil Field of 140,000 acres, harboring some five billion barrels of oil. And this came on the heels of hardly less spectacular strikes in the Permian Basin of west Texas. Oil plummeted to only a dime a barrel, but at a time when a dime could be the difference between bread and hunger for many, Texans were slow to realize that producing more and more oil for less and less money hurt more than it helped. Some of Texas's most bitter conflicts during the Great Depression were over the legality of regulating oil production and black-market resistance to it.

Was the Dust Bowl really as awful as depicted by John Steinbeck in *The Grapes of Wrath?*

If anything, it was worse. Steinbeck destroyed his first two attempts at writing this novel because after interviewing refugees from Texas and Oklahoma in California camps, he was so undone at the discrimination and abuse they endured that the book became more a social justice manifesto than a novel. Texas Panhandle singer Woody Guthrie captured something more of their plight in his song "So Long, It's Been Good to Know You." Dust storms increased each year: in 1934 there were twenty-two, forty in 1935, sixty-eight in 1936, and seventy-two in 1937. Women who caulked their windows with dish towels still wound up with grit in their bread. More than one automobile, overtaken by a dust storm, emerged with the paint completely sandblasted away.

How did Texas wind up with so much New Deal aid?

It was no accident. Texans still held bitter memories of Reconstruction and were determined never again to be at the mercy of the federal government. Their method was to build up such impregnable seniority in Congress that they would be the ones laying terms. At the beginning of 1933, Texan John Nance Garner was vice president, but he still held enormous influence in the House, where he had served fifteen terms, the last one as speaker. In the House, six Texans held committee chairs, including Marvin Jones at agriculture and James Buchanan at appropriations. Texas received New Deal aid at about 30 percent per capita above the national average.

If Texas politicians were so conservative, why did they milk the New Deal like that?

There was indeed a good amount of hypocrisy in play. Most of them had little use for Roosevelt and were shocked at the notion of appropriating funds for public relief. However, with the New Deal a reality, they were determined that Texas should do well by it. Moreover, by cooperating with FDR and with Garner as his vice president, they stood to inherit even greater power when Roosevelt left office. When FDR dumped Garner and ran for a third term with a new running mate, the Texas delegation was scalded, and it turned on him almost completely. To the hundreds of thousands of Texans on some form of relief, though, FDR was a saint.

How did the "Chicken Ranch" get its name?

It was a thriving business since the Republic of Texas was a brothel in La Grange, in Fayette County. To the legislators in Austin and students at Texas A&M, it was close enough to be accessible and far enough away to be discreet. Since 1905, it had been the enterprise of Miss Jessie Williams, the *nom de la nuit* of Faye Stewart of Waco. The brothel provided basic service, a place where men in need could "four-get" their troubles—get up, get on, get off, get out—for three dollars. When the times turned bad, she cut that rate in half, but many customers still could not manage it. Finally, she began accepting a chicken as payment instead.

Why was such an immoral business as a brothel tolerated?

Fayette County was settled largely by Czech immigrants—Bohemians—whose lives revolved around hard work and minding their own business. The law in La Grange was

---

Is it true that John Nance Garner said the vice presidency wasn't worth a pitcher of warm spit?

No. He said it wasn't worth a bucket of warm piss. It was the news reporters who toned it down.

made up of the Loessin brothers, one the city marshal and the other county sheriff. Twice a year, they went to the grand jury, who made sure that Miss Jessie's girls got regular medical checkups. Beyond that, they didn't care. When times turned bad, Miss Jessie spread her purchases around town fairly, gave generously to local charities, and even bought uniforms for local little league baseball teams. A photo of FDR graced her parlor, and she brooked no criticism of him.

What precision dance team brought pretty Texas girls to national attention?

In 1939 Dr. B. E. Masters, dean of Kilgore College, wanted his school's football games to feature some halftime activity that would keep fans in their seats instead of congregating beneath the bleachers to drink. He hired Gussie Nell Davis, who directed the cheerleading squad at the high school in Greenville. Instead of the usual girls' drum-and-bugle corps, Davis created a precision dance team, scantily clad in dresses above the knee. Female enrollment at Kilgore College went up, which was another of Masters's goals, and the Kilgore Rangerettes went on to worldwide performance and fame.

Where did the phrase "Pass the Biscuits, Pappy" originate?

Burrus Mill of Fort Worth hired a salesman, Kansas native Wilbert Lee "Pappy" O'Daniel (1890–1969), who had a knack for advertising. He hired a local musician named Bob Wills who was in between gigs, and he sponsored the band's music on local radio. O'Daniel loathed the band's country music, but the company's flour sales went through the roof. O'Daniel still fired them, for blasphemy, when he heard a song punctuated with "Lord, Lord!" Wills kept his band at work by offering to let O'Daniel pitch his flour on live radio, spots that O'Daniel expanded into segments of cracker-barrel philosophy and then electioneering, as he won the election for governor in 1938. "Pass the Biscuits, Pappy" had been a line from his Light Crust Flour commercials. He ran for office on the Ten Commandments and the Golden Rule, plus the promise of a $30-per-month state pension for the elderly. He won 473,000 votes, his Republican opponent got 11,000, and no pension ever came of it.

WORLD WAR II

How much did Texas contribute to the war effort?

Texas's famous oil was the greatest material value to the country. German submarines were a constant threat in the Gulf and the Atlantic Seaboard, and Interior secretary Harold Ickes foresaw this issue more than a year before Pearl Harbor. Surprisingly, his requests for steel to build new pipelines from Texas to the East Coast were denied. Once the United States was in the war, the "Big Inch," a twenty-four-inch crude oil pipeline from Texas to New Jersey, was completed in only a year and ten days, followed by the "Little Big Inch," a twenty-inch pipeline constructed to transport refined products. Bombers were assembled in Dallas and Fort Worth; hundreds of minesweepers, destroyer escorts, landing craft, and "Liberty Ships" slid down the ways in southeast Texas—some into waterways so narrow they had to be launched sideways. The war effort was universal; more than five hundred companies in the Houston area alone held defense contracts of some kind.

How many Texans served in World War II?

About 728,000—the highest proportion of any state in the Union.

What African American sailor became a hero for his gallantry at Pearl Harbor?

Doris "Dorie" Miller was a twenty-two-year-old mess attendant serving breakfast on the battleship *West Virginia* when the Japanese attack began. Anchored outboard

Born in Waco, Doris Miller became a hero at Pearl Harbor, becoming the first African American to receive the Navy Cross.

of the *Arizona*, the *West Virginia* was struck by six torpedoes and two bombs before the *Arizona* blew up. Miller helped carry his mortally wounded captain out of harm's way before firing a machine gun at attacking planes. Although he was never trained to use one, he downed one enemy aircraft and possibly a second. He was awarded the Navy Cross but never left the kitchen, either on the cruiser *Indianapolis* or on the escort carrier *Liscome Bay*, on which he died in November 1943 after the ship was torpedoed by a Japanese submarine.

How did the German Texans fare during war with Germany this time?

It took nearly a hundred years for the animosity of American Texans toward German immigrants and their descendants to dissipate, but they did not suffer the brutalization and suspicion that they were subjected to in 1917. Of course, it no doubt helped that the admiral commanding the U.S. Pacific fleet, Chester Nimitz (1885–1966), who was of German heritage, was from one of Fredericksburg's more prominent families.

What special qualities did the Texan Nimitz have that brought him to the fore?

After Pearl Harbor, President Roosevelt promoted Nimitz over twenty-eight flag officers senior to him. One thing that brought him to FDR's attention was Nimitz's authorship, in 1926, of a paper predicting that America's next major war would begin with a sneak attack by Japan. (Nimitz admired Japanese admiral Togo Heihachiro, and he knew that was how the Japanese had opened the Russo–Japanese War in 1904.) Nimitz had also seen the widest possible sea duty in submarines, gunboats, destroyers, cruisers, and battleships, and he understood the revolutionary possibilities of the aircraft carriers. He was personally brave, once in a port leaping overboard to save a sailor who could not swim; they were swept out to sea together and found only by chance. Perhaps most importantly, he was smart enough not to accept command of Pearl Harbor before the war, knowing that whomever was in charge there would be made the scapegoat for an attack.

Who were the WASPs?

The WASPs were the Women's Air Service Pilots. The vast number of male pilots who were scooped up into military service left a crippling shortage of personnel available for necessary noncombat flying, such as ferrying supplies, moving planes to bases where they were needed, even test-flying aircraft that had been repaired after battle damage. The Ferry Command was thus ordered to begin accepting women for such duties, but army brass was so hostile to the notion, they did whatever they could to sabotage the program. First, they set entry requirements so high that almost no women could qualify, and then when a training program was begun at the Houston airport, the female cadets suffered from wretched housing, lack of food, and often no transportation from barracks to airfield. Still, they stuck with it. Training was moved to Avenger Field near Sweetwater, west of Abilene, whose isolation, not to mention barracks crawling with scorpions and rattlesnakes, helped generate a 40 percent washout rate. By the end of the war, however, the WASPs had performed brilliantly.

Why are World War II vintage aircraft often seen over Brownsville?

Beginning with the purchase in 1957 of a P-51 Mustang, a group of vintage aircraft enthusiasts began what they called the "Confederate Air Force" in light mockery of their shoestring operation to preserve historic airplanes. Other enthusiasts, and the public, responded to their effort in a huge way, and in 2001, they changed their name to the Commemorative Air Force, which better reflected their mission. For many years, they were based in the nearby towns of Mercedes and then Harlingen, and their vintage planes were a frequent sight over the Valley during their air shows. As they have continued to

How did Fredericksburg become a center for the study of World War II?

Oddly for a Hill Country town where the deepest water is pools in the Pedernales River (which often runs dry), Fredericksburg was the hometown of Fleet Admiral Chester Nimitz, mastermind of the U.S. victory in the Pacific in World War II. His family owned the Nimitz Hotel, which is now the center of the National Museum of the Pacific War, which spreads over several blocks of indoor and outdoor exhibits. It is a world-class facility and great surprise to many tourists who are expecting a small-town, hole-in-the-wall effort.

expand and add more planes, the group has dispersed into "wings" in different parts of the state. They now fly some 130 vintage planes, with another thirty in various stages of restoration—an incomparable service to aviation history.

What formidable Texas woman took on the U.S. Army in the matter of equal treatment for women in the service?

That would be Oveta Culp Hobby. In 1929, former Texas governor William P. Hobby, who served from 1917 to 1921, was widowed; two years later, he married the much younger Oveta Culp. She was the long time parliamentarian of the Texas House of Representatives, then a journalist, and he was publisher of the *Houston Post*. They began adding radio stations to their empire, and while in Washington for Federal Communications Commission meetings, General George C. Marshall invited her to take charge of a Women's Interest Section of the army's public relations office. American women were deluging the service with letters, up to ten thousand a day, asking how they could be useful. Intelligent, determined, and well connected, Oveta Hobby parlayed the assignment into the Women's Army Auxiliary Corps ("Auxiliary" was later dropped, forming the WAC acronym). She wrote the code of conduct, raised admission requirements, designed modest, no-nonsense uniforms, and molded the unit into one that commanded respect from the rest of the military. She hectored the army into defining 239 substantial tasks that women could be rated to perform, important jobs like keeping air-raid lookout and folding parachutes, not just manning USO cantinas. When the brass decreed dishonorable discharges for WACs who got pregnant "without permission," she bridled, insisting that men suffer equal punishment, but the rule was eased instead. Oveta Culp Hobby rose to the rank of full colonel and was the only woman to receive the Distinguished Service Medal in World War II.

What Texan was the single most decorated soldier in World War II?

Audie Murphy (1925–1971) of Farmersville grew up in the grinding poverty of tenant farming, one of twelve children whose father had abandoned them. Small for his age, he enlisted as soon as he turned eighteen. Murphy fought his way through North Africa, Sicily, Italy, and southern France, was wounded three times, and was

After his storied military career during World War II, Farmersville native Audie Murphy became an actor, starring in movies such as 1951's *The Red Badge of Courage* and several Westerns.

promoted to lieutenant on the battlefield. Near Holtzwihr, France, on January 26, 1945, Murphy called in an artillery strike on his own position while holding off a German attack from his machine-gun position. When asked how close the enemy was, Murphy yelled, "Hold the phone, I'll let you talk to one of the bastards!" An acclaimed hero, Murphy was given virtually every decoration within his country's gift, but the rest of his life was haunted by what is now called post-traumatic stress disorder (PTSD).

What Texas seaman may have been the most decorated sailor of the war?

Much less famous than Audie Murphy was Commander Samuel David Dealey (1906–1944), nephew of *Dallas Morning News* founder George B. Dealey and commander of the U.S. submarine *Harder*. In conventional submarine warfare, submarines flee destroyers, which are designed to hunt and kill submarines. Dealey, however, realized that the Japanese navy was top-heavy with capital aircraft carriers and battleships but acutely short of destroyers. Eliminate their destroyers, he reasoned, and the rest of the Imperial Navy would be virtually defenseless against subs. Dealey indulged a vendetta against them, sinking five and possibly six, in addition to enemy merchant ships, until *Harder* was lost, with all hands on its sixth cruise on August 24, 1944.

What ship was known as the "Gray Ghost"?

After the sinking of the carrier USS *Lexington* (CV-2) at the Battle of the Coral Sea in World War II, a new carrier that was already under construction (CV-16) was renamed *Lexington* to honor the one that was lost. One of many *Essex*-class carriers, it is 872 feet (266 meters) long and displaces 36,380 tons (33,003,381 kilograms) under full load, and

The aircraft carrier USS *Lexington* is preserved at Corpus Christi.

137

> ## With the carrier *Lexington* preserved in Corpus Christi, are there any other World War II-era ships to see in Texas?
>
> **A** highly interesting grouping of vessels from the Second World War can be toured in Galveston, at Seawolf Park. The submarine USS *Cavalla* (SS-244) had a gallant career: commissioned early in 1944, it located, tracked, and relayed information on a Japanese task force that led to its defeat in the Battle of the Philippine Sea and torpedoed and sank the carrier IJN *Shōkaku*, which was one of the six that participated in bombing Pearl Harbor. Equally daring, it attacked two Japanese destroyers on the surface, sinking the *Shimotsuki* and escaping the second. Also in the park is the USS *Stewart* (DE-238), a 306-foot (93-meter), 1,250-ton (1,133,981-kilogram) destroyer escort. Just north of the park lies the hulk of an equally interesting ship, the SS *Selma*, an oil tanker launched in 1919, and one of a dozen experimental ships constructed during the wartime steel shortage of ferro-concrete. It was less than a year old when it tore a hole in its side on a jetty in Tampico and was scuttled in a hole dredged to receive it when repairs proved impossible.

much more for more modern duty. During an active career in the Pacific War, the Japanese reported it sunk four different times, resulting in its nickname, "The Blue Ghost." It was retired in 1991 after the longest service career of any ship in its class and permanently moored in Corpus Christi as a museum ship.

Why was Texas the site of so many prisoner-of-war camps?

Curiously, the Geneva Convention required that prisoners of war be maintained in conditions similar to the place where they were captured, not to their country of origin. U.S. troops first saw action in North Africa, which is not dissimilar from west Texas. By June 1944, Texas contained thirty-three POW camps, later consolidated to twenty-one, and held nearly eighty thousand prisoners, mostly German. Many Texans were indignant at how well German prisoners were kept and griped about the "Fritz Ritz," but most German POWs caused no trouble. They were delighted to have survived the war and be well treated until they could be repatriated. They worked amiably in local agriculture, earning credits to spend on personal supplies. Only twenty-one ever escaped, most of whom did it on a lark, with very few holding any thoughts of making it home; all were recaptured. No acts of sabotage were attributed to them.

What was unique about the Crystal City internment camp?

During the war, Texas hosted about thirty prisoner-of-war camps, but Crystal City's facility housed noncombatants, both enemy aliens and U.S. citizens descended from nationalities that America was fighting. Typically, this meant Japanese Americans, but Crystal City also interned German and Italian Americans, including U.S. citizens. Far less known was that countries throughout Latin America were allowed to deport Axis nationals and citizens of their own countries who were of foreign descent. About 80 percent of the Japanese held in Crystal City were Peruvian citizens, who Peru refused to take back even after the war. Most of them were eventually deported to their "home" country of Japan, even though they spoke Spanish and had never seen Japan. Legal tangles kept the camp open until February 1948; the site is now listed on the National Register of Historic Places.

What conflict with the military authorities almost led to a rupture in Texas-U.S. relations?

During the war, there was a nationwide speed limit of thirty miles per hour, partly to conserve gasoline but more importantly to conserve tires, for the United States had no domestic source of rubber. Pappy O'Daniel advanced to the U.S. Senate, and the new governor, Coke Stevenson, almost went to war with Interior secretary Harold Ickes over the latter's criticism of how far Texans would drive to attend high school football games. Stevenson had to threaten to mobilize the Texas Rangers to take on the feds, as not even a war would interrupt Friday night football.

POST WAR TEXAS

What happened to the battleship *Texas*?

After expending more than a thousand rounds of a 14-inch (2.5-centimeter) shell at Okinawa and with more third-generation super battleships coming into action, the *Texas* stood down. It participated in Operation Magic Carpet, ferrying troops home from the Pacific before arriving on the East Coast and being deactivated in June 1946. Unlike its vintage sisters, the *Texas* escaped the breakers and was presented to the state of Texas as a memorial on San Jacinto Day 1948. It remains the only surviving dreadnought to have fought in both world wars, and it is permanently berthed off the Houston Ship Channel at the San Jacinto battleground.

What horrific event in Texas City is considered the worst industrial accident in American history?

On the morning of April 16, 1947, the SS *Grandcamp*, a repurposed Liberty ship now with the French line, was ready to sail from Texas City with a cargo of machinery, sisal twine, small arms ammunition, and 2,200 tons (2 million kilograms) of ammonium nitrate fertilizer. Fire was discovered in the cargo hold at about 8:00 A.M., and an hour of fighting to contain it lost ground. At 9:00 the captain ordered steam pumped into the hold to smother the fire, which made it worse because ammonium nitrate contains its own oxygen, and the steam converted some of the nitrate into nitrous oxide. The entire Texas City fire department combatted the fire, as water around the red-hot ship boiled.

The SS *Wilson B. Keene* lists in the Texas City harbor after a second explosion ripped through the port.

At 9:12 the *Grandcamp* blew up in one of the most powerful non-nuclear explosions in history. People in Galveston ten miles away were knocked off their feet, and the blast was felt 250 miles away. *Grandcamp*'s five-ton anchor was hurled a half mile, and flaming debris rained down on Texas City, destroying five hundred homes and damaging many more. The official death toll was 567 but was surely higher. Fifteen hours later, the freighter *High Flyer*, carrying another 960 tons (approx. 871,00 kilograms) of ammonium nitrate, also blew up. A legal firestorm of nearly equal fury followed, as six years later, the U.S. Supreme Court held the government not liable under the Federal Tort Claims Act, and victims had to wait four years more for Congress to appropriate relief.

What bitter conflict between Texas and the federal government harkened back to Texas claims under Spanish law?

When Texas joined the Union in 1845, the United States accepted the new state to the limit of its territorial claims, which included a 3-league (10.35-mile) strip of territorial waters instead of the 3-mile limit of the English-speaking world. That was fine until oil was discovered, at which time the federal government asserted jurisdiction over the tidelands and the right to grant leases and take the income. It was an issue that affected all coastal states, but Texas's position was unique. The legal battle waged by Texas attorney general (soon to be governor) Price Daniel was fierce. It did downplay the issue of secession and readmission, but more than three hundred federal court precedents backed him up. The U.S. Supreme Court dropped a bombshell when it ruled in favor of Washington on the basis of its paramount right to provide for national defense. Texas used its congressional muscle to get bills passed overturning the decision, twice, each time vetoed by President Harry S. Truman, who Texans had come to hate anyway over such acts as desegregating the army. The tidelands issue was prominent in the 1952 presidential campaign. The Republican nominee, Dwight D. Eisenhower, announced his support for Texas and won the state, and he made good on his word by signing a tidelands bill in May 1953. However, it gave Texas tidelands oil only to three miles; winning back its original Spanish boundary took another six years.

Who was the only Texas governor to die in office?

If cotton, cattle, and oil were the pillars of the Texas economy, the family of Beauford H. Jester (1893–1949) was as Texan as one could get, producing all three on their lands near Corsicana. Jester wore several hats, including University of Texas regent, director of the state bar, and a member of the Railroad Commission before being elected and re-elected governor. After years of the stingy Coke Stevenson, Jester presided over Texas's first billion-dollar budget, which included education reforms, state park expansion, rural road construction, and other necessities that had been languishing. While traveling by train from Houston to Austin, Jester was felled by a heart attack on the night of July 11, 1949. Although married and the father of three, Jester expired in the arms of his mistress. The train was stopped, and the governor's paramour, a Miss Roget, was ejected. "They were mean," said a friend of hers many years later. "They threw her off and didn't even give her bus fare home." One of his unrealized projects was the creation of a better university for black Texans.

DESEGREGATION

How did the University of Texas try to avoid integration?

Since 1896, racial segregation in the field of education had been permitted under the doctrine of "separate but equal," predicated upon equal quality of education, which was a joke. Houston postal worker Heman Sweatt (1912–1982) decided to attend law school to better combat racial discrimination in the U.S. Postal Service. Texas provided no law school for African Americans, so Sweatt applied to the University of Texas. After the university denied his application due to race, the NAACP filed suit for him in May 1946. The state trial court granted Texas six months to provide a law school for blacks, but what materialized at the Texas State University for Negroes was so inferior that in 1950, the U.S. Supreme Court in *Sweatt v. Painter* required his admission to the University of Texas. (Sweatt's case there was argued by NAACP attorney Thurgood Marshall, who later served on the U.S. Supreme Court.) Because of the relentless stress and public recrimination, Sweatt never finished law school, but his case was a foundation on which national school integration was built.

What Texas school district was ordered to integrate, a year before the Little Rock, Arkansas, incident, and managed to defy the order?

The Tarrant County town of Mansfield, twenty miles southeast of Fort Worth, had a school district of some seven hundred white students and sixty black students, who were bused to an inferior school in Fort Worth. With *Brown v. Board of Education of Topeka* now the law of the land, the Texas NAACP sued to integrate the Mansfield public schools and quickly won a federal court order. The school board moved to comply, but citizen outrage boiled over. As schools prepared to open in the fall of 1956, a white mob surrounded Mansfield High School as others manned roadblocks to keep "outside agitators" away from the town. Governor Allan Shivers sent Texas Rangers to keep order, not enforcing integration but enforcing the previous order of things. The Texas NAACP appealed to President Eisenhower, who was sworn to uphold the laws and constitution. Eisenhower was gearing up for reelection and could not succeed without Texas. He did nothing; the state was allowed to defy the federal court order. After Ike was safely in his second term, the identical circumstance presented itself in Little Rock, Arkansas, and federal troops were sent to enforce integration there. Mansfield did not desegregate until 1965.

POLITICAL AND SOCIAL TURMOIL

Why did the Kennedy assassination seem to reflect so badly on Dallas?

Presidents Abraham Lincoln and James Garfield were shot in Washington, D.C., and

William McKinley in Buffalo, New York, but those assassinations did not discolor those

A photo taken minutes before President John F. Kennedy's assassination in Dallas shows the First Lady as well as Texas governor John Connally and his wife, Nellie.

cities to nearly the degree that Dallas was shamed by the murder of John F. Kennedy in Dealey Plaza on November 22, 1963. It is difficult to imagine now how deeply conservative Texas was. In the 1940s, Martin Dies Jr. was the first chairman of the House Un-American Activities Committee, and he became to the House what was Joe McCarthy became to the Senate, pointing at communists behind every bush while attacking his real enemies: liberals, New Dealers, and labor unions. The John Birch Society was a political force; in fact, Dallas was the home of celebrity General Edwin Walker, famous for the inverted American flag that flew outside his house, who left the service when he was forbidden to continue recruiting Birchers from within his command. (Kennedy assassin Lee Harvey Oswald attempted to kill Walker at his home in April 1963, but his shot missed him.) Even Oveta Culp Hobby, who had proven her sense of justice where women and minorities were concerned, turned stunningly conservative. To Texas reactionaries, John Kennedy, despite his strong anticommunist stances, had three strikes against him: he was from Boston, he was a Catholic, and he was a liberal—who had put Texan Lyndon Johnson on his ticket for geographical balance, to get the powerful and cantankerous Johnson out of the Senate, where he was majority leader, and to have some hope of carrying Texas. On the day of Kennedy's visit to Dallas, oilman H. L. Hunt took   143 out a full-page ad in the *Dallas Morning News* telling the president he was not welcome there. A handbill circulated the day before depicted Kennedy in full face and profile over the legend "WANTED FOR TREASON." The thundering crowd that cheered Kennedy's motorcade put the lie to any notion that he was universally hated, but so many Dalla-sites wanted Kennedy dead that they had plenty of reason for soul searching after he was shot.

How did Texans respond to one of their own as president of the United States?

Ever since Lyndon Baines Johnson attached himself to FDR and the New Deal, ce-menting his fealty by hitching a ride from Texas to Washington on Roosevelt's train dur-ing the 1936 campaign, he had walked a tightrope. On one side was his deep sense of social justice and sympathy for the poor and downtrodden, and on the other side was his knowledge of the kind of people who must vote for him if he wanted to stay in office. He became a master of campaigning conservative and governing liberal, of cutting the ground out from under open Texas liberals such as Senator Ralph Yarborough even as he sought similar ends. In his long years as Senate minority and then majority leader, he came to understand much more than Kennedy the use of power. Nationally, Johnson gained credit for social progress—Medicare, the Voting Rights Act, the Great Society—while suffering bitter criticism over his deeper involvement in the Vietnam War. In Texas, his support fell exactly the opposite way. To Johnson's lasting reputation, his conscience won out in securing passage of the Voting Rights Act, a stroke of justice that he predicted would cost the Democrats the South for decades, which it has.

What other terrible shooting, three years after the Kennedy assassination, drew national attention back to Texas?

On the morning of August 1, 1966, occasional University of Texas student Charles Whit-man—blond, handsome, clean-cut, an ROTC candidate, and marksman—woke up, mur-dered his wife, visited his mother and murdered her, then lugged a heavy trunk of arms and ammunition up the University of Texas tower, clubbing a secretary to death and

---

What U.S. president's life is celebrated in Johnson City?

Although President Lyndon B. Johnson bore the name of his family's long time Texas home, their connection to it predates his life by a long stretch. Within Johnson City, his childhood home is maintained by the U.S. National Park Service, and nearby, a much older cabin and stone house reflect the town's earlier period. Johnson's great-grandfather, George Washington Baines, was a trusted friend of Sam Houston, and Baines's son was the town founder. Several miles west in Stonewall (pop. 526) is the president's LBJ Ranch, the "Texas White House," also part of the National Historic Park.

Where was the political movement of La Raza Unida born?

Located in an area long remote from judicial oversight and in a culture in which the political disenfranchising of Hispanics was accepted even in areas where they formed an overwhelming majority, Crystal City was a natural candidate for the creation of the most strident new organizations for social justice in the turbulent 1960s. With roots in the Mexican American Youth Organization, La Raza held its organizational meeting in Crystal City on January 17, 1970, and only three months later won numerous local races there and in neighboring Cotulla and Carrizo Springs. The party reached a statewide zenith in 1972, but with the activism of the sixties fading, and La Raza's uncompromising views drawing criticism from other Hispanics as well as sympathetic Democrats, the party was no longer a force after 1978.

shooting those he encountered on the stairs. For the next two hours, he shot people from the observation deck, killing fourteen more and wounding more than thirty, before Austin police officers Houston McCoy and Ray Martinez gained the observation deck and dispatched him. An autopsy discovered a walnut-sized brain tumor, which, when added to Whitman's confused notes about his inexplicable violent urges and attempts at getting psychological help, make it apparent that he was becoming deranged.

Why did the 1960s, as a social protest movement, largely pass Texas by?

Texas in the 1960s offered no climate in which to indulge in social protest. Those who felt the urge were better off leaving the state, as did singer Janis Joplin (1943–1970) of Port Arthur. Unable to brook the restraints of small-town southeast Texas, she moved to Austin, where she began singing at a popular roadhouse called Threadgill's. Mocked and named ugliest man on campus by resident University of Texas frats, she relocated to San Francisco.

Did Texas have no "flower children"?

In Texas, the most visible manifestation of the love movement was the presence of the Children of God, which was a California group that settled in a commune near Stephenville. The cult required its young members to cut off contact with their families and turn over all their possessions to the group. In 1970, they spread their gospel on the University of Texas campus while wearing sackcloth and ashes, but they lost their home base when it was discovered that their recruitment was aided by what they called "flirty-fishing," or the promise of sex in exchange for membership.

What was the Armadillo World Headquarters?

As the Austin music scene took root, it needed some large venue as a home base, especially after a previous location, the Vulcan Gas Company, shut down in 1970. Attention 145 focused on an abandoned National Guard armory, located on a principal intersection just across Town Lake (now Lady Bird Lake) from downtown. The venture to turn the ugly, echoing building into a concert venue was a cooperative effort among the father of the founder of local band Shiva's Headband and others who cleared legal and real estate hurdles. Local artist Jim Franklin illustrated the choice of the armadillo for the building's totem and indeed was instrumental in making his whimsical renditions of that tough but harmless little animal the principal emblem of the city. The venue opened in August 1970 and rocketed in popularity among countercultural music fans who did not mind sitting on carpet swatches. Dope smoking there became legendary, but it was never raided because, in one account, officers did not relish the prospect of hauling in city officials and fellow cops.

Port Arthur native Janis Joplin was an iconic figure of 1960s music and counterculture scene.

The 'Dillo's pride of place was attested in a 1974 *Time* magazine piece that compared it to the Fillmore's importance to rock. The hippie clientele, however, had little money to spend, and the 'Dillo was almost always in financial straits. The final concert was on the last night of 1980, and the land was sold to build a high-rise of city offices.

What was the revolution that brought down the government in Crystal City?

Although the Hispanic community found its political voice in Crystal City in 1970, a continuing battle with ousted Anglo politicians and the informality and lax oversight of city affairs led to the continuation of a vivid political scene. By 2016 the stench had become overpowering. An undercover federal investigation discovered that rampant corruption had crossed ethnic boundaries, and in February 2016 the mayor, mayor pro tempore, the city attorney, and one present and one past city council member were all arrested on a slate of charges from abetting illegal gambling to taking bribes from contractors. Only one person on the city council escaped the dragnet.

MODERN TEXAS

What was the financial scandal that caused Texas voters to clean house in 1974?

The Sharpstown Scandal was unprecedented, even by Ma and Pa Ferguson standards. A Houston banker with the singularly appropriate name of Frank Sharp got into financial straits and put out word that legislators who supported his bill to aid his bank would be allowed to borrow from a fund he set up to buy stock in Sharp's insurance company, whose value Sharp would take care to inflate before they unloaded it. Among his takers were the speaker of the state House, Gus Mutscher, and Representative Tommy Shannon of Fort Worth. Governor Preston Smith was an unindicted, unnamed coconspirator, but the prosecutor made sure his name was leaked. About half of the Texas House either discreetly retired or were thrown out in the next election. Smith actually vetoed the Sharp bill but was humiliated in his bid for a third term, and even Lieutenant Governor Ben Barnes, untouched by the scandal, was unseated by William P. Hobby Jr., son of Texas's World War I governor.

What African American representative from Texas fascinated the country with her brilliance during the Watergate hearings?

The 1960s as a social phenomenon bypassed Texas, but liberals there did enjoy a brief resurgence, aided by the Texas Supreme Court that struck down the state's poll tax, which encouraged minority turnout. In Texas, Barbara Jordan (1936–1996) had been relegated to attending Texas Southern University, which until recently had been Texas State University for Negroes. She held her own as a national debate champion against the Ivy League and attended Boston University Law School. Politically, she accepted the patronage of Lyndon Johnson, and in the state House and Senate, her skill, preparedness, eloquence, and patience raised her high, as she was unanimously elected president pro tempore of the Texas Senate before being elevated to the U.S. House. There, her introductory comments at the House Watergate Hearings that "my faith in the Constitution is whole, it is complete" silenced the nation and helped convince the accused, President Richard Nixon, to resign. Later, President Bill Clinton desired to name her to the U.S. Supreme Court, but her health was prematurely failing; she was only fifty-nine when she died in Austin.

Who was Texas's second woman governor?

Texas state treasurer Ann Richards shone in the national spotlight as the keynote speaker at the 1988 Democratic National Convention. Her piercing accent, white bouffant hair, and rapier wit gave the country a look at a Texas original. Her campaign for governor in 1990 was aided by disastrous gaffes on the part of her op-

Ann Richards was only the second woman to become Texas's governor, some sixty years after Ma Ferguson.

ponent, Midland oilman Clayton Williams, but she still only barely won. She increased female and minority representation on state commissions, but with Texas becoming palpably more conservative, she governed to the right, expanding the prison system and police powers, criminalizing gay sex, and tightening the state budget. Still, caught among a massive influx of mostly conservative tech workers from outside the state, organized hysteria against President Clinton within the state, and her own lackluster campaign, she was soundly defeated for reelection by George W. Bush, managing partner of the Texas Rangers baseball team with no political background other than being the son of former President George H. W. Bush.

What caused the terrible tragedy in Waco in 1993?

Texas soil has long been fertile ground for religious separatism, providing vast, empty spaces for lunatics with messiah complexes to go off and follow their own doctrines and recruit followers without having to answer to outsiders. In the late twentieth century, the addition of antigovernment militia paranoia made an explosive chemistry. In 1982 a troubled ex-Baptist and peripheral Seventh-day Adventist named Vernon Howell (1959–1993) joined a splinter group called the Branch Davidians, who lived in a compound called Mount Carmel, 13 miles (21 kilometers) east of Waco. In 1990, believing himself a prophet and sort-of reincarnation of Hebrew king David and Persian king Cyrus, Howell changed his name to David Koresh and accelerated his takeover of the Mount Carmel cult. His dominance included the right to take as his own wives of other men in the cult as well as girls he chose. An investigation by Texas Child Protective Services uncovered no proof of sex with underage girls. Koresh vehemently preached an approaching apocalypse, and the presence of illegal firearms and explosives led to the involvement of the FBI and Bureau of Alcohol, Tobacco, and Firearms (ATF). The ATF raided the compound on February 28, 1993, resulting in the deaths of six Branch Davidians who resisted and four ATF agents. A siege then began that lasted fifty-one days. Acting to end what they considered a hostage crisis, the ATF and FBI used a battering ram to insert tear gas into the main building and force those inside into the open. In-

---

What is Midland's presidential connection?

Midland began as a rail stop marking the halfway point on the Texas and Pacific line's route from Fort Worth to El Paso. (The town was first named Midway, but the U.S. Post Office declined to approve it because there was already a Midway, Texas.) It was founded in 1881, and with no other supply and marketing center nearby, it quickly became established and grew exponentially with the discovery of Permian Basin oil. In the 1950s, future president George H. W. Bush lived in Midland during his formative years in the oil industry; he and his wife, Barbara, and their family, including their future presidential son, lived in a modest, two-bedroom home from 1951 to 1955, which is now preserved as the George W. Bush Childhood Home.

An aerial photo shows the Branch Davidian compound during the 1993 siege.

stead, cult leaders incinerated the complex, resulting in the deaths of fifty-nine adults and twenty-two children. Twenty of the dead perished of gunshot wounds, indicating a confusion of murder and suicide within the flames.

Was there anything to the "Republic of Texas" claim that U.S. annexation had never been constitutional?

No. Arguments that Texas's joining the Union was unconstitutional are not new. The Constitution is a general guideline for the formation of a government; it does not specify details of how that government will function. Its only provision for the acquisition of new territory, in Article IV, Section 3, is that new states cannot be admitted to the derogation of the rights of existing states. U.S. representative (and former president) John Quincy Adams's arguments against Texas annexation in 1837 had no merit, nor did those of the so-called "Republic of Texas," a clot of antigovernment protesters who moved into the Fort Davis area in 1993. Their contention was that Texas had had the status of an occupied nation since the end of the Civil War and that they were the true provisional government of the Republic of Texas. They began terrorizing their neighbors with a flood of bogus tax liens and other "legal" filings. The leader of one of their three factions, Richard McLaren, progressed to kidnapping in 1997, at which point their compound near Fort Davis was surrounded by Texas Rangers and local police. One "Texian" was killed trying to escape, and McLaren and five others received hefty prison terms. The incident revealed the thin line between truculent, antigovernment militia posturing and domestic terrorism.

Why did the government raid the Mormon compound near San Angelo?

As with Waco in 1993, authorities don't much care what religion people follow, but some cult practices such as sex with children will trigger intervention. In 2003 a group that had broken away from the Fundamentalist Church of Jesus Christ of Latter-day Saints (FDLS) acquired a 1,700-acre (7-square-kilometer) property near El Dorado in Schleicher County, about 45 miles (72 kilometers) southwest of San Angelo. It was one of the emptiest corners left in Texas, and it promised refuge for practices that were being scrutinized even on the remote Utah-Arizona border. It was purchased as an executive hunting resort, but extensive construction revealed a cult compound housing about seven hundred church members, including a 29,000-square-foot (2,694-square-meter) house for leader Warren Jeffs and a huge temple that he dedicated on New Year's Day 2005. Three years later, an alliance of state and local authorities, including Texas Child Protective Services (CPS), raided the compound on the strength of an anonymous (and spurious) tip and removed children from families in a saga of court battles that lasted over two years. Extensive DNA testing revealed in April 2008 that of fifty-three girls in the compound who were between fourteen and seventeen years old, thirty-one had borne children or were pregnant. Seven adult men of the "church" were convicted of various permutations of child sex and sentenced to prison. Jeffs, who had had sex with girls as young as twelve, was given life plus twenty years. Thus, while Texas CPS may have overreacted to the initial report made by a woman known to make false accusations, it could not have been more correct in following its instincts that something terrible was ongoing in El Dorado. Under a statute that allowed land acquired for certain felonious purposes to be seized, in 2012 the State of Texas took the 1,700 acres and extensive buildings that were valued at almost $20 million. When no one from the FDLS appealed the seizure, it passed to state ownership in 2014.

How many antigovernment militias operate within Texas?

In 2017, the Southern Poverty Law Center enumerated thirty-seven "extreme antigovernment" groups active in Texas of a national total of 689. (This was down from a total of 1,360 in 2012.) However, this thirty-seven includes hot-air propaganda operations such as *InfoWars* and does not include any number of loosely organized informal gun toters who harbor antigovernment sentiments.

How did a conservative bastion like Texas come to find itself on the forefront of establishing GLBT rights in the United States?

Given many Texans' outright hatred of the gay and lesbian communities, it really makes sense that the test case that declared the anti sodomy statutes of the remaining fourteen states that had them unconstitutional would have originated there. In suburban Houston in September 1998, a jealous boyfriend falsely reported a domestic disturbance at an apartment where his paramour was staying with a friend. When cops arrived, they entered the apartment, which was unlocked, discovered the couple having sex in their bedroom, and arrested and jailed them for violating Texas's sodomy law. Based on such outrageous facts, the federal courts could hardly rule otherwise than to declare the Texas law unconstitutional. In fact, from the trial court upward, judges and prosecutors cooperated with defense counsel in laying the framework for appeals. When *Lawrence v. Texas* reached the U.S. Supreme Court in 2003, the vote was 6–3, with Justice Anthony Kennedy's opinion finding that even gay people have a right to privacy in their own bedrooms. Justice Sandra Day O'Connor concurred but on the grounds of equal protection of the laws because Texas had continually legalized heterosexual sodomy. Justice Antonin Scalia dissented passionately, claiming that the Court had backed itself into eventually allowing gay marriage, which it did in *Obergefell v. Hodges* in 2015.

Has Texas followed the law on gay sex and marriage?

No. In fact, Texas re-upped its sodomy statute in the wake of *Lawrence v. Texas*, although it cannot be enforced, and Governor Rick Perry theatrically signed an amendment to the Texas Constitution banning recognition of gay marriages even when valid in other states. The Texas Supreme Court ruled in a 2017 decision that the "full constellation" of marriage benefits thrown open to legally married same-sex couples by *Obergefell* would not include survivor benefits of widowed state employees.

Who is the longest-serving governor in Texas history?

Rick Perry, a native of the tiny ranching community of Haskell, near Palo Pinto, had been a six-year state representative and eight-year agriculture commissioner when he was elected lieutenant governor in 1998. Only two years into that term, Texas governor George W. Bush resigned to assume the presidency, elevating Perry to the Governor's Mansion. After winning three terms on his own, Perry stepped down after fourteen years—a Texas record.

TEXAS REGIONS

How do Texans tend to organize their state by region?

Texans regard their huge state to have seven distinct regions:

1. The Gulf Coast (or Coastal Plains)
2. The Piney Woods
3. The Brush Country (sometimes called South Texas Plains)
4. The Trans-Pecos (or Big Bend Country)
5. The Hill Country (or Edwards Plateau)
6. The Panhandle-Plains
7. Blackland Prairies

THE GULF COAST

What major cities lie in the Gulf Plains?

Texas's largest city, Houston, with its metropolitan population of nearly seven million, lies on the border between the Gulf Plains and the Piney Woods, exerting great impact on both. On a lesser scale, the same is true of Beaumont, and the urban areas of Galveston, Corpus Christi, and Brownsville all impact the Gulf Plains.

What endangered species are present in the Gulf Plains?

The whooping crane, the tallest bird in North America, was once reduced to only twenty-one wild birds but is making a comeback (detailed below). The Attwater's prairie chicken has not yet been so lucky. This native grouse was once one of the most common game birds in Texas, but overhunting and loss of habitat reduced its numbers from an esti-

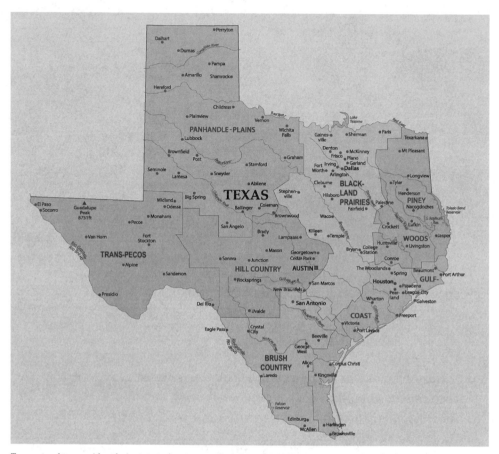

Texans tend to consider their state to have seven distinct regions: Trans-Pecos, Panhandle-Plains, Hill Country, Blackland Prairies, Piney Woods, Brush Country, and Gulf Coast.

mated one million in 1900 to 8,700 in 1937 to fewer than 50 in 2003. Captive breeding programs were started at seven different Texas zoos and research facilities, which was lucky because Hurricanes Rita (2005), Ike (2008), and Harvey (2017) reduced the wild population to about a dozen. They, and the Kemp's ridley sea turtle that breeds on Padre Island, are the endangered species that have the highest public visibility.

What are the principal threats to the Gulf Plains ecology today?

With so many parks and refuges located along the coast, one would think that the habitat is well protected. Its threats are larger than that, however, centering on beach erosion and the increasing salinity of the brackish marshes that shrimp and shellfish need to breed. These are issues that only get worse with the increase in sea level, which makes it all the more remarkable how many Texans have been persuaded that climate change is not occurring. The other continuing threat is pollution from offshore oil wells. Oil, drilling failure on the scale of the Ixtoc 1 blowout in 1979 that fouled 160 miles of U.S.

Gulf beaches, or the Deepwater Horizon blowout in 2010, cannot be predicted and are not adequately prepared for.

What parks and reserves protect the Gulf Plains today?

The Gulf Plains are home to one large installation of the national park system, the Padre Island National Seashore, which protects the bulk of the longest single barrier island in the world. The coastal marshes in which huge numbers of ducks and geese winter are protected in a whole string of National Wildlife Refuges (NWR).

Anchoring the coastal refuges in the southeast corner of the state is an inter governmental complex that exemplifies the magnified benefits of cooperation. Adjoining the McFadden NWR (58,861 acres [238 square kilometers]) are Sea Rim State Park (4,141 acres [17 square kilometers]), with 5 miles (8 kilometers) of beach that connect it with the Texas Point NWR (8,952 acres [36 square kilometers]), the J. D. Murphree State Wildlife Management Area (three tracts totaling 24,498 acres [99 square kilometers]), and abutting McFadden on the west is the Anahuac NWR (about 34,000 acres [138 square kilometers])—more than 200 square miles (518 square kilometers) of protected or managed habitat. Wintering snow geese in McFadden sometimes top 70,000 in number.

Further southwest, across Trinity Bay, Galveston has the benefit of Galveston Island State Park (2,019 acres [8 square kilometers]) that tries to balance recreational demand with ecological needs. Galveston Island is quite new in geologic time, only perhaps 5,000 years old, and is fragile, given to closing for long periods of time to repair repetitive hurricane damage. Further down, the Brazosport group of cities separate the Brazoria and San Bernard NWRs. Brazoria's contiguous 44,414 acres (180 square kilometers) extend well inland from West Bay, providing a variety of habitat for its remarkable species list since 1966: more than 400 different birds, 95 amphibians and reptiles, and about 130 butterflies and dragonflies. Brazoria is important for the extent of its brackish marshes, bordering fresh water and salt, where great blue herons, roseate spoonbills, and other wading birds that resonate with visitors live. West of the Brazosport urban area, the 54,000-acre (219-square-kilometer) San Bernard NWR is important for still more reasons, not least for Dance Bayou, one of the largest remaining blocks of old growth coastal hardwood in Texas.

What iconic bird species in danger of extinction was saved by the Aransas National Wildlife Refuge?

The tallest bird in North America, the whooping crane, stands up to 5 feet (152

Once nearly extinct, the whooping crane can now be found in Texas's Gulf Plains and marshes.

centimeters) tall, with a 7.5-foot (229-centimeter) wingspan. It is one of only two crane species on the continent. By 1941, rampant overhunting and loss of habitat reduced the population to just twenty-one wild birds, plus two in captivity. President Franklin D. Roosevelt created the Aransas Refuge on the southwest side of San Antonio Bay, north of Corpus Christi, by executive order on the last day of 1937 to protect more than 50,000 acres (202 square kilometers) of cranes' wintering ground. (They breed in Canada's Wood Buffalo National Park, where they are also fully protected.) Clawing its way back from the edge of extinction, 266 whooping cranes wintered at Aransas in 2007, with a world population now of about 400, and a separate breeding group has been established that winters in Florida.

What recent refuge increases the effectiveness of the Aransas NWR?

In 1994, the Interior Department reached an agreement with the Texas Parks and Wildlife Department to combine their holdings, thus adding more than 56,000 acres (227 square kilometers) to Aransas that stretch along 38 miles (61 kilometers) of Matagorda Island, just across the lagoon from the mainland refuge. Aransas is now about double its original size at 114,657 acres (464 square kilometers). That acreage is divided almost equally between upland habitats and coastal beach and marsh, and the lack of public access to Matagorda Island creates one of the most effective sanctuaries anywhere on the southern coast. Although Matagorda is maintained in its original state, there are further recreational opportunities nearby at the 3,954-acre (16-square-kilometer) Mustang Island State Park at Port Aransas, which has public amenities. The same can be said of Goose Island State Park at Rockport, which is home to the famous "Big Tree," once considered the grand champion coastal live oak with a trunk circumference of 35 feet (11 meters) and a 90-foot (27-foot) crown spread. It has since been dethroned, but it is still a mighty tree to behold.

Where is the largest remaining section of Gulf Prairie?

The most authentic look that one can have at what pioneers would have seen as the original grasslands inland from the Gulf marshes remains at the Attwater's Prairie Chicken NWR, 60 miles (97 kilometers) west of Houston. The World Wildlife Fund purchased the first 3,000 acres (12 square kilometers) in the mid-1960s to have some chance at saving that critically endangered bird, then donated that land to add to the federal wildlife refuge that was established in 1972, for a total of 10,528 acres (43 square kilometers).

Where is the largest hummingbird garden in Texas?

There are eighteen species of hummingbird found in the United States, of which half occur in Texas. Thousands of individual birds migrate through Aransas Pass, which has set aside Newbury Park in the middle of town as a place for them to rest and feed before flying on. The park is dominated by numerous wind-sculpted coastal live oaks, and it also attracts numerous butterflies.

Can one find a remnant of Gulf Prairie closer to Houston than that?

Yes. Again using 1970 bond money, Texas Parks and Wildlife made a brilliant purchase of 5,000 acres (20 square kilometers) of river frontage for Brazos Bend State Park. Purchasing began in 1976, facilities were developed, and the park opened in 1984. It is only 35 miles (56 kilometers) from Houston and barely 10 miles (16 kilometers) from its western edge. Here, there are also dense stands of coastal prairie in addition to bottom forest. It is all the more interesting because it is on land that was part of the original colonial grant on which Stephen F. Austin settled his pioneers, and one gets a sense of what they encountered when they first arrived.

What is the Welder Wildlife Refuge?

Not far from Aransas is the headquarters of the Rob & Bessie Wildlife Foundation, which carries on research programs and hosts recreational activities on its 7,800-acre (32-square-kilometer) refuge, a bequest from the founders.

What kind of nature opportunities are there near Corpus Christi?

Padre Island National Seashore is closest, but just for freshwater recreation, Texas Parks and Wildlife has a long-term lease on Lake Corpus Christi State Park.

What is going on with the Laguna Atascosa Refuge?

The Laguna Atascosa NWR, whose 97,000 acres (393 square kilometers) is a keystone of the coastal chain, is now being assimilated into the Lower Rio Grande NWR, which is described in the section on the Brush Country. Established in 1946 mainly as wintering grounds for migratory birds, just like other coastal refuges, its mission was expanded to suit its geographical importance. It is a key refuge, where the Coastal Plains merge into the thorn scrub of the Brush Country. It has a longer bird list than any other refuge in the federal system, and that is saying a lot, and it is home to the largest population of ocelots in the United States as well as typical south Texas species such as javelinas. In 2000, the refuge began a laborious program to restore degraded coastline and bring back former patterns of water flow, which won the refuge the 2007 National Wetlands Conservation Award.

THE PINEY WOODS

What are the characteristics of the Piney Woods?

The so-called Piney Woods of east Texas are the westernmost extension of the softwood forest that blankets the south all the way to the Appalachians. The dominant communities are of loblolly and longleaf pine, with mixed hardwoods especially along the stream corridors. Both types have dense understories of woody shrubs and wildflowers.

157

The American paddlefish (*Polyodon spathula*) is a rare and unusual fish that looks like it has a spatula for a nose. Attempts are being made to reintroduce it to Caddo Lake.

What endangered species are present in the Piney Woods?

The last known sighting of the famous ivory-billed woodpecker was in the tangled Big Thicket that is the southern end of the Piney Woods. Having already been listed as extinct and lamented by a local newspaper editor, an annoyed local woodsman went out, shot one, and thumped the body on the editor's desk. That was the last one seen, but a few may still exist. An effort to reintroduce the increasingly rare American paddlefish into the Caddo Lake area began in 2013 with the release of tagged individuals to research their life cycle. The exceptionally weird and ancient fish can top 5 feet (152 centimeters) in length and weigh more than 100 pounds (45 kilograms).

What current hazards present threats to the Piney Woods?

There is little to be done about poor forestry or agricultural practices on private land. East Texans are among the most conservative in the state, a heritage that dates back more than two hundred years, when much of the Piney Woods was considered international No-Man's Land and was settled by extra legal squatters. Of more acute concern to existing parks is an infusion of aggressive invasive aquatic plants such as hydrilla, water hyacinth, and especially giant salvinia that choke out native vegetation.

How was Caddo Lake formed?

Caddo Indians maintained that there was no Caddo Lake on Big Cypress Bayou before December 16, 1811, when the entire middle of the United States shook with the New Madrid earthquake, which was so powerful that it caused the Mississippi River to run backward. Scientists, however, tend to think that the lake's shallow basin was flooded by water backed up from the "Great Raft," a logjam 100 miles (161 kilometers) long in Louisiana. The Caddo Indian story cannot be entirely dismissed, for Tennessee's Reelfoot Lake was indeed created by the New Madrid quake.

Is Caddo Lake still in its natural state?

Yes and no. It is the largest naturally occurring lake in Texas but has not been kindly treated. As recently as 1942, the U.S. Army established the Longhorn Army Ammunition Plant on its banks, and the pollution associated with manufacturing explosives was dumped freely into the lake. After the plant closed, the site passed to the U.S. Fish and Wildlife Service, which in 2000 opened the Caddo Lake NWR. Right away, there was recognition of the lake's importance for wildfowl, as it was named one of only thirteen (at the time) "wetlands of international significance" under the Ramsar Convention. A downstream dam stabilized water levels to a large degree, and the 8,493 acres (34 square kilometers) of the refuge offer high-quality bird-watching as well as premier fishing, as the lake holds eighteen species of game fish in addition to nearly seventy nongame fish. Caddo Lake State Park is also in the vicinity, one of the first state parks, dating from 1933, and like most Texas parks of that era, its facilities were constructed by companies of the Civilian Conservation Corps. The state park covers only 468 acres (2 square kilometers), but it is a good spot to camp while exploring the environs. Caddo Lake lends itself especially well to canoeing—it is shallow, calm, and allows close inspection of the park's gigantic cypress trees.

Is anything else going on for the protection of the Caddo Lake Area?

Government purchases have traditionally been keyed in to what land was available or had been discarded from another agency rather than concentrating on what key features needed to be saved. Once again, the Nature Conservancy has stepped in with two key sanctuaries: one is the Caddo Black Bayou Preserve of 656 acres (2.6 square kilometers) just across the state line in Louisiana. It is remarkable for its preservation of an almost incalculably rare relict sandhill forest that contains no fewer than fourteen rare or endangered plants. Because of its extreme ecological value, as well as being surrounded by private property, it is not open to the public. Second, realizing that this jewel of an ecosystem was still being short-shrifted in protection, the Conservancy partnered with Texas Parks and Wildlife to purchase 7,000 acres (28 square kilometers), which they added to two previous preserves to create the TPWD's Caddo Lake Wildlife Management Area.

What is the Big Thicket?

Originally covering more than 2 million acres (8,094 square kilometers), the Big Thicket is a tangled, and in some places impenetrable, forest in Texas's southeast corner. Renowned as a biological "crossroads," the Thicket contains plants from many regions of North America as well as relict species such as ivory-billed woodpeckers and carnivorous sundews and pitcher plants left over from the last Ice Age. Attempts began as early

159

Big Thicket National Biological Preserve in southeastern Texas is a tangled wilderness with a treasure trove of interesting species such as carnivorous pitcher plants and the endangered ivory-billed woodpecker.

as 1927 to preserve the area as a national park, but the timber companies that owned most of the land, keen to harvest the gigantic virgin pine and cypress trees, opposed the park furiously. A Big Thicket National Biological Preserve (the first of its kind) was finally declared in 1968 and gazetted in 1974. It covered only 68,000 acres (275 square kilometers) but has since increased to 112,500 acres (455 square kilometers).

Timber companies replant as much as they cut; why was it necessary to take the land for a national preserve?

As a biological "crossroads," the Big Thicket harbors a tremendous variety of species, both plant and wildlife. "Tree farms" are managed for maximum lumber production and ease of harvest. By planting straight rows of loblolly pines and keeping the brush clear for mechanical harvesters to eventually lop them off, there is no variety of habitat or food source for the wildlife, resulting in an all but sterile landscape.

What is special about the Sandyland Sanctuary?

Back in the pioneer days, more than 90 million acres (364,217 square kilometers) of longleaf pine forest covered the South from Virginia to Texas. Ninety-seven percent of that is gone, and it is still shrinking. During creation of the Big Thicket Preserve, the park was opposed tooth and nail by resident logging giants Time and Temple-Eastex. In

1977, however, they stepped up and donated 2,138 acres (8.6 square kilometers) to the Texas Nature Conservancy, which was more than doubled in 1994 with a donation from Temple-Inland and a further parcel from Gulf States Utilities. Located in the heart of the major park units, the 5,654-acre (23-square-kilometer) Roy E. Larsen Sandyland Sanctuary preserves an incomparable relic of longleaf pine forest, plus beech and magnolia forest, swamp, and 6 miles (9.6 kilometers) of Village Creek. The Thicket's rampant diversity is on full display, with 340 species of wildflowers and more than 500 different butterflies and moths.

Are there any national forests in the Piney Woods?

There are four units of the National Forest System in Texas: the Angelina, Davy Crockett, Sam Houston, and Sabine National Forests.

Why is there so much private land within the national forests in Texas?

The same thing is true of national forest land within Texas as is true of national parks: Texas joined the Union in 1845 as an independent nation and retained its public domain. The federal government does not own vast tracts of land to set aside for conservation as it does elsewhere in the West. In other national forests, there might be only 2 or 3 percent of it in private hands; in Texas, the federally managed acreage might be only 40 percent of the total within the unit boundaries.

Where can Houston kids go to have a fun lesson in the local ecology?

At 2,800 acres (11 square kilometers) in northeast Harris County (basically suburban Houston), Sheldon Lake State Park is large enough to be considered a nature park, but the greatest emphasis is placed on nature education both through programs and at the 82-foot (25-meter) observation tower. The park is a good example of repurposing, as the main lake was dammed by the federal government in 1942 to provide water resources for war production. Texas Parks and Wildlife acquired the land as a management area in 1952 and transformed it into a state park and environmental learning center in 1984, and environmental restoration commenced in 2003.

Where is a good place to take in the history of the Piney Woods?

Montgomery County is one of Texas's oldest and most historic. The county seat of Conroe is a convenient combination of recreation at Lake Conroe; artistic revitalization in the downtown area, such as restoration of the Crighton Theatre; and historical preservation, in the Heritage Museum of Montgomery County, which documents, among other history, the life of the designer of one of Texas's Lone Star flags, Charles B. Stewart.

What other state parks are available in the Piney Woods?

There are many other state parks that are geared primarily for outdoor recreation, including:

Atlanta, Daingerfield, Huntsville, Lake Bob Sandlin, Lake Livingston, Martin Creek, Martin Dies Jr., Tyler, and Village Creek.

THE BRUSH COUNTRY

What are the characteristics of the Brush Country?

Located in a wedge of south Texas inland from the Gulf Coast and south of the Hill Country, the Brush Country is typified by heavy thornscrub of mixed grassland with plentiful mesquite, brasil, and blackbrush, but it also includes communities of cedar breaks and gallery forests. The dominant communities of the Hill Country and Gulf Prairie can give way gradually and intermix with Brush Country foliage, creating a jumble of different species.

What endangered species are present in the Brush Country?

Because the Brush Country represents to some degree a "spillover" of both plant and animal species from across the Rio Grande, many are found in the United States only in this ecosystem, which almost by definition makes them listable for protection in this country. These include two Central American cats, the ocelot and the jaguarundi; birds such as the green jay, chachalaca, and northern aplomado falcon; cacti such as the star and the black lace; and many others.

What are the principal threats to the Brush Country ecology today?

It would seem obvious that the ecology of the lower Rio Grande depends upon an adequate flow of water in the river. Over many years, however, too much irrigation drawn from the stream, made worse by drought and by Mexico's failure to release water from upstream tributaries as stipulated by treaty, resulted in periods in which no water at all from this once powerful river ever even reached the Gulf. In 2016, a new ecological threat appeared in the form of the anti-immigration border wall that was promised by the incoming

More common south of the border, the jaguarundi is a wild cat also found in the Brush Country. They can weigh up to 20 pounds (9 kilograms) and be about 2.5 feet (77 centimeters) long.

federal administration. Impermeable to wildlife, it would limit the utility of the Rio Grande Valley NWR (discussed below) to fulfilling its intended purpose.

Why should an anti-immigration wall affect wildlife?

One feature of the landscape on the U.S. side of the border is the *ramaderos* community—deep arroyos that cut inland from the river, sometimes for miles. Wildlife has always used these deep gullies to move from the river inland and back. Clearly, building an impermeable wall along the river will limit their movements and even cut off their access to water.

What parks and reserves protect the Brush Country today?

Perhaps the most gentle introduction to the Brush Country is at Choke Canyon State Park, about halfway between San Antonio and Corpus Christi, a property leased from the Nueces River Authority on the shore of a reservoir that supplies water to Corpus Christi. There are 1,485 acres (6 square kilometers) in two units. This is the westernmost limit of the alligator range and, in a way, east meets west when gators share a shore-line with javelinas. Of some note: the shoreline of Texas's prehistoric sea lay about where the Choke Canyon Dam is now.

What is easily accessible from Laredo?

They don't have far to go, for the closest Brush Country park experience to Laredo is at the Lake Casa Blanca International State Park on the east side of town, formerly run as a city-county park. Its 525 acres (2 square kilometers) are primarily managed for recreation, but hiking trails are maintained year-round for easy bird-watching, and encounters with local wildlife such as javelinas and jackrabbits are possible.

What is the special importance of the Rio Grande Valley NWR?

Early in the twentieth century, almost all the land in the lower Rio Grande Valley was converted to truck farms and fruit orchards, decimating the original Rio Grande jungle habitat. For many years, about the only remnants of that ecosystem were at Santa Ana NWR, Bentsen-Rio Grande State Park, and a small Audubon sanctuary at the mouth of the Rio Grande. Taken all together, it was well less than 3,000 acres (12 square kilometers)—a pitiful remnant of a once fascinating landscape. With more than twelve hundred plant species growing at this convergence of four different botanical zones, the tragedy could not be ignored. Recognizing the need to plug this hole in the system of U.S.-protected areas, plans were broached in 1979 to begin cobbling together units that, taken together, could re-create some of what was lost and link them with wildlife corridors. The plan was given greater impetus when a devastating freeze in the Valley devastated citrus orchards, and wildlife officials sensed an opportunity to buy up that land affordably and hired the ruined growers to convert their acreages back to native vegetation. The result has been that one of the most endangered ecosystems in the United States is now one of the best protected.

At only 1,900 acres (7.7 square kilometers), Santa Ana was still the largest protected remnant of the original Rio Grande Jungle, the only place in the United States where one could see Central American species such as coati mundi, ocelot, jaguarundi, and exotic birds such as chachalaca and Mexican green jay. It is now incorporated into the vastly larger complex of the Rio Grande NWR.

What other steps have been taken in preserving the Valley ecology?

The Nature Conservancy has extended protection over two sanctuaries in the Valley. The first is the Lennox Foundation Southmost Preserve on 1,014 acres (41 square kilometers) along an old oxbow lake, or *resaca*, near Brownsville. It is home to numerous rare and endangered species, including the southern yellow bat, Texas tortoise, black-spotted newt, Texas racer, the Mexican white-lipped frog, and the sheep frog. Most importantly, the tract preserves one of only two intact stands of Mexican sabal palm in the United States. (The Texas Audubon Society has saved the other at its 557-acre [2.3-square-kilometer] Sabal Palm Sanctuary on the Rio Grande delta. This is quite a humble fate for a plant community that once dominated more than 40,000 acres [162 square kilometers] of the Valley.) The second protected sanctuary is the Chihuahua Woods Preserve, a 349-acre (1.4 square-kilometer) relic of the original Tamaulipan thornscrub. Concerned local citizens began raising money to purchase the tract in 1988, and when they raised half, the Conservancy stepped in and supplied the rest. This tract is noted especially for its rare cacti and the recent sighting of a rare predatory bird, the hook-billed kite, nesting.

What is the World Birding Center?

This is a joint project of the U.S. Fish and Wildlife Service and Texas Parks and Wildlife to provide an organized bird-watching experience along a trail of nine different parks and refuges from the coast upstream as far as Roma, about 100 miles (161 kilometers) in. The facilities include boardwalks and viewing stands to give birders a chance to log some of the more than five hundred species recorded here. Three of the nine units are state parks of long standing: Bentsen-Rio Grande of 587 acres (2.4 square kilometers), originally preserved by the powerful Bentsen family because of their fondness for the native ebony trees; Estero Llano Grande, a 230-acre (0.93-square kilometer) wetland in Weslaco; and Resaca de la Palma, 1,200 acres (4.9 square kilometers) northwest of Brownsville, away from the river, that was once at least partly a historic park preserving a battle site from the opening of the Mexican–American War, where hiking trails through the semitropical brush give a fair idea of its original appearance. Altogether, the nine units provide more than 10,000 acres (40 square kilometers) of wildlife viewing experience.

The headquarters building for the World Birding Center in Bentsen-Rio Grande State Park, where the mission is to preserve birds and other wildlife and educate the public about them.

THE TRANS-PECOS

What are the natural features of the Trans-Pecos?

The largest feature of the Trans-Pecos is an extension from Mexico of the ecological region known as the Chihuahuan Desert, which is one of four desert types that scientists recognize in the American Southwest. Although dry, of course, the Chihuahuan is in its natural state a "lush" desert, with a profusion of such species as prickly pear and cholla cactus, yucca, ocotillo, and sotol. In its western portion, isolated mountain ranges rise to over 8,000 feet (2,438 meters), and with the increase in elevation, the desert gives way to meadows and oak forests and, in the highest places, ponderosa pine and quaking aspen, which reveal these to be a southern extremity of the Rocky Mountains.

What major cities are in the Trans-Pecos?

El Paso is the only large urban area in the region. After that, the largest towns are Pecos (population 8,800), Fort Stockton (8,500), and Alpine (5,900).

What endangered species are present in the Trans-Pecos?

Some of the species that are marked for special protection are the tiny Mexican long-nosed bat, which weighs less than 1 ounce (28 grams) and subsists on pollen and nectar taken from cacti and succulents. The Texas desert bighorn sheep was hunted to

165

extinction sometime around 1958. However, other closely related desert bighorns from further west have been introduced to fill that niche in the ecology. This ecosystem's top predators, the mountain lion and black bear, were hunted out many years ago but with greater protection are staging a comeback, especially the cougars, which have come to threaten local stock. The rare Hinckley oak, a miniature oak tree that seldom grows more than 5 feet (152 centimeters) tall, is federally listed as threatened. It is evergreen, its leaves have evolved into thornlike points like holly, and its acorns emerge as deep red before turning brown with age. Found in only two U.S. counties, most of its population lies in Big Bend Ranch State Park. The American spadefoot toad is also listed as threatened. The Comanche Springs pupfish hangs on in the acequias at Balmorhea State Park.

What are the principal threats to the Trans-Pecos ecology today?

Within Big Bend National Park, the illegal collection of endangered cacti for the house plant trade continues to be a problem. Overgrazing and poor land management have been problems ever since the area was settled, but landowners in west Texas are especially protective of their property rights. The Texas Parks and Wildlife Department website treads very softly, emphasizing its support of and cooperation with private landowners. To bridge this gap, private conservation groups such as the Nature Conservancy have stepped in with the purchase of conservation easements where purchase might not be welcome. Still, it manages crucial preserves such as the 19,740-acre (80-square-kilometer) Independence Creek in Terrell County, which protects pure springs that provide 40 percent of the flow of the upper Pecos River, up to 5,000 gallons (18,927 liters) per minute.

What parks and reserves protect the Trans-Pecos today?

The fact that the Trans-Pecos is one of the better-protected ecosystems not just in Texas but in the whole United States is a product not so much of any long-standing commitment to preservation but because the land was so commercially unproductive and forbidding to begin with. As one early settler remarked, "Every plant out here either sticks, stings, or stinks." There is one large and one smaller national park: Big Bend (1,252 square miles [3,243 square kilometers]) and Guadalupe Mountains (135 square miles [350 square kilometers]). Both parks are only part of larger protected complexes: Guadalupe Mountains adjoins wilderness study areas in New Mexico that connect with Carlsbad Caverns National Park. Big Bend N.P. adjoins Big Bend State Park (at 486 square miles [1,259 square kilometers], it is the largest Texas state park), the Black Gap Wildlife Management Area (161 square miles [417 square kilometers]), and a companion nature reserve across the Rio Grande in Mexico. Large tracts within both national parks have been more strictly protected under the Wilderness Act to limit human impact. The state installations are not as strictly protected as the national parks, but the Texas Nature Conservancy in 2008 purchased a 7,000-acre (28-square-kilometer) inholding within Big Bend State Park with plans for nature restoration.

What is unique about Balmorhea State Park?

Although covering only 46 acres (0.19 square kilometers), this park is important to the region. It centers about the large, permanent San Solomon Springs, which have been dammed to form a swimming pool up to 25 feet (7.6 meters) deep and is 1.3 acres (5,261 square meters) in extent, holding 3.5 million gallons (13.2 million liters) of water—making it the largest spring-fed pool in the world. The water is not chlorinated, as the springs' 15 million gallons (57 million liters) or more cycle through every day and keep the water clean. Originally, the springs emptied into a lush oasis in the desert that was frequented by the Mescalero Apache (hence its original name, Mescalero Springs), and from this wetland, Spanish settlers dug irrigation ditches called *acequias* to water crops. Interference with the natural order was mechanized in 1927 by the Bureau of Reclamation to funnel water directly for human use and further when the State Parks Board acquired the site in 1934, and the Civilian Conservation Corps began construction of the pool the following year. These activities destroyed the natural oasis, which has now been partially recreated to benefit native species, including the endangered Pecos gambusia and Comanche Springs pupfish. San Solomon is only the largest of a complex of springs in this area. Another important one, Sandia Springs nearby, is protected in a Nature Conservancy preserve.

Why is access so limited to the Devil's River?

Perhaps the outstanding effort by the Texas Parks and Wildlife Department and preserving wilderness in west Texas is, in two units, the 37,000-acre (150-square-kilometer) Devil's River State Natural Area. It lies on the border of the Hill Country and the Trans-Pecos; the area is extremely remote and rugged along the Devil's River above where it empties into Amistad Reservoir. Access is limited to maintain its wilderness aspect, although "limited" still means that more than 8,000 visitors are allowed in each year, who must pack in all their needs and leave nothing behind. The park contains Dolan Falls, which has the greatest water volume of any in Texas. Fifty-three ancient rock shelters have been identified, many with pictographs. Ecologically, the park is a convergence zone of the Hill Country with both Chihuahuan and Tamaulipan deserts. Several endemic small fish inhabit the river, which is isolated enough that even the bass and catfish in it are developing unique genotypes.

Scenic Dolan Falls along Devil's River, which is a valuable water resource for the state.

The state acquired the 19,000-acre (77-square-kilometer) upstream unit in 1988, and the 18,000-acre (73-square-kilometer) downstream parcel as recently as 2010—a laudable effort to preserve one of the last true wildernesses in the state.

Where is the best place in Texas to see Indian pictographs?

The middle Rio Grande was a rich site to view ancient Indian art, but much of it was lost with the damming of Amistad Reservoir. After intense lobbying by citizen activists, the state of Texas acquired 2,172 acres (9 square kilometers) along the Rio Grande that contains much of the best of what is left. It is in Val Verde County, not far from the Devil's River Natural Area. Panther Cave holds some of the oldest native art in North America, believed to date from about 7000 B.C.E.

What recreational opportunities are there in the Davis Mountains?

Lying about halfway between the Big Bend and the Guadalupe Mountains, the Davis Mountains State Park (2,709 acres [11 square kilometers]) was first envisioned when the state parks system was created, but with no appropriation and no donation, it took the ruin of the Depression for a local family to donate the first 560 acres (2.3 square kilometers). The first amenities were built by the CCC starting in 1933 and have acquired something of a historic status of their own. The park's primary use is recreational, but a section that is separated by a state highway is somewhat better protected as the Limpia Canyon Primitive Area. Although they are not contiguous, a hiking trail links the park to the nearby Fort Davis National Historic Site, which preserves the frontier cavalry post and also has a perimeter nature trail. Also nearby is the McDonald Observatory, operated by the University of Texas, which hosts "star parties" a couple of times a month, when visitors can observe distant galaxies and see lasers bounced off a reflecting plaque on the moon. Recognizing that the state park is not adequate for habitat protection, the Nature Conservancy has stepped in by acquiring the Davis Mountains Preserve of 33,075 acres (134 square kilometers), with conservation easements contracted on a further 102,675 acres (416 square kilometers)—a godsend for the local ecology, including top predators of mountain lions and black bears, which must patrol an extensive range, and numerous birds rare in Texas, such as Montezuma quail, various raptors, and ten species of hummingbirds.

What are the Hueco Tanks?

Several of the mountains in the Trans-Pecos are so isolated and so high that they create their own miniature weather systems. When desert wind is forced to rise over a mountain, it squeezes out what little moisture there might be in it. At times, motoring through the desert reveals that each mountain has its own thunderstorm. The runoff collects in rock basins, forming waterholes that both wildlife and the native Indians came to rely on. The Hueco Tanks, 30 miles (48 kilometers) east of El Paso, were such a gathering place for ancient peoples that they left metates ground into the stone and petroglyphs now preserved in the Hueco Tanks State Park (860 acres [3.5 square kilo-

Indian pictographs such as these can be discovered at Hueco Tanks, about 30 miles east of El Paso.

meters]). Because of the park's small size and fragile ecosystem, visitors are limited in number and are cautioned not to disturb the rock pools that shelter the threatened American spadefoot toad and the freshwater shrimp described as a living fossil. The unique syenite granite of the outcroppings has made the park a mecca for rock climbers from around the world, who are limited to seventy per day and must procure an approved guide to access most of the park.

Why isn't the Sierra Madera Meteor Crater better known than it is?

Of Texas's three impact craters, the Odessa Crater gets the lion's share of the attention because it is located near a major highway and city, is open to the public, and has an onsite museum. The Sierra Madera crater southwest of Pecos is located on private land. It is also so large, some 8 miles (13 kilometers) in diameter, that it is difficult to recognize for what it is. Indeed, its origins were only recognized by a geologist who discovered that the layering of rocks in the Sierra Madera, a range of hills 1.5 mile (2.4 kilometers) across and up to 800 feet (244 meters) high, could only be explained as a rebound structure from a meteor impact.

THE HILL COUNTRY

What defines the Hill Country?

Different authorities define it differently, but to simplify, it can be said to include the Edwards Plateau, which basically is the limestone bed of Texas's prehistoric inland sea, and the Llano Uplift, an ancient exposure of Precambrian volcanic rock about 90 miles (145 kilometers) across, with granite, schist, and gneiss interspersed with the newer limestones. This exhibits radically different geology from the surrounding country, including minerals found only here.

What major cities lie in the Hill Country?

Oddly, there are major urban areas on the boundary of the Hill Country—Austin on the east and San Antonio on the southeast but not within 45,000 square miles (116,549 square kilometers) of its interior. Even the smaller cities of San Angelo on its north and Del Rio on its southwest lie on its fringes. This has helped preserve the rural character of the Hill Country, while the larger towns within it, such as Fredericksburg (pop. 11,000), provide convenient access to it.

What brought the Hill Country to national notice?

In the presidential election of 1960, Democrat John F. Kennedy selected a Texan, Senate majority leader Lyndon B. Johnson, to be his running mate. *Life* magazine assembled a feature story on the soon-to-be vice president, turning a spotlight on his family ranch near Johnson City. The *Life* article referred to Johnson's bucolic surroundings as "God's country" to the amazement of the hard working farmers and ranchers. After Johnson became president, his ranch on the Pedernales River became the "Texas White House," U.S. Highway 290 west from Austin was improved, and the Hill Country found itself less isolated.

What endangered animal species are present in the Hill Country?

The two most prominent endangered species are birds that depend upon mature juniper habitat, the Golden-cheeked Warbler and Black-capped Vireo. Less visible but more numerous are the many endemic and endangered cave-dwelling insects and spiders that inhabit the maze of caverns that underlie the Hill Country's limestone karst—some probably yet to be discovered. Hanging on in the very heart of Austin is the endemic Barton Springs salamander, first described to science in 1993 and placed on the endangered list four years later. Other small endemic fish in other streams are federally protected, and they perennially madden would-be developers.

Where can one find Texas wild rice?

First cousin to two other species of wild rice in North America, including the one harvested by Menominee Indians in Wisconsin for sale as a table delicacy, Texas wild rice (*Zizania texana*) is critically endangered. It is found in 140 patches and strips totaling only about 0.3 acre (1,214 square meters) along the uppermost 2 miles (3.2 kilometers) of the San Marcos River. It is a bright green, willowy grass that grows in water 1 to 6 feet (30 to 183 centimeters) deep, completely submerged except for flower heads that rise above the surface. The peculiar needs of its reproductive biology make it vulnerable to changes in water level and quality. While botanists at nearby Texas State University watch vigilantly over this last remnant, they cannot control recreational use of the stream or its commercialization.

> ## What is being done to save the fountain darter?
>
> Ironically, one favored habitat for this endangered, 1-inch- (2.5-centimeter-) long fish is among the long, ribbon like leaves of Texas wild rice. In addition to the upper San Marcos River, it is also found in the headwaters of the Comal River several miles to the southwest, but that population has been infested with an exotic parasite, so its future is uncertain. As a precaution against extinction, the National Fish Hatchery and Technology Center located in San Marcos maintains a captive population of about five hundred individuals. The fountain darter's liberal breeding habits are in its favor, which is lucky because its life span is less than two years.

What are the principal threats to the Hill Country ecology today?

The presence of two of the largest cities in the United States—San Antonio and Austin—at the eastern edge of the Hill Country has prompted the provision of so many parks and preserves that it ought to be considered one of the most protected areas of the state. However, some threats to the quality of life in and around it, such as the quality of drinking water on which San Antonio depends, are affected by more than the reservation of parkland and require a more general legislative approach. In the eastern portion of the Hill Country, loss of habitat to rampant urban sprawl has been inevitable for two of the United States' fastest-growing cities. The biological health of the Highland Lakes above Austin has come under serious threat recently by the presence of zebra mussels, a highly aggressive, invasive mollusk.

What parks and reserves protect the Hill Country today?

Despite its ecological interest, nothing in the Hill Country recommended itself to protection on a federal scale until the establishment in 1992 of the Balcones Canyonlands National Wildlife Refuge. The purchase of 27,500 acres (111 square kilometers) of expensive land on the very outskirts of development-mad Austin was an achievement, and it partnered with a complicated web of state, county, and city purchases for either habitat or groundwater protection. Still, the density of state parks in the Hill Country is the most in Texas.

How did Enchanted Rock get its name?

About 90 miles (145 kilometers) west of Austin, the Enchanted Rock State Natural Area contains the second-largest exposed rock, called a *batholith*, in the United States (Stone Mountain in Georgia is larger). The pink, granite dome rises like the top of a colossal skull, looming 425 feet (130 meters) above the surrounding terrain and covering about 1 square mile (2.6 square kilometers). The 1,642-acre (6.6-square-kilometer) park that surrounds it has a perimeter hiking trail and a campground that a 2017 survey ranked as the best in Texas. The exfoliating dome expands during the heat of the day, and there

The exposed stone of Enchanted Rock is approximately 1 billion years old and is the second-largest *batholith* in the United States.

can be audible groans at night as the rock cools back into place. This prompted Comanche Indians to believe that the place was haunted, hence its name.

How did the Lost Maples get lost?

Lying astraddle the border of Real and Bandera counties in the most rugged heart of the Hill Country, Lost Maples State Natural Area protects 2,906 acres (12 square kilometers) of the upper Sabine River. Acquired by the state in 1974 using money from the 1970 bond passage, the park is managed for wildness but has thirty campsites and 11 miles (17.8 kilometers) of hiking trails. The most interesting part of the botany is the presence of bigtooth maples, which exist far outside their normal range, and in the autumn provide a spectacular leaf change. Scientists have come to believe that this species at one time existed commonly in this area but died out as conditions changed, leaving this sheltered remnant behind.

What other state nature parks exist in the Hill Country?

Many outstanding examples of the Hill Country have been preserved throughout. They include natural areas: Devil's Sinkhole, Hill Country, Honey Creek, and Government Canyon State, and state parks: South Llano River, Kickapoo Cavern, Garner, Colorado Bend, Inks Lake, Longhorn Cavern, Lyndon B. Johnson, Pedernales Falls, Blanco, Guadalupe River, and McKinney Falls.

With all this state protection, have private organizations turned their attention elsewhere?

Not at all; the Nature Conservancy took upon itself the job of acquiring the Eckert James River Bat Cave, which houses a colony of some four million Mexican free-tailed bats, and also the 2,508-acre (10-square-kilometer) Love Creek Preserve. It is located in a distinct subsystem known as the Bandera Canyonlands along more than 2 miles (3.2 kilometers) of Love Creek, which is a tributary of the Medina River. The water is home to various rare small fish and even a freshwater jellyfish. Rare plants listed by the Conservancy include Texas mock orange, sycamore leaf snowbells, darkstem noseburn, spreading least daisy, and many others. The preserve was acquired through the generous and amiable cooperation of the previous owners, who recognized the area's importance. In cooperation with federal and state authorities who administer nearby parcels, the Conservancy also manages the 4,084-acre (16.5-square-kilometer) Barton Creek Habitat Preserve in the Austin suburbs.

Why are so many of the state parks centered about caverns?

Geologically, the Hill Country is predominantly limestone karst—that is, an ancient bed of rock that was lifted up and, as rainwater soaked through fissures, created an acid that ate rock away and formed caverns, many of them large and containing formations of national importance. Other important karst regions in the United States include the Ozark Mountains of Arkansas and southern Missouri and much of Puerto Rico. Those fissures in the limestone also create pathways for underground water, which flows east and erupts from the Hill Country in massive springs along its edge, which is called the Balcones Escarpment. These include Comal Springs in New Braunfels, San Marcos Springs in San Marcos, and Barton Springs in Austin.

Are the famous Caverns of Sonora open or locked up?

It is not easy to know because they have been both. Local ranchers had known of the cave since the early 1900s, but the property owner did not give permission to explore it until 1955, and four spelunkers from Dallas made their way through 7 miles (11 kilometers) of passages. What they saw took their breath away, as these caverns have one of the best collections of rare calcite formations on earth—soda straws, "bacon and eggs," helictites that issue from the walls—and the site became world famous. Many formations are so delicate they can be, and have been, dislodged at the slightest touch, and some of the most extraordinary features have been destroyed. The cave was closed to the public for

Which cave or cavern should someone explore first if their time is limited?

The largest cavern in Texas is Natural Bridge, 8 miles (13 kilometers) west of New Braunfels. Not discovered until 1960, the cave has 2 miles (3 kilometers) of passages that have been found so far. The deepest part open to the public is 180 feet (55 meters) below ground but extends at least another 80 feet (24 meters) lower than that. The largest chamber yet discovered is about 100 feet (30 meters) wide, 100 feet (30 meters) high, and 350 feet (107 meters) long. As remarkable as the cave's size is its collection of rare calcite formations, and it is a "living" cave, still being formed by the action of rainwater dissolving the limestone. The natural bridge for which it is named is not within the cavern but above ground near the entrance, a 60-foot (18-meter) span formed by a collapsed sinkhole. For further natural history, the Natural Bridge Wildlife Ranch is 7 miles (11 kilometers) west of the cavern.

The Caverns of Sonora contain some spectacular formations. Unfortunately, it is not always possible for visitors to explore this natural wonder.

many years, but finally it was decided that the best protection was to offer tours—limited and strictly monitored. In Sonora proper, the Old Ice House Ranch Museum interprets local history and tells the story of one of Butch Cassidy's Wild Bunch, Will Carver, who was killed here in 1901.

Why was the Colorado River dammed so extensively?

Because of the vivid rainstorms that plague the Hill Country, the largest stream to drain out of that region, the Colorado River, was subject to cataclysmic floods. Downtown Austin was inundated in 1900, when a city dam and power plant were washed away, and again in 1935, with further floods in 1936 and 1938. Even before the 1935 flood, the Lower Colorado River Authority was formed to tame the Colorado, moved by the imperative of flood control, the availability of federal money through the Works Progress Administration, the desirability of providing rural electrical power, and the possibility of recreation. The first and farthest upstream, Buchanan Dam, is over 2 miles (3.2 kilometers) long, was finished in 1939, impounding a lake of 875,000 acre-feet. Downstream, three pass-through dams were built, Inks, Wirtz, and Max Starcke, before reaching a

second large flood-control at Mansfield Dam, impounding Lake Travis of some 1.2 mil-

When Mansfield Dam was constructed near Austin in 1942, it created Travis Lake Reservoir, which controls flooding and is also a popular recreational area.

lion acre-feet (1.42 billion cubic meters). Farther downstream, two more pass-through dams, Tom Miller and Longhorn, aided control before returning the Colorado to its natural processes below Austin. The system proved its worth during a break in the 1951 drought when shattering rainstorms in the upper basin raised the giant Lake Travis 57 feet (17 meters) in just 14 hours. A similar scenario plays out on the Medina River above San Antonio, whose Medina Lake can change from nearly empty to brimful overnight.

THE PANHANDLE–PLAINS

What are the natural divisions within the Panhandle-Plains?

Northwest of the Hill Country and Blacklands (Prairies and Lakes region) lies a southern extremity of the Great Plains of two major types. In the east and rising slowly toward the west are the Rolling Plains, predominantly mixed-grass prairie with stands of mesquite and shinnery oak, thickly sprinkled with prickly pear cactus, and with gallery forests along the streams of pecan, willow, and cottonwood. The region terminates in the west, where the headwaters of the Red River meet the Caprock, atop which lie the Staked Plains, an almost weirdly flat plain of shortgrass, playa lakes, and almost no trees whatsoever.

175

What Texas cities lie in this natural region?

Fort Worth might be considered to lie at the eastern border of the Rolling Plains, although technically it is in a Cross Timbers belt of the Blacklands. Abilene and Wichita Falls lie in the heart of the Rolling Plains, San Angelo on its southwestern border. Midland and Odessa lie at the southern edge of the Staked Plains, Lubbock 130 miles (209 kilometers) north of there lies in its heart, and 120 miles (193 kilometers) farther north, Amarillo is still nearly 100 miles (161 kilometers) from the state line, with the Staked Plains extending across the borders into New Mexico and Oklahoma.

What exactly is the Caprock?

A few feet beneath the lush shortgrass prairie of the Staked Plains lies a layer of "hardpan"—a rock like band of calcite formed by the interaction of rainwater reacting with the abundant minerals in the subsoil. This hard layer retards erosion, which is limited to its edges and along major streams. As the soil outside the hardpan has washed away over eons, the resulting cliffs rise in places more than 1,000 feet (305 meters) in height. This exposed flat edge of the hardpan at the top of the cliffs is called the Caprock.

How did the Staked Plains get their name?

There are different accounts. The most likely dates from the Coronado entrada of 1540. Coming from the west, they mounted the Caprock and entered a prairie almost weird in its flatness, carpeted in almost impenetrable grass, but with no trees. One diarist wrote how unnerving it was for their huge expedition—a thousand men, plus stock and attendants—to cross this prairie and leave no more trail than if they were sailing on the ocean. The only way to mark the way they had come was to drive stakes in the ground or else raise cairns of bones and refuse.

What are "playa lakes"?

The Staked Plains are so notoriously flat that rainwater has little path to run off but collects in circular, wetland mini habitats called playa lakes. There are about 19,300 of them, covering about 2 percent of the Staked Plains area. They vary in size from 15 to over 800 acres (0.06 to 3.2 square kilometers), but the great majority are under 30 acres (0.1 square kilometers) in size. In earlier times, bison favored the mud in playa lakes for lying down and cooling off—hence, "buffalo wallow" was a playa lake that had been scooped out and deepened by that usage. With the beginning of panhandle agriculture, farmers and ranchers modified playa lakes by dredging deeper pits within them to concentrate the water, creating water holes for livestock and water for furrow irrigation. Only more recently have researchers learned that playa lakes are a principal source of recharge for the Ogallala Aquifer, which has been over pumped for agricultural irrigation. Scientists are now working to convince landowners to fence off playa lakes and provide a grassland buffer, allowing them to perform their natural ecological function.

Does any wildlife make use of playa lakes?

The native grasses such as millet and smartweed that crowd the edges of playa lakes in wet years produce abundant seeds for consumption by migratory birds, and the Texas Panhandle is a crucially important winter home for them, second only to the Gulf Coast in the size of its wintering flocks. Snow geese and Canada geese can number over three hundred thousand, plus migratory ducks such as northern pintails and mallards.

Have any refuges been provided to protect Panhandle waterfowl?

Two units of the National Wildlife Refuge System have been established in the Panhandle. Buffalo Lake NWR was established in 1958 southwest of Amarillo on 7,664 acres (31 square kilometers) managed for waterfowl and also for the protection of year-round native species, such as prairie dogs and the burrowing owls, ferrets, and other species that utilize their abandoned burrows. The land was originally bought up to dam Tierra Blanca Creek to provide water for irrigation, but that scheme was foiled when the water table fell so low that the creek dried up and the land was given over to the refuge system to do the best it could with it. In addition to providing a winter home for hundreds of thousands of migratory ducks and geese, the refuge protects some of the last best remnants of the Staked Plains' original shortgrass prairie. Some 175 acres (0.7 square kilometers) of it is so pristine, it has been designated a National Natural Landmark. Similarly, the Muleshoe NWR on 6,440 acres (26 square kilometers) near the New Mexico line, northwest of Lubbock, protects wintering waterfowl in addition to a huge number of lesser sandhill cranes, about 15 percent of the entire species population. Migrating in from northern Canada, they stand about 3 feet (91 centimeters) tall, with a 6-foot (183-centimeter) wingspan. Muleshoe was the first national refuge in Texas, established in 1935, so its remnant of shortgrass prairie is also remarkably undisturbed.

What other parks and reserves play a role in protecting the Panhandle-Plains ecology?

As with other regions of Texas, most state parks exist for recreational purposes, although maintenance of naturalistic settings and values are always a consideration. Three state parks, however, are large enough to provide significant ecological benefit. Palo Duro Canyon State Park, east of the city of Canyon, was recently enlarged to 28,000 acres (113 square kilometers) but still covers only a tiny portion of the largest gorge on the eastern side of the Staked Plains. Similar terrain 40 miles (64 kilometers) to the southeast is protected in the 15,300 acres (62 square kilometers) of Caprock Canyons State Park. Like Palo Duro, the land was once part of the vast JA Ranch run by Charles Goodnight. Lower down on the Rolling Plains near the town of Quanah, 1,900 acres (7.7 square kilometers) is contained in the Copper Breaks State Park.

What endangered species are present in the Panhandle-Plains?

The Texas Parks and Wildlife Department currently lists fourteen animal species as the objects of some degree of concern, most of which fortunately have not yet progressed too far down the road toward extinction. Some of them not discussed elsewhere include the kit fox, the smallest of the North American foxes, also known as the swift fox. Their numbers have been reduced in part to their being poisoned by bait set out for coyotes; the cave myotis bat, which originally hibernated in gypsum caves but has now appropriated urban habitats such as carports and bridges; the Palo Duro mouse, whose range is limited to juniper-dotted canyon walls along the Caprock; the Texas kangaroo rat, whose favored burrowing site is at the base of a mesquite or similar tree; the sand dune lizard, whose range is confined to the limited number of active sand dunes; and the Texas horned lizard—the iconic Texas horny toad—which was once very common but whose loss of habitat has shrunk their numbers until they are now classed as threatened within the state. The lesser prairie chicken, whose numbers are only 3 percent of what they were a century ago, is also the subject of concern in Texas. While no facility dedicated to them lies in the state, just across the New Mexico line from Muleshoe NWR lies the Nature Conservancy's 18,500-acre (75 square kilometers) Milnesand Prairie Preserve, which works to keep that species around.

Where are there sand dunes for that lizard to dig in?

At the southern end of the Panhandle-Plains, one place that is ideal for the sand dune lizard is the 3,840-acre (15.5-square-kilometer) Monahans Sandhills State Park, which covers only a small portion of a 200-mile (322-kilometer) dune field that extends far into New Mexico. Another feature of the park, where the dunes have stabilized, is the shin oak, a dwarf tree that is only 4 feet (122 centimeters) tall at full maturity. There are also much smaller dune fields near Lubbock.

What are the principal threats to the Panhandle-Plains ecology today?

More than half the original extent of the Panhandle-Plains has been converted to agriculture, with much more given over to stock grazing, whose damage to the ecology is less visible. Very little unaltered ecosystem is left. One serious threat to prairie ecology that escapes common notice is the spread of invasive species, especially redberry juniper and Eastern red cedar on the Rolling Plains, and salt cedar and Russian olive on the Staked Plains. Replacement of native grasses with plantings of a single monoculture such as bluestem does no favors for the environment, either.

How old is the Odessa Meteor Crater?

The Odessa Meteor Crater was formed about 62,000 years ago. It is over 500 feet (152 meters) in diameter and was originally over 100 feet (30 meters) deep, but it has infilled over time to where it is only about 15 feet (4.6 meters) deep at its lowest point. It was first recognized as a meteorite impact by scientist Daniel Barringer, who also first realized the origin of Meteor Crater in Arizona. While not nearly as spectacular as that one, the Odessa Crater has unique features that the larger one does not. It is only one of several impact craters in the immediate vicinity. They were formed when a shower of iron-nickel bolides fell as a shower in the same event—an extremely rare phenomenon. The smaller craters filled in completely over time and were discovered only by excavation. Drilling established that there was no main meteor mass buried in the floor of the main crater. It exploded upon impact; the largest piece ever found weighs 330 pounds (150 kilograms) and the original meteorite is estimated to have weighed 70 tons (63,503 kilograms) and blew out about 100,000 cubic yards (76,455 cubic meters) of rock upon impact.

A piece of the mostly iron meteor that created the crater near Odessa is on display at the Meteor Crater Museum.

What happened at the Alibates Flint Quarries?

Thirty miles north of Amarillo, there is an area of about 10 square miles (26 square kilometers) straddling the Canadian River, where outcroppings of a rock known in the vernacular as flint—actually an agatized dolomite—from which the earliest proto-Indians fashioned tools and weapons began perhaps 12,000 years ago. The wide distribution of locations in which Alibates artifacts have been found attest that there was widespread trade in these implements. Hundreds of pits to quarry the flint were dug, which are still extant along with village sites. In 1965, 1,079 acres (4.4 square kilometers) were reserved by the federal government as the Alibates Flint Quarries National Monument, which is open to the public but to protect the sites can be visited only on tours guided by park rangers. The site was first investigated and named by a geologist named Charles Gould in 1907, who was unaware that a local creek was actually named for rancher Allie Bates.

BLACKLAND PRAIRIES

What characterizes the Blackland Prairies?

There is actually a complicated intermingling of habitats, including not just the Blackland Prairies but also Post Oak Savannah in the east, belts of cedar breaks in its middle, south of Dallas and Fort Worth, and two belts of the Cross Timbers in its western portion. This is the most heavily agriculturalized portion of the state, with rapidly increasing population and with wilderness values reduced to camping in lakeside parks leased from the reigning water authority.

What major urban areas are located in the Blacklands?

The Dallas-Fort Worth "Metroplex" with its population of over seven million is certainly the largest. After that, one must look down the list as far as Bryan and College Station in the southeast, Temple in the south, and Waco north of there. Unlike west Texas, where the bulk of a county's population lives in the county seat, the countryside of north-central Texas is heavily settled with family farms or vacation homes, giving the whole a prospect that is pastoral but not wild at all.

What endangered species are present in the Blackland Prairies?

The Texas Parks and Wildlife Department concedes in one of its publications that wildlife long ago extirpated from north-central Texas is adequately protected in other portions of the state, implying that it would be an uphill battle to justify the expense of trying to reintroduce them to their former range.

What parks and reserves protect the Blackland Prairies today?

There is a plethora of state parks in the Blacklands/Post Oak/Cross Timbers areas today, but to say that they "protect" the ecology would be rather a misnomer because most of them are primarily geared to recreational activities. They include Bonham, Cedar Hill, Cleburne, Cooper Lake, Eisenhower, Fairfield Lake, Fort Boggy, Fort Parker, Lake Mineral Wells, Lake Somerville, Lake Tawakoni, Lake Whitney, Lockhart, Meridian, Purtis Creek, Ray Roberts Lake, and Stephen F. Austin.

Aren't there any exceptions to that rather tame prospect?

Partly, yes. In the very western portion of the Cross Timbers, bordering on the Rolling Plains, Possum Kingdom State Park, on 1,528 acres (6 square kilometers) acquired from the Brazos River Authority, covers some very rugged scenery. Still, most of the possible activities revolve around lake recreation. Also, 90 percent of the park burned in a wildfire in 2011, the same year as the Bastrop fire, and it will take time to recover. Also in the Cross Timbers near Granbury, Dinosaur Valley State Park, on 1,524 acres (6 square kilometers) on the Paluxy River, is one of the few places anywhere that one can see the tracks of all three major types of dinosaurs: giant, three-toed chicken tracks of predatory theropods, the wedge-shaped tracks of the duck-billed dinosaurs, and the enormous circular impression of the sauropods. Another interesting exception is Mother Neff State Park, which has a scenic walk along the Leon River.

Is the Hagerman National Wildlife Refuge worth visiting?

Lying only about 50 miles (80 kilometers) north of Dallas, the Hagerman NWR is about the closest place that residents of the Metroplex can find much in the way of wildlife. The

Hagerman consists of 11,320 acres (46 square kilometers) "overlaid" on the Big Mineral arm of Lake Texoma. It is managed primarily for migratory waterfowl, and appreciable gatherings of ducks and geese can be seen—and hunted—in season. Still, there is a mixture of wetland and upland habitats, so visiting off-season can provide some peace and quiet on the hiking trails. Several hundred acres of the refuge are farmed, though, to provide forage for the wintering fowl, so the wilderness experience will not be uninterrupted.

Why are the state parks around Bastrop so unique?

Bastrop and Buescher state parks are heavily geared toward outdoor recreation but also protect stands of the "Lost Pines" loblollies. And at Palmetto State Park on 270 acres (1.1 square kilometers) near

Loblolly pines are part of the verdant forest at Bastrop and Buescher state parks, but Lost Pines marks an area of some 100 miles where the land is devoid of the trees before reaching Piney Woods.

Gonzales, one can see dwarf palmettoes at the western extremity of their range. The bird watching there can be interesting, as it is a known "hot spot" with 240 recorded species, including prothonotary warblers and crested caracaras, a large scavenger with a 4-foot wingspan. The latter can be interesting to watch, as they are one of the few birds of prey (albeit usually dead prey) that forage on foot.

What is meant by the "Lost Pines"?

From 30 to 40 miles (48 to 64 kilometers) east of Austin, in a belt that extends from north of U.S. Highway 290 east of Elgin to south of State Highway 71 at Bastrop, the ecology is dominated by a verdant forest of loblolly pine trees. The mystery is that there is a separation from the Piney Woods of more than 100 miles (161 kilometers) in which there is hardly a pine tree to be seen. The trees of the Lost Pines have been shown to be genetically related to those of the eastern woods. One recent theory has it that it is really the Bastrop forest that is the parent of the Piney Woods, not the other way around, that a genetic bottleneck created by the last glacial retreat is what reforested east Texas. We may never know for certain, but the question was almost rendered moot by the Bastrop wildfire of 2011 that devastated most of the Lost Pines.

What is unusual about the Marquez Crater?

Although it is one of only three major impact craters in Texas, the Marquez Crater has no trace on the surface of the ground and escaped detection until geologists in the 1980s

181

who were more interested in petroleum realized that rocks brought up showed that what they thought was a salt dome was not. Early settlers knew that the land was not right; there was no water when they dug wells where there should have been plenty; the soil was black gumbo where it should have been red and sandy, and it contained chunks of yellow limestone, for which there was no explanation whatsoever. Now it is known that all of that is a result of rebound from a deep meteor or comet strike. Sixty million years ago, this part of the shallow sea was vaporized in the creation of a crater about 9 miles (14.5 kilometers) across as revealed by the presence of melted shocked quartz.

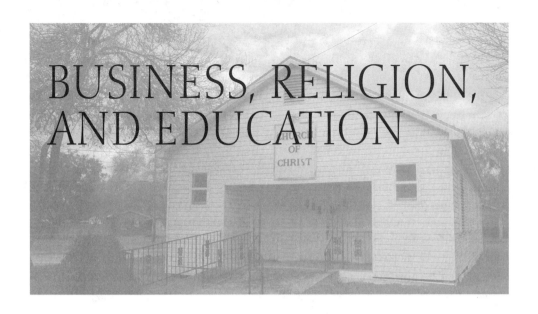

BUSINESS, RELIGION, AND EDUCATION

ECONOMICS AND LARGE COMPANIES

How large is the Texas economy?

If Texas were an independent country, its economy would be the tenth largest of all the world's countries. That is a gross domestic product of about $1.7 trillion, or about the size of Canada's. As ranked by the International Monetary Fund, it is slightly less than the GDP of Brazil or Italy and a bit larger than those of Russia or South Korea. Texas generates a GDP that is about 8.75 percent of the total U.S. GDP of $19.4 trillion.

What are the most profitable Texas-based companies?

The following table lists the largest companies based in the Lone Star State according to a 2014 report issued by the governor's office. As you can see, oil is still king in Texas.

Top Texas Companies Earning over $20 Billion Annually

Name	Industry	Public/Private	Headquarters	Revenue
ExxonMobil Corp.	Oil and Gas	Public	Irving	$407.6 billion
Phillips 66	Oil Refining	Public	Houston	$166.2 billion
Valero Energy Corp.	Oil and Gas	Public	San Antonio	$137.7 billion
AT&T Inc.	Telecommunications	Public	Dallas	$128.7 billion
ConocoPhillips	Oil and Gas	Public	Houston	$59.4 billion
Dell Inc.	Computers/IT Service	Private	Round Rock	$56.9 billion
Energy Transfer Equity	Oil and Gas	Public	Dallas	$48.7 billion
Enterprise Products Partners L.P.	Oil & Gas Pipelines	Public	Houston	$47.7 billion
Sysco Corp.	Wholesale Foods	Public	Houston	$44.7 billion
Plains GP Holdings	Oil & Gas Pipelines	Public	Houston	$42.2 billion

Top Texas Companies Earning over $20 Billion Annually (contd.)

Name	Industry	Public/Private	Headquarters	Revenue
Tesoro Corp.	Oil Refineries	Public	San Antonio	$39.2 billion
Halliburton Comp.	Oilfield Services	Public	Fort Worth	$29.4 billion
Fluor Corp.	Engineering	Public	Irving	$27.3 billion
American Airlines	Airlines	Public	Fort Worth	$26.7 billion
National Oilwell Varco	Oilfield Equipment	Public	Houston	$22.8 billion
Baker Hughes Inc.	Oilfield Equipment	Public	Houston	$22.3 billion
Kimberly-Clark Corp.	Paper Products	Public	Irving	$21.1 billion
USAA	Insurance	Public	San Antonio	$20.9 billion
H.E.B. Grocery Corp.	Grocery Stores	Private	San Antonio	$20.3 billion
HollyFrontier Corp.	Oil Refineries	Public	Dallas	$20.1 billion

Source: "Texas Top Tier: The Largest Companies Headquartered in Texas." Office of the Governor, Economic Development and Tourism, 2014.

How is wealth distributed in Texas?

Figures vary according to the methodology used, but in general, the average per capita income in Texas is a little less than $20,000, with a median average family income of just under $50,000. In one hundred Texas counties, per capita income is less than this; in 154 counties, it is more. The poorer counties are concentrated in the Rio Grande Valley, with the poorest, Zavala County, having a per capita income of just over $10,000. About 4.7 million Texans live below the poverty line.

Where do the richest Texans live?

Data showing where Texas's wealthiest citizens live is somewhat skewed toward sparsely populated rural counties where income is kept high by oil royalties. Setting that aside, most of Texas's rich people live not in the major cities but in affluent satellites of those major cities, whose taxes are not burdened with urban blight. Again, depending on the methodology used, here are the thirty wealthiest communities in Texas, listed by the metro area in which they are located:

Wealthiest Texas Communities

Rank	City	Neighborhood	Per Capita Income
#1	Fort Worth	Southlake	$176,000
#2	Austin	Barton Creek	$110,000
#3	Fort Worth	Westover Hills	$98,000
#4	Dallas	Highland Park	$97,000
#5	Houston	Hunters Creek Village	$88,000
#6	Houston	Bunker Hill Village	$86,000
#7	San Antonio	Hill Country Village	$77,000
#8	Near Corsicana	Mustang	$75,000
#9	Houston	West University Place	$69,000
#10	Houston	Hillshire Village	$66,000

Wealthiest Texas Communities (contd.)

Rank	City	Neighborhood	Per Capita Income
#11	San Antonio	Olmos Park	$65,000
#12	Dallas	University Park	$63,000
#13	Austin	The Hills	$61,000
#14	Houston	Southside Place	$57,000
#15	Austin	West Lake Hills	$55,000
#16	Austin	Onion Creek	$54,000
#17	Galveston	Tiki Island	$54,000
#18	Dallas	Parker	$54,000
#19	Corpus Christi	Lakeshore Gardens	$52,000
#20	Austin	Rollingwood	$52,000
#21	Houston	Hedwig Village	$52,000
#22	Austin	Lost Creek	$52,000
#23	Dallas	Heath	$51,000
#24	Fort Worth	Colleyville	$50,000
#25	San Antonio	Shavano Park	$47,000
#26	Houston	Sugar Land	$47,000
#27	Houston	Bellaire	$46,000
#28	Austin	Lakeway	$45,000
#29	Lubbock	Ransom Canyon	$45,000
#30	San Antonio	Alamo Heights	$45,000

What is unique about the founding of the town of Corsicana?

Now with a population of twenty-one and one of the smallest towns in Texas, Corsicana was incorporated in 1973 for the purpose of legally selling alcohol in otherwise dry Navarro County, which clung to its "blue law" as most of the state was giving up such anachronisms.

Texas has long been famous for its oil production, but petroleum is still a finite resource—how is production holding up?

Texas produced about one billion barrels of oil per year in every year from 1966 to 1978 when a slow decline began. Some production was lost almost every year from 1979 and bottomed out at only 336,222,000 barrels in 2007—just over a third of what it had been thirty years before. Starting in 2008, new technology (including horizontal drilling and, yes, "fracking") made abandoned wells profitable again and sparked new exploration. So, despite the Great Recession, production began to increase dramatically, over 30 percent per year in 2012, 2013, and 2014, and leveled off back at a billion barrels per year since 2015.

Where does that rank nationally?

When oil was discovered on the North Slope of Alaska, it was feared that the Texas oil industry might be eclipsed, but production there has fallen to three hundred thousand barrels per day, which is less than 10 percent of Texas production. Texas now produces about one-third of all U.S. oil, ranking first by far, ahead of North Dakota, California, Alaska, and Oklahoma. Texas also has more proven reserves (10.5 billion barrels) than any other state and more refineries (twenty-six) than any other state. Petroleum is still very much "Texas tea."

Just how many oil wells are there in Texas?

As of 2017, there were 187,139 producing oil wells in Texas—about thirty-four thousand more than when the industry hit bottom in 2007. The era of uncontrollable gushers is gone, however. Those wells produce an average of just over fifteen barrels per day each.

Texas is also a large supplier of natural gas—does its history track that of petroleum?

Yes. Texas has over 130,000 producing gas wells, a number that has been on the decline since 2012, about double the number of second-place Pennsylvania and just under one-quarter of the gas wells in the country, which is about a quarter of the proven U.S. reserves. Texas gas production is about 5.6 trillion cubic feet of natural gas per year.

Where will they look when that is gone?

In recent years, scientists have discovered prodigious amounts of natural gas frozen as methane hydrate beneath the deep seabed. It exists in a volatile balance of temperature

A natural gas pipeline compressor station. Natural gas is also plentiful in Texas.

and pressure, and Texas researchers are trying to figure out how to recover it without triggering a catastrophic methane release that would send the world's climate back to the age of the dinosaurs.

Oil and gas must still run out one day—has Texas established itself with any renewable energy resources?

Texas's tall mountains are found in the desert west, so what hydroelectric power there is, about 1,100 megawatts, is generated from reservoirs such as those that tamed the Colorado River. However, Texans have found a way to make those relentless Panhandle winds useful, as the state is home to the third-largest wind farm in the United States, which churns across four counties and generates 782 megawatts of electricity. In fact, Texas contains four of the United States's ten largest wind projects and overall generates about 21,000 megawatts, or about one-quarter of all the wind power in the country.

How much does Texas export?

Counting both agricultural products and manufactured goods, Texas exports to foreign countries far more than any other state—more than $260 billion per year, much of it from the Port of Houston, which in cargo volume is the sixth largest in the world.

What industries are Texas's leading employers?

In 2017, Texas's aggregate work force of 12.5 million was broken down into the following broad categories:

- 1,972,000 in government (only 200,000 for the federal government, 417,000 state, 1,355,000 local)
- 1,680,000 in health and education (including teachers and medical employees)
- 1,670,000 in professional services (including science and technology and management)
- 1,327,000 in leisure and hospitality (including bartenders, wait staff, and hotel workers)
- 1,314,000 in retail
- 488,000 in transportation (including airline employees, truck drivers, and couriers)
- 215,000 in oil and gas and related support industries

Conservative politicians perennially run on the need to lower taxes, but how heavily are Texans actually taxed?

Texas nationally has the seventh-lowest tax burden of the fifty states. It is one of only eleven states not to have a state income tax. The state sales tax is 6.25 percent, although local entities (cities, school districts) can add as much as another 2 percent to that, as many have been forced to do as sleight-of-hand federal and state tax "cuts" really just shift the burden for essential services to local governments.

What was the deal with Enron?

Texas energy players celebrated after they managed to get the industry deregulated, and Enron was the ultimate upshot of grand larcenous schemes. It was an energy company formed by the merger of Houston Natural Gas with another entity, which through financial frauds of staggering proportions loaded its debt into subsidiary shell companies and absorbed other companies like an amoeba as its execs cashed in stock options worth hundreds of millions. When the house of cards collapsed, thousands of little employees lost pensions and savings, the once powerful accounting firm of Arthur Andersen was destroyed, and there was even talk that perhaps some government oversight was not a bad idea—but that soon passed.

How large a component of the Texas economy is the defense industry?

It is astronomical. In addition to the direct spending by the Department of Defense through two large army installations (Fort Hood and Fort Bliss), six Air Force bases (Lackland, Randolph, Laughlin, Dyess, Goodfellow, and Sheppard), and three naval air bases (in Corpus Christi, Kingsville, and Fort Worth), the list of giant corporate defense contractors is withering: Lockheed Martin, Bell Helicopter, Boeing, Vought, Raytheon, Hewlett Packard, Alliant Techsystems, Rockwell Collins, and many, many others.

Has the advent of high-tech industries had a great effect in Texas?

Although the integrated circuit, without which the modern computer would be impossible, was invented in Dallas, and there has always been a hi-tech presence there, much

Computer and IT services company Dell is headquartered in Round Rock.

What is the largest military base in the United States?

Fort Hood, named for the Civil War's Texan tactical wizard John Bell Hood, located outside Killeen at the border of the Hill Country with the Blacklands, is one of the largest military bases in the world with some 214,000 acres (866 square kilometers). It is the home base of the U.S. Army's III Corps and First Cavalry Division and is the most populous U.S. military installation anywhere, with about fifty-five thousand soldiers and civilian employees. At the beginning of World War II, the U.S. military needed an expansive property with open ground on which to test and train with its new tank destroyers. The initial 108,000 acres (437 square kilometers) was bought, and facilities built, within nine months of Pearl Harbor. While no one doubted Texans' patriotism, many local land-owners who had lived there for generations were very unhappy about the forced sale. Regimental museums on the post interpret Fort Hood's history.

of the industry's growth and development took place in the San Francisco area ("Silicon Valley"), and it was only with an influx of those companies to Texas that the full weight of the hi-tech revolution struck home. Austin, which was once virtually recession-proof because its economy was so diversified, is now so dependent on the computer industry that it is called "Silicon Hills," and about half of the city's entire payroll is now tied to some aspect of the industry. Both Dell and Apple, head-to-head competitors in the computer market, are docked there, as well as Freescale Semiconductor, Cirrus Logic, Silicon Labs, AMD, and many others. Compaq is in Houston, Datapoint and Rackspace in San Antonio, and EDS, Perot Systems, and Texas Instruments in Dallas. The arrival of so many new people with specialized skills and no experience with Texas culture has had a profound impact not just on the economy but on politics and society as well.

AGRICULTURE

How many farms are there in Texas?

The whole enterprise of enticing settlers to come to Texas was to create a rural yeomanry of family farms and ranches, and that was the anchor of both Texas's economy and society for generations. Now, however, economic realities are changing that. In 1940, there were 420,000 farms in Texas; in 2016, there were 241,500, so nearly half of them are gone. Nevertheless, Texas still ranks first nationally in the number of farms and in several other agricultural indices but only third in cash receipts, behind California and Iowa. The impact of the decline in the number of farms has fallen most heavily on the family operations, as many have been absorbed into larger, more mechanized, corporately owned "agribusiness." Agriculture contributes some $24 billion to Texas's annual economy, but this efficiency has come at great cost to a way of life.

What is the "Winter Garden"?

The Winter Garden is a term that refers to the agricultural area of the south Texas Brush Country, made productive by irrigation, and with an extraordinarily long growing season that allows up to three crops per year of some vegetables.

Texas as an antebellum state was dependent upon cotton for its economy. Is cotton still "king"?

Texas still leads the United States in cotton production, yielding 9,322,000 bales at 480 pounds each in 2017, or nearly 4.5 billion pounds of cotton, which is about 40 percent of all U.S. cotton. Most of it is exported around the Pacific Rim as well as to Turkey and Mexico.

Texas produces more cotton than any other state in America.

Texas is famous for its cattle and cotton, but how much does it produce of other crops?

Figures on agricultural production must always be read with the caution that good years and bad years mix with each other unpredictably. One year of bumper crop is seldom followed by another. Pecan production, for instance, swings wildly from one year to the next depending upon rainfall, pest control, and other factors. Nevertheless, a one-year cross-section of the farming industry reveals Texas as an engine of absolutely staggering agricultural production. In 2017, Texas contributed to the national table and for export:

Texas Agricultural Production 2017

Crop	Production
Corn	313,650,000 bushels
Sorghum	94,500,000 bushel
Wheat	68,150,000 bushels
Sugar Cane	1,552,000 tons
Rice	1,146,000,000 pounds
Potatoes	849,000,000 pounds
Peanuts	756,000,000 pounds
Watermelons	638,000,000 pounds
Grapefruits	384,000,000 pounds
Cabbage	183,000,000 pounds
Spinach	98,400,000 pounds
Pumpkins	87,750,000 pounds

Texas Agricultural Production 2017 (contd.)

Crop	Production
Cucumbers	68,000,000 pounds
Pecans	38,000,000 pounds
Grapes	32,140,000 pounds
Carrots	26,400,000 pounds
Oranges	1,690,000 boxes
Peaches	5,000,000 pounds

How did Texas wine get to be such a big deal?

Actually, Texas wine always should have been a big deal. Padres with some of the earliest Spanish entradas planted grapevines so there would be wine for Holy Communion, and they were planted more than a hundred years before they appeared in California. When the first German immigrants arrived in the Hill Country in the 1840s, they were surprised by its similarity—fertile river plains flanked by limestone hills—to the Rhine River region, which was famous for wine. Texas viticulturalists such as Thomas Munson gained worldwide reputations. Evangelical tambourine banging for Prohibition, effected in 1918, brought all that crashing down. A new industry grew slowly, helped by a cabernet from the Llano Estacado Winery (now the state's second largest) winning a double gold medal at an international competition, and by the efforts of an outspoken agriculture commissioner, Jim Hightower, who promoted the effort tirelessly (and gained attention with jokes about "The Grapes of Erath County"). Today, Texas ranks fourth among the states in wine production, with over 4,000 tons (3,628,739 kilograms) per year from about two hundred wineries.

Haven't Texas "blue laws" passed from the scene yet?

Not at all. About one-quarter of Texas counties are dry either whole or in part. Originally, blue laws prohibiting any commerce on Sundays were intended to push people into church but eventually were limited to restricting sales of cars and alcohol. Today, the law is a byzantine patchwork of state and local legalism: a restaurant may serve alcohol after 10 A.M. on a Sunday if and only if it comes with the availability of food, but stores that sell for off-premises consumption may not sell alcohol between 1 A.M. and noon on Sundays. The argument against liquor has always been religious, while the arguments in favor of it are based on economics and personal liberty. In Texas, this can get confused with moralists' claim to the right to regulate the behavior of others.

Why is the Texas pecan industry so volatile?

In addition to the hazards of pests, drought, and hailstorms, it is in the genetics of pecan trees that one year of heavy production is almost inevitably followed by an off year. At least the large orchards are more automated now, with harvest done by mechanical tree-shakers and the cracking and shelling also done by machine. In former years, pecan shelling was done by hand, and one of the most contentious labor actions in Texas history was in 1938, when the predominantly Latino membership of the pecan shellers' union struck. They were led by twenty-one-year-old firebrand Emma Tenayuca (1916–1999) of San Antonio. Herself not Hispanic but Comanche, whose family had lived in the area since before Anglo settlement, she organized the workers, but her communist party membership was so controversial that national labor figures assumed local control. The conditions that they struck against were appalling: they were paid seven cents per pound for shelled pecan halves (six cents for pieces) in factories in which there were no restrooms and pecan dust brought on tuberculosis at triple the national rate. The strike succeeded and then failed. After a

Pecans are a popular cash crop in Texas, as well as a favorite in the state's famous pies, but the orchards are vulnerable to bad weather and insects.

three-month shutdown, federal arbitrators granted the shellers a wage of 25 cents an hour, which made pecan production unprofitable. The owners then mechanized the operation, throwing ten thousand shellers out of work.

With traditional agriculture being such a presence in the Texas economy, has organic farming gained any large foothold?

Not so much. According to the Agricultural Statistics Service, there are only 178 certified organic farms in Texas, which is 0.07 percent of the total number of Texas farms. This ranks seventeenth among the states, with California by comparison having 2,632 organic farms, or 3.38 percent of their total. Texas ranks ninth in organic acreage, however, with over 125,000 acres and is sixth in value of organic products, with about $200 million.

With such a small commitment, does Texas lead in any kind of organic production?

Texas grows about 90 percent of all the organic cotton in the United States on about 10,800 acres (44 square kilometers), not in the traditional southeastern cotton counties but on the western plains. This is because the drier humidity is a natural deterrent to many pests and the cold winters completely kill and dry out the previous year's plants, which otherwise would have to be done chemically. Texas also grows about 95 percent of U.S. organic peanuts on nearly 5,000 acres (20 square kilometers) and leads the country in organic rice acreage, just under 20,000 acres (81 square kilometers), closely followed by California.

When one thinks of organic farms, table vegetables typically come first to mind. Is this not a large component of Texas organics?

Actually, no, but it used to be. Today, there are fewer than 1,500 acres (6 square kilometers) of organic veggies grown in Texas, which is less than 1 percent of the U.S. total. Largely, this is due to economic globalization, which makes it cheaper at the supermarket to import produce from abroad. Organic vegetable farming can also be quite labor intensive.

Texas ranches were founded upon cattle; does the state still lead the country in that department?

Within Texas, about half of all agricultural cash receipts arise from the sale of beef cattle. The Texas herd of about 12.3 million animals—although this can vary considerably from year to year based on drought conditions, cost of hay, and market prices—is roughly 13 percent of all the cattle in the United States. Annual sales total is in excess of $11 billion. In addition, the raw milk from Texas's half-million-strong dairy herd brings in another $1.8 billion.

It seems like pigs were a necessity on every frontier farm; is Texas now a leading pork producer?

Texans do love their bacon and sausage for breakfast but seem mostly content to let others raise the hogs. At the end of 2016, Texas held only about 1.25 percent of the U.S. swine herd. However, the more than two million head of swine that were slaughtered supplied nearly 370 million pounds (167,829,177 kilograms) of pork.

A range war was once fought between cattlemen and sheep men—are sheep still raised extensively in Texas?

What night-riding cowboys were unable to effect in the 1880s, market conditions have now accomplished instead. While vast swaths of west Texas and the Hill Country remain ideally suited for the raising of sheep and goats, that industry seems to be nearing the end of a steep decline. In 1880, there might have been six million sheep in Texas; from

---

Organic farming seems pretty trendy— are most of these farmers younger?

Not at all; only 9 percent of Texas organic farmers are even under thirty-five, and more than two-thirds of them are over fifty. What this means is that Texas farmers are pragmatic. Since farming is a risky business anyway, they always have their eye open to make a higher profit margin with a different kind of operation, and organic food does sell at a substantial premium above the regular market.

193

a high of ten million in 1940, Texas sheep now number only about seven hundred thousand, producing about 1 million pounds (453,592 kilograms) of wool. Goats in Texas number about nine hundred thousand for all kinds, only eighty thousand of them Angora goats from which mohair is clipped—although that is about half the entire remaining world production.

CLOTHING INDUSTRY

Speaking of cattle and leather, who have been the greatest Texas boot makers?

Connoisseurs of fine boots have their own favorites, but it is hard to top the heritage of Nocona Boots. Starting in 1879, master leather worker H. J. Justin (1859–1918) of Indiana settled in Spanish Fort, where the Chisholm Trail crossed the Red River, borrowed $35 from the local barber to open a boot shop, and hit upon an admirable scheme. Cowboys driving cattle northward would stop in, get their feet measured for new boots, and pick them up on the return trip. After the Katy Railroad came through nearby Nocona, Justin moved there, pulled his sons and daughter Enid into the business when they were old enough, and by 1908, they were selling boots (averaging $11 per pair—a whopping $288 in current value) in Mexico, Cuba, Canada, and twenty-six states. After Justin's death in 1918, his sons heeded a call of the Fort Worth Chamber of Commerce to relocate there. Enid, however, felt so strongly he would have wanted them to stay that she remained in Nocona, borrowed $5,000, and started Nocona Boots with seven employees who stayed with her. Enid Justin was a superior business-woman, drumming up new retail markets, seizing upon automation when it made sense, and she was adaptable. With the oil boom, she began manufacturing lace-up boots 16 inches (41 centimeters) tall that the roughnecks loved. Her company and that of her brothers' reunified in 1981, have since been acquired by Berkshire-Hathaway, and remain a force in Texas boot making.

In central Texas, a strong case could be made for Sam Lucchese (1868–1929), a Sicilian immigrant who settled in San Antonio, another stickler for quality whose shop was turning out thirty-five pairs of custom boots per day in 1919. As with the Justins, Lucchese Boot Company was a family operation for a couple of generations before going corporate. Lucchese's grandson and namesake became a boot maker to Hollywood movie stars from John Wayne to Gary Cooper (and Zsa Zsa Gabor), as well as for Lyndon and Lady Bird Johnson. In 1970, he sold out to the holding company Blue Bell, Inc.

Did anyone get similarly famous making cowboy hats?

Yes, but the famous Stetson "Boss of the Plains" model was not made in Texas. There was a sickly haberdasher named John B. Stetson (1830–1906) in Philadelphia who traveled to the frontier in the 1860s for the dry air and designed the broad-brimmed hat to keep the sun out of his eyes and channel the rain away from his face. The Texas Rangers were among the first to recognize the hat's virtues, and Stetsons became the cowboy wear of choice. The company stayed in business for about a century, then ceased making hats and licensed out its famous name to other products, such as cologne, before going under in 1986. That design has been widely appropriated, of course, and there are master hatters in Texas who customize headgear for the discriminating. None have more experience than Texas Hatters in Lockhart, which has been in business for more than ninety years, fitting out celebrities from the cast of *Lonesome Dove* to the Prince of Wales.

John B. Stetson is credited with inventing the classic cowboy hat, which he produced in the company he founded in 1865.

How did Texas become a manufacturing center of men's slacks?

The late 1800s brought a new wave of immigration that sometimes brought in nationalities previously rare or unknown in Texas. Among them were Maronite Christians fleeing religious discrimination in the Mediterranean coast of the Ottoman Empire. Unlike their European counterparts who maintained close-knit ethnic communities, these Lebanese-Syrians blended quickly into the Texas population and for the most part made a success of their adventure. Nahim Abraham, for example, went all the way to the Panhandle, where he operated the Fair Store in the city of Canadian for decades, and Abraham Dabaghi settled in Huntsville, where he became a city fixture as the long time proprietor of the Raven Café (named for Sam Houston) on the courthouse square. Some were skilled haberdashers. Joseph Haggar began manufacturing slacks in Dallas, holding down costs by sending out piece work to local women to do at home. The brothers Mansour and Abihider Farah set up business in El Paso to utilize cheap Mexican labor there. Both of those companies expanded to become major players in American menswear.

Not much clothing is more associated with Texas than blue jeans. Aren't they a Texas invention?

Nope. Denim work pants reinforced with copper rivets originated with Bavarian immigrant tailor Levi Strauss in California.

Does Texas have any leading jewelry companies?

The flood of European immigrants in the nineteenth century brought a number of skilled jewelers and watchmakers to Texas, but by far, the more astonishing story is a modern one. Wisconsin native Kendra Scott moved to Austin and began designing jewelry in 2002 on a shoestring budget, cold-calling stores and boutiques and taking orders, needing to sell samples to buy materials to fill the orders. From a beginning in her spare bedroom, she now runs a $1 billion-dollar business with seventy-five retail outlets of her own and vends to hundreds of others. An important aspect of her brand is her generosity to a spectrum of charities.

Similarly, James Avery of Kerrville began crafting jewelry in his mother-in-law's garage in 1954. Much of his work had a strong Southwestern motif and proved immensely popular. The collection grew to over eleven hundred pieces, produced in five studios scattered around the Hill Country, and sold in some fifty of his own stores around the country. His pieces are bought avidly in the various church retreat camps of the area, and the company also has bestowed a lot of money to charities. Avery was ninety-six when he passed away in 2018.

RELIGION

How religious are Texans compared to the rest of the United States?

According to the U.S. religion census of 2010, Texas ranks first among the states in the number of Protestant evangelicals with nearly 6.5 million (at that time), and it also ranks first with another 1.5 million "nondenominational" evangelicals, which takes in those who attend independent "megachurches." Texas ranks second (after Pennsylvania) in the number of nonevangelical Protestants, which includes Episcopalians and Presbyterians. Officially, Texas ranks third in the number of Catholics (after California and New York), but that number may be higher because the preponderance of undocumented immigrants not counted in the census are undoubtedly Catholic. Perhaps surprising, Texas has more Muslims than any other state, with over 420,000, and is second in Hindu population, third in Buddhists, and fifth in Mormons.

The Bishop's Palace is the most opulent mansion in Galveston, but aren't Catholic clergy supposed to live simply?

What is now known as the Bishop's Palace began as a home for Galveston congressman Walter Gresham, his wife, and nine children. Begun in 1887 and finished in 1893, it is an almost gaudy Romanesque revival fantasy of 19,082 square feet (5,816 square meters) on four floors, built of rusticated stone and finished inside with rare woods. The Galveston diocese acquired the home in 1923 to house the bishop, but it is also used for other functions. The diocese opened the house for tours in 1963, with income used to help Catholic students at the University of Texas Medical Branch nearby, and the upper floor was used to house seminary students. The massively strong structure sheltered hundreds during the Great Storm of 1900, while most of those who took refuge in nearby St. Mary's Cathedral were killed when the roof collapsed.

How did Texas become such a locus of evangelical churches?

The evangelical movement known as the Second Great Awakening began in the upper Appalachians in the early 1800s. It was highly emotional, highly Pentecostal, and placed little emphasis on formal education. It spread down the Ohio and then the Mississippi, and it reached Texas at just about the same time as independence and freedom from enforced Catholicism. Typical of the early missionaries who reached Texas was Sumner Bacon (1790–1844), a Cumberland Presbyterian. After being denied a license by the Arkansas Presbytery for being illiterate, Bacon sneaked into Texas anyway to distribute Bibles. The more prosaic Presbyterian, Episcopal, and Congregationalist denominations were slow to respond to calls to send missionaries to Texas, and the evangelicals' emotional, accusatory revival preaching struck home on the frontier, where many men were leading such morally impeachable lives that the fear of hell's fire could affect a conversion where theological discussion could not.

Did racism not play a role in the entrenchment of evangelicalism in Texas?

Sadly, it did. Two factors reinforced each other: first, the widespread anti-Hispanic feeling that followed the revolution; and second, the antipathy of evangelical missionaries toward any practice but their own, but especially Catholicism, which was the religion of Latin America. Evangelical Americans, however, were equal-opportunity loathers and treated the Germans and central and eastern Europeans (Poles, Czechs, Moravians) little better. The Southern branches of evangelical Protestantism—particularly the Southern Baptists—split from their Northern churches over supporting slavery, which made those congregations bastions against racial progress that lasted for generations.

What is the world's largest seminary?

Located between Fort Worth and suburban Arlington, the Southwest Baptist Theological Seminary has a faculty of about one hundred and more than three thousand students. Ironically, one of the buildings on campus was a notorious speakeasy during Prohibition.

When did the Church of Christ first come to Texas?

The Second Great Awakening informed a related "Restoration" movement that carried scriptural legalism almost to its logical extreme. Springing simultaneously from Pennsylvania and Kentucky, this was a sect that advocated a return to the Christianity of the first century. Hence, mem-

The Church of Christ came to the Texas frontier in the late nineteenth century thanks to people like reformer Alexander Campbell.

bers became notorious for their austere services, especially the lack of an organ or piano to accompany the singing, and later (after a schism in the 1880s) for their stance that they are the elect of God and the only ones going to heaven. In this denomination, churches split and lives were wrecked over such issues as whether the communion wine must be shared from one cup or could be served in separate portions and who, after temperance became a national call, built a scriptural case that the wine in the Bible was not "wine" at all but unfermented grape juice. Adherents of the reformer Alexander Campbell, they were often known as Campbellites. Frontier Texans did not know about Campbell, but they knew that there were camels in the Bible, and when they first showed up in Nacogdoches, one diarist noted that the "Camelites" had come to town. To his credit, one of the movement's founders, Barton W. Stone, was an abolitionist, and as the Churches of Christ observed the splits in the Methodist and Baptist churches, they preached that slavery was a secular political issue and ought not to divide fellowships.

How did the Episcopal Church come to Texas?

The earliest attempts to establish the Episcopal Church in Texas fell apart; members of that denomination in Mexican Texas were forbidden to practice their faith openly, as were all Protestants. During the Revolution, New York minister Reverend Richard Salman undertook to start an Episcopal colony, but his land grant proved to be bogus, and once he got to Texas the locals refused to accept him. The Episcopal hierarchy also got in the way, as the first two applications to be foreign missionaries to Texas were turned down. The first Episcopal congregation in Texas was established with Christ Church in Matagorda on January 27, 1839, followed by a second church in Houston six weeks later. Although the interior of east Texas was quite thickly settled, attempts to get a minister there proved fruitless for years. Not until 1855 did Frances ("Fanny") Cox Henderson, the formidable wife of Texas's first governor, James Pinckney Henderson, take matters in hand. The vestrymen of San Augustine provided her with credentials, she journeyed to Philadelphia (which was her hometown, anyway), and she became the first woman to address the diocese. They were too shocked by her boldness to refuse, and Texas soon gained Episcopal congregations in Nacogdoches, San Augustine, Rusk, and Palestine.

Did any new religious denominations actually begin in Texas?

In the hothouse of evangelical fervor, denominations seemed to compete with each other in loudness to demonstrate their holiness. But for some reason, the Cross Timbers around Fort Worth became a locus of different stripes of dissent. On February 2, 1884, the Reverend Henry Renfro (1831–1885), a former pupil of Rufus Burleson (a founder of Baylor University, who had baptized Sam Houston) and founder of the town of Burleson, was put on church trial for infidelity. Renfro had admitted to reading unapproved authors, such as Jewish-Dutch philosopher Baruch Spinoza, and questioned whether doctrinal purity was all that important in light of scriptures such as Micah 6:8, in which all that God requires of a person is to live out justice, mercy, and humility. A few years thereafter, a group of Seventh-day Adventists, an offshoot of end-timer Millerites, whose destruction of the world

---

What is meant by the "Texas painted churches"?

When Central Europeans began arriving in Texas, they alleviated their home-sickness by painting their modest new frame churches in a spectacular way to remind them of the ancient cathedrals they had left behind. The best examples are in the towns of Dubina, Praha, High Hill, and Ammannsville, and there are organized tours available through the Chamber of Commerce in Schulenberg. That town was founded in 1842 and settled largely by Czech and German immigrants. Their culture is preserved not just in the availability of kolaches in local bakeries but also in the Schulenburg Historical Museum and, perhaps more festively, in the Texas Polka Music Museum.

---

had not come to pass, materialized down the road from Burleson and started the town of Keene, later the location of an Adventist college. Throughout these years, Texas grew thick with unaffiliated "holiness" and "perfectionist" churches to whom all previous religious regimens were insufficient for salvation. In 1904 they signed a compact near the little town of Rising Star, north of Brownwood, creating the Church of the Nazarene, and they added more than one hundred congregations in a merger signed at Pilot Point near Denton four years later. There are now well over three hundred Nazarene congregations in Texas.

Who were the Sanctified Sisters?

Martha White McWhirter (1827–1904) was the wife of Belton miller and grocer George McWhirter, resident in the county since 1855. Together, they established the Union Sunday School, which welcomed people from all denominations, although the McWhirters were themselves Methodists. Their marriage began to fray after the deaths of two (and eventually six) of their twelve children and her suspicion that he was trying to initiate an affair with one of their servants. Persuaded that God was punishing her, she prayed fervently for guidance and emerged convinced that she had received the holy spirit and been "sanctified." She should continue her household chores, but she declared herself freed from any more intimate contact with the unsanctified, including her husband. Mrs. McWhirter shared this revelation with ladies in her Sunday school, a number of whom shortly also received the gift of the spirit so they could stop having sex with their husbands. As Mr. McWhirter moved into an apartment above his store, "Sanctified Sisters" began moving into their house to escape the wrath of their jilted husbands. Belton was scandalized and gossip flew, but Martha organized the Belton Woman's Commonwealth, which became self-supporting through crafts, dairy products, and her inheritance of her husband's estate upon his death in 1887. Eventually, the group opened a hotel downtown, and in time, they gained such financial clout that Mrs. McWhirter was invited to take a seat on the Belton Board of Trade. She withdrew from active management at seventy-two but accompanied the members when they sold out their holdings in Belton and established themselves in comfort near Washington, D.C.

Who were the "Holy Jumpers"?

Early on in the Anglo frontier, Methodists were the most fervent Protestant evangelists. Stephen F. Austin, tasked with keeping his colony Catholic, wrote that the "Methodist excitement" caused him more trouble than horse thieves. By the end of the 1800s, however, Methodists had retired to the back bench and let others do the shouting. That sat ill with some in the church, and they broke away to form the Metropolitan Church Association, better known as the Society of the Burning Bush, whose followers withdrew into religious communes. Backed by a wealthy patron, a chartered train pulled into Tyler in 1913 with 375 society members, who moved onto a 1,575-acre (6.4-square-kilometer) farm about 15 miles (24 kilometers) south of town. They constructed modest houses for married couples and dormitories for the unmarried, they took their meals in a common dining hall, and visitors were treated hospitably, but mixing was not encouraged. They built a large tabernacle. Worship centered on demonstrations of the spirit, especially back flips, although the tabernacle was floored with several inches of sawdust to ease the landings of those who were not quite as possessed as they thought. When they sang praises, they hopped up and down, which led to their local nickname, the Holy Jumpers. Members who were caught in a sin were not punished but were taken into the tabernacle and wailed over. Despite fruit and pecan orchards having been planted before their arrival, they seem to have been better at back flips than farming; a local grocer sued them for $12,000 in arrears, and the property was seized and sold for debt in 1919.

What is the "Cowboy Camp Meeting"?

When Presbyterian missionary William Bloys (1847–1917) arrived at Fort Davis in 1888, it was still an active cavalry post, high in the desert mountains, amid large ranches scattered so thinly that at first sight, the land seemed uninhabited. Bloys had applied to be a foreign missionary, but he was turned down because of lung disease and was sent to the desert partly to restore his health. Ranchers who came into the fort appealed to him to provide something in the way of services. So Bloys preached a circuit—exhausting in this vast area—and in 1890, he organized a camp meeting at Skillman's Grove, 16 miles (26 kilometers) west of the fort, first attended by forty-three people under a brush arbor. It became an annual event; Bloys purchased the site for $2 an acre, built a tabernacle in 1912, and in 1913 the attendance topped 1,000 for the first time. The event blossomed in both popularity and good fellowship among those who attended; apparently, the closest thing to a controversy erupted when Blind Merriman, the piano tuner, accidentally fell into the Baptists' baptizing hole, and there was fervent discussion over whether or not he had been saved.

What makes the Cowboy Camp Meeting so unique?

Reverend Bloys was an amazingly practical man. When he first began preaching in west Texas, the population was so thinly settled and there were so few preachers that he would baptize people into whatever denomination they wanted. After starting his camp meetings, he insisted that all contributions had to be truly voluntary, so he never passed a collection plate, and he allowed no buying and selling on the grounds. In starting an association to help run the whole enterprise, he directed that it must move by consensus, and all members' decisions had to be unanimous. (This they were, including their decision not to let Bloys retire; he was seventy when he died in 1917.) The Bloys Camp Meeting spun off numerous other revivals around the Southwest on the same model, and the original still thrives, now attended annually by about three thousand people, who keep his traditions intact.

Who was Don Pedrito?

From the nineteenth and well into the twentieth century, medical care was scarce in the south Texas Brush Country. At a time when only one medical doctor lived

A faith healer at a time when medical care was hard to come by in south Texas, Don Pedro Jaramillo was called "the healer of Los Olmos Creek."

between Laredo and Corpus Christi, the predominantly Latino population turned to *curanderos*, faith healers whose fame spread by word of mouth. They specialized in their methods, whether an *oracionista* who worked through prayer, a *yerbero*, or herbalist. In South Texas, the most famous became Don Pedro Jaramillo, a Tarascan (also called Purépecha) Indian from Guadalajara, in the Mexican state of Jalisco, who settled on the Los Olmos Ranch in 1881. "Don Pedrito" charged no fees to the poor but was well supported by donations. After the founding of the nearby towns of Alice in 1888 and Falfurrias in 1895, he purchased food by the wagonload, which he dispensed to the needy along with his cures. He was noted for the prominence of the number nine in his prescriptions—to repeat a ritual nine times or take a certain medicine for nine days. After his death in 1907, Jaramillo's grave in Falfurrias became a shrine, and he is regarded as a folk saint, although never canonized by the Catholic Church.

EDUCATION

Who was the "Father of Texas Education"?

In some aspects of his leadership, the Republic of Texas's second elected president, Mirabeau Lamar, was an impractical and ineffectual dreamer, but he put education in Texas on a solid footing as the Texas Congress passed a law setting aside 3 leagues of land (which equaled 13,285 acres [54 square kilometers]) in each county for the support of public schools and a single reserve of 50 leagues (221,420 acres [896 square kilometers]) to eventually fund a public university. Education, however, was considered a local matter, and the Republic did not involve itself in it.

Where does Texas rank nationally in high school graduation rate?

Texas has by far more schools, nearly three hundred, with a 100 percent graduation rate, than any other state in the nation, although that is partly a function of the huge number of school districts, more than eleven hundred. (However, eleven states have *no* schools with 100 percent graduation.) Overall, Texas's graduation rate of 90.9 percent ranks sixth, after Nebraska (93.7 percent), Kentucky (93.1 percent), Iowa and Missouri (93 percent), and Massachusetts (91.2 percent).

The second president of the Republic of Texas, Mirabeau Lamar, is remembered as the "Father of Texas Education."

What was the Robin Hood Plan?

Up to 1983, Texas funded its public schools through a patchwork of the Permanent School Fund, plus the proceeds of the state lottery, a tiny portion ($0.0025) of the state sales tax, and whatever supplement might be passed by each legislative session. This resulted in enormous disparity in the quality of education between wealthy school districts and poor ones. In response, MALDEF (the Mexican American Legal Defense Fund) filed suit against the state education commission, alleging that the arrangement violated the Texas Constitution's mandate for an efficient program of public education. The Texas Supreme Court agreed unanimously but then also threw out the legislature's first two attempts to rectify the injustice. In 1993 it came up with a plan that did pass Court scrutiny, under which a wealthy school district could arrange to give part of its tax revenue to a poor district (hence, "Robin Hood") or else enter a byzantine schedule of taxes, caps, and state recapture to redistribute the wealth.

What happened to "Robin Hood"?

In 2005 the Texas Supreme Court changed its mind. Robin Hood's effect was that this transfer of wealth forced many school districts to increase local property taxes to the statutory limit as to amount to a state property tax, which was unconstitutional. Moreover, the legislature, instead of dedicating recapture money to needy districts, siphoned off $2.8 billion to finance a cut in business taxes. In 2011 the legislature slashed school spending by about $5 billion; further lawsuits prompted the Supreme Court to step away, ruling that school financing met "minimum constitutional standards," but was a mess. As results made themselves felt in students' declining test scores, into the breech stepped a proliferation of entrepreneurial "charter" schools, privately run but taking a share of dwindling state money. As parents pulled children from public schools into charter schools or opted for "home-schooling," public districts, whose share of state money is allocated by enrollment, suffered even more financial pressure: not only do they have fewer students than they would without competition from charter schools, but state spending per student has declined nearly 20 percent in the past decade. When the nightmare will end is anyone's guess.

What is "No Pass, No Play"?

At the same time the legislature revamped the school finance system under order of the Texas Supreme Court, it also took note of declining scores of Texas students on college entrance standardized tests and took some stern action. One regimen was called "No Pass, No Play," under which students who were failing a subject were suspended for six weeks from participating in sports or other extracurricular activities, which could resume once they pulled their grades up. In a state where high school sports is often the lifeblood of a community and where people recognized that a school's best athletes were not necessarily the brightest scholars, this was soon regarded as too draconian, and the suspension was reduced to three weeks, with students still allowed to practice their skills, just not publicly perform. Similarly, school districts also began requiring students to pass end-of-year academic skills tests in certain grades before being passed through. Here, too, the initial targets came to be seen as too rigorous and were relaxed, but teachers still complained with good reason that now they had time in the classroom only to drill in the rote facts of the tests while neglecting such other essential concepts as critical thinking.

How did higher education get started in Texas?

The first colleges in Texas were founded by religious denominations, and just as in the competition for souls, the Methodists and Baptists were the leading contenders. The first was

---

What was the worst school disaster in American history?

With bringing in the East Texas field, new towns sprang up in the area like mushrooms, each with new families and children. All the towns in western Rusk County combined into a single school district, whose pride and joy was the New London Consolidated School, a $300,000 marvel that included administration offices, a gymnasium and sports complex, and, best of all, seven oil wells right on the campus. However, even with all that wealth behind them, the contractors built the school on the cheap, deciding not to vent the heating radiators into proper flues but just emptying exhaust into the walls and crawl spaces. Gas began leaking, and at 3:20 P.M. on Monday, March 18, 1937, the school blew up like a bomb, and bricks pelted down a quarter mile away. The death toll was 293 children, which would have been much higher if the lower grades had not already gone home for the day.

Rutersville College, located in the town founded by Methodist evangelist Martin Ruter, in 1840. Baylor University began in 1845 in the town of Independence, not far from the Republic's capital in Washington, and later moved to Waco. The Presbyterian Austin College was not far behind, having begun in Huntsville in 1849 and since moved to Sherman.

Where was the first Protestant church college in Texas established?

The town of Rutersville lay 7 miles (11 kilometers) northeast of La Grange in Fayette County, and there the Republic of Texas chartered the country's first institution of higher learning. The college was the project of Methodist missionary Martin Ruter, who had to give up the school's religious affiliation to win government backing. At its height, the two-story school taught nearly two hundred students in 1844.

How many colleges and universities are there in Texas now?

That depends on who is doing the counting and how they count them, but about 175; 63 of them are private and 112 are public. Texas A&M University is the oldest, opening in 1876; the University of Texas is the largest, with more than fifty thousand students; Rice University in Houston is probably the most prestigious in the most fields. Total enrollment in Texas colleges for both juniors and seniors is about 1,550,000.

What is the Permanent University Fund?

At the same time that the Congress of the Republic of Texas set aside three leagues of land in each county to finance public schools, the fifty leagues of land set aside to fund a state university became the nucleus of a permanent endowment. In 1858 this was in-

Texas A & M University in College Station is the state's oldest public university. It has a student body of nearly sixty-nine thousand and an endowment approaching $10 billion.

Is Baylor University really as morally strict as its reputation holds?

After his two terms as Texas governor, Pat Neff served as president of Baylor from 1932 to 1947, famously denying coeds permission to wear nylons or makeup. Dancing had also been forbidden since the school's inception in 1845, thus it was rather a shock to the nation when that ban was lifted in April 1996. Fifth Street—the heart of the campus—was blocked off, and Baylor president Robert Sloan (1949–) and his wife, Sue, inaugurated the event, for which Sloan confided that they had learned the minuet. The school's morals did not deteriorate completely, for revelation of a culture of sexual assault among the football team that became public in 2015 hit the campus like a bomb. The scandal led to the firing of head coach Art Briles and the resignations of university president Kenneth Starr and athletic director Ian McCaw, among others, and criminal prosecutions of players.

creased with $100,000 in U.S. bonds, increased with another million acres of land under the 1876 Constitution, and another million acres when the University of Texas opened in 1883. Income from these lands—rents, grazing leases, water and mineral rights—was to be divided between the state's two flagship universities, two-thirds to the University of Texas and one-third to Texas A&M. The land was mostly in west and southwest Texas brush and was not worth much per acre, but oil was discovered when the Santa Rita No. 1 rig blew on May 28, 1923, and made the PUF vastly wealthy. The market value of its assets doubled from $6 billion in 2003 to $12 billion in 2008 before losing about 25 percent of its value in the recession that began in 2008. Beneficiaries have been expanded to include all sixteen units of the University of Texas system and all eleven units of the Texas A&M system. In 1984 a second endowment was established to contribute to Texas's other public universities, which are constitutionally ruled out of the PUF.

How many libraries are there in Texas?

According to the Texas Library Association, Texas has a total of 884 public libraries, comprising 550 principal installations and 334 branches and mobile units. Among the other states and District of Columbia, Texas ranks forty-first in state spending on libraries, forty-second in local spending, and forty-eighth in total operating revenue. As of the time of the publication of this book, Texas libraries welcome a total of 70.8 million visits from the public, or fewer than three visits in a year from each Texas resident, and these patrons borrow over 116 million items.

What was the first library in Texas?

There have always been some Texans who valued books and reading. When Dr. Ashbel Smith arrived in Texas in 1837 with trunks of medical texts and classics, President Sam Houston made him surgeon general of the Texas Army—and his roommate. Today, for an activity that is not a high priority for a majority of Texans, there is surprising competition for the honor of being Texas's first library. One of the more insistent claimants is the Dr. Eugene Clark Library in Lockhart, which was founded in 1899, the gift of a visiting New Orleans physician who took a liking to the town. While not Texas's first library, it is the oldest to still be housed in its original building. When steel magnate Andrew Carnegie undertook his philanthropic program to build libraries across America, Texas benefited greatly, with thirty-four Carnegie Free Libraries. The first grant of $5,000 went to the small town of Pittsburg in 1898; the oldest one still in operation is in Bryan, which opened in 1903. The first public library in Texas was the Galveston Mercantile Library, which opened in 1871. Henry Rosenberg (1824–1893), a Swiss immigrant who became immensely wealthy in Galveston commerce, left $600,000 to provide free library services to the city. The Rosenberg Library Association was formed in 1900, and while their aim to build a majestic library was stalled by the Great Storm of 1900, the present building opened in 1904. Having absorbed the collections of the then-Galveston Public Library, the Rosenberg also functions as a major historical repository. Texas's leading cities all seemed to get the idea at about the same time: the Dallas Public Library was founded in 1901, the same year as the Fort Worth Library; El Paso in 1902; and San Antonio in 1903—in each case with assists from the Carnegie Foundation. A Houston library opened in 1895 and obtained its own building in 1904, with a Colored Carnegie Library following in 1913. Austin was behind the curve, opening its first library in 1925 after the local chapter of the American Association of University Women went door to door in the city soliciting money and books.

How many presidential libraries are located in Texas?

Three because two U.S. presidents were from Texas, and one preferred that association to his own native state. They are: the Lyndon Baines Johnson Library and Museum in Austin

at the edge of the University of Texas campus, which opened in 1971; the George Bush Presidential Library, which opened in 1997 on the campus of Texas A&M University in College Station; and the George W. Bush Presidential Library and Museum, which opened on the campus of Southern Methodist University in Dallas in 2013.

Why did some people refer to the LBJ Library as "Ozymandias Hall"?

After retiring from office in 1969, former President Johnson knew that he was in failing health. It was uncertain how long he would live, but he wished to survive long enough to see his presidential library dedicated. Designed as ten rearing stories

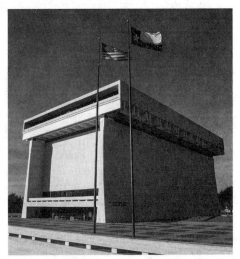

The Lyndon Baines Johnson Library and Museum in Austin is nicknamed "Ozymandias Hall" because of its imposing, grandiose architecture.

of travertine marble, located on the University of Texas campus near the LBJ School of Public Affairs and across the street from the law school, it was built quickly and dedicated in May 1971, with Johnson in attendance, and he died less than two years later. Local wags, noting the monumental scale of interior bronze bas reliefs of Johnson and that the construction began to deteriorate before anyone anticipated, called the structure Ozymandias Hall, a reference to the Percy Bysshe Shelley poem about a self-proclaimed king of kings whose only monument protruded from lonely desert sands.

ENVIRONMENT AND NATURE

PHYSIOGRAPHY, CLIMATE, AND WEATHER

What is Texas's general physical description?

There are a great many ways to characterize Texas from the most simplified routes of scenic topography for tourists to highly detailed maps of geology, hydrology, or ecology. The latter lends itself to the most useful combination of being detailed yet accessible. For simplicity, we have divided the state into seven biological regions: (1) the Gulf Coast, which includes tidal marshes and covers about 10 million acres in a band along the 370-mile (595-kilometer) general curve of the Gulf Coast; (2) the Piney Woods, which extend over about 16 million acres (64,750 square kilometers) in a broad belt running up the east side of the state; (3) the Brush Country, about 21 million acres (84,984 square kilometers) of semiarid scrub inland from the southern coast; (4) the Blackland Prairies and Post Oak, a patchwork of related ecosystems totaling about 34 million acres (137,593 square kilometers) between the Brush Country and Piney Woods, extending north to the Red River; (5) the Hill Country, a 25-million-acre (101,171-square-kilometer) complex of broken hills, plateaus, and a large, ancient volcanic uplift; (6) the Trans-Pecos, a desert-dominated region of 16 million acres lying west of the Hill Country; and (7) the Panhandle-Plains of predominantly grassland in the northwest of the state, of two types: the first is 19 million acres (76,890 square kilometers) defined as the Rolling Plains that extend west to an escarpment known as the Caprock, which vaults 1,000 feet up to the second type, the Staked Plains, which spread over 24 million stunningly level acres (97,125 square kilometers).

What have the temperature extremes been in Texas?

Oddly, both the extreme high and extreme low temperatures in Texas have been recorded twice, many years apart. The highest temperature ever measured was 120 degrees

Fahrenheit (49 degrees Celsius) at Seymour in Baylor County, southwest of Wichita Falls, in 1936, and at Monahans in Ward County, near the southeast corner of New Mexico, in 1994. The lowest temperature ever recorded was -23 degrees Fahrenheit (-31 degrees Celsius) at Tulia in Swisher County, about halfway between Lubbock and Amarillo in 1899, and at Seminole, in Gaines County, southwest of Lubbock, in 1933. All are located in areas of exposed prairie: Seymour on the Rolling Plains and the other three on the Staked Plains.

How has climate change affected temperatures in Texas?

Whether or not one accepts the notion of planetary warming, there is no doubt that Texas has been getting dramatically hotter. In Austin, for instance, since the city began recording temperatures in the nineteenth century, it has experienced an average of eleven days over 100 degrees each year; in the past two decades, this has accelerated, the worst being 2011, with ninety days over 100 degrees Fahrenheit (38 degrees Celsius) and also a new all-time temperature record of 112 degrees Fahrenheit (44 degrees Celsius). The increase is so dramatic that some local weathercasters now begin calculating an average back only a half century or so, which gives people a frame of reference with their lifetimes but obscures the scale of the difference.

What is the average winter snowfall in Texas?

Even as the growing season increases from north to south, the average amount of snowfall decreases from north to south. In an average year, Amarillo receives about 18 inches (46 centimeters) of snow, Lubbock 8 inches (20 centimeters), and San Angelo 2.4 inches (6 centimeters). In central Texas, it is more common to have an ice storm than snow, but Austin averages 0.6 inches (1.5 centimeters) per year and San Antonio 0.5 inches (1.3 centimeters). South of there, years with no snow are not uncommon.

How much does rainfall vary in Texas?

From desert in the Trans-Pecos to the humid Piney Woods, Texas rainfall increases steadily and dramatically from west to east: El Paso averages about 9 inches (23 centimeters) of rain per year. Alpine, in the high Chihuahuan Desert, averages 14.8 inches (37.6 centimeters); Abilene, on the Rolling Plains, 23.3 inches (59.2 centimeters); Dallas, in the Blackland Prairies, gets 29.5 inches (74.9 centimeters); Austin, at the edge of the Hill Country, receives 31.5 inches (80 centimeters); Bryan, 90 miles (85 kilometers) east of there, 39.1 inches (99.3 centimeters); Houston, in the Piney Woods, 44.8 inches (113.8 centimeters); and Beaumont, in the southeastern corner, 52.8 inches (134.1 centimeters).

Why are Austin and San Antonio so peculiarly subject to flash floods?

These two cities' susceptibility to flooding are a result of their geography, situated at the eastern edge (the "Balcones Escarpment") of the Hill Country. Warm, moist winds course in off the Gulf of Mexico and then suddenly rise upon meeting this barrier. When this coincides with the arrival of a cold front and an upper-level disturbance to trigger storms, the result can be devastating "rain bombs" of 10–12 inches (25.4–30.5 centimeters) or more. With the exponential growth of those cities, with the loss of natural ground cover or streets and buildings, and inadequate preparation to handle urban runoff, the resulting floods can be horrifying.

What is considered the most powerful rainstorm ever in Texas?

A rain event that lasted from September 8 to September 10, 1921, occurred at the edge of the Hill Country from San Antonio to north of Georgetown. Central San Antonio was left in as much as 9 feet (274 centimeters) of standing water. The community of Thrall, 20 miles (32 kilometers) east of Georgetown, endured 36.4 inches (92.5 centimeters) of rain in 18 hours—the heaviest rainfall event in U.S. history.

How bad can Texas's famous hailstorms get?

When he first became president, Texan Lyndon Johnson said that the situation in Vietnam made him feel like a hitchhiker caught in a Texas hailstorm: "I can't run, I can't hide, and I can't make it stop." The year 2016 was particularly bad for hail in Texas, as there were forty-five days in April and May in which at least one damaging hailstorm occurred within the state, with submitted insurance claims of more than $5 billion, $1.2 billion of that from a single event in San Antonio on April 12. This annual total shattered the previous record for hail claims of $1.9 billion, set only the year before in 2015. In June 2017, one thirty-minute hailstorm in Odessa generated $480 million in insurance claims.

How big can hailstones get?

Texas hailstones do not hold the U.S. records for either weight or diameter. Hailstones form in updrafts within thunderclouds into super-cooled atmosphere; as they fall, they are layered with more moisture or bond with other hailstones, are caught in another updraft, and repeat the process to grow. It takes only a 20-mph (32-km/h) updraft to create pea-sized hail and a 40-mph (64-km/h) updraft to make quarter-sized hail. Functionally, about the largest hail that can form in a supercell is about the size of softballs, or grapefruit, as in the 2017 Odessa storm; they require updrafts of more than 100 mph (161 km/h) to form. Wind-driven hail that size can kill people, pierce house roofs, and destroy whole lots of new cars at dealerships. Big hail causes the injuries, but they are not

Texas is somewhat infamous for its hailstorms that generate large, damaging balls of ice.

necessarily the most destructive storms. The "Black Friday" hailstorm of August 1979 in the Texas Panhandle flattened 550,000 acres (2,226 square kilometers) of crops with hail no bigger than marbles.

Would these not qualify as natural disasters?

Large hailstorms might elicit a federal disaster declaration, but that is mostly to ease the path for victims to refinance and fix the damage. Hailstorms in Texas, even bad ones, are so common that people just take them in stride. In Dallas–Fort Worth, for instance, hail caused $1.21 billion in damage on April 28, 1992; $656 million on April 28, 1995; $1.63 billion on May 5, 1995; $1.14 billion on April 5, 2003; and $905 million on June 13, 2012.

What is the most dangerous element of thunderstorms?

The greatest ambient threat from a thunderstorm is its lightning. The sultry, hot hair that gets pushed above an advancing cold front creates prodigious amounts of static electricity that has to be discharged, and in finding the path of least resistance to the ground, lightning can strike out several miles from the edge of the storm. This is why meteorologists caution people that if they can even hear thunder, it is time to move indoors. Waiting too long can prove fatal, as in 1979, when three people near Plainview were struck down together while in the very act of fleeing to shelter. Boaters in the middle of a lake are particularly vulnerable, with no other target within perhaps hundreds of yards, and the added threats of an exploding gas tank, and drowning.

Where does Texas rank nationally in lightning danger?

In 2017, Texas was first in the United States in the number of cloud-to-ground strikes with about 3.3 million. Florida, which is much smaller, finished a close enough second that it ranks first in the density of lightning strikes. While nine out of ten people who are struck by lightning survive, during the decade 2007–2016, Florida led the nation in lightning-struck fatalities with fifty-one, while Texas finished second with twenty-one.

What other damage can lightning cause?

Secondary damage is a significant aspect of lightning bolts. Every year, thousands of acres of forest and range land are lost in fires caused by lightning. In 1974 lightning

Just how many tornadoes does Texas have in a year?

The United States has an average of 1,224 tornadoes annually, and 147 of them—12 percent of the total—touch down in Texas. This is 55 more than second-place Kansas and 82 more than third-place Oklahoma. Almost never are there fewer than 80 (except for the terrible drought of the early 1950s, when there were fewer than 20 in 1951 and 1952), and sometimes (1982, 1995, 2007), there are more than 200. The record is 232, set in 1967.

struck an oil tank in Port Neches, burning up 150,000 barrels of petroleum before the fire could be put out. In a similar incident five years later in Nederland, lightning hit an oil tanker. An empty bunker full of fumes exploded, killing two and injuring sixteen. Other frequent casualties of lightning include stock in fields and barnyards and communications towers and cables.

NATURAL DISASTERS

Why does Texas seem to get more than its share of tornadoes?

Long ago, meteorologists described a swath of the Great Plains as "Tornado Alley," which begins in Texas and funnels through Oklahoma and Kansas. The principle is the same that leads to spectacular thunderstorms along the Balcones Escarpment, except on a continental scale: hot, humid air bounded by the Front Range of the Rocky Mountains creates the atmospheric conditions that spawns a disproportionate share of the twisters in North America. In south Texas, tropical storm rain bands also spawn tornadoes, such as the 115 that spun out of Hurricane Beulah in 1967.

What is the most active season for tornadoes?

April and May are the most risky months, with a smaller, secondary season in autumn. Enumerated by months, Texans can expect five tornadoes in January, three in February, eleven in March, twenty-nine in April, forty-four in May, twenty-two in June, three each in July and August, five in September, nine in October, eight in November, and five in December.

What have been Texas's deadliest tornadoes?

Counting down the ten worst tornadoes in Texas history:

Why did people in Lubbock believe for so long that their city was immune from tornadoes?

The interposition of Yellow House Draw canyon between the town and the prevailing direction of storms was supposed to break up severe weather before reaching the town. This was proven false on May 11, 1970, when a massive F5 tornado ripped through the central business district. Twenty-six people were killed, the twenty-story Great Plains Life Building was twisted a foot out of level, and the $250 million in damage made it the most expensive windstorm in U.S. history to that time.

10. Jarrell, north of Austin, May 27, 1997, 27 dead, 12 injured. Usually in such a storm, there are more injured than killed, but this rare F5 tornado tore even masonry homes from their foundations and in places sucked pavement from the roads.

9. Saragosa (20 miles [1.6 kilometers] south of Pecos), May 22, 1987, 30 dead, 121 injured. This F4 storm was half a mile (.8 kilometers) wide; two-thirds of the deaths occurred at an indoor graduation ceremony, as adults protected children with their bodies.

8. Zephyr (near Brownwood), May 30, 1909, 34 dead, 70 injured. This storm struck in the wee hours of the morning in the era before warning sirens.

7. Kenedy, May 6, 1930, 36 dead, 60 injured. The flimsy housing in this rural area never stood a chance.

6. Hill and Navarro counties, May 6, 1930, 41 dead, 200 injured. The same day that Kenedy was devastated in south Texas, this long-lived tornado plowed through the Blacklands south of Fort Worth and Dallas. It claimed casualties in the towns of Frost, Rankin, Bardwell, and Ennis.

5. Wichita Falls, April 10, 1979, 42 dead, 1,700 injured. Calculated to be an F4, this was one of the largest tornadoes recorded, at times 1.5 miles (2.4 kilometers) across. Three thousand homes were destroyed, and more than half the fatalities were killed in their cars.

4. Glazier-Higgins, April 9, 1947, 68 dead and 272 injured in Texas, many more as it crossed into the Oklahoma Panhandle and then into Kansas. First dropping to the ground near Pampa before roaring northward through the Panhandle, this massive storm was over 2 miles (3.2 kilometers) wide.

3. Rocksprings, April 12, 1927, 74 dead, 205 injured. This 1-mile-(1.6-kilometer)-wide F5 tornado destroyed 235 buildings in the town; 12 survived. The dead and injured comprised about a third of the town's population.

2. Goliad, May 18, 1902, 114 dead, 250 injured. This powerful F4 storm arrived in Goliad after leaving a path of devastation 15 miles (24 kilometers) long.

1. Waco, May 11, 1953, 114 dead, 597 injured. This F5 storm was about .3 mile (.5 kilometers) wide, with wind estimated at an almost incomprehensible 300 miles (482 kilometers) per hour. It crossed the city from south to north, destroying 600 buildings, damaging 1,000 more, and 2,000 vehicles. This was the storm that inspired the Texas Tornado Warning Conference and closer cooperation among business, academia, and the government. This twister originated in Lorena, several miles to the south, but many Waco residents declined to take shelter, having grown up with a local Indian tale that a tornado would never strike the city.

How often do hurricanes strike the Texas coast?

The odds are that any 50-mile (80-kilometer) stretch of Texas beach will be hit by a hurricane once every six years on average. The weather service calculates that somewhere in Texas is struck by a hurricane at a rate of 0.8 per year. Since before the Civil War, it is estimated that Texas has experienced sixty-five hurricanes. The greatest number strike in August, although the most destructive storms tend to come in September; the traditional hurricane seasons, runs from June 1 through the end of November. The earliest to strike Texas was on June 2; the latest was on November 5. Although there is usually a lengthy respite between hurricanes, in 2005, Hurricane Rita deluged southeast Texas only three weeks after Hurricane Katrina largely destroyed New Orleans. The longest intermission between Texas hurricanes lasted from October 1989 to August 1999.

What have been Texas's most notorious hurricanes?

- Carla, September 1961—Second-largest hurricane in history, with winds up to 175 mph (282 km/h) and a staggering 22-foot (6.7-meter) storm surge. The storm made one feint at the coast before backing up and circling a loop, which gave a quarter of a million Texans time to evacuate. In fact, this was part of the largest peacetime evacuation in U.S. history to that time, with some small towns being completely depopulated and up to 80 percent of the people in larger cities having fled. While a terrible disruption, the evacuation limited deaths in Texas to thirty-four. Because of the size of the storm, there was extensive damage up to 200 miles (322 kilometers) to the east (on the "strong" side). It also held together with remarkable tenacity, spawning tornadoes as far north as Tulsa, Oklahoma, generating heavy rains in the Midwest, then Canada, and its remnants finally exhausted themselves east of Labrador.

- Beulah, September 1967—Third-largest hurricane in history, struck near Brownsville, tracking up the Rio Grande for over 100 miles (161 kilometers) before turning south into Mexico. Hurricane-force winds extended north to Corpus Christi, there was catastrophic flooding in San Antonio, and the storm spawned 115 tornadoes, which was a record. Padre Island was riddled with 22 new cuts into the Laguna Madre that had to regenerate by natural processes. Wind gusted to 136 mph (219 km/h), and there was a 20-foot (6-meter) storm surge.

- Allen, August 1980—The most powerful storm in the Caribbean up to that time, Allen had wind gusts up to 185 mph (298 km/h) and a minimum pressure of only 26.55 inches (67.44 centimeters). Heading consistently west-northwest toward Brownsville, meteorologists persistently forecast a rightward turn, but the sheer mass of the storm defied the atmospherics, and it plowed straight ahead into Brownsville. Fortunately, so much of

Hurricane Ike struck the hapless Galveston in 2008, killing eighty-four people.

215

the storm crossed over land before the eye-wall did that the storm backed down from its peak intensity before coming ashore. Having recovered from Beulah, Padre Island now suffered 68 new cuts between the Gulf and lagoon.

- Alicia, August 1983—Remembered mostly for the flooding and destruction wrought in Houston, where downtown streets were blocked by glass blown from office towers.

- Charley, August 1998—Although only a tropical storm that never reached hurricane strength, Charley's path west from Corpus Christi ended a catastrophic, multiyear drought in the Brush Country. The storm was almost unique in not delivering its biggest punch along the coast but holding it until reaching the middle Rio Grande. Nearly a foot of rain fell in Del Rio, sending two-thirds of the city underwater and nearly inundating the International Bridge.

- Bret, August 1999—Remarkable for its size more than its intensity, Bret's gale force winds extended from Brownsville north to Corpus Christi. Coastal grassland absorbed much of the near-biblical rainfall, estimated at some 40 inches (102 centimeters) in northeast Kenedy County, and the storm is credited with replenishing shrunken reservoirs and helping the region's drought recovery that began with Tropical Storm Charley a year before.

- Allison, June 2001—Notable for its early development before Gulf waters had a chance to reach their peak temperature, for reversing course from north to south after reaching as far inland as Lufkin, allowing it to take a second swipe at Houston, which saw catastrophic flooding, and, after it exited eastward out of Texas, for forming a new eye over dry land, which almost never happens.

- Rita, September 2005—Striking so soon after Hurricane Katrina devastated New Orleans and only a couple hundred miles to the west at Sabine Pass, this storm extended the season's coastal devastation well into Texas, with $10 billion in damage and fifty-nine direct and indirect fatalities. Power was lost in much of Houston for several days, causing thousands to relocate inland until conditions improved.

- Ike, September 2008—Yet another storm to rake across Galveston and Houston, a freak of circumstances allowed Ike's winds to strengthen without benefit of a decrease in pressure. With direct and indirect deaths numbering eighty-four and nearly $20 billion in damage, Ike remains one of the most destructive storms on record.

With lightning strikes so common, do wildfires ever escalate to disaster status?

Indeed they do. The most destructive wildfire in Texas history began on September 4, 2011, north of Bastrop State Park, most likely started by sparks from an electrical line. It took over a month to put out, destroyed much of the botanically unique "Lost Pines" area, destroyed 1,645 homes, claimed two lives, and charred 34,068 acres (138 square kilometers). And that was just one fire. The 2011 drought was so catastrophic that across the state that year, more than thirty-one thousand fires burned nearly 4 million acres (16,187 square kilometers), which was almost half the total land nationally that was lost in fires that year.

Does Texas have earthquakes?

Texas sits on historically stable sedimentary rock of an ancient seabed and is not often subject to earthquakes. However, Caddo Lake in the northeast was formed by the cataclysmic New Madrid quake of December 16, 1811, which was centered in southeastern Missouri. There are very occasional tremors in the desert mountains of the Trans-Pecos. Since the advent of "fracking," which is the forcing of water under high pressure deep underground to widen fissures in order to extract oil or gas, numerous small earthquakes have occurred in north-central Texas. Although first used in Texas in 1949, the technology was widely applied in the 1980s on the Barnett Shale formation around Fort Worth, resulting in an onset of minor temblors.

GEOLOGY

Are there any gemstones found in Texas?

Only one diamond has ever been found in Texas, a one-quarter-carat, chocolate-brown stone found in 1911 in Foard County near the Wichita River. No one has a clue how it got there. The state gem is the Texas Blue Topaz; they are found primarily in the Llano Uplift of the Hill Country, in the very heart, appropriately, of the state. A special cut was devised for this stone, through which a five-pointed Lone Star is visible when viewed from above through the flat table. The largest Lone Star topaz weighs 176 carats—about the diameter of a half-dollar coin—and of similar depth. Some uncut crystals have been much larger. This unique geological area has also yielded garnet and amethyst. Less important deposits of semiprecious stones exist in the desert Trans-Pecos.

What about precious metals?

It is ironic, since the Spanish explored Texas in the hope of finding gold, that very little gold actually exists in Texas. Most of what was produced was just the by-product of a lead mine near Presidio in the Trans-Pecos, which also yielded a small amount of silver. As one might expect of an area with quartz veins, a tiny amount of gold has been found in the Llano Uplift but nothing to justify panning creek gravel. Alamo casualty Jim Bowie was said to have known the location of a lost Spanish silver mine, but evidence of it has never been found (and some people have noted that one of Bowie's main incomes was from land fraud).

The state gem is the Texas Blue Topaz, which is found primarily in the Hill Country.

217

Is it true that there are pink pearls?

Surprisingly, yes. As the Spanish scoured the region in the sixteenth-century quest for gold, they were shocked to discover native Indians around the Concho River wearing pearl ornaments in various shades of pink, lavender, and purple. The Concho (Spanish for "shell") hosts the native Tampico pearly mussel (*Cyrtonaias tampicoensis*) that bears them; the exact shade of color depends on the mineral content of the water. Only about one animal in twenty-five contains a pearl; they are located by wading through murky water, feeling for them with one's toes—and hoping not to encounter a snapping turtle or water moccasin instead. Large, spherical or baroque pearls are very rare and costly. Because of the decline of the species, the state now licenses commercial pearl operations, of which there are about a half dozen.

Are there many fossils in Texas?

In the time when dinosaurs roamed the earth, most of Texas was beneath a shallow, inland sea. Thus, most Texas fossils are of the marine variety; most impressive is the Onion Creek Mosasaur, a 30-foot (9-meter) top predator excavated from a stream bed south of Austin in 1935. It is on display in the Texas Memorial Museum on the University of Texas campus along with an impressive collection of other Texas fossils. Fossils of large mammals from the Ice Age are more common.

Where are the best places to view Texas fossils?

An exposed section of the Paluxy River bed near Glen Rose, southwest of Fort Worth, was once the shore of that ancient sea. There, Dinosaur Valley State Park preserves tracks in the limestone of all three different major dinosaur types: large, three-toed predators, of which Tyrannosaurus Rex is the most famous; wedge-shaped tracks left by duck-billed dinosaurs; and large, circular impressions of titanosaurs, such as the since renamed Brontosaurus. In 2002, a flood on Canyon Lake near New Braunfels topped the spillway and scoured out a huge ravine down to the Guadalupe River, exposing a wide variety of marine fossils from 110 million years ago, before there were dinosaurs. These can be viewed via locally organized hiking tours.

Have there been any other recent discoveries?

In 1971, archeologists working in Big Bend National Park discovered the first known remains of Quetzalcoatlus, a gigantic, flying pterosaur. On its hind legs, it stood 10 feet (3 meters) tall and had a 36-foot (11-meter) wingspan—about twice that of the better-known Pteranodon. In 1978, individuals searching for arrowheads near the confluence of the Bosque and Brazos rivers, northwest of downtown Waco, discovered the first bone of an eventual twenty-four Columbian mammoths that perished in three separate events. Heeding local requests, President Barack Obama created the Waco Mammoth National Monument, operated in tandem with Baylor University and the city of Waco.

A computer-generated reconstruction of a Quetzalcoatlus, a species whose fossils were first found in Big Bend National Park.

What has made Texas such a rich source of petroleum?

Texas had so much oil for the same reason there is such an abundance of marine fossils: prehistoric, inland sea. Oil was formed from decaying marine biomass—dead plants and tiny organisms such as plankton—which sank to the bottom of the sea in an ever-thickening layer. Over eons, they sank deeper into the crust, and under the right conditions of temperature and pressure, petroleum was formed. It is an oversimplification, but generally, when the process happened on dry land, the result is coal; when it happened in seabeds, the result is oil. There is an infinite variety of details in how an oil deposit is formed, resulting in many different kinds of petroleum of varying densities and colors. During the decades that Texas oil dominated the world market, "West Texas Intermediate Crude" was the standard benchmark against which the quality, and price, of the world's different petroleums are measured.

Are any other minerals commercially mined?

A number of minerals were discovered in Texas in quantities that were once thought to be commercially usable, but the deposits proved to be so small that they were mined out, or else mining them ceased to be profitable when market prices fell. This was the fate that befell Texas production of silver and its by-products, lead and mercury, as well as zinc, tin, and others. A small amount of uranium is mined in south Texas, and low-grade iron ore is processed in north Texas, although for purposes other than steel production, such as to provide a mineral supplement in animal feed.

What do people study at Study Butte?

Located a couple of miles west of Big Bend National Park (now in the gap between the national park and Big Bend Ranch State Park), the village of Study Butte was founded in c. 1900, and its fortunes have always been tied to the nearby mercury mines. It has opened and closed at various times in the past century, depending upon whether market conditions made mercury extraction profitable. Study Butte's population has swelled when there is work and dwindled, sometimes down to a dozen or so, when there isn't. The butte, and town, are named for early mine manager Will Study, and the surname is pronounced with a long "U." Today the mine is closed, but the reservation of Big Bend Ranch State Park has generated an influx of tourism and created a more stable base for the town—a dramatic example of how conservation can benefit a local economy.

What are the abundant minerals in Texas?

Texas is a leading U.S. producer of sulfur, which is obtained both from large native deposits associated with oil deposits near the Gulf Coast and by recovering it during purification of natural gas. Also associated with natural gas is helium, which is one of the most abundant elements in the universe, but is exceedingly rare on earth. The natural gas in the Panhandle is almost unique for containing recoverable quantities of helium. Salt and gypsum are widely distributed, mined, and vended.

How is Texas fixed for groundwater?

A map of Texas aquifers presents an exceedingly complex picture, as the state is underlain by at least thirty different sources of groundwater. The most significant of them are:

1. The Ogallala Aquifer. The water beneath the Staked Plains is the southernmost extension of this giant formation that extends under much of the Great Plains. It is ancient water that began accumulating during the Miocene Era eight to ten million years ago. For many years, agricultural irrigation has been drawing water out far faster than it can recharge, resulting in the water level falling as much as 4 feet (122 centimeters) per year, forcing farmers to deepen their wells and worry when they might hit the bottom. Research in recapture, more efficient use, and increased recharge is ongoing with urgency.

2. The Edwards Aquifer. Some Texas cities, such as Dallas and Austin, have been provident in constructing reservoirs to provide for people's water needs. Other cities, such as San Antonio, have continued to rely on wells that now supply 90 percent of the city's needs. San Antonio, and the cities at the edge of the Edwards Aquifer, such as New Braunfels and San Marcos, drastically affect the health of this aquifer, whose level can vary as much as 80 feet (24 meters) between wet years and dry ones. Strict water rationing is now an accepted way of life during droughts.

3. The Hueco-Mesilla Bolson Aquifer. This small but deep aquifer in the western Trans-Pecos for many years was the sole source of water for both El Paso and Cíudad Juarez, Mexico. Overpumping finally so affected the quality of the water that workers began scrambling for other sources, including construction of the largest inland water desalinization plant in the world, which is fed by underground brine. A couple of wildcatters who made their fortunes drilling for oil have begun buying up water rights elsewhere in the desert to pump water to El Paso, to the fury of local residents whose personal wells stand to run dry. Texas property law never foresaw this emergency or took into account the shared nature of water in aquifers, so there has been little to stop them.

PLANTS AND ANIMALS

You always hear that Texas has more than five thousand different kinds of wildflowers. Isn't that at least a *little* exaggeration?

Actually, no, it isn't. One of the best Texas wildflower guides divides the state into no fewer than nine botanical regions from beaches to pine forests to plains, mountains, deserts, and relict botanical "islands." Of all species of plants that bear flowers, Texas really does have more than five thousand.

How greatly do planting times vary in different parts of the state?

The U.S. Department of Agriculture classifies Texas as lying within "hardiness zones" six through nine but that is a very general measure. Texas nurseries subdivide those four into nine, from the northwestern Panhandle, which receives its average first freeze the second week in October. Moving south, Amarillo has its average first freeze on October 24, Lubbock on November 2, Midland and Abilene on November 13, Waco on Novem-

Is Texas stone commercially valuable?

If there was another thing, besides petroleum, that that prehistoric seabed was good for, it was for laying down vast deposits of limestone. It is now widely quarried for building stone, or else crushing for gravel, for cement manufacture, and other uses. It comes in various forms, most interesting of which is the Cordova shell limestone, which is shot through with a thick array of small but amazingly distinct fossils. Within the thousands of square miles of limestone, igneous intrusions left large deposits of high-quality granite, some gray, and the most valuable a distinct dusty, rose red. It is avidly quarried, and what is not suitable for dimension stone is crushed for use in landscaping.

ber 25, Austin on December 2, Houston on December 6, Corpus Christi on December 11, and Brownsville on December 17, if it has a freeze at all.

What is significant about Texas's wild grapes?

"Mustang" grapes (*Vitis mustangensis*) grow rampant across much of the state. They are small and sour, although edible. Pioneers made jam and jelly from them, with the addition of lots of sugar, and also wine, about which the less is said the better. They did, however, prove to be of incalculable value to the world. Beginning in the mid-nineteenth century, the French wine industry began to wither as a result of an

Vitus mustangensis, or "Mustang" grapes, grow wild commonly in Texas and can be credited with saving the wine industry in the state.

unstoppable epidemic of phylloxera aphids, which likely came from the United States. For thirty years, no treatment proved effective, and then a Texas viticulturalist, Thomas Munson, proposed grafting French vines onto hardy mustang roots, which were resistant to the pest. It worked like magic, the French wine industry was saved, and a deputation made its way from France to Denton, Texas, to decorate Munson with the Legion of Honor.

Do people really eat cactus?

Yes, there is no need to starve if lost in the desert. The tender, young pads of the prickly pear are known by the Spanish name *nopalitos* (or *nopales* for the adult pads). Skinned to remove the tough hide and thorns, they are most commonly sliced and cooked in scrambled eggs. The taste vaguely resembles squash. One cup of prickly pear contains about a third of the daily recommendation for Vitamin C and magnesium, about a fifth of the daily fiber, beneficial allowances of calcium, potassium, and copper, and a smaller portion of B vitamins and other minerals, with only 9 carb grams.

Why doesn't one read about "cedar fever" among early Texas settlers?

Probably because the Ashe juniper, also known as mountain cedar, which is the culprit in the "cedar" fever that afflicts millions, did not used to be so common. It is native, not invasive, but it is opportunistic. In the Hill Country which it now dominates, it moved out onto the grassy prairies only after early ranchers overgrazed them. And once established, the cedar trees' huge root systems soak up virtually all the water, choking out other plants and becoming the dominant species. In areas where the cedar has been removed and the original range grasses have been restored, springs that ran dry generations ago have come back, and the variety of plants has led to an increasing population and variety of wildlife. This is true not just of protected parkland. Ranchers who care-

What is the "Cactus Capital of Texas"?

The bleakness of the countryside was well depicted in Cormac McCarthy's *No Country for Old Men*, and the predominance of prickly pear prompted the city to get the legislature to designate Sanderson as the state's Cactus Capital. There is a self-guided nature trail outside of town, and every fall is the Prickly Pear Pachanga, a dinner that raises funds for cultural activities.

fully manage their grazing to the grasslands' natural carrying capacity have found their land to regain a health and vigor they never imagined.

How did mesquite become so popular for meat smoking?

Smoked meat first became prevalent among German immigrants in the Hill Country. In the beginning, they used hickory wood, but those trees became so scarce that they turned to mesquite as a substitute.

What are some of Texas's grand champion trees?

The U.S. Department of Agriculture has identified 679 native tree species in the United States, of which nearly half, 319 species, exist in Texas. Of the state's most characteristic and identifiable trees, some of those currently recognized as the largest are:

- American Elm, Bastrop County, 95 feet (29 meters) tall, 91-foot (27.7-meter) crown spread, 5.5-foot (1.7 meter) trunk diameter
- Ashe Juniper, Comal County, 41 feet (12.5 meters) tall, 49-foot (15-meter) crown spread, 3.7-foot (1.1-meter) trunk diameter
- Bald Cypress, Real County, 68 feet (20.7 meters) tall, 99-foot (30.2-meter) crown spread, 8-foot (2.4-meter) trunk diameter
- Blackjack Oak, Henderson County, 65 feet (19.8 meters) tall, 80-foot (24.4-meter) crown spread, 3.1-foot (0.9-meter) trunk diameter
- Burr Oak, Tarrant County, 81 feet (24.7 meters) tall, 105-foot (32-meter) crown spread, 5.8-foot (1.8-meter) trunk diameter
- Eastern Cottonwood, Falls County, 101 feet (30.8 meters) high, 106-foot (32.3-meter) crown spread, 8.5-foot (2.6-meter) trunk diameter
- Honey Mesquite, Real County, 56 feet (17.1 meters) high, 87-foot (26.5-meter) crown spread, 4.8-foot (1.5-meter) trunk diameter
- Loblolly Pine, Rusk County, 130 feet (39.6 meters) tall, 49-foot (14.9-meter) crown spread, 4.4-foot (1.3-meter) trunk diameter
- Longleaf Pine, Sabine County, 118 feet (36 meters) high, 38-foot (11.6-meter) crown spread, 3.2-foot (1-meter) trunk diameter

- Pecan, Parker County, 87 feet (26.5 meters) high, 118-foot (36-meter) crown spread, 7-foot (2.1-meter) trunk diameter
- Plains Cottonwood, Armstrong County, 96 feet (29.3 meters) high, 93-foot (28.3 meter) crown spread, 6.6-foot (2-meter) trunk diameter
- Southern Live Oak, Brazoria County, 67 feet (20.4 meters) high, 109-foot (33.2-meter) crown spread, 10.2-foot (3.1-meter) trunk diameter (note: the famous "Big Tree" at Goose Island State Park, which was long recognized as the largest live oak in the state, was dethroned after the discovery of this one).
- Southern Magnolia, Smith County, 66 feet (20.1 meters) high, 87-foot (26.5-meter) crown spread, 6.1-foot (1.9-meter) trunk diameter
- Sycamore, Walker County, 104 feet (31.7 meters) tall, 80-foot (24.4-meter) crown spread, 6.9-foot (2.1-meter) trunk diameter
- Texas Live Oak, Young County, 48 feet (14.6 meters) tall, 91-foot (27.7-meter) crown spread, 9.6-foot (2.9-meter) trunk diameter
- Texas Mulberry, Presidio County, 37 feet (11.3 meters) tall, 43-foot (13.1-meter) crown spread, 2.7-foot (0.8-meter) trunk diameter
- Texas Walnut, Jeff Davis County, 48 feet (14.6 meters) tall, 56-foot (17.1-meter) crown spread, 3.7-foot (1.1-meter) trunk diameter
- Water Tupelo, Jasper County, 110 feet (33.5 meters) tall, 61-foot (18.6-meter) crown spread, 4-foot (1.2-meter) trunk diameter

How big do alligators get in Texas?

An alligator captured by lasso (!) in Liberty County in 2016 set a new state record at 13 feet, 8.5 inches (4.2 meters) and weighed an estimated 900 pounds (408 kilograms). This is perhaps 2 feet (0.6 meters) and 100 pounds (45.4 kilograms) short of the U.S. record. It was captured by wranglers from Gator Country near Beaumont, named "Big Tex," and trucked away for display. 500 pounds (227 kilograms) is more typical for a bull gator, with 200 pounds (91 kilograms) and 8.5 feet (2.6 meters) long typical for a female.

Have gators fully recovered from their bout with near-extinction?

Yes, the alligator is one of American conservation's greatest success stories. Early Spanish explorers in Texas recorded with consternation that at the coastal rivers, one

Once in danger of extinction, the alligators in Texas are now thriving again.

Why are there camels in Bronte?

Before the Civil War, the U.S. Army was diligent in extending its control over the arid reaches of west Texas, and beginning in 1855 it began acquiring several dozen camels, along with Arab and Turkish drivers, to evaluate their suitability for transport duty. Eventually, they acquired more than sixty, and in every trial they proved themselves superior pack animals, outperforming the army's standard mules at every turn. The Civil War brought an end to the experiment. Camel headquarters was at Camp Verde near present-day Leakey in Real County, but as that fort is now a scatter of ruins on private property, the restored Fort Chadbourne, near Bronte, hosts a living history exhibit on camels and the army. Although the town was indeed named for British novelist Charlotte Brontë, in Texas the "e" is silent.

could almost walk from shore to shore on the backs of alligators. One early Anglo colonist wrote in the 1820s that families along the Lavaca River had trouble keeping dogs because "many was the thirsty canine who went down to the river to drink, and never thirsted more." A century of relentless overhunting and loss of habitat brought the big reptiles within sight of that slide toward extinction, and they were placed on the list of the Endangered Species Act of 1973. With hunting banned, greater public awareness of their importance to the southern riverine habitat, and stricter protection even outside of parks, they bounced back dramatically and were removed from the endangered list in 1987.

Do Texas restaurants serve alligator meat?

Alligators are edible. Most of the meat is in the tail, but it must be ruthlessly trimmed of its rank-tasting fat. The powerful jaw muscles that snap the mouth shut are the best eating for their lack of fat. Numerous regional-fare restaurants in Texas now serve deep-fried gator as a novelty appetizer. This is more sensible now that meat is required to come from licensed gator farms, which eliminates the nastier, flavor-impacting things gators might eat in the wild.

Were buffalo ever successfully domesticated?

Only partially. Soon after the close of the frontier, rancher Charles Goodnight experimented with them and even crossed them with domestic cattle. Some buffalo raised by hand can be ridden, but they never proved to be practical agricultural animals. They are now commonly raised on farms for meat, however.

While one often reads of rural Texans shooting and eating opossums, are they really any good to eat?

Yes, but first, one must overcome the nausea that often accompanies the mere thought of eating one of the ugly little things. In fact, 'possum could be the single most nutrient-packed game meat there is. One modest, meal-sized portion of 100 grams (3.5 ounces) contains 60 percent of the daily requirement for protein, a quarter of the iron, selenium, and phosphorus, more than 100 percent of the vitamin B12 and from 20 percent to 40 percent of other B vitamins, and good shots of potassium, zinc, and copper—and no carbohydrates in 220 calories.

What happened to all the prairie dogs?

Vast numbers of prairie dogs (which are not dogs at all but burrowing rodents) used to live in "towns" spread across the Panhandle-Plains. At least half a billion of them lived on the Staked Plains alone. In many areas, there was a hazard while riding horseback of one's mount stepping into a burrow and breaking a leg. It was the arrival of farming in this region, which had previously been thought suitable only for ranching, that spelled doom for the prairie dogs. Drowning them was not practical, for their burrows penetrated the hardpan into the porous sands beneath; one rancher drained a whole stock tank over one village, which was under-water for only half an hour as the prairie dogs sought refuge in underground air pockets. They are edible, but Anglo pioneers would not eat anything with the word "dog" in it. Eventually, they were done in by teams of professional exterminators with poison grain and gas.

Where in Texas can you go to see prairie dogs close up?

Mackenzie State Recreation Area, named for Ranald Mackenzie, the army officer who was instrumental in clearing Indians from the Staked Plains, is Lubbock's largest, embracing riding trails, an amusement park, and a golf course. Prairie dogs can be intimately viewed at the walled prairie dog town.

Is it true that armadillos can pass leprosy to humans?

Technically, yes. Aside from humans, most of whom have a genetic resistance to leprosy, or Hansen's disease, the nine-banded armadillo is the only other mammal known to harbor the pathogen that causes it. While it is true that occasional youthful pranksters will chase down an armadillo on foot (armadillos cannot run fast) to see it curl into its defensive ball, one would have to pick it up and handle it, and even then, the risk of transmission is low.

Armadillos are a fascinating species, but one thing to be wary of is that they can sometimes transmit leprosy to humans if handled.

What poisonous snakes are there in Texas?

Because of its large area, Texas is one of the few states that hosts a full complement of all the poisonous snake species found in North America: rattlesnakes, copperheads, water moccasins, and coral snakes. The last named are the most poisonous but fortunately have a timid demeanor. The other three, from the pit viper family, can be quite aggressive.

PARKS AND RESERVES

Why does Texas have so few national parks compared to other large Western states?

Throughout the West, land for national parks, monuments, and forests was provided by withdrawing it from the vast store of federal public domain. Texas was alone among the states in having transformed directly from independent country to state, and it was allowed to keep its public domain to help defray the Texas national debt. Thus, the federal government did not start off owning any land in Texas.

How many national parks are there in Texas?

The U.S. National Park Service administers a wide array of lands of varying designations, such as historic sites and recreation areas, of which Texas has several, in addition to the separately administered National Wildlife Refuges. Of the large natural wilderness areas associated with the term "national park," Texas has four: Big Bend and Guadalupe Mountains national parks, both in the Trans-Pecos, Padre Island National Seashore, and the Big Thicket National Preserve in the Piney Woods. There are also four national forests, also in the Piney Woods, and five national grasslands, four in the Panhandle-Plains and one in the Blacklands. The characteristics of the individual national wildlife refuges, forests, and grasslands are considered in the following sections on their natural regions.

What was the first national park in Texas?

With its scenic powers already well known, the Rio Grande canyons were brought into the state park system in 1933, and the Chisos Mountains that tower more than 5,000 feet (1,524 meters) above the desert were added the following year. The National Park Service advocated creation of a national park in the so-called "Big Bend," the 107-mile (172-kilometer) bow in the flow of the Rio Grande, with facilities to be constructed by the Civilian Conservation Corps. Not everyone was convinced, however; many questioned whether the empty Texas desert really held wonders on the scale of Yellowstone or the Grand Canyon. (Indeed, as political by-play, one reason Texas officials pressed for a Big Bend National Park was because of the law that requires that federal parks be approached by paved roads, and they saw a way to get the federal government to pave a route through the Trans-Pecos!) President Franklin D. Roosevelt, who was known for his foreign policy initiative to leave interventionism behind and be a "good neighbor" to Latin America, saw a park in the Big Bend as an opportunity to develop a cross-border natural area and lent his support. In 1935 Congress reluctantly passed the act, creating Big Bend National Park, but stipulated that no federal money could be used to acquire it. Six years later, the legislature called its hand with a $1.5-million appropriation, which was supplemented with a fund raising campaign among Texas schoolchildren. The park opened in 1944 with a $15,000 budget and staff of five; in 1972, Congress relented with an appropriation to purchase the last of the private inholdings. The long time lack of commitment to recreational facilities proved to be a blessing, as most of the park was declared to be a roadless area and placed within the protection of the Wilderness Act.

Has Big Bend in fact pulled its weight as a national park?

Now extending across more than 800,000 acres (3,237 square kilometers; about the size of Rhode Island), Big Bend harbors more than a thousand plant species, including several cacti that are so endangered that preventing poachers from digging them up is a constant task. Some 434 bird species have been recorded, which is more than half of the total in North America and more than in any other national park. Plant communities high in the mountains have been discovered to be relics of the last Ice Age, and in 1976, Big Bend was declared a world biosphere by UNESCO. It is now considered a jewel of the national park system. It only ranks forty-second in visitors at just over three hundred thousand per year, but that number can still strain the fragile ecology, as hikers' feet tread ever deeper into the sandy soil of the trails.

Big Bend National Park affords some of the most spectacular views in Texas.

How is it that Guadalupe Mountains National Park and Padre Island National Seashore were created so closely together in time?

Both projects were dear to the heart of Texas's last liberal senator, Ralph Yarborough (1903–1996), one of the last "happy warriors" of the New Deal era, and represented rare victories for him at a time when his influence was being undercut by Lyndon Johnson and John Connally. Created in 1968 and opened in 1972, Guadalupe Mountains hosts only about 170,000 visitors per year (about half the number that visit nearby Carlsbad Caverns), but that is beneficial to the fragile ecology and heightens the reward for hikers who reach its central feature, McKittrick Canyon, with its springs and forest of ash, oak, and bigtooth maple. The park began with a private donation of nearly 5,000 acres (20 square kilometers), and the remaining 81,000 acres (328 square kilometers) of desert did not break the federal budget. The park contains Guadalupe Peak (8,749 feet; 2,667 meters), the highest point in Texas, and the mountain range comes to a spectacular southern point at the cliff of El Capitan, which rises 3,000 feet (914 meters) above the desert. Padre Island was created in 1962 as the nation's fourth national seashore, protecting 70 miles (113 kilometers) of the earth's longest coastal barrier island, which provides nesting areas for the Kemp's ridley sea turtle, the rarest marine turtle in the world. Unlike South Padre with its miles of condominiums and party life, much of Padre Island's 130,000 acres (526 square kilometers) remain pristine except for continuing petroleum exploration—a concession necessary to getting it protected at all.

How many national wildlife refuges are there in Texas?

Sixteen—although this is a flexible number, and new tracts of wildlife habitat are always being added to the chain of wildlife refuges in Texas. The greatest number, eight, protect coastal wetlands. Three more are in the Piney Woods, one in the Gulf Plains, one in the Hill Country, one on the Rolling Plains, and two on the Staked Plains. Most exist to provide habitat for water-fowl, as Texas sits under the great Central Flyway of North Amer-

What was revolutionary about the Big Thicket National Preserve?

While the United States has traditionally supported the creation of parks in other countries based on a location's ecological value, it never took its own advice. National park qualification at home was almost inevitably about scenery: the tallest mountain, the deepest canyon, and the like. Advocates for federal protection of the dense botanical tangle in southeast Texas known as the Big Thicket had to convince Congress to change its stance. When they finally succeeded in 1974 after more than forty years of effort, the Big Thicket National Preserve, along with a sister preserve in Florida, were the first parks of their kind in the country. This was another park for whose creation Texas senator Ralph Yarborough had to vigorously campaign.

ica's migratory ducks and geese. Both the national parks system and the wildlife refuges are administered by the U.S. Department of the Interior but are run separately and under different guidelines. The greatest difference is that most of the refuges are managed for controlled and sustainable hunting but with permanent protection of habitat.

How do the national forests and national grasslands in Texas differ from being parks?

The national forests and grasslands are administered by the U.S. Department of Agriculture and are managed for multiuse. So, unlike national parks, there are hunting, timber harvest, and grazing leases issued to private ranchers—but all managed for sustainability. Texas has four national forests, all within the Piney Woods, and each with an area of about 160,000 acres (647 square kilometers) within their declared boundaries, but those boundaries also enclose a large amount of land still in private hands:

1. Angelina National Forest, 153,160 acres (620 square kilometers), including two protected wilderness areas, Upland Island and Turkey Hill.
2. Davy Crockett National Forest, 160,633 acres (650 square kilometers), including the Big Slough Wilderness Area.
3. Sabine National Forest, 160,798 acres (651 square kilometers), including the Indian Mounds Wilderness Area.
4. Sam Houston National Forest, 163,030 acres (647 square kilometers), including the Little Lake Creek Wilderness Area.

There are five national grasslands, four of which are in the Panhandle-Plains and one in the Blacklands. They are:

1. Rita Blanca National Grassland, 92,822 acres (376 square kilometers)
2. Black Kettle National Grassland, 31,300 acres (127 square kilometers)
3. McClellan Creek National Grassland, 1,449 acres (6 square kilometers)
4. Lyndon B. Johnson National Grassland, 20,313 acres (82 square kilometers), which is administered jointly with the one unit in the Blacklands
5. Caddo National Grassland, 17,873 acres (72 square kilometers)

Why was Texas so late in providing a state parks system?

From the time of its earliest settlement, wilderness in Texas was something to conquer, not something to be preserved. Empty land was seen as an economic opportunity, a heritage that manifests itself in the attitude of today's "sagebrush rebellion," that preserving a piece of land for everybody is really taking that opportunity away from somebody.

How did Texas state parks originate?

Texas did not provide a legal foundation for state parks until 1923, and even then, it came with crippling restrictions. A Texas parks board was authorized only to accept land for parks, and there was no provision for the state to purchase parkland or to develop parks from the land that was donated. Nevertheless, Texans so supported the parks concept that in two years, the state received the gifts of sixty parcels of land, one as large as 7,000 acres (28 square kilometers). Development came only with the New Deal, that national regime that the Texas political establishment loved to hate. Laborers from the Works Progress Administration, the National Youth Administration, and especially the Civilian Conservation Corps built facilities in thirty-one parks by 1941. Eventually, the Parks Board was allowed a budget. There were fifty-eight state parks by 1958, and five years later, administration was improved by merging the Parks Board with the Game and Fish Commission to form the Texas Parks and Wildlife Department, which is the governing authority today. In 1970, voters passed a large bond package that accelerated growth of the parks system.

What was Texas's first state park?

Creation of the Texas system of state parks is closely associated with Pat Morris Neff, governor from 1921 to 1925, who was widely known as a nature lover and who kept pet deer on the grounds of the Governor's Mansion. His mother, Isabella Eleanor Neff, bequeathed 6 acres (24,281 square meters) of their family's scenic Coryell County farm, along the Leon River southeast of Gatesville, to the state in 1916. As governor, Neff called a special session of the legislature to consider his message that the proliferation of the automobile had created a widespread "back-to-nature" movement, and the state owed it to them to provide parks for them to retreat to "where the bees hum, the birds sing, the brooks ripple, the breezes blow, and the flowers bloom." With his mission accomplished, Neff donated a further 250 acres (1 square kilometer) of the family farm to form Mother Neff State Park.

Why does Texas allow hunting in its state parks?

While most states even in the West administer their state parks as game sanctuaries, as is the international standard, in Texas, the gun culture and the tradition of hunting for food and sport is insuperable. However, there is a better and more rational reason for it. For generations, ranchers, especially in the Hill Country, have supplemented their incomes with the sale of deer leases and have managed large tracts of land to maximize the deer population. The result is that today, the Hill Country has several times the number of deer than the land could naturally support. Deer in several parks would have to be culled annually anyway to prevent them from starving, and sport hunting creates revenue and public support.

Governor Pat Neff played a huge part in establishing Texas's state park system.

Is the smallest state park really a single grave?

It isn't now, but it used to be. For many years, the smallest was Acton State Park, 0.006 acre (24 square meters), the grave of Davy Crockett's second wife, Elizabeth Patton Crockett (1788–1860). With her two sons, she came to Texas in the mid-1850s to take possession of the land grant that was due his survivors after he was killed at the Alamo. She died at age seventy-two and is buried in the Acton Cemetery near Granbury. Her imposing monument was raised in 1913 with a legislative appropriation and later passed to the Texas Parks Board. In 2007, the Texas Legislature stripped Acton and seventeen other state historic sites from the parks system and transferred them to the Texas Historical Commission (THC) after criticism for poor maintenance. For many years, the legislature had raided state park revenues and pirated them away for general revenue, so their criticism had dubious merit. Nevertheless, the result, which streamlined park lands under the Parks and Wildlife Department and historic properties under the THC, was not a bad thing.

What is the largest state park?

Before passage of the 1970 bond issue, the reigning largest park was Palo Duro Canyon with just over 15,000 acres (61 square kilometers), later just eclipsed by Sea Rim State Park near Beaumont, but much of that land was transferred to the federal wildlife refuge system. In the years following the development of Big Bend National Park, scientists and nature buffs realized that the park boundaries left out the region's most important geology, a circular, 50-square-mile (129-square-kilometer) feature that looks like a meteor crater but is really the remains of a prehistoric magma intrusion between two layers of limestone. The resulting interest led to the creation of Big Bend Ranch State Park of 311,000 acres (1,259 square kilometers), by far the state's largest, augmenting the ecological protection of the national park but protecting additional important features.

With the presence of four large national forests, what is the purpose of the Texas State Forest System?

To a greater degree than the national forest, the Texas State forests promote research and demonstration projects. There are five small tracts administered by the Texas A&M Forest Service, which is a state agency founded in 1915 that is also tasked with coordinating fighting forest fires in the state and identifying the largest trees of their species in Texas. Unlike the national forests, which are managed for multiuse including hunting, the state forests are also animal sanctuaries. No hunting is permitted, but other outdoor recreation, including picnicking, hiking, and camping, generally are (with some local exceptions). The five state forests are: the E. O. Siecke State Forest, the first, established in 1924 on 1,724 acres (7 square kilometers) in Newton County; the I. D. Fairchild State Forest near Rusk, 1925, at 2,740 acres (11 square kilometers) the state's largest; W.

Goodrich Jones State Forest, 1926, on 1,733 acres (7 square kilometers) south of Conroe; the John Henry Kirby Memorial State Forest, 1929, on 600 acres (2.4 square kilometers) donated by lumber magnate J. H. Kirby and others in Tyler County; and the Paul N. Masterson Memorial Forest, 1984, 519 acres (2.1 square kilometers) in Jasper County, donated by his widow.

Who was Hackberry Jones?

W. Goodrich "Hackberry" Jones was about as international as a Texan could be to have been born in 1860. His father was a watchmaker and jeweler in Galveston his mother was the sister of French composer Jacques Offenbach. He spent his early teens in Germany, exulting in walks through the Black Forest with his father, talking with professional foresters and marveling at how the forest was kept in continuous production through judicious harvesting and continual replanting. Back in Texas, Jones became a successful banker in Temple and began agitating for wise timber management on the German model. He gained local fame for his project of planting hackberry trees for shade in Temple. Hackberries grow quickly and provide shade, but they are also brittle, short-lived, maddeningly fecund, and are considered a nuisance. The slight, bespectacled man was mocked about town as "Hackberry" Jones. He was a little ahead of his time. When he approached Governor "Farmer Jim" Ferguson, who was also from Temple, for a $10,000 appropriation to begin a Texas forest service, the governor was horrified. "Ten thousand dollars?" he exclaimed. "Why, for five hundred dollars I can get you a good man to cut all the trees you want!" But he saw the service established and is considered the father of forestry science in Texas.

Are national and state parks the only alternatives for nature protection in Texas?

No, both the Nature Conservancy and the Audubon Society own significant tracts of property that scientists deem to be ecologically important. They are considered in the separate sections on Texas's natural regions that follows.

THE BIG FIVE CITIES

HOUSTON

What is the current population of Houston?

As of 2018, the latest figure is 2,340,814.

How did Houston get its start?

As Santa Anna's army marched across Texas, they burned virtually every town they came to. After Santa Anna's humiliation at the Battle of San Jacinto, the only settlement nearby that had even a few intact buildings was Columbia. Later that year, the brothers John and Augustus Allen purchased a half league of land on Buffalo Bayou, declared a new town that they named Houston in honor of the president, and reached an agreement with the Congress to provide a capitol building if they would relocate the government there. The transfer occurred in the spring of 1837, although the Capitol was not quite finished and tree boughs were lashed in the rafters for shade. With the arrival of the government in May, the population increased from twelve to fifteen hundred, the city was incorporated in June, and the Allens' fortune was made.

When Houston was founded specifically to be the national capital, what was early society like?

One young immigrant named William A. A. Wallace (1817–1899), of Scottish heritage and in fact a descendant of the famous William Wallace, was horrified by what he saw. When he learned that his sister was considering a move to Texas, he wrote his family that in Houston, "such a sight I never saw . . . worse society could not be found on the globe. People kill each other here every day. . . . I would rather see a sister of mine in the grave than in Texas." (Wallace later became a celebrated Texas Ranger, better known by his nickname, Bigfoot.) When painter John James Audubon passed through on one of his bird-collecting expeditions and sought out President Houston, he found him in the executive mansion, a two-room shanty, warming his fingers at a tiny fire. On cold days, a public fire was kept burning in the street before the principal business, a bar, hotel, and brothel called the Mansion House, kept by a tough-as-nails virago named Pamela Mann.

How did Houston grow?

The city's two years as the nation's temporary capital gave businesses time to take root. The economy was heavily rural and agricultural, and Houston became the marketing center. Then, importantly, Texas railroads began in Houston, so all the cotton bound for export passed through the city, and it became an important destination for the flood of immigrants arriving in the new nation. The first U.S. census in Texas was for 1850, which enumerated 2,396 in Houston, and that doubled by 1860 and doubled again by 1870.

What was the first railroad in Texas?

Politics in the Republic of Texas mirrored that in the United States, which was experiencing the full vivid turmoil of Jacksonian populism, including its distrust of national banks and chartered corporations. Transportation in Texas was at the mercy of the ele-

Houston is a vibrant city that includes a robust downtown and beautiful parks and waterfronts.

ments, internal improvements were needed desperately, and railroads were only ten years old and could not be built without cooperative financing of some kind. Nevertheless, the popular hatred of banks sank the first attempt at chartering a Texas railroad. It was the success at attracting Northern capital that led to the chartering of the Buffalo Bayou, Brazos, and Colorado Railway Company early in 1850, which was the second railroad west of the Mississippi. The railroads that followed mostly began or ended in Houston, and it was the city's primacy as a rail hub that guaranteed its economic success.

With all that emphasis on business and wealth, did Houston ever cast an eye toward historical preservation?

Oh, yes. Houston set aside its first park in 1899 at the west end of downtown. Over time, Sam Houston Park became a relocation depository for many of the city's significant early homes. That ongoing effort is overseen by the Heritage Society, which was formed in 1954. The effectiveness of historical programs in the city was accelerated by the formation of the Houston History Alliance in 2005, a confederation of the former Houston History Association with numerous other organizations.

What Texas university is the hardest to get into?

A scion of the Gilded Age (1870s to 1900) who proudly listed his occupation as "capitalist," William Marsh Rice (1816–1900) was eighty-four when his butler administered chloroform to him as he slept at the behest of Rice's lawyer, who wanted his money. They almost got away with it, but it became the first sensational murder trial of the twentieth century. Marsh left most of his fortune to found an institution of higher learning in Houston, where he had formerly lived. Rice University opened in 1912 and is now a research university with a $5.3 billion endowment, is ranked first in the world in materials science research, has a 6:1 student-faculty ratio, and sponsors more than $140 million in research funding each year. It is also noted for its programs in business, the arts, and music—especially a marching band known as "The Mob" that can generate outrage on opponents' football fields.

What Houston businessman was so powerful that President Franklin D. Roosevelt referred to him (behind his back) as Jesus?

At the time the stock market crashed, Jesse H. Jones (1874–1956) was probably Houston's sharpest businessman, with interests in lumber, real estate, finance, banking, and insurance in addition to owning the *Houston Chronicle*. A conservative Republican with a well-founded reputation for dour arrogance, it was undoubtedly a step down for him to accept President Herbert Hoover's request that he chair the Reconstruction Finance Corporation. Despite their political differences, incoming president Franklin D. Roosevelt was impressed by Jones's ability and retained him in that post, later making him secretary of commerce as well. Jones therefore played a large role in putting the country back to work during the Great Depression and also ramping up for the war effort.

Roosevelt's respect for him did not make Jones any easier to bear, and FDR was heard often to refer to him in private as Jesus H. Jones.

How did Houston leaders respond when they learned that Dallas had beat them out to host the Texas Centennial celebration?

They published a book listing Dallas's contributions to the revolution. Its pages were blank.

Since Houston could not host the Centennial, what did it undertake to honor the century since Texas independence?

City leaders settled upon constructing a monument at the site of Texas's decisive battle at San Jacinto.

Is it true that the San Jacinto Monument is taller than the Washington Monument in Washington?

Built in 1936–1939 during the height of New Deal work relief, the $1.5 million cost was shared by the State of Texas and the federal government. There was said to have been some resentment in the nation's capital at funding a memorial that, rumor had it, would be taller than the Washington Monument's 555-foot obelisk. The Texans in Washington (including Jesse Jones) managed to secure the money, partially on the assurance that the finished structure would only be 533 feet tall. This was true; they merely omitted mention of the 34-foot (10-meter), 220-ton (199,581-kilogram) Lone Star that would surmount the structure, making the whole assemblage 567 feet (173 meters) high and the tallest monument column in the world. The shaft is 48 feet (15 meters) square at the base, tapering to 31 feet (9 meters) at the observation room; it is built of reinforced concrete faced with Cordova shell limestone. The base contains a theater, library, and museum of Texas history that is visited by over a quarter of a million people a year.

The impressive San Jacinto Monument, which honors the decisive battle of the Texas Revolution, stands at 567 feet, 12 feet taller than the Washington Monument.

What Houston businessman sketched out the idea to rebuild Europe after World War II?

Jesse Jones was not the only influential Houston tycoon in Washington. Will Clayton (1880–1966), who owned the world's largest cotton concern, became undersecretary of state for economic affairs shortly after World War II ended. He wrote a persuasive argument that the United States should use its status as the world's only reigning power to quickly rebuild Europe. Secretary of State George C. Marshall read it, endorsed it, and launched the Marshall Plan in June of 1947.

How did the nation's premier center for cancer treatment come to be?

Will Clayton's brother-in-law, Monroe Dunaway Anderson (1873–1939), moved to Houston in 1907 to help run the Clayton empire. He was a Democrat and a Cumberland Presbyterian, but personally he was a near-recluse. He never married and lived alone in one hotel or another for thirty-two years. He amassed considerable wealth and had a charitable disposition. Before his death, he willed most of his money to a foundation, with a directive to care for "the sick, the young, the aged, the incompetent and the helpless among the people." The ultimate result was the MD Anderson Cancer Treatment Center. It is the heart of the largest medical complex in the world, nesting more than forty institutions on a 640-acre (2.6-square-kilometer) section of land that includes the Texas Dental College, the Baylor College of Medicine, the Memorial Herrmann Hospital, and many others.

What was the largest hotel built in the United States during the 1940s?

Houston's Shamrock Hotel was the project of Texas oilman Glenn McCarthy (1907–1988). It had eighteen stories and eleven hundred rooms, and it was built at a cost of $21 million. It also featured a thousand-car garage, a 25,000-square-foot (2,323-square-meter) exhibition hall, and a 142-by-165-feet (43-by-50-meter) swimming pool. In an homage to McCarthy's Irish roots, the interior color was predominantly green in the Art Deco style that had long since fallen from fashion. There was green room décor, green bellhop uniforms, green everywhere.

McCarthy also honored his Irish ancestors by having the Shamrock's lobby built in sixty-three shades of green. How did the great architect Frank Lloyd Wright respond when he saw it?

Wright is alleged to have said many things about it. One was that he found it very interesting because he had always wondered what the inside of a jukebox looked like. Another was that he pointed to the ceiling and said to his apprentice, Euine Fay Jones, "That, young man, is an example of the effects of venereal disease on architecture."

What all happened at the Shamrock's grand opening?

The opening, night party on St. Patrick's Day 1949 cost $1 million. The week before the opening, McCarthy purchased an airliner from Howard Hughes and flew in some 150 Hollywood celebrities, including Errol Flynn, Ginger Rogers, and Hedda Hopper. The public, however, also felt themselves invited, and more than fifty thousand people jammed the grounds, two thousand paid $42 for dinner, and the corridors were jammed with another thousand of the curious, causing such pandemonium that headliner

Dorothy Lamour's broadcast was cut off the air, and the city's mayor, Oscar Holcombe, and his wife, Mary, were stranded in a hall for two hours.

Did the Shamrock make money for its owner?

McCarthy had told Jesse Jones of his plan to build a magnificent hotel on Main Street but 3 miles (4.8 kilometers) south of downtown at a site where McCarthy also envisioned a grand shopping center named after himself and a large medical center. Jones expressed his doubt that businessmen would want to make the trek to the edge of town. Jones turned out to be correct; the Shamrock always had difficulty attracting enough business to pay the more than one thousand staff members. In 1954 it was sold cheap to the Hilton Corporation, who also could not make it pay. It remained popular as a venue for society gatherings, but Hilton eventually unloaded it on its neighbor, the Texas Medical Center, and the Shamrock was demolished on June 1, 1987.

Where are U.S. astronauts trained?

When President John F. Kennedy announced on May 25, 1961, America's commitment to place a man on the moon by the end of the decade, the NASA Space Group had already been in existence for two and a half years. A year later, Kennedy spoke at Rice University, outlining both the Apollo program and construction of a manned spaceflight center to be built in Houston. Once space exploration began, missions after launch in

A replica of the International Space Station is on display at the Lyndon B. Johnson Space Center in Houston.

Florida were handed over to Houston, whose voice of "Mission Control" became familiar to millions over television. The facility was renamed the Lyndon B. Johnson Space Center within a few weeks of the former president's death in 1973 and continues its mission today in addition to being a leading tourist destination.

What was the world's first enclosed, air-conditioned sports stadium?

The Astrodome in Houston was the child of Roy Hofheinz (1912–1982), who was a political force in Houston from 1934 to 1955. An avid baseball fan, he was instrumental in winning an expansion National League team by boldly pledging to build a covered stadium for them to play in. His motive was practical as much as boastful, for watching baseball in Houston's humid summer heat, often washed out by rainstorms, was a trial. On a visit to Rome with his daughter, Hofheinz was captivated at the Coliseum by descriptions of the retractable awnings that kept part of the crowd in the shade. Hofheinz led the consortium that made the new stadium happen. Officially named the Harris County Domed Stadium, it was informally known as the Astrodome for the city's new baseball team. It was touted as the Eighth Wonder of the World, and visitors that first year found little reason to quarrel. Built in three years and three months at a cost of $35 million, it could seat forty-eight thousand. The playing surface was excavated to 25 feet (7.6 meters) below ground level, 208 feet (63 meters) beneath the height of the dome, which is 708 feet (216 meters) across. The entire structure covered over 9 acres (0.04 square kilometers). People who were accustomed to sweltering on metal benches to watch sporting events now sat under air-conditioning on plush theater seats. The upper rim was lined with luxury skyboxes. When it opened on April 9, 1965, it was the only domed sports arena on earth as well as the largest dome in the world. The opening event, an exhibition game between the newly named Houston Astros (formerly known as the Colt .45s) and the visiting New York Yankees, was the first game played on an artificial surface.

What happened to the Astrodome?

The concept of the domed stadium was so phenomenally successful that before long, the Astrodome was the *smallest* domed stadium in the country. It was also worn out by repeated use, hosting not just baseball but professional football, wrestling matches, even concerts. After the Astros moved to Minute Maid Park in 2000, the Astrodome faced an uncertain future. Demolition to repurpose the valuable property was not out of the question, but its status as an architectural icon was beyond dispute. In 2017 the Texas Historical Commission accorded the structure a designation as a state antiquities landmark, which prevented it from being torn down, and on May 29, 2018, it received a plaque designating it as a National Historic Landmark, which also provides tax incentives to restore it.

What visionary indoor shopping mall set a new standard for the concept when it opened in 1970?

Glenn McCarthy was never able to get his planned shopping center off the ground at the Shamrock, but the concept struck a chord with Gerald D. Hines, the legendary Houston developer who went on to build such landmark structures as Pennzoil Place and the Transco Tower. Hines began planning a lavish retail destination, an indoor shopping mall, that would have such amenities as an ice skating rink on the ground floor. He would locate it on busy Westheimer Road, several miles west of downtown. Hines's Galleria debuted in November 1970 with 600,000 square feet (55,742 square meters) of retail space. Its main axis featured three levels of retail stores beneath a barrel-vaulted skylight; its success was smashing. Hines's Galleria was barely open when plans went forward to expand it. Galleria II opened in 1976, then Galleria III and IV. Today, the Galleria complex hosts 375 stores in 2.4 million square feet (222,967 square meters) of retail space, anchored by the swankiest retailers in the country: Tiffany & Co., Versace, Prada, Yves Saint Laurent, and high-end department stores. The Galleria now is touted as the most visited attraction in the city, with more than thirty-five million visitors per year.

What was the Galleria designed after?

While the Galleria's three-story, barrel-vaulted arcade revolutionized the concept of indoor shopping in the United States, it was really modeled on the Galleria Vittorio Emanuele II in Milan, Italy, which was built—a barrel-vaulted indoor arcade—during the 1860s.

Why does Houston's urban sprawl seem so disorganized?

Like most Texans, people in Houston do not like being told what they can or cannot do, and they have never supported zoning laws. Such propositions were defeated by popular vote in 1948, 1962, and 1993. This dedication to *laissez faire* property ownership has led to such anomalies as middle-class houses lying just across the fence from towering skyscrapers or an erotica store being in business right next to a high-end Dillard's Department Store. This attitude has tended to flavor Houston's ambient brashness and braggadocio with a touch of chaos—which is not an inaccurate portrait of the city in general. Those who find Houston's sprawl and cacophony otherworldly will not be surprised that "Houston" was the first word spoken from the moon in 1969.

SAN ANTONIO

What is the population of San Antonio?

As of 2018, the population is 1,541,456.

How did San Antonio get its name?

A seventeenth-century expedition of missionaries and explorers reached the current site, the domain of Indians they named the Payaya, at a place the Indians called "Yanaguana," or refreshing waters. It was June 13, 1691, the feast day of St. Anthony of Padua, hence, San Antonio.

What recommended this location for a settlement?

The Indians had named the place accurately, for it had abundant water pouring from springs at the eastern edge of the Hill Country. During Spain's seemingly interminable series of wars with France, New Spain and French Louisiana found their fates tied to whether there was war or peace in Europe, but news was so slow to reach North America, they never knew what was going on in Europe. Spain established a road, El Camino Real, that ran eastward through the heart of New Spain to a new capital they had declared, Los Adaes, which actually lay far inside Louisiana. San Antonio lay about halfway between the established towns in Mexico and the Louisiana frontier.

How did San Antonio become the colonial capital?

The Spanish had settled on a general fort-and-mission system of settling remote parts of their New World empire, establishing with each step a mission for conversion of the Indians, and a fort, or presidio, to protect priests and European settlers, especially in Texas, to keep the French from getting any ideas. Trouble was indeed brewing with the French, who were annoyed that the Spanish located their pretended capital in territory they claimed. So missionaries, settlers, and troops were sent to the San Antonio area and founded the Misión San Antonio de Valero on May 1, 1718, and the Presidio San Antonio de Béxar four days later. When the French retook Los Adaes in 1719's "Chicken War," Spain pulled back all the way to San Antonio, which began functioning as the provincial capital.

The Alamo is, of course, a must-see for any tourist visiting San Antonio.

So, the Alamo was built in 1718?

No, the original Misión San Antonio de Valero was built in 1718. The structure that is known today as the Alamo was the second rebuilding of the church, which dates from the 1770s; it had been secularized and was in ruins by the time of the battle.

When did San Antonio begin to have a functioning civilian government?

Because of its remoteness and the danger posed by hostile Indians, the Spanish government had difficulty convincing civilians to move to the frontier to populate it. When the Villa San Fernando de Béxar began functioning in 1731, most of the settlers had been imported from the Canary Islands and were unfamiliar with the frontier.

How fast did the settlement grow?

From this nucleus of fifty-six Canary Islanders, adding soldiers' wives and families and immigrants from the Mexican interior, over the next fifty years, the population of San Antonio grew to 642 adult civilians, with 605 children plus the garrison soldiers and priests.

Did San Antonio attract Indians to the missions?

Yes, the church's commitment to try to civilize the native Indians, however arrogant we see the effort now, even prompted the addition of new missions in the same area: Nuestra Señora de la Purísima Concepción, Misión San Juan Capistrano, and Misión San Francisco de la Espada, which were moved there from other locations in 1731; and the Misión San José y San Miguel de Aguayo, which was moved to this location in 1760. Taken together, what is now called the "Missions Trail" is a U.S. National Historic Park and was named a UNESCO World Heritage Site in 2015. They form an important tourist destination for modern San Antonio and provide an important context for interpreting its history.

How did the citizens of San Antonio respond to the Texas Revolution?

When Antonio López de Santa Anna ran for president of Mexico in 1833, he ran as a liberal federalist, promising a system in which central power would be shared with the country's several states. This was widely supported in San Antonio, as in Texas. After his election, he abrogated the Constitution and began ruling by decree, and this divided the Hispanic community. Many felt ties of loyalty to the mother country, whatever form of government was imposed; many others, especially the educated element, felt betrayed and supported Anglo colonists in their bid for independence. In this they were joined by other Mexicans from the interior who revolted against the Santanista dictatorship and were defeated.

How badly was San Antonio divided by the revolution?

In some instances, it was not much different from the American Civil War. Families were divided and even had brother fighting brother. In one instance, Gregorio Esparza perished along with several other Latinos, fighting with the Americans in the Alamo. After the battle, his body was discovered by his brother, Francisco, who was in Santa Anna's army.

What is La Villita?

When San Antonio was first established, the soldiers and their families lived in brush *jacales* along the south bank of the San Antonio River. These huts washed away in subsequent floods and were replaced by sturdier but still modest homes. It became an ethnically mixed neighborhood with the arrival of Germans, Alsatians, and other nationalities and remained humble in its appearance. At the time the WPA began developing the River Walk during the Great Depression, it was recognized that this historic district needed to be preserved, whatever state it had fallen into. Today, it is a colony of artists, jewelers, and craftsmen who live in and sell their work on-site; it is listed in the National Register of Historic Places.

What is Fiesta?

In a full calendar of enjoyment, Fiesta is the largest festival that happens in San Antonio. It occurs over seventeen days every April, features more than one hundred separate events, staged by some seventy-five thousand volunteers, with a total of more than three million participants, and contributes over a third of a billion dollars to the city's economy. It began in 1891 as a way to honor those who fell at the Alamo; 2016 was the 180th

The annual Fiesta celebration in San Antonio lasts over two weeks and includes over a hundred exciting events!

anniversary of the battle as well as Fiesta's 125th anniversary. In 2018, San Antonio celebrated its tricentennial.

How did the Battle of Flowers get its name?

It was not because the name "Tournament of Roses" was already taken, although the Pasadena event does predate San Antonio's Fiesta by one year. In 1891 women converged before the Alamo in all manner of flower-bedecked buggies and bicycles and began throwing flowers at each other—hence the name. It is now the oldest element of Fiesta's seventeen days and the only major parade in the United States staged entirely by women—although they do accept help from the Texas National Guard for security and crowd control. It is held on Fiesta's second Friday and typically attracts a crowd of about 350,000.

What historic event happened at the Menger Hotel?

At the beginning of the Spanish–American War, the assistant secretary of the Navy, Theodore Roosevelt of New York, resigned to take an active command in the U.S. Army. He had visited Texas and the Menger before on a hunting trip and, being a former cowboy, he well knew Texans' reputations for toughness and horsemanship. Thus, he came to recruit Texans for his First U.S. Volunteer Cavalry, better known as the Rough Riders. TR joined his regiment on May 16, and the hotel's bar became the volunteers' preferred watering hole. It is now the Roosevelt Bar, presided over by a bull moose, which was the totem of his 1912 presidential run. The bar and the adjoining corridor now house a museum of memorabilia from the Spanish–American War.

Wasn't the Menger already famous before this?

Indeed yes, it was considered the finest hotel in the Southwest. German immigrant William Menger opened a brewery on the site in the early 1840s, which proved so popular that he and his wife built a boarding-house to augment it. That also made money, so they commissioned a two-story stone hotel that opened in 1859 and almost immediately built a forty-room addition. It became the preferred place to stay in San Antonio and hosted President Ulysses S. Grant, General Phil Sheridan, and other luminaries. Its "Colonial Restaurant" was famous for its menu of turtle soup (with turtles caught fresh locally), wild game, and mango ice cream. The bar, which was renovated in 1887 with cherry paneling and French mirrors, was even more famous for its mint juleps served in cups of sterling silver, hot toddies, and, in a nod to Menger's original brewery, beer chilled in the Alamo's own *acequia*. The Menger never slowed down; it expanded again in 1951, now occupying almost the whole block immediately south of the Alamo, and in 1976 was added to the National Register of Historic Places.

Is it true that Roosevelt and the Rough Riders liked to ogle animal trophies in San Antonio?

Yes, local trophy collector Albert Friedrich (1864–1928) opened a saloon on Dolorosa Street in which he displayed a freakish seventy-eight-point rack of antlers, along with other curiosities that he had bought. By 1896 he needed a larger saloon, the Buckhorn; after more changes of location and owners, it remains in business as the Buckhorn Saloon and Museum, to which fins and feathers were later added.

What was the first air-conditioned skyscraper in the United States?

The Milam Building opened in downtown San Antonio in 1928, named for Colonel Ben Milam, the Texan officer who led volunteers in capturing the city in 1835 and in whose honor the only flag on the building is that of Texas. At twenty-one stories, it was when it opened the tallest in the country built of brick and reinforced concrete and the tallest to be air-conditioned. The system was designed after that used in a German mine, with the chilling unit aided by chunks of ice in the basement.

What was the occasion for the HemisFair?

In 1968 San Antonio threw a gigantic party, a world's fair celebrating the 250th anniversary of the city. Its iconic structure was the Tower of the Americas, a 750-foot needle topped by a revolving restaurant and observation deck. That concept had been used six years before by Seattle's Space Needle for that world's fair, but San Antonio's tower, predictably for Texas, was 250 feet taller. It opened on April 6, 1969—only two days after Martin Luther King Jr. was assassinated and angering many in the African American community that the opening went on as scheduled. Putting on the fair cost $156 million and stayed open for six months, losing, on the bottom line, over $6 million.

Hemisfair Park with the Tower of the Americas in the background.

Is the Tower of the Americas still in use?

Yes, it is still a favored venue for people to celebrate special occasions and to enjoy the view.

Why on earth is there a SeaWorld park in San Antonio, so far from the ocean?

Central Texas is a destination for amusement parks, which also includes Six Flags Fiesta Texas nearby and the Schlitterbahn in New Braunfels. That, plus the presence in San Antonio of a world-class zoo, made San Antonio a likely market for both entertainment and marine life education, thus a logical choice for one of SeaWorld's inland parks.

What powerful San Antonio congressman predicted the savings and loan crisis of the early eighties?

While Ronald Reagan was a hugely popular president in Texas, the push toward deregulating the savings and loan industry alarmed the powerful chairman of the House Banking Committee, Henry B. González. As a state senator in 1960, he had delivered Texas to Kennedy and the Democrats, as his Viva Kennedy-Viva Johnson clubs had delivered more than their margin of victory in the state. He went to Congress in 1962, where his intelligence and integrity were a thorn in the side of the business greed emblematic of the Reagan era. He not only predicted the S&L disaster, whose bailout cost hundreds of billions of dollars, but before he retired, he also predicted the collapse of the peso following the North American Free Trade Agreement (NAFTA).

DALLAS

What is the population of Dallas?

As of 2018, the population stood at 1,359,133.

How did Dallas get its start?

In 1839, the area that became Dallas was far off the beaten path, well to the west of the stream of settlers coming from the United States via Arkansas and 200 miles (322 kilometers) north of the action in the settled areas of the Republic of Texas. One man, John Neely Bryan, born in Tennessee on Christmas Eve 1810, saw his future there. He was an Indian trader, and here, where the Trinity River branched, was an advantageous location to pursue that and also operate a ferry, which would become steady work with more settlers. Bryan explored the area with a Cherokee companion named Ned, left his name on a stake where Dealey Plaza is now, and returned to Arkansas to organize his affairs so he could return permanently. When he came back two years later, Texas had fought the Cherokee War, and the north Texas Indians were gone. Making the best of it, he decided to stay and take advantage of trade on the Preston Trail that the Republic was blazing

The sparkling skyline of Dallas is reflected off the Trinity River at night.

from Austin to the Red River. Bryan had the area that is now downtown surveyed, but he needed settlers. He invited people from Bird's Fort to join him, and luckily, there were other people available in the Peters Colony whose affairs were a mess. The first crops were planted in 1842; Bryan was instrumental in getting the settlement made a county seat when it was created in 1846.

Has Dallas really managed to preserve its very first house?

Well, not really, although most people who see the Bryan cabin in Founder's Plaza assume it must be. Bryan built his cabin overlooking the Trinity River, and it was destroyed in a 1930 flood. This replica was probably built soon after.

Who was Dallas named for?

Surprisingly, that is not known for certain. There are several candidates, the most prominent being Senator George Mifflin Dallas of Pennsylvania, soon to become vice president of the United States under James K. Polk; Bryan had Scottish ancestry, and there was a town in Moray named Dallas. Most likely, however, there was an early settler named Dallas, and Bryan later told his son that he named the town after "my friend Dallas."

How did Dallas get its start as a business capital?

Bryan had picked a favorable, fertile, and well-traveled location. Records indicate that the first doctor came in 1843, the first lawyer two years later, and by the time Texans

What was La Réunion?

There was a French philosopher of the time, Charles Fourier, who was publishing his doctrine of utopian communism. This was not unusual, but Fourier's thinking was more advanced in advocating the full participation of women. One of Fourier's disciples, Victor Prosper Considerant of Lyon, put together a colonial venture and settled about two hundred French, Swiss, and Belgian people just a few miles south of Dallas. When the colony started to break apart, as utopian ventures were wont to do, many relocated to Dallas, which gained such skills as brewing and watchmaking that diversified the community.

voted on whether to join the United States, there were thirty-two registered men (the vote was 29 to 3, in favor). Bryan nursed his colony attentively, and his cabin became the courthouse, post office, and supply store even as traffic increased on his ferry. Like many Texans, Bryan caught the gold fever and disappeared to California but quickly returned, and he saw his little town gain some cultural diversity and new skills with the breakup of the nearby colony La Réunion.

How did Reconstruction turn Dallas into a city?

By 1860, Dallas boasted a photographer and a barber, and the population had increased to about 678 but with about twice that number in the surrounding area. With the debate raging about secession, Dallas was a center of the "Texas Troubles," a largely hysterical rumor that slaves and their abolitionist sympathizers were about to rise up. A fire in the central business district moved a mob to hang three slaves, and the city voted 741–237 for secession. After the war, Dallas was one of the least touched cities in the former Confederacy, and refugees came looking to start over. The population more than tripled from three thousand in 1870 to ten thousand in 1880.

How did Dallas get the railroads to come?

Dallas was healthy and growing, but city leaders could not risk the town getting left behind by the railroads; Texas by now had several examples of settlements whose residents had spurned rail transport, which led to them drying up. As construction neared, a Dallas deputation visited officials of the Houston and Central Texas Railway with $5,000 to move their planned route from Corsicana to Dallas. Unable to bribe the Texas and Pacific, Dallas leaders resorted to some political chicanery, getting an amendment tacked onto a bill that made the T&P run its route through "Browder Springs," which really turned out to be Main Street. The dirty play worked. Dallas's population during the 1870s increased by seven thousand, more than half of whom arrived in 1872, within a year of the railroad. Dallas now had a rail junction where north-south tracks crossed east-west, it was a jump-off for travelers headed west even as it was a market for buffalo robes being shipped east, and by the mid-Seventies, it had city water, gas, and a volunteer fire department.

What turned Dallas to manufacturing?

Dallas had gone far down the road toward being a business center, but the national Panic of 1893 hit the city hard. Banks failed, and the markets in lumber, wheat, and especially cotton fell. It occurred to some city leaders that they would do well to give some attention to actually making things that people must have. As the economy slowly improved, Dallas found itself a world leader in producing farm machinery, saddles, and other goods. Their heart was never in it, though, and they returned to their love of business and finance.

What was the first skyscraper west of the Mississippi?

Appropriately for a city that prided itself on its business atmosphere, it was the fifteen-story Praetorian Building at 1607 Main Street in Dallas, built at a cost of $800,000, begun in 1905 and opened in 1909. The Praetorians were one of the many fraternal benefit orders of the day that existed to provide insurance benefits for its members, and Dallas was on its way to becoming an insurance capital. The building was a wonder of modernity, with its interior finished with marble and mahogany. There was steam heat, elevators, hot and cold running water in every office (supplied by two artesian wells), and complete wiring for telephone, telegraph, and electricity. Taller buildings soon followed, but the Praetorian held its own, renovated and doubled in size in 1961. Its history notwithstanding, the Praetorian Building was eventually considered an obstacle to progress, and it was demolished in 2013.

What powerhouse American high-end retail store began in Dallas?

Herbert Marcus (1878–1950) was born in Kentucky but moved to Texas at fifteen to be near his brother, and he clerked in a general store in Hillsboro. He later moved into sales, relocated to Dallas, and made a name for himself. Then, with his sister Carrie (1883–1953) and her husband Al Neiman, they moved to Atlanta to work promotions for Coca-Cola, at which they were so good they sold their business for $25,000. Pooling their money, they returned to Dallas and opened an exclusive shop of ladies' ready-to-wear in Dallas, relying on Carrie's impeccable taste and willingness to counsel customers through purchases. Carrie divorced Neiman two

The Neiman-Marcus headquarters building is in downtown Dallas.

years later, and brother and sister created a retail legend. One important way their fame spread was, beginning in 1926, the publication of an annual Christmas catalog, featuring gifts of epically expensive whimsy. (In recent years, these have included his-and-hers service robots and a personalized submarine.) That same year also saw Neiman-Marcus begin the first regularly scheduled fashion shows in the United States. Their other innovations included the first in-store gift wrapping service and the first customer rewards program. Later, the founder's son, Stanley Marcus, began issuing the Neiman-Marcus Award to outstanding designers; Coco Chanel became a dedicated customer. Neiman-Marcus was acquired by Bergdorf Goodman in 1972 and spun off again in 1989.

What was the first self-contained shopping center in the United States?

Realizing that many Dallasites already aspired to be just a little better than regular people, developer Henry Exall bought land north of Dallas in 1889, intending to create a verdant neighborhood of well-appointed homes along Turtle Creek. He named the development Philadelphia Place after his hometown, which was known for its network of parks, and he dammed Turtle Creek into Exall Lake to help the project along. The scheme evaporated in the Panic of 1893. In 1906 meatpacking magnate John Armstrong bought the land, to develop much along the same lines, under the name of Highland Park. By 1913 there were five hundred residents, who petitioned Dallas to annex them, but were rebuffed. Highland Park prospered, and second and third developments were opened and filled. Dallas realized its error and sought to annex the city, but by then Highland Park wanted none of it. In 1931 the city featured Highland Park Village, the first self-contained shopping center in the United States, with dozens of retail venues and a theater behind a unified Spanish colonial façade.

Why did wealthy Dallasites move into the Park Cities?

North of Highland Park, University Park had its beginnings to house families connected with the new Southern Methodist University, which opened in 1915. It was larger than Highland Park at 515 acres (2 square kilometers), attracted a population of over 20,000 by 1945, and was no less exclusive, but unlike Highland Park the city government was amenable to be annexed to Dallas when they came calling. This time it was the citizen referendum that defeated the unification. Through the 1950s, officials saw no need to intermingle with Dallas. It was one of the wealthiest cities in the country, and it had superb schools which, because University Park took no federal money, did not have to deal with desegregation, especially since there were no African American residents within the city limits. Most recently, the enclave twins had a population of 8,564 in Highland Park and 24,905 in University Park. They were the #1 and #2 best educated cities in Texas and combined still have one of the highest per capita incomes not just in Texas but nationally.

How did Dallas win the right to host the official Texas Centennial Exhibition?

It was not hard—they threw money at it. For all Texans' chauvinism, they were late in preparing for the one-hundredth anniversary of their independence, especially after it was found that government involvement meant passing an amendment to their micro-managing 1876 Constitution. By the time the wheels began turning in 1934, they had less than two years to pick a site, design and build a venue, get entities invited and accepted, and open the gates. The Centennial Commission appointed a Centennial Corporation to get it done, and three of its directors were Dallas bankers, who cobbled together a gift of land, bonds, and cash to the amount of $10 million.

After it won the job, how did Dallas celebrate the Centennial?

Dallas architect George Leighton Dahl (1894–1987), whose local portfolio consisted of the Cotton Bowl and the Neiman-Marcus Building, was given the job of getting the buildings up in time. He devised a new style of architecture that he called Texanic, which may have been for publicity purposes because it was straight-up Art Deco with an inflection of ancient Karnak: clean-lined, massive, and therefore fast to build, with human figures of giant, pointy-breasted goddesses and ripple-chested men with small heads. There were fifty structures, most of them lining an interminable reflecting pool. With ten thousand men at work and happy to have jobs, most of the grounds were finished for the June 6 opening. The exhibitors and organizers knew how to delight a crowd. The National Cash Register Company was housed in a giant cash register; the French exhibit was in a mock ocean liner. A broadcasting studio allowed the public to see exactly how all that worked. And men on their own, or who slipped their wives, could take in Paris Peggy and Corinne the Apple Dancer. Despite the availability of so much feminine allurement, the Centennial's actual opening was a much more chaste affair, featuring six-year-old Madge Thornall, great-granddaughter of Sam Houston, done up as an In-

The Music Hall at Fair Park in Dallas is just one of several buildings designed by architect George Dahl for the Centennial that are still in use today.

dian princess. The exposition also marked some social milestones. The Cotton Bowl football stadium, which predated the Centennial buildings, hosted the Texas Centennial Olympics and were integrated, which was a first anywhere in the South. One of the popular exhibits was the Hall of Negro Life, another first for an exposition of this scale.

After the Centennial was over, how did Dallas continue to capitalize on its fairgrounds?

The country had only just begun recovering from the Great Depression, but the Centennial's impact on the Dallas economy helped considerably. It had attracted more than 6.3 million people, nearly all of whom had spent at least a little money. With that in mind, they decided to turn the stiles one more time and reused the buildings for a "Greater Texas & Pan American Exhibition" the following year. It was rather a bust, as many of the key exhibitors such as automobile companies did not return, and it attracted only a third the number of visitors as the Centennial. Dahl's buildings, however, were there to last, and continued to be used annually for the Texas State Fair, which is the largest in the United States. Thirty of them now survive and are considered one of the finest collections of Art Deco structures in the country.

After the war, how did Dallas manage to diversify its economy and stay in the forefront?

Luckily for them, a whole new industry developed with the arrival of the integrated circuit, invented by Jack Kilby at Texas Instruments, which helped Dallas become the third-largest technology manufacturer in the United States. Dallas still never took its eye off the sales ball for long, opening a giant complex of consumer ware vendors starting with home furnishings in 1957, the Trade Mart in 1959, Market Hall in 1960, the Apparel Mart in 1964, and the World Trade Center in 1974. Taken together, they formed a combination of shopping mall and permanently evolving exposition—but only for wholesalers and "qualified" buyers who then distribute the wonders to consumers.

Dallas has long held itself out to be such a business capital; just how big is big business there?

Very, actually. As the number of Fortune 500 companies headquartered in Houston fell from twenty-four to twenty, the number in DFW grew to twenty-two—a small difference, but it carried bragging rights. Those headquartered in Dallas proper include AT&T, which relocated there in 2008; Energy Transfer Equity; Tenet Healthcare; Southwest Airlines; Texas Instruments; Jacobs Engineering, which moved in from Pasadena in 2016; HollyFrontier; and Dean Foods. In the suburbs, ExxonMobil is headquartered in Irving along with five others, including Celanese and Kimberly-Clark; four in Plano, including Alliance Data Systems; and GameStop in Grapevine. Other powers to reckon with are Neiman-Marcus, which began in Dallas and never left, Zale Corporation, 7-Eleven, Comerica Bank, Mary Kay Cosmetics, and many, many more.

> ## How does Dallas maintain such a strong business engine even in bad times?
>
> Its greatest key to success is diversification. Dallas hosts so many different kinds of business that trouble in one or a few leave it relatively unaffected. Houston was hurt by the oil downturn in 2014, but as far as Dallas was concerned, women will always wear makeup and people will always need insurance.

Have any of Dallas's grand dreams come crashing down?

A few. More than a century of never-say-die efforts to channelize the Trinity River and turn Dallas and even Fort Worth into seaports turned into one boondoggle after another. During the presidency of Texan (by way of Connecticut) George H. W. Bush, there was the Superconducting Super Collider gambit, an underground nuclear particle accelerator more than 50 miles (80 kilometers) in circumference south of Dallas that would have been far more powerful than Europe's Large Hadron Collider. The project was abandoned after spending more than $2 billion; contests were held for ideas on how to find a use for the miles of unfinished tunnel; one of the better entries was for a mushroom farm. When the metro area finally outgrew Love Field on Mockingbird Lane for its airport, speculation was rife on where the giant new regional airport would be located. Much of the smart money bet on a southerly location between the two cities, which meant east of Burleson and west of Ennis. Investors began buying up land with a fever, driving up prices into a bubble. When the true location was ultimately announced northwest of Dallas between Plano and Denton, the well-diversified investors took it in stride, but plenty of wannabes lost their shirts—winning zero sympathy from local dirt farmers who had either seen their taxes skyrocket or accepted deals they couldn't refuse.

AUSTIN

What is the current population of Austin?

Austin is just shy of one million at 983,366, according to 2018 surveys.

How did Austin get its start?

As with many aspects of Texas history, there are different stories. The more official version is that the Republic's second president, Mirabeau B. Lamar, wished to found a new capital city in the interior where, as he estimated, north-south trade routes would intersect with east-west. Unofficially, when he was inaugurated, the capital was in Houston, a new town named for his predecessor, Sam Houston, whom he hated with a passion, and he refused to conduct the government from there. His commissioners as-

Austin was founded to be a center of trade routes in Texas. Settled in 1835, it was incorporated four years later and now has a population of nearly one million people.

cended the Colorado River to a village called Waterloo near a massive, booming spring of cold, fresh water. A new town was laid out north of the river, named in honor of Stephen F. Austin, and received the government in 1839.

What violent incident assured Austin's survival?

When Sam Houston was elected president again in 1842, moving the capital back to Houston city would have been too obvious. After the Mexican invasion, he began conducting the government from the former capital at Washington. Residents of the new town were alerted that something was afoot, and local boardinghouse keeper Angelina Eberly spied Rangers loading the national archives into wagons in the dead of night on December 31. A loaded cannon was kept in the street nearby as a defense against Indians, and Eberly fired it to alert the townspeople. Citizens turned the gun on the archives building and fired seven more shots as the Rangers jumped into their wagons and rumbled away. They were overtaken by a posse the next day on Brushy Creek, and the national papers were recovered after a brief gunfight rather grandly termed the "Archives War" and stored for safekeeping in Eberly's cellar. The government returned to Austin for good in 1844.

How did Austin finance its first government building boom?

Texas joined the Union in 1845 to the extent of its national claims, which extended into what is now central Wyoming. Following a dispute over the extension of slavery, the United States paid Texas $10 million. With these funds, Texas was able to build a Greek revival capital and a fireproof land office in which to store those most valuable of government records (whose architect, Conrad Stremme, was German, hence its resemblance to a Bavarian castle). Finally, the government hired local architect Abner Cook (1814–1884) to design and build the cavernous Greek revival Governor's Mansion.

What old government buildings are still in use in Austin today?

The Land Office building continued in that function until 1918, when it became a dual museum for the Daughters of the Republic of Texas and the United Daughters of the Confederacy. Extensive restoration began in 1989; since then it has functioned as the Capitol Visitors Center, with exhibits and educational programs. The Governor's Mansion is now the fourth oldest in the United States to have been lived in continuously since its construction. In 2008 the house was heavily damaged in an arson attack. However, it was in the midst of an extensive renovation, so its collections of art, priceless antiques, mementoes, and even architectural elements such as mantels and the stair banister, were safe in storage. After a $22 million rebuilding, the house is substantially as it was.

What innovation did Austin bring to the craft of law and order?

During the 1870s, downtown Austin became increasingly unruly, owing to a growing number of saloons, gaming halls, and the commerce in "Guy Town," a prostitution district. One of the worst characters was Englishman Ben Thompson (1843–1884), a gambler, knife fighter, and saloon owner who had been tried several times for murder but always gotten off and who was well known as a "mean" drunk. In 1880 the citizens elected Thompson to be city marshal. Once he switched to the good side of the law, the dangerous element, unwilling to tangle with the most dangerous bastard in town, quietly slipped away or else behaved themselves, and Austin enjoyed a period of unprecedented quiet. Along with fellow psychopath King Fisher, Thompson was gunned down in San Antonio in 1884, aged forty.

What is the largest state capitol building in the United States?

In 1856 Texas built itself a new capitol with money from its settlement with the United States for selling it excess territory claimed by the Republic. The building was homely and inadequate, never popular, and after twenty-five years of use, its replacement was planned, a process that was accelerated when the existing building burned to the ground in November 1881. A competition was held to present the state with a capitol suited to its majesty and ambitions, and the winner was Elijah Myers of Chicago, who had already designed four capitols throughout the West. The building was colossal, nearly 200 yards (183 meters) across and 100 yards (91 meters) through, with four stories having 22-foot (6.7-meter) ceilings. It was a feast of inventiveness, including strategically placed glass floors to let light into the nether reaches,

An 1888 photograph shows the Goddess of Liberty statue as it is prepared for installation at the Capitol building in Austin.

pierced tin vents in the ceilings of the House and Senate chambers to encourage a flow of air, and its centerpiece, a 302-foot- (92-meter-) high dome of cast iron, painted to match the pink granite.

Why was the Capitol built out of pink granite?

The original design called for construction using white Texas limestone, but after the contractor delivered 60 tons (54,431 kilograms) of it and construction began, it rained, and brown-red streaks were observed on the stone. It seemed that the local limestone had iron crystals in it, which rusted in the rain. That stone was consigned to the foundation and interior rubble, and a search was undertaken for a replacement. Learning of the dilemma was a partnership of ranchers at Granite Mountain in Llano County. Their land turned out to be useless for either farming or ranching, as it was a rock. One even tried to trade the place for a horse but was turned down. They offered their expanse of pink granite as building stone, the state built a railroad from Austin to Llano, rounded up teams of convicts from state prisons to do the quarrying, and one of the nation's most beautiful capitols acquired its distinctive color.

How was the Capitol nearly lost?

In February 1983, Lieutenant Governor Bill Hobby's daughter and some of her friends were watching television in his apartment located behind the Senate chamber. Faulty wiring caught fire, and the blaze spread to gut most of the east half of the building. One guest was killed, and a policeman and four firefighters were hurt. The tragedy was the beginning of a triumphant, $98-million restoration that took the building back to its original grandeur and also a $75-million underground expansion.

Who was the first known serial killer in the United States?

From December 1884 to December 1885, Austin was terrorized by a series of grisly attacks in which seven women and one man were murdered, and six women and two men

---

Who was Andrew Zilker?

Indiana native Andrew Jackson Zilker (1858–1934) is said to have arrived in Austin with 50 cents in his pocket. He found his fortune as an ice manufacturer and bought up land across the river from downtown, including Barton Springs, whose water he used to make his ice. He went into banking and became the city water and light commissioner and a member of the school board. To benefit the latter, he sold 366 acres (1.5 square kilometers) of his land holdings, including Barton Springs, to the city, with the proviso that their payments go to the school district—the land that is now Zilker Park, crown jewel of the city park system. Though public-spirited, he was prickly, once starting a brick making company in hopes of ruining a rival, and encouraged later political figure Tom Miller to run for mayor to spite the incumbent.

were wounded. A suddenly enlarged police force augmented by vigilante volunteers saturated lower downtown's "Guy Town," and the murders ceased. The term "serial killer" did not exist yet, and the authorities could not conceive that one perpetrator had unleashed all this mayhem. One report said that during the course of the year, four hundred men were taken in for questioning; there were two trials and one conviction, which the Texas Supreme Court overturned for manifest lack of evidence. Not until reinvestigated for the television show *History Detectives* in 2014 was a convincing theory put forward. The likely killer was Nathan Elgin, nineteen, a black cook who worked in the vicinity of the murders, who had a club foot that matched an evidentiary bloody print—and who was killed by police while in the act of assaulting a girl with a knife.

What is the longest-running musical show on American television?

Austin City Limits is a live-performance music presentation recorded at KLRU television, an affiliate of the Public Broadcasting System, on the University of Texas campus. Having first aired in 1975 (featuring Willie Nelson) and continuing to the present, it is the longest-running musical show in American television history. The first forty years of programs have been digitally archived by the Rock and Roll Hall of Fame in Cleveland, Ohio.

Why does Austin think of itself as the live music capital of the world?

Austin has long been the place to go in Texas for musicians to go to try to make a career for themselves. In the past, roadhouses such as Threadgill's, which launched Janis

The Austin City Limits Festival is an October event full of fun and music.

Joplin, arguably seedy venues like the Armadillo World Headquarters, and Alliance Wagon Yard (both now gone) gave the country Willie Nelson, Kris Kristofferson, and many other practitioners of an identifiable local sound. Today, would-be musicians make their bids at the long line of bars down the 6th Street "Music District," and a full calendar of music festivals include the South by Southwest and Urban festivals in March, Reggae Festival in April, and the Austin City Limits Festival in October.

What are "Moonlight Towers"?

Many American cities have nicknames. New York is the "Big Apple." New Orleans is the "Big Easy." In 1894, Austin leaders decided that the city needed a similar sobriquet and decided that it should be the "City of Perpetual Moonlight." Other cities had used "moonlight towers" before, and Austin purchased thirty-one discards from Detroit, creating a network of 165-foot-tall metal towers, each topped with a cluster of carbon-arc lamps that illuminated a 1,500-foot (457-meter) radius and made any nighttime stroll seem as though it were under a full moon. Of the original thirty-one towers, fifteen survive (six in their original locations), most famously the one in Zilker Park, which becomes the nation's tallest artificial Christmas tree every December. They are the last known moonlight towers in the United States and are a National Historic Landmark.

Who was responsible for transforming the downtown lake from an unofficial city dump into a premier urban park?

Just southeast of downtown, Longhorn Dam on the Colorado River was built in 1960 to form Town Lake, actually a cooling reservoir for the Holly Street Power Plant. The dam is only 36 feet (11 meters) high, creating a long, slender thread of a lake 6 miles (58 kilometers) long through the central city, where isolated spots of the shoreline became strewn with refuse, used tires, and old refrigerators, even a toxic waste dump. In the early 1970s, discontent reached a critical mass; private initiatives to clean it up didn't work, the city council stepped in to organize something, and television station KTBC did a story about it. KTBC was owned by Lady Bird Johnson, former first lady and icon of American beautification. With her influence, some phone calls, and nearly $20,000 of her own money, she was largely responsible for making Town Lake Park happen. City officials offered to name the park for her, but she refused. Within a month of her death in 2007, the city overrode her wishes and renamed it Lady Bird Lake.

How long did it take to complete the Hike-and-Bike Trail around the lake?

Following various fires and malfunctions, the Holly Street Power Plant was deactivated and later demolished, adding that land to the park; a water treatment facility at the edge of downtown was taken offline in 2008. Motorboats have long been banned on the lake, making it a haven for paddle boards, kayaks, and a training center for the University of Texas rowing team. Pesticide contamination finally flushed out, and the ban on eating fish caught in these waters was lifted, in 1999. Swimming is still prohibited, owing to treacherous currents and dangerous debris from previous floods. It took until

What is Hippie Hollow?

Long known for its laissez faire attitude toward people's personal predelictions, Austin took little notice when remote coves on the north shore of Lake Travis became frequented by naturists indulging in nude sunbathing and "skinny dipping." The practice increased greatly during the countercultural revolution of the late 1960s and early 1970s. After the wealthy began building mansions on the overlooking hilltops, complaints about the nudity increased. (A county sheriff's deputy reportedly told one complainant that if she did not like what she saw, she should put the lens cap back on her telescope!) Beginning in October 1985, Travis County has managed the area as the only clothing-optional swimming area in Texas. Use is age-restricted to eighteen and over, and having sex in the open air is still illegal.

2014, and completion of a 1.3-mile (2.1-kilometer), $28 million boardwalk, to finish the 10-mile (16-kilometer) Hike-and-Bike Trail that loops around the lake. The trail was recently named for former mayor Roy Butler, who was instrumental in creating the park, and his wife, Ann.

How did bats come to be such an important cultural icon in Austin?

About 1.5 million Mexican free-tailed bats live in the chinks and crevices under the Congress Avenue bridge across Lady Bird Lake. They are the largest urban colony in the United States, and watching their nightly departure to forage for insects in the pastures east of the city has become a favored activity. Crowds line the bridge, boats are chartered, and once each summer, traffic is shut off for the Bat Festival that takes place on the bridge. Their impact on the tourist industry has become almost as significant as their devouring tons of mosquitoes and other insects every night.

How does Austin demonstrate its good will toward the bicycling community?

According to *Forbes*, Austin is the third most bicycle-friendly city in the United States, after Philadelphia and Tucson. Dedicated bike paths include the 10-mile (16-kilometer) loop around Lady Bird Lake and the 7.3-mile (11.7-kilometer) Walnut Creek Trail. There is also the Veloway near the Wild Flower Center and forty stations of the recent "Austin B-cycle" bike-sharing program. Dozens of miles of city streets, some with quite heavy traffic counts, have seen car lanes reduced to accommodate dedicated bike lanes, some with their own miniature traffic signs. It is a common feeling among the populace that only Austin would spend $1 million to build a curving, landscaped pedestrian and bicycle bridge across Lady Bird Lake, right next to the Lamar Boulevard bridge, to protect them from the traffic. This is often followed by a second feeling that only in Austin would cyclists continue to clog traffic on Lamar to demonstrate their power.

Austin is a very bicycle-friendly city that features miles of bike paths.

How manic are Austinites about their physical fitness?

Despite burgeoning gym memberships and the daily jam of joggers on the Hike-and-Bike Trail, Austin only ranks twelfth nationally among the fittest cities, according to the American College of Sports Medicine. That is, however, the highest rank among Texas cities. One marker of Austin's traditional alienation from the rest of Texas might be that it is the twelfth fittest city in the center of the eleventh fattest state.

How many people participate in the Austin 10K?

With 23,200 runners in the 2018 Austin 10K, it was the largest in Texas but only sixth largest in the nation. This has been an annual early-April event since 1978 and is only one of many competitive and charitable running events in the city, including a mid-February marathon held since 1991. RunGuides has calendared ninety different events for 2018, twenty-three of which expect more than one thousand entrants.

With the state legislature still dominated by rural representatives, how do they feel about convening in such a city?

Like they are in hostile territory and count themselves lucky that the Constitution requires them to meet for only 140 days once every two years. They find ways of showing their disdain, such as saddling Austin with a higher proportion of toll roads than other major cities. Another recent trick was to deprive Austin of congressional representation. After the 2010 census, Austin was sliced like a pie into five different districts that reach far out into rural conservative territory that dominates the vote.

What is meant by the oft-repeated mantra "Keep Austin Weird"?

In many ways, Texas's capital city is atypical of the rest of the state and always has been. It was the largest city to vote against seceding from the Union in 1861, and rural hayseed governors tried to cleanse the university of liberal egghead professors in 1917 and 1944. During the 1960s, Austin was virtually the only city in Texas in which it was relatively safe to be counter cultural, and "slackers" have been a part of the local fabric ever since.

Ubiquitous on bumper stickers and endlessly invoked on live radio talk, the city's unofficial motto seems to be a way of embracing Austin's stubborn culture of personal laissez faire, of rejecting enforced conformity to bourgeois social norms, and of celebrating artistic creativity even when the art isn't very good. "News of the Weird" is a standard feature of Austin's alternative weekly newspaper, the *Chronicle*, and since 2007 there has even been a Museum of the Weird in the heart of the 6th Street entertainment strip. It is housed in a portion of Lucky Lizard Curios and Gifts as the owners' homage to P. T. Barnum's American Museum and the generation of carnival attractions and dime museums that it spawned.

The commitment to weirdness has also taken such forms as lionizing a bearded, thong-wearing homeless cross-dresser named Leslie Cochran (1951–2012) into an ever-present reproach for the plight of the homeless and the embracing of the informal "Graffiti Park," a hillside of concrete retaining walls, the only reminder of an abandoned condo project west of downtown, that was surrendered to daily new art and tagging.

How fast is Austin growing?

Every day, about forty people move away and about 150 newcomers arrive, causing a chronic strain on city services and infrastructure.

The motto "Keep Austin Weird" can be seen on signage and tourist shop souvenirs around the city.

FORT WORTH

How many people live in Fort Worth?

There are 893,997 people living in that fair city as of 2018.

What is Texas's most populous suburb?

If it were located elsewhere than on the edge of Fort Worth, Arlington's position as Texas's seventh-largest city would rate it as a major urban area. However, its interminable sprawl of housing and lack of a central downtown, and being the largest city in Texas that is not a county seat, makes it Fort Worth's largest satellite in most people's eyes.

How did Fort Worth get started?

Fort Worth is the largest Texas city to have actually had its beginnings as a military fort. It was built on the upper Trinity River. In 1843 the Republic of Texas agreed with local Indian tribes that no Anglos would pass west of a line of trading posts that would be established, one of which was at the junction of the West Fork and the Clear Fork of the Trinity. After statehood and the Mexican–American War, the commander of the Department of Texas, General William Jenkins Worth, recommended a picket line of ten forts, from the Rio Grande north to the Indian Territory, of which seven were built. The site of the Trinity River trading post was the most northerly. Worth died of cholera in south Texas, and Major Ripley Arnold, when he established the camp on June 6, 1849, named it for the late General Worth.

What Indians lived in the Fort Worth area?

The Rolling Plains immediately west and north of Fort Worth were Comanche country, so one needed to be alert for a raiding party. However, they were not the principal Indians in the area; that was a western branch of the Caddo. They had moved into Cross Timbers and Cedar Breaks south of town because it had turned into a curious Native no-man's land. The Tonkawa of the Brazos Valley would not go west of there because they knew the Comanche were better fighters than they were; the Comanche did not go east of there because they knew if any of them were killed in a fight, the Tonkawa would eat them, which they found to be the worst degree of demoralizing.

How did the panther become such a social totem in early Fort Worth?

The economic recession of 1873 hit the cattle industry, among others, hard, and Fort Worth fell on hard times. When the railroad decided to end its construction for the time being in Dallas, the local newspaper editor indulged in a little mockery of their upstart to the west. He quoted an attorney, late of Fort Worth, who said that business there was so slow, he had seen a panther sleeping near the courthouse. Instead of taking the insult, Fort Worth wore the name proudly, a "Sleeping Panther" statue was erected, and the businesses and clubs proudly used "panther" in their names.

Established in 1849 and incorporated in 1873, Fort Worth is Texas's fifth-largest city and once had one of the largest livestock markets in the United States.

How did Fort Worth acquire the nickname "Cowtown"?

Cattle from Texas had been driven up the Shawnee Trail to Missouri until they began to be turned back because they carried Texas fever, a disease borne by ticks to which the Texas cattle were immune but which was highly fatal to northern cattle. Therefore, the north-bound traffic was diverted west to a route from San Antonio, through Waco and Fort Worth, to the Indian Territory and on to Kansas. The railroad reached Fort Worth in 1876, and the intersection of the Chisholm Trail with railroads had the same explosive effect on commerce there as it had in Kansas when herds had to be driven all the way up there.

How was Fort Worth affected by this influx of cowboys, buffalo hunters, and freighters? One imagines they did not come here for Sunday school.

No, in fact, the ward between the rail yard and the courthouse became known as Hell's Half Acre, a warren packed tight with saloons, brothels, dance halls, and gaming houses. Over the years, it attracted such sketchy types as Bat Masterson, Sam Bass, and Butch Cassidy and the Sundance Kid. (Yes, Etta Place was with them.) James Earp, brother of Wyatt, Morgan, and Virgil, tended bar at the Cattlemen's Exchange. City fathers were conflicted by the presence of so much vice literally down the street from the courthouse. They disapproved of it, but they couldn't deny how much money it brought into the city, so it was tolerated.

Where is the last major stockyard in the United States?

It was all very well to ship cattle off to eastern markets, but business leaders realized how much more profitable it would be to process the beef—and pork and mutton as well—there in town. The various small stockyards near the rail terminal were consolidated on

The Fort Worth Stockyards, a popular tourist stop, is on the U.S. National Historic District list.

a site of more than 200 acres (0.8 square kilometers) north of town and organized as a clearinghouse for buying and selling livestock in 1890. The leading national meat packing companies, Swift and Armour, were invited in and opened plants, and by 1907 the yard was moving through more than a million head per year. The frenzy lasted for half a century before the business gave way to a more automated process. The nearly fifty buildings are preserved as a U.S. National Historic District; many have been converted into shopping or entertainment venues, although the Stockyards' stables still offer full-service horse care and boarding.

What was Quality Hill?

This was an eminence overlooking the Trinity River south and west of the central business district, which Fort Worth's cattle barons dotted with the gaudiest mansions their architects could devise. Few of them survive, but the ones that do, such as Thistle Hill and the Eddleman-McFarland House, testify that they were not shy about flaunting their social station over the little people.

What Fort Worth cattle heiress received an eighteen-room mansion as a honeymoon cottage from her father?

Electra Waggoner (1882–1925) was the daughter of W. T. Waggoner (1852–1934), one of the biggest land-owners in north Texas. She was traveling in the Himalayas broadening her horizons when she met Albert Buckman Wharton of Philadelphia and married him in 1902. Her father built a home for them, named Thistle Hill, on Quality Hill, a Georgian revival of 2.5 stories and eighteen rooms in 11,000 square feet (1,022 square meters). When Electra and her husband moved away to take over management of her share of the Waggoner Ranch, they sold Thistle Hill in 1911 to fellow land barons Winfield and Elizabeth Scott for $90,000 (over $2.3 million in current value). Scott improved the house to even grander pretense, replacing the green wood roof with green tile and swapping out wood columns for stone. For at least this group of society swells, though, money could not buy happiness. Electra divorced, married twice more, and died when she was only forty-three. She had two sons, each of whom led a turbulent life and met a tragic death. Winfield Scott died before his remodel was even complete; his son burned through the family money, and he sold the house on the cheap to the Girls Service League of Fort Worth for only $17,500. Later, it sat vacant from 1968 to 1975 but today is open to the public and available for events.

Who was the first celebrity televangelist?

After the turn of the twentieth century, Hell's Half Acre continued its vice but without the romance of its frontier association; it was just a seedy plot of urban blight. The Progressive Era brought with it a backlash in fundamentalist religion, whose leading light was the Reverend J. Frank Norris (1877–1952) of the First Baptist Church in Fort Worth. Unlike the previously famous Billy Sunday, who was a great revivalist but concentrated on personal preaching, Norris mastered radio to inveigh against modern evil—not just evolution but everything from moving pictures to lipstick. Norris made Hell's Half Acre his special target, and he was instrumental in mobilizing public support for shuttering the dens of vice.

Who were the "T-Patchers" and "Tough 'Ombres"?

On July 18, 1917, units of the Texas National Guard were organized in Fort Worth as the 36th (Texas) Division, followed a month later by the 90th Division, who adopted a badge emblazoned T-O, for Texas-Oklahoma, with the sobriquet Tough 'Ombres. T-Patchers took part in the liberation of Rheims, taking twenty-six hundred casualties in twenty-three days; the Tough 'Ombres lost nearly ten thousand in Saint-Mihiel, the Meuse-Argonne, and other bloody battles.

How did the U.S. Army help bury Hell's Half Acre?

The U.S. entry into World War I meant a sudden upsurge in military training camps, one of which was Camp Bowie, just outside Fort Worth. There was a time when sex and liquor contributed to the economy, but military spending promised even more, so local police had no objection when the Army imposed martial law to close Hell's Half Acre down.

What sustained Fort Worth's economy after the return to peace?

After very nearly abandoning the drilling effort as hopeless, a massive oil strike was made in Ranger, about 100 miles (161 kilometers) west of Fort Worth. Several one-horse villages such as Burkburnett, Desdemona, and Breckenridge, in addition to Ranger, became gaudy boomtowns, and Fort Worth became not just a center for their business dealings but also the location of several refineries that processed their crude.

Who was the chief booster of Fort Worth's rivalry, not to say enmity, with Dallas?

At the age of thirteen, Amon Carter (1879–1955) struck out on his own, leaving his native Crafton, Texas, and hustling a living by selling "chicken" sandwiches in the rail station in Bowie. He was a born deal-maker; he was only twenty-six when he got a job selling advertising for the *Fort Worth Star*, which was in financial trouble, and he engineered the purchase of its more profitable rival, the *Fort Worth Telegram*, and made it a success. It was he who originated the catchphrase that Fort Worth is "where the West begins," and he often enjoyed adding that Dallas, which he loathed, was "where the East peters out." Although he often commuted the 30 miles (48 kilometers) to Dallas, Carter famously carried a sack lunch, and he could boast to his dying day that he never spent one thin dime in Dallas.

Didn't Amon Carter leave a philanthropic legacy that extended beyond Fort Worth?

In addition to being honored by Texas Christian University, Carter's name was also placed on the main entrance of Texas Tech University in Lubbock, which he was instrumental in creating, and the Texas A&M Law School Auditorium.

How did Fort Worth respond to the torrent of tourists who poured into Dallas for the Centennial Exposition?

Simple: they staged a rival and much more low brow event called the Frontier Centennial Celebration and smothered Dallas with advertising that proclaimed "Dallas for Culture—Fort Worth for Fun."

Just as Dallas's Fair Park buildings continue in use, did Fort Worth's Centennial make any lasting contribution to the city?

Amon G. Carter was too good a salesman not to give his city something to remem-

Amon G. Carter was the founding editor of the Fort Worth *Star* and was renowned as a booster for the city.

ber. In addition to the Wild West show and carnival midway, which everyone expected, its centerpiece was Casa Mañana, a lavish, outdoor entertainment venue that seated four thousand and featured the world's largest revolving stage, whose curtain was a wall of water from jets that shot up from the surrounding moat. He then obtained the services of Billy Rose to produce his "Show of Shows." The whole assemblage was a smash hit, and plans were laid to turn the venue into a regular summer entertainment, but that scheme proved too expensive. Casa Mañana was taken apart and its materials contributed to World War II scrap drives.

Doesn't Fort Worth still have Casa Mañana?

Over the years, nobody forgot what fun it was, and in 1958 the president and manager of the Fort Worth Opera Association won city backing to bring back Casa Mañana, this time as a theater-in-the-round set in a futuristic geodesic dome that seated eighteen hundred. The new venue debuted that July with a production of *Can-Can*, and Casa Mañana has been expanding and adding programs ever since. It is now home to a full-time arts school with training in the performing arts for children as young as four.

Wait—what was a place like Fort Worth doing with an opera association?

Surprisingly, "Cowtown" is home to the oldest continuously performing opera company in Texas, having presented Verdi's *La Traviata* in November 1946. (It was performed in the Stockyards, but still, it was opera.) Over the years, keeping the productions coming has involved almost as much drama off the stage as on, but young singers who built their résumés by performing there included tenor Placido Domingo and coloratura soprano Beverly Sills. The company switched to a spring festival format starting in 2007 and now stages not just classical warhorses but world premieres of new works as well.

What Fort Worth pianist conquered Soviet Russia and then brought that fame home to start a competition of his own?

After the Soviet Union achieved a technological coup over the United States by launching the Sputnik satellite in 1957, the Khrushchev government decided to demonstrate its cultural renown as well by inaugurating a new piano competition named for Pyotr Ilyich Tchaikovsky. One of the contestants was a twenty-three-year-old Texan named Van Cliburn (1934–2013), whose performances of that composer's B-minor concerto and Rachmaninoff's infamously hard Third Concerto brought the audience to their feet. Chairman Khrushchev himself approved awarding Cliburn the gold medal when the judges acknowledged his performance the best. Four years later, Cliburn instituted a piano competition that was held at Texas Christian University and is still held every four years.

Where is the greatest collection of Western art located?

When he was not engaged in boosting Fort Worth, Amon Carter indulged his personal passion for collecting Western art, especially the works of Frederic Remington and

269

The Amon Carter Museum of American Art includes collections of such popular Western artists as Frederic Remington and Charles M. Russell.

Charles M. Russell, of which he assembled more than 250 pieces. Carter funneled much of his wealth into the foundation bearing his name in 1945; he made his wish known in 1951 to create a museum to house the collection. After his death, his daughter engaged New York architect Philip Johnson to design the building, which opened in January 1961. Since then, the collection has grown exponentially, displaying all phases of the artistic experience—first of the frontier and then of the American experience. To reflect its broader collecting reach, the name was modified in 2011 to the Amon Carter Museum of American Art. It now also houses a massive collection of Western photography.

What world-class art museum opened in Fort Worth and further eroded the city's reputation for being uncouth?

Less showy than the career of Amon Carter, Fort Worth businessman Kay Kimbell (1886–1964) assembled a business empire scarcely less impressive. Indeed, having been born in Leon County and begun work as a granary's office boy, he came as far as Carter did in transcending his roots. Kimbell's cultured wife, Velma, shared his passion for collecting old masters. They began their foundation in 1935, Louis I. Kahn was engaged in 1966, and the facility he designed caused a sensation in the art world. Displayed are works of Rembrandt, Goya, Rubens, El Greco, and others in a world-class collection.

What sensational Fort Worth murder case riveted Texas's attention in 1976?

While Fort Worth's cultural scene was making colossal strides away from its frontier roots, the seamy side of Fort Worth money came to the surface in the trial of oil millionaire Cullen Davis, who was accused of attempting to kill his soon-to-be ex-wife, Priscilla Davis, and killing his stepdaughter and Priscilla's lover. Davis hired celebrity attorney "Racehorse" Haines, who got Davis acquitted despite multiple eyewitness accounts.

What futuristic water garden was featured in a classic science fiction movie?

In 1961, Fort Worth began planning a large convention center. (Yes, it once again meant to compete with Dallas, which opened such a venue in 1954.) The obvious thing to do was demolish what remained of Hell's Half Acre for the facility, which resembled a flying saucer and opened in 1968. In 1974 a 4.3-acre (17,401-square-meter) water garden was added as an amenity on the south side, another gift of the Amon G. Carter Foundation and a return engagement for architect Philip Johnson. Its three main pools and tumbles of cascades were meant to blunt the intrusiveness of the urban surroundings and were featured in the 1976 film *Logan's Run*.

With all the business frenzy in Dallas and with Fort Worth determined not to become Dallas, has it been left behind in commerce?

Not really. There are only two Fortune 500 companies that are based in Fort Worth, but they are no slouches: D. R. Horton, the biggest home builder in the United States, and American Airlines.

With the business paradise of Dallas right next door, how has Fort Worth managed to convince major companies to locate there?

For years, it let Amon Carter do the talking. He is credited with personally jawboning such kingpins as Bell Helicopter, the major employer in the northeast quadrant of the county, and several oil companies into staying. In recent years, it has not been difficult to demonstrate the many ways in which Fort Worth has transformed its rowdy frontier tackiness into a cultural center that lacks Dallas's frenetic and high-strung overcrowding.

GOOD TIMES, TEXAS STYLE

SPORTS

What did people do for sport in early Texas?

One of the favorite activities in Spanish Texas was to bury a rooster up to its neck. The first rider to gallop by, lean down from his saddle, and snatch off its head was the winner. Bullfighting, which was imported from Spain during the colonial period and is still practiced in Mexico (although it is increasingly controversial), never really caught on in Texas, first probably because of the lack of blooded stock and second because after independence, anything that hearkened back to Latin culture fell into extreme disfavor.

What recreation was there after the Anglo arrival?

On the Anglo frontier, sports and betting have always been two sides of the same coin. Stephen F. Austin forbade gambling among his colonists, but he did permit horse racing as an incentive to improve stock. Other sports often had a practical end as well, such as hunting out bee trees for the honey. After Austin passed from influence, gambling became ubiquitous, and there were also contests of physical strength and horsemanship. On the early Anglo frontier, balls were popular as social mixers, and they were athletic affairs. Pioneers sometimes mocked later dances such as waltzes, where couples would just "glide around"; in their day, the success of a party was measured by how many floorboards were broken with such steps as "Cut the Pigeon's Wing." The advent of evangelical religion put a damper on such festivities, however. Among children, Blind Man's Bluff and Hide-and-Seek were well known.

Does Texas have a sports Hall of Fame?

Texas indeed was the first state to conceive of a hall of fame for its most distinguished sports celebrities. In 1949 the all-star game of the Texas High School Coaches Association was played in Beaumont, and the local newspaper's sports editor, Thad Johnson, gave a speech advocating such a step. Two years later, the Texas Sports Hall of Fame was founded with its first inductee, baseball legend Tris Speaker. A physical museum opened in Grand Prairie in 1981, was reconstituted in a new museum in Waco in 1993, and expanded in 2010. Of special note is the gallery dedicated to the Southwest Conference, which was a college football powerhouse from 1914 until its dissolution in 1996. While mostly showcasing athletes and coaches, the museum also recognizes the importance of sports impresarios, such as honoree Lamar Hunt (1932–2006), who guided enterprises as disparate as the Kansas City Chiefs, World Championship Tennis, and the Dallas Burn/FC Dallas soccer franchise.

RODEOS

What was the origin of rodeos?

For a sport that is so deeply associated with the Texas frontier, rodeos actually became organized into a sport quite recently. Some of what became standard events, such as saddle bronc riding, steer wrestling, and calf roping, derived straight from the working life of the cowboy; others, such as bull riding, were added later for excitement and showmanship. The very term "rodeo" came into use later; at first, rodeos were more often called "cowboy contests." The first rodeo to award prizes—and hence arguably the first professional contest—took place in Pecos in 1883. This was the year after the premiere

Hugely popular in Texas, as well as many other states, the rodeo has its origins in the daily life of cowboys working with horses and cattle.

of Buffalo Bill Cody's "Wild West Show," which also showcased western riding skills. Rodeos moved indoors for the first time in Fort Worth in 1917 and after the war gained immeasurably in national publicity and popularity with the advent of lengthy rodeos in Boston and New York. In the hyperbole of showmanship, many cowboy contests claimed that their winners would be world champions, and rodeos as a competitive sport did not really become organized until the formation of the Rodeo Association of America in 1929, which standardized events and scoring systems. With organization came conflict, and in 1936, the performing cowboys staged a successful strike for better prize stakes in Boston. Between 1938 and 1946, a veritable alphabet soup of organizations were formed and re-formed until the emergence of the Professional Rodeo Cowboys Association in 1975.

How did Texas cowboys fare after rodeo became a national sport?

They more than held their own. Bull rider Harry Tompkins of Dublin, Texas, won the national title five times, in 1948, 1949, 1950, 1952, and 1960. He succeeded Fort Worth's Dick Griffith, who won the title each year between 1939 and 1942. Toots Mansfield, who was the first president of the Rodeo Cowboys Association, won seven national calf roping titles between 1939 and 1950.

What made Bill Pickett such a rodeo sensation?

Bill Pickett (1870–1932) was an African American cowboy born near Liberty Hill in Williamson County, north of Austin. About one-third of the cowboys on the ranching frontier were either black or Latino (a fact missed by silver-screen Hollywood westerns), and Pickett left school after fifth grade to be one. Pickett's fame lay in a precursor of steer wrestling that was known as bull dogging: leaping from his horse onto a running steer, grappling with its horns, and wrestling it to the ground. His particular variant was to bite the steer on the upper lip, a maneuver that the animal found so painful that it would

Whatever happened to the Texas Prison Rodeo?

Starting in 1931, the Texas prison system began staging a rodeo that featured inmates competing in standard competitive events such as calf roping and bull riding but also gag events such as bareback basketball and wild cow milking. It was held at the Huntsville Unit, the oldest prison in the Texas system, which opened in 1849. The annual event was enormously popular with the public, it provided inmates with much-needed distraction, and it was an important source of funding for educational materials and recreational equipment for the prisons, which the tough-on-crime legislature would not adequately fund. The 1986 event was cancelled, owing to safety concerns with the stadium. The legislature did not appropriate the money needed to fix the structure and federal funds became available for inmate programs, so the rodeo was allowed to pass into history.

become docile, so much so that Pickett could dog a steer without using his hands. (It is rather the same reason that a ring is inserted through a bull's nose.) Billing himself as "The Dusky Demon," Pickett hired himself out to wild west shows and became a major attraction. Ironically, it was only after he retired that he was fatally kicked in the head by a horse.

BASEBALL

What was the Texas League?

Baseball was a sport that united all Texans. The competitive Texas League started in 1888 and rose from Class D in 1902 to Class A in 1921. One of the dominant teams early on was the Corsicana Oilers. They enjoyed a winning streak of twenty-seven games and one of the most lopsided wins, a 51–3 thrashing of the Texarkana Casketmakers. Later, the Fort Worth Panthers came to the fore, winning six pennants in a row from 1920 to 1925. A "Texas leaguer" as a name for a single hit that passes just over the heads of the infield may be a misnomer, for it was not in use during the League's heyday. The modern-day Texas League consists of eight minor-league affiliates of Major League Baseball teams.

Who was the first Texan to be inducted into the Baseball Hall of Fame?

Tristram Edward (Tris) Speaker (1888–1958) was born in Hubbard, Texas, in Hill County north of Waco. As a boy, he little imagined that when he fell from a horse and broke his right arm, being forced to become left-handed would be his fortune. He played one year of college baseball and honed his skills in the Texas League before being sold to the Boston Americans in 1907 (they became the Red Sox the following year)—being vociferously opposed at every step by his mother, who equated being "sold" to a team with slavery, and desired him to come home and take up ranching. In 1912, Speaker stole 50 bases and hit 50 doubles (the first player to ever do so) and enjoyed three hitting streaks of 20 games or more. Once again, his mother urged him to come home and work for his living. Speaker played with Boston through 1915, then Cleveland, Washington, and Philadelphia. Over his twenty-

Nicknamed "The Grey Eagle," Hall of Famer Tris Speaker played for teams in Boston, Cleveland, Washington, and Philadelphia and had a batting average of .345.

two-year career, Speaker amassed 3,514 hits (ranking fifth all-time), with a .345 batting average (sixth), and hit 792 doubles (first). He also holds records for double plays and assists. Speaker entered the Hall of Fame in 1937 on the second ballot, the first Texan to be inducted and seventh overall. "The Grey Eagle" finally did go home, and he died of a heart attack after a fishing trip on Lake Whitney.

Did Tris Speaker have any rivals from Texas?

Perhaps one, the "Magnificent Rajah," Rogers Hornsby (1896–1963), eight years younger than Speaker, born to a San Angelo branch of a family who settled near Austin in frontier days and had a bend of the Colorado River named after them. Hornsby was the National League batting champion from 1920 to 1925 and again in 1928. During his career, he slammed 302 home runs with a batting average of .358—less than his single-season record of an astonishing .424 in 1924 and second highest in all of Major League Baseball after Ty Cobb at .367. Like Cobb, Hornsby was famously foul tempered, but he was dedicated to his physical condition. He read no type smaller than headlines lest it weaken his eyes and did not smoke or drink but freely indulged his one vice, betting on horses. After his playing days, he managed six different major-league teams but was fired from each for being headstrong and disagreeable.

What is the most winning NCAA Division I baseball program in the United States?

The University of Texas began playing competitive baseball in 1894 and since then has compiled an aggregate winning percentage of .727, comprising 3,558 wins, 1,323 losses, and 32 ties. UT's number of total wins is second to Fordham University, but that school began playing baseball in 1859—35 years before UT. UT's record embraces six national championships (second to the University of Southern California with twelve), six second-place finishes, and a record thirty-six appearances at the College World Series. Texas has won more CWS games with 85 (11 more than USC), more NCAA Tournament games won with 240 (58 more than second place Florida State and Miami), and has more NCAA Tournament appearances with 59 (3 more than Florida State) than any other school. While in the Southwest Conference (1915–1996), UT won the championship sixty-four times in eighty-one years and then eight Big 12 championships through 2018. More than one hundred UT baseball players have gone on to careers in the major leagues.

In the earlier days of UT baseball, what slightly sneaky home-field advantage did they have?

Before UT baseball moved to Disch-Falk Field in 1975, games were played at Clark Field, which featured a limestone bluff up to 30 feet (9 meters) high in center field known as Billy Goat Hill. UT players were well schooled in the footholds to scamper up the cliff; indeed, some UT center fielders chose to play their position atop the bluff and could often hold opposing players to a double if they hit a ball up there. UT players, on the contrary, if they hit a long fly ball to center field, they could count on an inside-the-park home run as opposing fielders tried helplessly to scale the cliff.

With all the installations celebrating sports in Texas, is there one place dedicated to Texas Rangers' legendary pitcher Nolan Ryan?

Yes, Ryan's home-town of Alvin, between Houston and Galveston, where he played Little League and high school baseball, is home to Ryan memorabilia as well as a theater and an interactive pitch-catch exhibit.

FOOTBALL

What does the phrase "Friday Night Lights" mean?

In the weekly autumn calendar of Texas football, high school games are played on Friday nights, college games on Saturdays, and professional games on Sundays. *Friday*

Born in Refugio in 1947, former Astros and Rangers pitcher Nolan Ryan was inducted into the Baseball Hall of Fame in 1999.

Night Lights was the name of a successful film (2004) and television series (2006–2011), set in small-town Texas and depicting the extraordinary degree to which a town's self-esteem is carried in the fate of its high school football team and the pressure placed on the team and its coach to win. The phrase does still evoke this culture, which is a harsh reality in much of Texas, both rural and urban.

What are the premier college football programs in Texas?

The most storied college program has to be that of the University of Texas, which began in 1893 and through 2017 has accumulated a .705 all-time winning percentage (897-366-33), four national titles (1963, 1969, 1970, 2005), 32 conference titles, and a bowl record of 27-24-2. Texas A&M is not far behind, opening play in 1894, with an all-time winning percentage of .602 (732-476-48), three national titles (1919, 1927, 1939) and two Heisman Trophy winners. They have won 18 conference titles, but their bowl record of 17-21 is not so good.

How did the UT mascot come to be named Bevo?

Sports fans in Austin were aware that other teams touted mascots but had never bothered to pick one of their own. In 1911, though, football team manager Steve Pinckney spied a distinctive longhorn steer colored dark orange and white, with a blaze on its forehead that with a little imagination resembled Texas. He talked some alumni into buying him, and the team became the Texas Longhorns. Since the beginning of league play, UT had formed a deep rivalry with Texas A&M, and in the 1916 game, UT upset A&M by a score of 21–7, which led to a plan to brand the score onto the new mascot.

Didn't UT also have an informal mascot in the 1920s?

They did indeed, a feisty little bulldog named Pig Bellmont, brought to the school as a puppy by athletic director L. Theo Bellmont and named Pig in honor of football center Pig Dittner, whom he was said to resemble. He was a big favorite with students for a decade, largely for his habit, when someone would prompt him, of growling "A&M!" On New Year's Day of 1925, Pig was run over on the Guadalupe Street "drag" to universal grief. He reposed in his small coffin beneath lilies and juniper boughs before being buried in a grove of oak trees just northwest of what is now the Graduate School of Business. His headstone read PIG'S DEAD. DOG GONE.

Word of this soon reached College Station, and six Aggie cadets searched over Austin until they found the steer's hiding place and branded 13–0 on him instead, which was the score by which they had beaten UT the year before. Not to be outdone, UT partisans altered the brand to BEVO, which was the name of a popular non alcoholic beer. All UT Longhorn mascots since then have been named Bevo.

Who was the outstanding player of Texas college football in that classic era?

If the limit is to pick only one, it would likely be Samuel Adrian Baugh (1914–2008), who played for the Texas Christian University Horned Frogs and was largely responsible for turning the team into a powerhouse. He punted, he played defensive back, but he was most gifted at quarterback, with a weirdly accurate sidearm throw that led them to a 1936 Sugar Bowl win and a victory at the first Cotton Bowl in 1937. Baugh was then drafted by the new Washington Redskins, who won the national championship in their debut season of 1937. Baugh was always torn between baseball and football, and his famous nickname of "Slingin' Sammy" was actually given him for his baseball throw. He stayed with the Redskins until 1952, winning another NFL championship in 1942 and being named NFL Player of the Year in 1947 and 1948. During these years, he regularly led the league in passing yards and completion percentage. His 1940 punting average of 51.4 yards still stands.

When did professional football come to Texas?

Coming to Dallas as a 1960 expansion team, the Dallas Cowboys were the first NFL team in the South since the demise of the Dallas Texans in 1952. During their glory years, the Cowboys logged twenty straight winning seasons between 1966 and 1985. The sobriquet that competitors find maddening, that the Cowboys are "America's Team," began as a tout in one of their own promotional trailers, but boosters always seemed to find a way to make it fit whether because of the squeaky-clean image of their early years under dapper head coach Tom Landry (for twenty-nine years "the only coach the Cowboys have

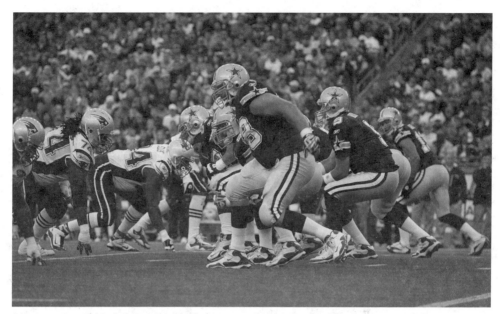

The Dallas Cowboys became Texas's first professional football team with staying power in 1960 after the one-season life span of the original Dallas Texans in 1952. They were a force to be reckoned with under coach Tom Landry, who led them from 1960 to 1988 (pictured is the 2011 team).

ever had"), later as they won five of their eight Super Bowl contests, or today as the first sports team in the world to be valued at $4 billion, generating some $620 million in revenue. The Houston Oilers began playing at the same time as the Cowboys as charter members of the AFC, but they moved to Nashville for the start of the 1997 season. This left Houston without professional football until the coming of the expansion Houston Texans in 2002.

AUTO RACING

Are any Formula 1 auto races held in Texas?

Circuit of the Americas, a Formula 1 circuit and site of the United States Grand Prix, opened just outside of Austin, welcoming aficionados of this most rarefied level of auto racing for the first time in 2012. The only other locations in the United States for such events have been in Las Vegas, Dallas, Detroit, Indianapolis, Phoenix, Riverside (California), Sebring (Florida), Watkins Glen (New York), and Long Beach. None of them currently host Formula 1 events, leaving Austin, Montreal, and Mexico City as North America's current F1 host cities.

What is Texas's most important auto-racing track?

The Gulf Coast Speedway, which hosts the Texas State Championships, is located in Alvin, south of Houston.

Whatever happened to Texas Stadium, where the Dallas Cowboys played?

From the start of their franchise in 1960, the Cowboys played at the Cotton Bowl in Fair Park, an aging venue in an increasingly unsafe part of town. Dallas turned down the team's request for a bond issue to build a new stadium downtown, which prompted the team to leave the city for Irving. Texas Stadium hosted its first game on November 24, 1971, and the team played there for thirty-eight seasons. Drawing most comment was the rectangular hold in the roof over the playing field, which was left as it was when it was discovered that the structure could not support the mechanism needed for a retractable roof. When asked about it, one Cowboy player quipped that they left the hole in the roof so that God could watch his team play. When a new venue, AT&T Stadium in Arlington, which could seat a third more spectators, was ready, Texas Stadium closed on Christmas Day 2008 and was demolished by implosion on April 11, 2010.

Is there a place where nonprofessionals can get a taste of racing?

The MSR Houston in Angleton is a 2.38-mile (3.83-kilometer), seventeen-turn course where members can try their hand in a Radical Sports Racer or stock car, and there is also a kart track.

TENNIS

What Dallas resident won the tennis grand slam and had her ground strokes favorably compared to a battleship?

California native Maureen Connolly (1934–1969) took up tennis because her divorced mother was unable to afford riding lessons. Her natural gift for the sport turned heads at once; when she was only eleven, a sportswriter was so impressed with the power and accuracy of her forehand and especially her backhand that he nicknamed her Little Mo. World War II was just ending, and "Big Mo" was the sobriquet of the battleship USS *Missouri*, under whose 16-inch (41-centimeter) guns the Japanese surrendered. At sixteen, she became the youngest player to win the U.S. championships, and she went on to win a total of nine Grand Slam singles titles, including the calendar Grand Slam of winning the Australian Open, French Open, Wimbledon, and U.S. Open in 1953. Only one other player, Don Budge, had ever accomplished this, in 1938. In 1954, two weeks after winning her third consecutive Wimbledon, her right leg was badly broken when the horse she was riding threw her after being spooked by a passing cement mixer. With her playing career ended, Connolly married, settled in Dallas, and was active in the tennis scene for almost fifteen years, becoming a journalist and Wightman Cup coach, founding an important foundation for the development of junior tennis, and penning a memoir in which she admitted that she had always thought tennis would be her "dark destiny," that her supreme accomplishment would be achieved through fear and loneliness. She was only thirty-four when she died of ovarian cancer in Dallas.

What was the most famous tennis match ever played in Texas?

By 1973, former tennis champion, showman, and proud sexual chauvinist Bobby Riggs had humiliated the great Australian Margaret Court and scheduled a "Battle of the Sexes" match with Billie Jean King, who was a top player and advocate for women's rights in general. They played on September 20, 1973, in the Astrodome, before a crowd of more than thirty thousand. It was gaudy, with King entering on a litter like Cleopatra and Riggs affecting the role of a

In 1973, former tennis champion Bobby Riggs challenged Billie Jean King in the "Battle of the Sexes" match at the Astrodome. King whooped his butt, scoring a morale-boosting victory for women everywhere.

sugar daddy surrounded by buxom, young women. King won, 6–4, 6–3, 6–3. King was terrified at the setback women's rights would suffer if she lost but instead, she paved the way to establish the Women's Tennis Association, equal pay, and Grand Slam tournaments.

HOCKEY

How did ice hockey come to a hot place like Texas?

The roaring twenties were good times in Texas, and people were game for new amusements and distractions. In San Antonio, San Pedro Springs Park was a popular recreational area, and near the end of 1925, local entrepreneur Joseph Tobin opened the Crystal Palace, an ice rink made possible by newly advanced refrigeration machinery. As a prelude to opening, the rink hosted what was likely the first hockey game ever played in Texas. After opening, Tobin formed a "house team" that played games against all comers from as far away as Canada. The Crystal Palace became a sensation; a local department store began selling calf-length "skating dresses" with kick pleats; and there were regular hours for open skating, "sweetheart" nights for pairs to skate to music, and exhibitions of trick skating and races. Even nonskaters were brought in with musical acts and offered beginners' lessons. The venue survived under different names and owners until 1963 and was instrumental in sparking interest in hockey.

When did professional hockey arrive in Texas?

There were various fits and starts. In 1941 a professional team called the Dallas Texans formed and had a promising debut before four thousand fans against the St. Paul Saints, but World War II aborted it, and after the war, the team ceased competing after only four seasons. The Chicago Blackhawks established a farm team that played in Dallas from 1967 to 1982. Finally, in 1993 the two-time division champion Minnesota North Stars moved their franchise to Dallas as the Dallas Stars. After a sputtering start and coaching change, they won the Stanley Cup in 1999 and remain a force in the sport. At least two dozen other hockey teams of various skill levels have come and gone around the state, and several minor-league teams are thriving.

GOLF

What did Harvey Penick bring to golf in Texas?

Harvey Penick (1904–1995) was a nonpareil golf teacher, whose instructional book published near the end of his life became the biggest-selling golf book ever written. Penick was born in and was a life long resident of Austin, and he was the golf coach at the University of Texas, where he led the team to twenty-one conference championships in his thirty-three years there. He taught and was idolized by such luminaries as Kathy Whitworth, Ben Crenshaw, and Tom Kite. Near the end of his life, he collaborated with Austin writer Bud Shrake to author *Harvey Penick's Little Red Book*, which became a sensation in the golfing world. A master of the mental game, Penick's sway over his students was such that, almost with his last breaths, he imparted some final tips to Crenshaw, who went out and became the second-oldest winner of the Masters Tournament.

What Texas golf course was built with no greens?

When cereal baron C. W. Post established his quasi-Utopian settlement of Post in Garza County, one of the amenities he provided was a three-hole golf course. However, the arid soil could not grow grass suitable for putting greens. Post therefore huddled with his chief stone mason, George Sampson, and they came up with a blend of sand and petroleum that served as a reasonable facsimile. Both men being good Scots, Post hired a band wearing kilts to serenade an event, but the Garza County sheriff arrested them for indecency.

OTHER SPORTS

How did Texan Jack Johnson set the world of boxing into a panic?

Prizefighting was illegal in most of the United States, including Texas, but the boxing culture thrived undercover and enjoyed an avid following. An oversized black janitor from Galveston, Jack Johnson, fought his way up the hierarchy until he defeated Tommy Burns of Canada in 1908 to become heavyweight champion of the world. Anglo Texans were appalled. Johnson was insolent, he drove and wrecked fast cars, and he took no responsibility for the damage he left in his wake. Worst of all, in many Anglos' minds, he consorted with white women. The boxing world opened the campaign to find a "Great White Hope," some manly, Anglo athlete who could put the obnoxious Johnson in his place. They settled on former champion Jim Jeffries, and the two fought in Reno, Nevada, on July 4, 1910. Johnson toyed with him and then destroyed him. The fight was covered by the adventure writer, reporter, and avid amateur boxer Jack London, who, though he personally lost a large sum of money on the fight, wrote what other white journalists would not: that Johnson was an astonishing athlete who had won the bout with superior quickness and technique. He did not lose the title until 1915, at age thirty-seven and in a condition in which he had no business fighting.

Is there any locale in Texas that celebrates bowling?

When the Germans began streaming into Texas in the 1840s, they brought with them their avidity for ninepins, which was considered suitable as a family activity. Among Anglo-American Texans, tenpins gained favor, as it was considered a masculine sport, and venues were often set up in or next to saloons. Texas's bowling mecca today is undoubtedly Arlington, just east of Fort Worth. There, one complex houses the International Bowling Museum, the Hall of Fame, and the U.S. Bowling Congress.

What Port Arthur native may have been the greatest female athlete ever?

Mildred Ella Didrikson (1911–1956) was born to Norwegian immigrants, who early gave her the nickname of Babe. She was no notable scholar, failing eighth grade and later dropping out, but her athletic prowess became evident early. After a flirtation with singing and acting, she worked for an insurance company so she could lead their basketball team to the 1931 Amateur Athletic Union championship. She also competed in AAU track and field, finishing first in six of ten events. She rocketed to international fame by winning two gold medals and one silver medal in the Los Angeles Olympics of 1932: gold in the javelin and 80-meter hurdles, silver in the high jump. Didrikson (Babe Didrikson Za-

harias after marrying) also loved baseball, and after some training by Dizzy Dean and Burleigh Grimes, she pitched in exhibition games for the St. Louis Cardinals and Philadelphia Athletics. Her greatest post-Olympic fame, however, came as a golfer, winning forty-one amateur tournaments before turning professional, then forty-one LPGA tournaments, seven of them majors, between 1940 and 1954. Even after she was stricken with bowel cancer, she won the U.S. Women's Open one month after undergoing surgery with a colostomy bag still attached to her side. Aside from her achievements, she also broke ground for the place of female athletes in the world of sport, regularly shrugging off criticism for her lack of modesty and femininity.

Born in Galveston, Babe Didrikson was a gold medalist in track who also excelled in golf, basketball, and baseball.

CHOW TIME!

What comprises Texas barbecue?

Barbecue is a dish that has many variations around the United States. Kansas City barbecue is as distinctive as Memphis, or Carolina, barbecue, and they are vastly different from one another. Texas barbecue is noted for being slow smoked over fragrant woods—hickory, until they used it all, now oak or pecan. It is a tradition that probably originates with the German and Polish immigrants who knew their smokehouses. Usually, the cooking involves both a "mopping" sauce for basting and a finishing sauce for the table.

Perhaps the most important question that can be asked in Texas: Where is the best barbecue?

This question, while of signal importance, is so subjective and so fraught with passionate personal loyalties as to be close to unanswerable. However, some famous eateries show up repeatedly in lists of the best barbecue. Whether judged by presidential patronage or by the daily wait of up to two hours, Franklin Barbecue in Austin, which opened in 2009, has been described by one knowledgeable food blog as "probably the most highly regarded barbecue joint in the world." Pitmaster Aaron Franklin is not without credentials, himself a winner of the James Beard Foundation Award for best chef in the Southwest in 2015 and his restaurant crowned as the best by both *Bon Appetit* and *Texas Monthly*. Franklin Barbecue survived a wicked kitchen fire in August 2017 that closed it for three months, but it has come back stronger than ever.

Smoking the meats slowly over burning hickory is how barbecue is done in Texas.

Texas Monthly's 2017 guide to the best barbecue in Texas could not narrow the field to fewer than fifty, but if one had to select a barbecue capital of Texas, it would likely be Lockhart, home to three different contenders: Black's, Smitty's, and the Kreuz Market. Each one has its uncompromising partisans, so the safe course is to just eat at all three. Among smaller cities, Belton might finish second, having both Miller's Smokehouse and Schoepf's. One of the most original single restaurants is the Salt Lick in Driftwood, thirty minutes southwest of Austin, a veteran of numerous appearances on televised food shows. It was begun by Thurman Roberts in 1967 on the family ranch along with his wife, Hisako. Their sauce, sold commercially, is brown-orange instead of the traditional red, and it derives from her Hawaiian ethnicity. If anyone knows how to cook pork, it is Hawaiians, and not without reason is the Salt Lick most celebrated for its pork ribs. Side dishes honor the German side of barbecue, with the coleslaw and potato salad prepared with vinegar and pepper instead of the ubiquitous mayonnaise and sugar. When Austin opened its new airport in 1999 at the revamped Bergstrom Air Force Base and the decision was made to lease food concessions to feature standout local fare over generic chains, it was the Salt Lick that got the barbecue nod.

Where is Texas's leading chili cook-off?

Carne con chile, as a dish of meat stewed in powdered chile peppers and usually finished with a thickening of *masa*, actually began in San Antonio, hawked by street vendors. Stories have persisted that there were informal competitions among them for who made the best chili in the early twentieth century, but actual records have proved elusive. The first documented chili cookoff was at the Texas State Fair in October 1952. Frank X. Tolbert (1912–1984) of the *Dallas Morning News* covered the event and began writing more about chili, culminating in his book *A Bowl of Red*. Disputes over chili's finer points led to a contest between Wick Fowler, Texas's acknowledged chili master, and a Hollywood chef who pulled out at the last minute and was replaced by best-selling humorist H. Allen Smith (1907–1976), who incurred the wrath of Tolbert with a magazine article claiming, "Nobody knows more about chili than I do." The shootout took place in Terlingua on October 21, 1967, and ended in a tie: one judge voted for Fowler and one for Smith, and the third gasped from a near-faint of indigestion that he could not vote. (Smith did add beans to his chili, which experts consider enough of a sin to disqualify it.) What began more or less as a tourist gimmick is now a major Texas event, drawing several thousand attendees from around the Southwest on the first Saturday of every November. For a time in the late 1970s, to mock U.S. government plans to reinforce the border fence and deter illegal immigration, the organizers added the "Mexican Fence-Climbing Contest."

How did Corsicana become famous for fruitcakes?

German immigrant August Wiederman settled in Corsicana and opened a bakery in 1896 that quickly gained a reputation for its fruitcakes, gaining devotees that included humorist Will Rogers and tenor Enrico Caruso. When the circus came to town in 1914, the Ringling brothers ordered fruitcakes as holiday gifts to be sent out by posts, and Wiederman saw the advantage to be gained by mail-order service. In 1947 he sold the Collin Street Bakery to L. W. McNutt, whose family still operates it. The bakery employs some six hundred people during the holiday season and includes celebrities and foreign royalty among its loyal customers.

What wildly popular American food entered the American diet thanks to a Texan?

Fletcher Davis, a short-order cook in Athens, Texas, in 1880 devised a grilled patty of ground beef sandwiched in Texas toast, which he prepared for a customer in a hurry. It proved so popular that Davis and his wife introduced the dish at the St. Louis World's Fair in 1904. Grilled ground beef had long gone by the name of Hamburg steak, and Davis called it a "hamburger." (Other sections of the country also have their entries for first hamburger, but Davis is the strongest contender.)

What brings tourists to Brenham today?

Although quite historic in its own right, Brenham lies on the highway between Austin and the Republic capital, and most people pass through. Many visitors seek out the legendary Blue Bell Creameries, which has been making ice cream since 1911, when it produced two gallons a day. The ice cream parlor shows a video about the company's history.

What favorite American soft drink entered the American diet in Waco?

The concentration of cattle drives to cross the Brazos in Waco, and the later arrival of the railroad, transformed Waco into a major frontier town, complete with a red-light district called "the reservation," which survived the relocation of Baylor University to the city in 1886. This was also the era of unregulated patent medicines, when any local pharmacist could bottle tonics that, whatever their medical claims, were at least rendered

The Blue Bell Creameries factory is in Brenham.

pleasurable with alcohol and opiates. Waco druggist Charles Alderton at Morrison's Old Corner Drug Store began experimenting with more benign fruit syrups at the store's soda fountain and eventually chanced upon a combination that his customers loved, as did owner Wade Morrison. As customers clamored to be served a "Waco," some suggested that Morrison give the new beverage a more distinctive name, and he decided to honor a Virginia pharmacist he had worked for in earlier years, Dr. Charles Pepper. The drink was a sensation at the St. Louis World's Fair in 1904 and went commercial. Contrary to legend, Dr Pepper (the period after "Dr" was not dropped until about fifty years later) is not the earliest carbonated drink in America. It predates Coca-Cola, just barely, but there is a ginger ale that is older. Today's Dr Pepper Museum in Waco is housed in the original 1906 bottling plant.

AMUSEMENT PARKS, ZOOS, AQUARIUMS, AND GAME PARKS

Where is Texas's premier water amusement park?

Although it opened in 1979, New Braunfels's Schlitterbahn has gained such fame it seems as though it has been around much longer. The name in German means "slippery road" for its chutes and water slides. As it has expanded four different times, the park has gained the world's first inland surfing ride, the first uphill water coaster, the first wave

The Schlitterbahn in New Braunfels has become one of Texas's most popular amusement parks. It's the perfect escape for the family on a hot day!

river, and now the world's longest artificial tubing stream, complete with rapids. The park won the Golden Ticket Award from *Amusement Today* magazine seventeen years in a row, and it employs two thousand seasonal workers. The corporation now operates three resorts, two indoor and five outdoor water parks, mostly in Texas but one in Kansas City, Kansas, and another planned for Fort Lauderdale, Florida.

What iconic American theme park empire began in Arlington?

Regional development entrepreneur Angus G. Wynne Jr. (1914–1979) realized the boon that a major amusement park could bring to the Dallas-Fort Worth area after he visited Disneyland in California. Planning began in 1959, construction started in August 1960, and one year later almost to the day, he debuted Six Flags Over Texas on 212 acres (0.86 square kilometers) between Arlington and the Trinity River. It was a pseudo-historical theme park, with six regions dedicated to Texas under one of the six national sovereignties that have reigned over Texas: Spain, France, Mexico, the Republic of Texas, the Confederacy, and the United States. There were forty-six rides and attractions, including a roller-coaster and its signature log flume, whose riders could expect to be soaked when the "log" in which they were riding plummeted down a flume into slower water

The first Six Flags amusement park debuted in Arlington in 1960. The name refers to the different governments that controlled the state over the years: Spain, France, Mexico, the Republic of Texas, the Confederate States of America, and the United States of America. There are now twenty-five Six Flags parks around the country.

at the bottom. The park was also the first in the country to feature musical shows and was a runaway success and the first of a new species of attraction.

When did Texas get a SeaWorld attraction?

SeaWorld is a chain of parks that includes rides, aquariums, and live animal shows. There are four parks (three in the United States and one in Abu Dhabi, United Arab Emirates). The one in San Antonio opened in 1988 and has over three million visitors a year. Live shows include animals such as dolphins, beluga whales, and the famous Shamu, the killer whale.

How many zoos are there in Texas?

Zoological gardens in the United States are accredited by the American Zoological Association (AZA). It certifies eighteen zoos and aquariums in Texas. Alphabetically by city, they are:

- Abilene Zoological Gardens
- (Brownsville) Gladys Porter Zoo
- (Corpus Christi) Texas State Aquarium
- Dallas World Aquarium
- Dallas Zoo
- El Paso Zoo
- Fort Worth Zoo
- (Galveston) Rainforest and Aquarium at Moody Gardens
- (Glen Rose) Fossil Rim Wildlife Center
- Sea Life Grapevine Aquarium
- Houston Aquarium
- Houston Zoo
- (Lufkin) Ellen Trout Zoo
- (New Braunfels) Animal World & Snake Farm Zoo
- San Antonio Zoological Society
- Sea-World San Antonio
- (Tyler) Caldwell Zoo
- (Waco) Cameron Park Zoo

In addition, the following fourteen nonaccredited institutions are open in Texas:
- Amarillo City Zoo
- (Amarillo) Wildcat Bluff Nature Center
- Austin Nature and Science Center
- Austin Zoo and Animal Sanctuary

- (Boyd) International Exotic Feline Sanctuary
- (Gainesville) Frank Buck Zoo
- (Houston) Cockrell Butterfly Center & Live Insect Zoo
- Houston Museum of Natural Science
- (McKinney) Heard Natural Science Museum and Wildlife Sanctuary
- (New Braunfels) Clearsprings Aviaries and Zoological Gardens
- (San Antonio) Natural Bridge Wildlife Ranch
- (San Antonio) Primarily Primates
- (San Antonio) Wild Animal Orphanage
- (Victoria) The Texas Zoo

There are also a number of small, privately owned safari parks and petting zoos:

- (Alvin) Bayou Wildlife Park
- (Clifton) Texas Safari Ranch
- (Grand Saline) East Texas Gators & Wildlife Park
- Grapeland Safari Park
- (Jacksboro) Hidden Lake Safari & RV Park
- (Jacksonville) Cherokee Trace Drive-Thru Safari
- (Johnson City) Exotic Resort Zoo
- (Pilot Point) Sharkarosa Wildlife Ranch

Are Texas zoos popular with the public?

Nationally, more people visit a zoo in a year than attend professional football, baseball, and basketball games combined. The Houston Zoo draws more than 2.5 million visitors per year, San Antonio 1.2 million, Fort Worth 1 million, Dallas 920,000 (plus another 650,000 visiting the Aquarium), and El Paso 350,000. Even smaller Texas installations typically attract double the number of the city's population each year, such as Waco's Cameron Park at 260,000, the Abilene Zoo with 220,000, and Lufkin's Ellen Trout Zoo at 130,000. The Fossil Rim Wildlife Center outside of Glen Rose, which is not in a large metro area, still prompts 230,000 people a year to get in a car and drive there.

Why would a Texas zoo not seek AZA accreditation?

Not being accredited does not necessarily mean that a wildlife facility is a roadside tourist trap. Maintaining a collection of exotic animals is a staggering expense and getting more so, and some zoos are hard up for cash to maintain memberships. Also, being a member implies a zoo's ability to participate in some of the more than 450 Species Survival Plans (SSP), which some are not equipped to do.

What Texas zoo pioneered the exhibition of animals in natural habitats without cages?

The Gladys Porter Zoo in Brownsville was founded as recently as 1971, so it did not have an outdated infrastructure of cages to demolish and improve. This zoo was the brain-child and passion of J. C. Penney heiress Gladys Porter and was built, stocked, and brought on line with funding from the family foundation before being given to the city of Brownsville. It was also one of the first zoos to concentrate on the breeding of rare and endangered species and has been a conservation showcase since it opened.

What was revolutionary about the "Herpetarium" at the Fort Worth Zoo?

At the time it opened in 1960, visitors who pulled open the door handles of cast bronze cobras entered the most advanced, state-of-the-art care facility for reptiles in the world. Housing more than 200 species in 175 displays, the 55-by-117-foot (16.8-by-35.7-meter) building features variable skylights, temperature-controlled water, and, to the horrified delight of the public, curved, non reflecting glass with plants on the outside that make it appear that giant boa constrictors could strike out at the public. An emergency alarm system was also installed—which was used to good effect when a king cobra disappeared. The incident was splashed all over the news before the snake was "found" in a secure area and, in zoo-management circles, was thought likely to have been a publicity stunt. In addition to the Herpetarium, the Fort Worth Zoo is counted as one of the U.S. flagship zoos, with more than 7,000 animals on 65 acres (6 square meters) and ongoing programs to create natural habitats.

Why do some Texas zoos seem to specialize in certain kinds of animals?

It is not an accident. As the AZA developed its Species Survival Plans, it took advantage of different zoos' areas of expertise. The San Antonio Zoo, for instance, over many years gained special skills in the care of large antelope so that its ungulate program is now one of the best in the country, featuring such rarities as giant sable antelope. It also manages the SSP for snow leopards and, at one time, cared for about 10 percent of all the remaining snow leopards on earth. The Fort Worth Zoo manages the SSP for golden lion tamarins and oversees attempts to reintroduce these beautiful and endangered monkeys back into the wild. Then, too, as zoos learn more from research about different species' spatial and social needs, specimens are shifted to facilities that can care for them better. Elephants, for example, are highly intelligent and socialized animals, and a zoo with a single animal will send it to another, where it can have some badly needed company.

What special attractions are there at the Houston Zoo?

In recent years, the Houston Zoo invested more than $40 million in a 6.5-acre (26,305-square-meter) African habitat for naturalistic display of white rhinos, chimpanzees, and a raised overlook where visitors can feed giraffes. Such public interaction is crucial in building wide support for wildlife conservation. With about 6,000 animals of 900 species,

An aerial view of the Houston Zoo, one of Texas's eighteen zoos and aquariums.

there is always plenty to experience. What happens on the grounds is only part of the Houston Zoo's mission. It also participates in conservation programs around the world for saving such endangered species as the clouded leopard, Bornean orangutan, Galapagos tortoise, and many others.

What is unique about the Austin Zoo?

Austin is Texas's capital, the nation's eleventh-largest city, and the biggest city in the country to not have a municipal zoo. Feelings against animal captivity have always run high in this famously liberal community, and past bond elections to establish a city zoo have failed—which is ironic now that zoos are in the forefront of preventing the extinction of numerous important species. Austin's current "zoo" actually prides itself on being an anti zoo, for it is really a rescue facility for abandoned and abused exotic animals. They include a former Baylor University bear mascot, rescues from pharmacological studies, and ex-circus animals. The Austin Zoo has, however, entered the international zoo mainstream by successfully breeding two lions that are believed to be of the north African Barbary subspecies, which is extinct in the wild. All the funding comes from admission fees and private donations of money, food, and supplies.

Why is the Austin Zoo so often approached by larger and more famous zoos to take animals off their hands?

For many years, the zoo community worldwide has undertaken what is called the "zoo revolution," deemphasizing its role in public amusement and recognizing its responsibility to keep endangered species from going extinct through research in genetics, breeding, and habitat requirements. Since adopting individual "Species Survival Plans," zoos coordinate with each other to provide genetic diversity within the existing captive population to avoid further wild captures. Given the limited space available, it has become difficult to house individual animals that are not suitable for breeding, and sometimes, such excess specimens—even of endangered species—are destroyed. The Austin Zoo is now famous as a rescue facility, and it receives incessant appeals from other zoos to take problem animals off their hands.

What purpose is served by having zoos in smaller cities?

Rural Texas has always been a bastion against social and political progress, and the presence of zoos in smaller cities, which has often been instigated by the activism of passionate individuals, has enlarged wildlife education to a much larger population than it would have reached otherwise. Moreover, the presence in smaller city zoos of such critically endangered species as black rhinos increases their chance of survival, first against poaching in the wild—which is especially true of rhinos because their horns are worth five times their weight in gold on the illegal traditional Chinese medicine market—but also lessens the risk of losing ground in saving a species by accident or disease in another zoo.

What is the largest aquarium in Texas?

When it opened in 1990, the Texas State Aquarium in Corpus Christi made the determination that it would not try to display exhibits from around the world but instead would interpret in depth the ecology of the Gulf of Mexico. Recent additions include a 400,000-gallon (1.5-million-liter) exhibit of the Caribbean Sea, including sandbar

The largest aquarium in Texas is the Texas State Aquarium in Corpus Christi.

sharks, that can be experienced by walking through an acrylic tunnel beneath the surface. A representation of the Flower Gardens coral reef off the Texas coast shows green moray eels and Atlantic tarpon. The aquarium has equipped itself to be an approved rescue facility for wildlife caught in marine disasters and is accredited by the Association of Zoos and Aquariums.

Isn't the Snake Farm in New Braunfels just a tourist trap?

It was at one time and was quite famous as a tacky attraction, but it is far more than that now. Established in 1967, the Snake Farm became almost a paradigm of roadside kitsch, but new owners took over in 2007 and began a transformation into a dynamic center for wildlife education and conservation. It is now fully accredited by the AZA and has quadrupled in size, with plans for such exhibits as a kangaroo "walkabout" and a safari park.

Speaking of drive-through safaris, why do African animals seem to thrive so well in Texas?

Drive-through game parks feature African savanna species—zebra, various antelope, giraffe, even endangered species such as rhino. One reason they seem so at home is that Texas is very similar to the east African veldt, in hot climate, in geology, and even with similar species in the botanical background: acacias are the dominant tree in the African savanna, a niche that in Texas is conveniently occupied by the mesquite, which is in the same family. They feel right at home.

HOLIDAY EVENTS, MUSICAL PAGEANTS, AND FESTIVALS

Did El Paso really host the first U.S. Thanksgiving?

The city has a good claim to it. On April 30, 1598, the conquistador Juan de Oñate reached the Paso del Norte, having marched for fifty days across the Chihuahuan Desert, thinking to blaze a shorter route to the pueblo country of present-day New Mexico. Unlike previous *entradas*, Oñate meant to bring settlers into the country and had with him some five hundred people and seven thousand head of livestock. After terrible privation, including almost no food or water for over a week, they reached the Rio Grande, rested for ten days, and participated in a feast of Thanksgiving twenty-three years before the pilgrims of Plymouth Colony.

What is celebrated on Cinco de Mayo?

Many Americans mistakenly believe that May 5 is Mexican Independence Day, which is actually September 16. May 5 is the anniversary of a Mexican army's victory over a much larger invading French force in 1861, sent to install an Austrian archduke, Maximilian von Habsburg, as Mexican "emperor." Cinco de Mayo has never been widely observed as a holiday in Mexico. In the United States, however, it gained popularity with the coming of the Chicano political movement. Its commercialization by brewers and leisure industries in the 1980s turned it into a widespread revel of Latino culture, whose actual historical roots are not particularly important.

What is the oldest outdoor musical pageant in Texas?

Albany native Robert Nail Jr. (1908–1968) was gifted in drama, and family oil money sent him east for a suitable education. At the Lawrenceville School; he studied under Thornton Wilder; at Princeton, he was at least as talented as his friends Jimmy Stewart and José Ferrer. Although a great future awaited in New York, Nail's family was devastated by the Great Depression, and he returned home to care for his mother. Back in Albany after such a heady experience, Nail became a theater director and produced a local pageant in which he encouraged waitresses and farmhands to take part, which eventually became the "Fort Griffin Fandangle," an annual production that features new songs and performers every year.

Why do tourists stream into Palo Duro Canyon every summer night?

They are bent on attending the *Texas* outdoor musical pageant, which has been a summer feature for over fifty years and has become an institution. It was written by Paul Eliot Green, a Pulitzer Prize-winning playwright who specialized in historical dramas and who came to Palo Duro Canyon at the invitation (and expense) of a group of culturally aware citizens. He willingly engaged to write a musical play to depict the history of the Panhandle-Plains. Outdoor theater in Palo Duro began with a visiting performance of the Fandangle from Albany, and it stirred the hearts of the city's culturally minded, who shared a vision of a musical pageant set against the huge backdrop of Palo Duro. A different play was staged from 2003 to 2005 to rejuvenate interest, but popular demand brought Green's *Texas* back for good.

Pulitzer Prize-winning author Paul Eliot Green wrote the musical pageant *Texas*, which is performed annually outdoors at Palo Duro Canyon.

What is celebrated in the Austin Kite Festival?

Austin's traditional kickoff to spring began in 1929, making it the oldest kite festival in the country. Traditionally held on the first weekend in March (with a rain date for the next weekend) on the Great Lawn at Zilker Park, thousands of attendees are shuttled across Lady Bird Lake on buses from parking downtown. Prizes are awarded for largest, highest-flying, strongest-pulling, steadiest, and most unusual kites, and the latter category alone is usually worth the visit.

Where is the Texas Folk Life Festival?

In another afterlife of HemisFair, the Texas Folk Life Festival is sponsored annually by the Institute of Texan Cultures, which is a wing of the University of Texas at San Antonio. Just as the institute, which began life as Hemisfair's Texas pavilion, documents Texas's bewildering tapestry of ethnicities and nationalities, the festival is an annual celebration of that diversity. It dates from 1972, which makes it rather ahead of its time. The institute itself, in addition to the museum, contains a research library of hundreds of oral histories and some three million historical photographs.

Does Texas have any ongoing folk music festivals?

There are many seasonal or ad hoc musical gatherings in Texas, but certainly, the most famous continuing folk festival is the one held since 1972 at Quiet Valley Ranch outside of Kerrville in the heart of the Hill Country. Beginning in 2008, it has been managed by the Texas Folk Music Foundation. It is held over eighteen days in early summer and attended by as many as thirty thousand people who feel free to buy a ticket for one day to listen to a favorite performer or camp out for the duration. Notable past performers have been as diverse as Willie Nelson, Mary Chapin Carpenter, and Peter, Paul, and Mary.

What annual livestock celebration still marches its stock down a town's main street?

In the south Texas town of Cuero, poultry processing has been a leading industry since a turkey dressing house opened in 1908. Capitalizing on a popular dance of the day, Cuero's city leaders organized a fair and "Turkey Trot," as the turkeys were marched from farm to packing house, to publicize the industry in 1912. It was presided over by Governor O. B. Colquitt and was considered a great success. Subsequent iterations of the Turkey Trot were less successful; as poultry raising became more automated, fat, pen-raised turkeys collapsed from exhaustion during the event. The trot was then limited to hardy, free-range birds. In 1973 the event transformed into the Cuero Turkeyfest, with such events as a turkey-calling contest (for the humans) and a beauty contest (for the turkeys). The highlight is a grudge race between a turkey from the poultry center of Worthington, Minnesota, who is always named Paycheck, and a local Cuero entry, who is always named Ruby Begonia.

What is so special about the Pecan Street Festival?

Where other Texas cities have devoted themselves to building up business—industry in Houston, finance in Dallas—Austin has always maintained a devotion to supporting the arts. While the music industry is well supported, Austin's other artists—painters, sculptors, jewelers, woodworkers, and other craftsmen—needed a venue to publicize their skills

What is Eeyore's Birthday Party?

Eeyore, of course, is the forever melancholy donkey in A. A. Milne's classic tales of *Winnie-the-Pooh*. A lynchpin of Austin's festival calendar and, like the Kite Festival, an indispensable spring ritual, this takes place (weather permitting) on the last Saturday of April in Pease Park in central Austin. It features beer, music, quirky costumes, beer, drum circles, face painting, and beer.

and vend their wares. This two-day festival has been held twice each year for more than thirty years—on the first Saturday and Sunday in May and the last Saturday and Sunday in September. Sixth Street (or Pecan Street in the original 1839 town plat) is closed down and divided into booths; competition to exhibit wares is so fierce that the festival has become juried. Sixth Street is closed to traffic while people indulge in live music, face painting, and food. It is sponsored by a consortium of downtown businesses called the Pecan Street Association, who in turn use festival proceeds to support many local causes.

For what annual festival is the Brazosport community of Clute recognized?

Texas's larger cities may have their gaudy fairs and carnivals, but only Clute has the annual Great Texas Mosquito Festival, which has been ongoing for more than thirty years, organized by the city SWAT Team. It features a 26-foot- (8-meter-) tall mosquito mascot named Willie-Man-Chew, a mosquito-calling competition, and a 5K race known as the Mosquito Chase.

Who started the Texas Book Festival?

Pecan Street is not a favorable venue for featuring the most quiet of the arts: writing. Austin is home to a vast literary community; the Austin Writer's League, before it morphed into the Writer's League of Texas, was the second largest in the United States. The festival, begun in 1995 by Texas (later U.S.) First Lady Laura Bush, the TBF takes place in the state capitol and spills off the grounds onto surrounding streets. Since its beginning as a showcase for Austin and Texas authors, the TBF is now a major stop on the U.S. book-publicity circuit, hosting about three hundred authors and attended by some fifty thousand people.

What happens at the Crystal City Spinach Festival?

Crystal City cannot display its oversized statue of Popeye, and be surrounded by thousands of acres of spinach, and not have a spinach festival. It takes place early each November, with food, music, and activities.

Where is the largest state fair in the United States?

The Texas State Fair, an annual autumn rite held in Dallas's Fair Park, takes advantage of a spacious physical plant: the buildings left from the Texas Centennial of 1936. They, plus a raucous midway, acres of livestock tents, competitive crafts and cooking, and the Cotton Bowl for the annual shootout between UT and OU football make this the largest fair in the country.

What is the largest annual historical reenactment that takes place in Texas?

On Palm Sunday of 1836, Colonel James Walker Fannin and nearly four hundred of his men were executed—the officers and wounded were within the chapel courtyards of the Presidio La Bahía, while the rank and file were marched a distance away and mown down. Today, on the weekend nearest to March 27, La Bahía, which is possibly the best preserved Spanish presidio in the country, hosts a two-day reenactment that is attended by thousands from across the country. "Living historians" explain period clothing and gear, equestrians demonstrate Mexican cavalry maneuvers, and there is musketry and cannon fire, so it is best to leave pets at home. Each day, a distinguished Texas historian discusses the Texas Revolution in the chapel where the Texians were held prisoner before their deaths.

What is the world record length for spitting a watermelon seed?

For over sixty years, every June, the agricultural marketing center of Luling (pop. 5,700, 40 miles [64 kilometers] south of Austin) has hosted the Watermelon Thump—named for the common method that shoppers employ to determine whether a melon is ripe. The event draws around thirty thousand visitors, and one competition not to be missed is the Seed Spitting Contest, which offers a $500 prize for the longest distance and an additional $500 for setting a new record. Local residents pride themselves on their tech-

---

To what small town does the University of Texas retreat to celebrate the unlikely combination of frontier history, classical music, and Shakespeare?

German settlers began arriving in the area in 1845 to live on the Nassau Plantation that the *Adelsverein* (German immigrants society) had purchased for them. Today, the Winedale Historical Center preserves a collection of buildings carefully curated to represent a cross section of mid-nineteenth-century life: there is a dog-trot cabin original to the property and a Greek revival residence. Most prominent is the Sam Lewis Stopping Place, a rare surviving example of the kind of residence that once dotted rural Texas, a private home that was enlarged to serve as a stage depot and inn for travelers. Founded by pianist James Dick, the Round Top Festival Institute gathers world-class musicians every June and July to teach and perform solo recitals, chamber music, and orchestral concerts on its grounds outside of Round Top. And at the end of July and into August, three Shakespeare plays are offered every year in the Winedale Theatre Barn.

nique and were humbled when a contestant from Houston set a record of 65 feet, 4 inches (20 meters), but in 1989, home honor was restored with a truly formidable spit of 68 feet, 9 inches (21 meters). In recent years, Jubilee melons—round, bright green, with dark red meat—have become the most profitable to grow for their great supermarket appeal. However, seeds for the spitting contest must come from traditional Black Diamond melons specially grown for the event.

When are the Buda Wiener Dog Races?

Hemmed in by the metropolis of Austin and the booming college town of San Marcos, the community of Buda began to lose its century-old bucolic atmosphere to suburban sprawl in the 1980s, and the population more than doubled from the seventy-two hundred in the 2010 census to more than fifteen thousand estimated in 2016. (The name is pronounced *Bewda*, as it is an Anglophone mangling of the Spanish *viuda*, named for the widows who cooked at an early hotel.) Unable to compete with its larger neighbors in athletic events but not to be outdone, in 1998, Buda began its now nationally known Wiener Dog Races, preceded by a Cutest Pet Parade. The annual fundraiser for the local Lions Club is held every April.

How many rattlesnakes are dispatched at the Sweetwater Rattlesnake Roundup?

The Rattlesnake Roundup held in Sweetwater in 2018 was the sixtieth iteration, and it is widely considered the largest event of its kind in the United States. The event attracts upward of thirty thousand people, who book up the motels a year in advance and who add $5 million to the town's coffers. It is held on the second weekend of March—just as the ground is warming up and the snakes are stirring from their dens. Like many sim-

The Buda Wiener Dog Races are held annually as a fundraiser for the local Lions Club.

ilar events, it also features music, a cook-off, carnival rides, tutorials on safe snake handling, and other attractions. The record haul of snakes was brought in 1982, just short of 18,000 pounds (8,165 kilograms).

While not enough to impact Texas's overall population of rattlesnakes, local ranchers who must beware of them every time they step outdoors, and who have to doctor snakebit dogs and livestock, do not miss them at all. (Rattlesnake actually does taste vaguely like chicken.)

ODDS AND ENDS

Is anything left of the famous Route 66 as it passed through the Texas Panhandle?

Located 40 miles (64 kilometers) west of Amarillo on I-40, the little town of Vega engaged national attention for perhaps the only time in its history when its billboard directing liberals to keep on traveling until they leave the state went viral in June 2018. The town began in 1903 when the local landowner sold right-of-way to the rail line that became the Rock Island, which caused the once prominent cowboy capital of Tascosa to begin drying up. While that era is preserved in the Oldham County Heritage Farm and Ranch Museum, it is "Dot's Mini Museum" that displays memorabilia from Route 66, the celebrated federal highway that ran from Chicago to Los Angeles, opened in November 1926, and came through Vega. There is also a restored Magnolia gas station from the period with further interpretation of those times.

What Texas city has a state boundary line for its main street?

Although founded in 1873 on the line between Texas and Arkansas as the most logical junction for competing railroads who were building in the same area, it ironically is not known who gave Texarkana its name. State Line Avenue is both its main street and the boundary between twin jurisdictions at the city, county, and state levels.

Does Texas preserve any tall ships?

Maintained by the Texas Seaport Museum, the three-masted barque *Elissa*, 141 feet (43 meters) long and 620 tons (562,455 kilograms), was launched in 1877, missing by three years being the oldest ship still regularly sailing. It sailed under many flags and actually carried cargo along the Texas coast at one time. It was slated for the breakers but was rescued in 1970. *Elissa* embarks on regular cruises from its berth at Pier 21 in Galveston and participates in tall ship reviews.

Why are early Texas frame houses so rare?

Early in the period of Anglo settlement, sawn lumber was a luxury in a place where tall, consistently straight pine trees could be easily felled and hewn into cabins. Milled boards were either imported, or there was a wait for a sawmill to be erected in a given locale.

West Columbia preserves several early Texas frame houses, most prominently the plantation house of Old Three Hundred pioneer Martin Varner (1785–1844), which became even more historic after it became the family seat of Texas governor Jim Hogg. The Ammon Underwood House located near the rebuilt Capitol is one of the oldest frame residences in Texas. Nearby, the Sweeny-Waddy Log Cabin is a rare survivor of early Texas slave quarters, and an early African American school room is preserved, attached to the Columbia Historical Museum, whose exhibits bring the local history through the oil and ranching eras, including period clothing.

What is the secret of the Ellis County Courthouse?

Built at a time when Victorian Romanesque Revival was all the rage in Texas architecture, the courthouse in Waxahachie was built in a great flight of fancy. It was finished in 1897 and cost a staggering $130,000— or $3.75 million today. The element that visitors try to find is in the sandstone carvings. One Italian sculptor who was brought in to carve the decoration fell in love with local girl Mabel Frame, whose angelic face graces the column capitals. After she jilted him, her visage changes into a terrifying harpy.

What is the Old Stone Fort?

Contrary to its name, it was not a fort in any defensive sense. The leader of the town's re-establishment, Antonio Gil Ibarvo, built the structure in 1779 or soon thereafter,

The stunning architecture of the Ellis County Courthouse in Waxahachie is the result of the popularity of the Victorian Romanesque Revival style in the 1890s.

using local adobe for the interior walls and locally quarried iron ore for the exterior. He used it as a mercantile and warehouse, but as he was also the civic leader, official functions were carried out from there as well. Volunteers assembled here to open the Revolution in 1825. After several decades of statehood, the historic structure had sunk to being a saloon and was torn down in 1902. The stones were stored by a local ladies' civic club until the Stone Fort was reconstructed, using the same rocks, as a Centennial project in 1936. It is now a museum and focus for Nacogdoches history and tourism. Incidentally, Nacogdoches and hence the Stone Fort were key objects of filibusters in the early 1800s, and the Green Flag rebels, the James Long expedition, and the Fredonian Rebellion all declared insurgent governments here—thus where six flags have flown over Texas, at least nine flags have flown over Nacogdoches.

Where in Texas can you find a stagecoach inn?

Built in 1860, Salado's stage stop was an important rest on the road and also proximate to drovers on the Chisholm Trail. Its register logs the names of Robert E. Lee (when he served in Texas before the Civil War), Sam Houston, George A. Custer (when he was military governor during Reconstruction), cattle baron Shanghai Pierce, outlaw Jesse James, and others. The inn is still in use as a restaurant. Elsewhere, Salado is known as one of Texas's best hunting grounds for antiques, and there are twenty sites in town with historical markers.

Where can one find a well-restored military fort in the Panhandle-Plains?

There are truncated remnants of many frontier Indian-fighting forts in Texas, such as Griffin and Richardson, but the most extensive is probably Fort Concho in San Angelo, with

The beautifully restored Fort Concho in San Angelo is a National Historic Landmark popular with many visitors to San Angelo.

What is the "littlest skyscraper in Texas"?

In 1912, the Burkburnett oil field turned that and surrounding towns into boom-towns, and the population of nearby Wichita Falls rocketed from 8,200 in the 1910 census to 40,079 in the 1920 census. Loose money and gullible wildcatters were everywhere. With office space in a critical shortage, Pennsylvanian J. D. McMahon began raising money to construct what he boasted would be a peerless high-rise, 480 feet (146 meters) tall. He soon had $200,000 in hand, and although his investors looked over his blueprints, not one of them noticed that the building was laid out in inches, not feet. The resulting Newby-McMahon Building had an interior dimension of about 9 by 12 feet (2.7 by 3.7 meters) and rose four stories (40 feet [12 meters]) high. The investors took him to court but obtained no relief, for as the judge noted, McMahon had built the exact building that he showed them, and the swindle gained national fame after being featured in *Ripley's Believe It or Not!* soon after. It is now part of the Depot Square Historic District in Wichita Falls. Nearby are the Wichita Falls Railroad Museum, which features a collection of vintage engines and cars, and the Museum of North Texas History, which showcases the region's unique blend of ranching and oil heritage (with some five hundred hats of various eras), and a Curtiss Jenny airplane in a satellite facility at the airport.

twenty-three original or restored buildings and extensive interpretive exhibits. Concho was the headquarters of the Fourth Cavalry under Ranald Mackenzie, who finally succeeded in clearing the Comanche off the Staked Plains. Go to fortconcho.com to learn more.

How did a rural county seat come to have a front-rank art museum?

Albany is the seat of Shackelford County, just northeast of Abilene. Founded in 1867, its first permanent structure was its jail, not surprising because of its proximity to Fort Griffin, which had a reputation for being one of the most unruly installations in the Army. Although Albany is in other respects like any small Texas town—chuckwagon breakfasts on the courthouse square during special events, 1A high school football played under "Friday night lights"—the Old Jail Art Center really is just one example of unexpected culture encountered there. There is also a bookstore, a publishing company, and art galleries. The Old Jail, with backing by local oil and ranching money, was expanded into a modern annex and turned into an art museum. At a time when Albany had one traffic light, residents could stroll into the museum and see oil paintings by Renoir, etchings by Rembrandt, and works of similar caliber.

Are there any quality planetariums in Texas?

Yes, there are numerous planetariums in Texas. One of the best is at Angelo State University in San Angelo, which is billed as the fourth-largest university planetarium in the United States, with a dome capable of displaying more than half a billion stars and other celestial features. It is also known for its outreach programs to schoolchildren.

Where is Texas's last twenty-four-hour staffed lighthouse?

The Lydia Ann Lighthouse near Aransas Pass is privately operated, but photographers find it a favorite subject from nearby vantage points and from offshore.

Which is the only historic Texas lighthouse open to the public?

After Texas joined the United States, the federal government bore the responsibility for safeguarding coastal navigation and began building lighthouses. The most southerly was the Port Isabel Lighthouse, near the mouth of the Rio Grande, northeast of Brownsville. Begun in 1852, the 82-foot (25-meter) brick masonry tower guided ships through the Brazos Santiago Pass and had the power of its lamps increased several times. Today, it is open to the public as a State Historic Site, as is a reconstruction of the keeper's cottage.

What was the longest single-span suspension bridge west of the Mississippi at the time it was built?

Untamed and unpredictable, the Brazos River could be an impediment to cattle drives on the Chisholm Trail. With the economy in the doldrums of Reconstruction, city leaders hit on the bridge project to reinvigorate the economy. A bridge company was chartered in 1866 through the legislature to have a monopoly on traffic for twenty-five years. Their agent traveled to New York in October 1868 to engage a contractor, and he settled

The Brazos River Bridge, built in 1870 as the longest suspension bridge west of the Mississippi at the time, is on the National Register of Historic Places.

on John A. Roebling's Sons Company of Trenton, whose more famous later project was the Brooklyn Bridge. The twin masonry towers on either side of the Brazos used some three million bricks, and the span across the river was 475 feet (145 meters). The nearest suitable machine shop was in Galveston 200 miles (322 kilometers) away, and it was 100 miles (161 kilograms) to the nearest railhead, but using materials hauled by ox teams over appalling roads, the work proceeded, and the bridge opened on New Year's Day of 1870. They charged drovers a nickel per head to drive their herds across the river and quickly recouped the $141,000 cost. Tolls were retired and the bridge conveyed to the county in 1889, two years early. The Waco bridge entered the U.S. Register of Historic Places in 1970, was retired from carrying automobile traffic the following year, and is now used as a pedestrian attraction.

What was the last U.S. military fort to have mounted cavalry?

When the Army returned to Texas after the Civil War, it established a picket line of military posts running from southwest to northeast, roughly along the edge of settlement. Its southwestern anchor was Fort Clark, originally established in 1852 and abandoned during the war. Strategically located to protect both from cross-border bandit raids and Indian incursions, Fort Clark saw intensive service throughout the frontier era and regained that importance during World War I and German meddling in Mexico. In February 1943, the fort hosted the Second Cavalry Division, which was the last vestige of horse cavalry, but it was mechanized before the end of World War II, and the fort stood down in 1946. It lies across U.S. Highway 90 southwest of the town. Several of its historic buildings are still recognizable, despite the gold course that crosses the parade ground, and its history is presented in the Old Guardhouse Museum.

QUIRKY TEXAS

REGIONAL SPEECH, Y'ALL

How did Texans come to speak such a distinctive dialect?

When organized Anglo settlement began in 1821, most of the immigrants came from the American South. At that time, many of those people came from areas where English was spoken with a strong Jacobean strain that continued back to the early arrivals from England. (Traces of this can still be found in southern Appalachia today.) Once in Texas, many settlers and small towns were so isolated from any other linguistic influence that their speech evolved with little outside disturbance. Of course, some Texans came from the Northeast and from Europe, whose speech added small amounts of their color as well.

Has anyone ever studied the roots of Texan English?

One important linguistic study of words that have become associated with Texas speech identified that 59 percent of them originated in the South and only 8 percent of them in the Northeast. Almost one-third of Texan words were traceable to the Middle Atlantic. Only 1 percent of Texas words had a foreign derivation, either Spanish ranching vocabulary or from the thousands of Germans who began arriving in the 1840s. However, the study also noted that Spanish terms soon began pushing English words out, from west to east, when they were more appropriate or convenient to use.

Among the latter are:

American term	Spanish-derived Texan
barnyard	corral
thornscrub or brush	chaparral
leggings	chaps (from chaparrados)
rope	reata

American term	Spanish-derived Texan
string of work horses	remuda
flat-topped hill	mesa
dry wash or gully	arroyo
celebration	fiesta
jail	hoosegow (from juzgado, or court)

How did the ten-gallon hat get its name?

This is also Spanish in derivation and has nothing to do with water-carrying capacity. Before the Anglo arrival, Spanish *vaqueros* or cowboys would affix ribbons, or *galones*, to their hats when attending a fiesta. A hat to which ten ribbons had been attached was considered especially festive. Equally, such a hat might be referred to as *tán galan*, or very dapper.

What is a maverick?

Today, this refers to a person who acts upon one's own independent thought, one who refuses to follow the patterns of a particular group. In early Texas, it referred to an un-branded calf. Early San Antonio mayor Sam Maverick, who was the final signer of the Texas Declaration of Independence, held a land grant on which he ostensibly raised cattle, but he became so involved in politics that he neglected his stock, and his annual increase in calves remained unbranded.

What has caused the Texan dialect to start fading away?

As regional speech patterns go, the Texas dialect has proven pretty resilient. However, the dialect of the mass media—television and radio—is American Middle Atlantic. That is what actors and announcers are trained to use. Young Texans who grow up exposed to it are more likely to adopt it and abandon words that their grandparents used. Also, owing to American population shifts in the past several decades, Texas has received millions of immigrants from other parts of the country who bring their own word usages and further dilute native speech patterns.

The Texan ten-gallon hat doesn't actually hold ten gallons of anything. The term most likely comes from Spanish, referring to a ribbon on the hat or the gallant style.

Why does the old-time Texan dialect sound so illiterate?

Largely because it *is* illiterate. As schools proliferated and education eventually became mandatory, many of the first "Texanisms" to fall from use amounted to nonstandard grammar that was drilled out of students. *Ain't* was once ubiquitous for "am not," "is not," or "are not," but now its use all but defines an ignorant person. Others fell from usage even more quickly, especially nonstandard past tenses of verbs: "throwed" for "threw," "riz" for "has risen," "clumb" for "climbed," "dremp" for "dreamed," and "holped" for "helped," for example. However, such words today in historical fiction or film scripts are used as colorful short cuts to create a frontier ambience.

What are some Texas words that have fallen from usage?

Here is a selection of words for which, as of the midpoint of the twentieth century, when the language of the mass media began to really have an impact, a majority of Texans still preferred to use their own term. A "Texan" was defined as born and raised in Texas.

American term	Texan term
skunk	polecat
over there	over yonder
Mom / Dad	Ma / Pa
dating	courting (sometimes sparking)
minister	parson
corn on the cob	roasting ears
breast bone (fowl)	pully bone
bedspread	counterpane
peanuts	goobers
skim milk	bluejohn
calf	dogie
sack	poke
covered porch	gallery
widow	widow woman
angered	riled up
redundant indicatives	where at, this here, that there
poor ignorant white person	peckerwood
completely	plumb
fatigued	tuckered out

The infrequency with which one hears the Texan terms today is a measure of how fast the local dialect has changed in two generations. However, some Texans, especially those in rural areas, still prefer their own terms for:

corn bread	corn pone
white bread	light bread
pancakes	flapjacks
green beans	snap beans
cottage cheese	clabber cheese
outhouse	privy
chest of drawers	bureau

Some "Texanisms" are still ubiquitous and sometimes the butt of humor when used elsewhere in the country. Among the most common are:

309

What is the difference between "chile" and "chili"?

Nothing, really. "Chili" is just an accepted Anglicization of "chile," although usage has seemed to divide generally between "chile" for the family of peppers and "chili" for the dish.

American term	Texan term
second person	y'all (not "you all"; that is from the Deep South)
second-person plural	all a' y'all
preparing to	fixin' to
greeting	howdy
farewell	so long

What is the origin of "howdy"?

One common formal greeting of a stranger today is "How do you do?" Two centuries ago, this could be expressed as a more hearty or familiar "How do ye do?" That was contracted to "How d'ye do?", then further to "Howdy do?", which became the Texan "Howdy!" Still later, when "hello" was often replaced with "hi," many Texans adapted to the even less formal and more friendly "Hidy!"

What is a "Texas Norther"?

Weather in Texas is notoriously changeable, although the American humorist Will Rogers made his remark "If you don't like the weather, just wait a minute, it'll change" in reference to Oklahoma, not Texas. In winter, Arctic cold fronts can come roaring down the Great Plains, unimpeded by mountains or forests, and arrive with terrifying speed and ferocity. Occasionally, a day of record heat can be followed by one of record cold, with a glaze of ice. Such a front may herald its arrival with a dark, blue-gray tint in the northern sky, hence it often being called a "blue norther."

POINTS OF INTEREST

Does Texas have any museums dedicated to the art of quilting?

Although it began as a frontier necessity and became an important venue of social bonding among far-flung farm women throughout the frontier, the craft of piecing quilts together from scraps of disparate material has developed into an avidly followed folk art. Behind its highly decorative storefront in downtown La Grange, the Texas Quilt Museum interprets the history of quilt making and also continues the tradition of providing a gathering place for those who follow the craft.

How is it possible to live in the ace of clubs?

Situated in the midst of a prosperous area, Texarkana was the hive of ambitious men looking to make their fortunes. James Draughon was a Confederate veteran and former prisoner of war, and he had known poverty and dependence. After the war, he worked his way up to own a mercantile, and when he was ready to go into the lumber business, he moved his family to Texarkana and prospered. The story is that when Draughon won $10,000 in a poker game on the ace of clubs, he had an architect design a mansion in that shape, two stories over a basement, of three octagonal rooms and one rectangular room clustered about a central hall. Built in 1885, the mansion later passed to other families before being preserved as one of the finest Italianate Victorian houses in the country. Among aficionados of house museums, the Draughon-Moore House, unofficially the Ace of Clubs House, is famous for the completeness and fidelity of its preservation, truly a time capsule of its years as a family residence through differing eras.

Prostitution was so common in Texas, but being socially unacceptable, it seems as though no one will acknowledge it; where can one learn about it?

Women in frontier Texas were commonly thought to need a "protector" and married with or without love to have a man. Exceptions were those who had the education to be a teacher, the skills to be a seamstress, or the opportunity to keep a boardinghouse. Many were forced into the sex trade, including Alamo survivor Susanna Dickinson, whose fourth husband divorced her for turning tricks in their barn. Miss Hattie's Bor-

Now a museum, the Ace of Clubs House in Texarkana is literally shaped like the card game suit.

dello Museum in San Angelo is located in a restored bordello with many original furnishings.

What is the "Cadillac Ranch"?

Amarillo was known for an eccentric arts patron named Stanley Marsh (1938–2014), who encouraged artists to challenge the common public concept of what art should be. In this piece of public art, ten Cadillac automobiles are buried to half of their length at the same angle as the great pyramid of Cheops. Passersby are encouraged to contemplate them (they are on the I-40 access road 12 miles [19 kilometers] west of downtown) and add their own colorful contribution to them.

Where are the world's largest cowboy boots?

In 1979, San Antonio artist Bob Wade used mostly donated materials to craft a pair of boots that have become a landmark that is displayed in a rock garden outside that city's North Star Mall. They are 35 feet tall and mimic the appearance of ostrich leather, which was a fad in Texas boot making around that time.

Where was the world's largest jackrabbit?

For years, the annual rodeo in Odessa featured a unique event: the jackrabbit-roping contest. To publicize the city and the rodeo, the Chamber of Commerce commissioned

Located near Amarillo, Cadillac Ranch was created in 1974 by artists Chip Lord, Hudson Marquez, and Doug Michels. The cars represent models from 1949 to 1963, and the installation was a way for the artists to challenge modern architectural conventions.

Artist Bob Wade created the world's largest cowboy boots, which can be seen next to the North Star Mall in San Antonio.

an 8-foot- (2.4-meter-) tall fiberglass hare in 1962. It was the project of the chamber's president, John Ben Shepperd, hence the sculpture's name, *Jack Ben Rabbit*. The Humane Society agitated to end the rabbit-roping competition and succeeded in 1978. The giant rabbit was moved into storage, but public demand brought it back, displayed with a historical marker in front of the school district headquarters, and bolted to the sidewalk since someone attempted to purloin it in 1997. Although Jack Ben Rabbit lost the world record title in 2017, it is still a popular photo spot.

Where is the world's largest jackrabbit now? Located in Crosby County just east of Lubbock, the Ralls High School athletic mascot is the jackrabbit, and for many years, the town cast an envious eye on the giant hare in Odessa as the world's largest. They could not, however, find a local artist willing to take on the project of making a bigger one until chainsaw artist Cam Dockery buzzed into four large elm trees to create a 2.5-ton (2,268-kilogram) rabbit in 2017. At 14 feet, 6 inches (4.4 meters) tall, it is almost twice the height of Odessa's former title holder, and it stands guard over the Ralls baseball diamond.

Why is there a giant statue of Popeye the Sailor Man in Crystal City?

Crystal City lies in the Winter Garden, an extensive area of commercial truck farms. Before irrigation, the land produced only brush and cactus, but plentiful water and the long growing season turned Texas into a national force in commercial vegetable growing. Spinach came late to the Winter Garden, but its need for deep, sandy soil and plen- 313 tiful, cheap labor made it a natural. First planted experimentally in 1917, ten years later, there were 5,000 acres (20 square kilometers) of it, making spinach a bountiful cash crop. Popeye the Sailor Man was a cartoon character introduced by Elzie Segar, a native of Uvalde, into his ongoing "Thimble Theatre" strip in 1929, and by the time the series was animated in 1932, Popeye had become the most popular character. The running gag was that every time Popeye got himself into some mortal peril, he would down a can of spinach, gain amazing strength, and vanquish his foes. In the five years leading up to 1936, industry estimates were that Popeye increased sales of spinach by one-third, and Crystal City honored the character with a statue in front of City Hall. Texas went on to become the United States's leading producer of spinach.

One expects such a historic city to have museums, but how did it come to open an entirely new collection not seen before?

The Bryan Museum, which opened in the restored Galveston Orphans Home in 2015, is a gift to Texas of Houston energy magnate J. P. Bryan, a collateral descendant of Stephen F. Austin. A lifelong collector of history, as was his father, Bryan's assemblage of books, art, documents, and artifacts are now curated into a cogent, 20,000-square-foot (6,096-meter) presentation of Texas history. Of special note are antique firearms, saddles, more than five hundred pairs of spurs spanning five hundred years, and some thirty-five hundred documents relating to Galveston history.

What is there to see and do in Columbus that enriches the Texas experience?

The town of Columbus on the Colorado River, 75 miles (121 kilometers) west of Houston, is one of the oldest in the state and was settled by Stephen F. Austin's original "Old Three Hundred" colonists. In few other places can one approach so close to the early Anglo frontier in Texas. It is the site of the Alley Log Cabin, which was built in 1836 and is furnished with artifacts from the Republic period. Equally interesting is the Dilue Rose Harris House Museum, which belonged to a woman who, as a nine-year-old girl, became a unique memorialist of the revolution with her reminiscences that were published in the early issues of the *Quarterly of the Texas State Historical Association*.

How did the Haley Memorial Library and History Center get started?

One of Texas's most celebrated historians, J. Evetts Haley (1901–1995), wrote a biography of Charles Goodnight, based partly on extensive interviews with the aged ranching legend, a history of the XIT Ranch, and other highly regarded books. He was long associated with West Texas State University in Canyon. He was also extremely conservative; in 1956, he ran for governor of Texas on the segregationist ticket and later eroded his reputation when he attacked Lyndon Johnson in a privately published screed, *A Texan Looks at Lyndon*, in 1964, which became the best-selling political book of all time thanks to bulk orders from the John Birch Society and others. He ended his relationship with West Texas State when they integrated, and he moved to Midland. Much of his later descent into extremism was likely a result of his dementia, and he did not touch the quality of the history collection he assembled, which includes the original bell cast for the Alamo mission in 1722 as well several items related to New Mexico's Lincoln County War and Billy the Kid.

With so much attention on Big Bend and on the lower Rio Grande, is there any place that preserves the heritage of the middle stretch of the valley?

Although the original town of Zapata had to be abandoned with completion of the Falcon Dam in 1953 and rebuilt on higher ground, the story of the middle Rio Grande is told in the Zapata County Museum of History and the La Paz County Historical Museum. That history is notable, as Zapata was part of the short-lived Republic of the Rio Grande in 1840.

Where else is Brownsville history preserved?

After the Mexican–American War, the Rio Grande was an international boundary and major navigable waterway, so river boatman Charles Stillman (1810–1875) went into partnership with Richard King and Mifflin Kenedy to establish a river trade. Stillman founded the town of Brownsville, less than 1 mile (1.6 kilometers) from Fort Brown. Stillman's house, built in 1850, is now the center of the Brownsville Heritage Complex. Further local history can be absorbed at the Historic Brownsville Museum.

Where can one find any reminders of U.S. Army life on the border?

Perhaps the best-preserved army installation on the Rio Grande is Fort Ringgold in Rio Grande City, which was established in 1848 and played a key role in the suppression of cross-border banditry of such figures as Juan Nepomuceno Cortina. Among the buildings maintained are the post hospital and the house, where Colonel Robert E. Lee held command of the Department of Texas before he resigned his commission and fought for the South in the Civil War. A reminder of a somewhat later period is the restored La Borde House Historic Inn. Built in 1899 for a French merchant who plied the Rio Grande in his trading steamer, the house adapts the French Creole style to the Mexican frontier.

Where in Texas can one catch a glimpse of the "Gilded Age" as it was experienced in the East?

Wealthy Texans of the late nineteenth century became almost a parody of the loud-mouthed, crude, ignorant, unsophisticated *nouveau riche*, and after the discovery of oil, Eastern money was present only as investments in large ranches or other enterprises. One exception was Ned Green, the son of famed New York miser Hetty Howland Green, "The Witch of Wall Street," whose stinginess cost Ned a leg when she proved too cheap to engage a doctor to treat an infection. Ned Green came west to manage his own railroad empire and gained fame, mostly for his debauchery. His sumptuous private rail car reposes in Ben Gill Park in Terrell.

315

LEGENDS

Where do the "Pecos Bill" stories come from?

Different American regions and industries have developed larger-than-life folk heroes, whether purely the creation of folklore such as Paul Bunyan the lumberjack or possibly stemming from real people such as John Henry the steel driver. Pecos Bill, the paradigm hero of Texas tall tales, may be neither but an example of "fakelore": the product of one writer's imagination that he claimed to be a traditional character. Pecos Bill—raised by coyotes after his family lost him crossing the Pecos River, rescued by a cowboy who persuaded him that he wasn't a coyote, who mastered a horse named Widowmaker, who lassoed a tornado, who spiked his whiskey with nitroglycerin, and who acquired a girlfriend in Slue-Foot Sue who was riding down the Rio Grande on a huge catfish—today is assumed to have originated among yarn-spinning cowboys. However, he does not appear to have an existence before author Edward Sinnott "Tex" O'Reilly (1880–1946) began writing stories about him in 1917. Whatever the origins of Pecos Bill, O'Reilly himself could almost have stood in as the subject of tall tales. In his youth, he was a soldier of fortune who fought in the Spanish–American War, the Boxer Rebellion, the Philippine Insurrection, and half a dozen other conflicts—and also fought with Pancho Villa in Mexico. He later became a writer, an editor at the *San Antonio Light*, and he published a Pecos Bill collection in 1935.

What is the legend of the chupacabra?

Literally, it means "goat sucker," and it refers to a vampirical beast alleged to stalk various regions of Latin America. It is of recent origin; the first alleged sighting was in Puerto Rico in the spring of 1995, reported by an individual who had seen the newly released film *Species*, who believed that the bug-eyed, spiny-backed creature in the movie was real and whose description matched the half alien in the film. Despite this dubious provenance, tales of chupacabra predation raced across Puerto Rico and spread to other parts of Latin America. In the American Southwest and especially Texas, stories of chupacabras slaughtering and draining the blood of hapless small livestock proliferated after being featured on crackpot cryptozoology programs on "reality" television. In Texas, a few individual animals have been shot or

An illustration of a chupacabra attacking livestock.

run over on highways and have proved to be either coyotes or large feral dogs, rendered hairless and debilitated by extremely advanced cases of mange.

What are the Marfa Lights?

Ten or twelve nights a year, not predictable by season or weather conditions, observers can see balls of light floating, drifting, or sometimes darting, usually above Mitchell Flat, an expanse of grassy desert east of Marfa, Texas. Sightings date from 1883, when a local cowboy said he took them for Indian campfires, although the Apache were evicted from the area three years previous, and no remains of fires could be found when searched for. Area ranchers confirmed that they too had seen the lights periodically. Different explanations have been put forward that could explain the Marfa Lights in part, but they have not proved definitive: electrostatic discharge, a fata morgana (an optical illusion caused by a temperature inversion of a type common in the area), a combustion of the right combination of hydrocarbon gases (methane and phosphine) seeping from the ground, or refraction of automobile headlights from the passing highway (which does not explain the early sightings). Whatever their origin, calling them the "Marfa Ghost Lights," paired with a good story about the spirits of early conquistadores still looking for gold, has proven good for tourism, and the Texas Department of Transportation has built an observation stand overlooking Mitchell Flat on U.S. 90 east of town.

Where are Texas's most haunted places?

Texas hauntings, like those anywhere, place one squarely in the realm of "the story is" without worrying too much over the factual predicate. Certain locations, however, have maintained a reputation for elevated creepiness for many years, long before they were hyped by tacky "reality" shows. Here is a short list of some of the most famous, alphabetically by city:

- Austin: Not many houses in Austin could better fit the bill as a haunted house as the Littlefield House, a turreted Victorian fantasy built in 1893 at the edge of the University of Texas campus. It cost $50,000 and is clad in bricks imported from Belgium at 50 cents apiece, built by UT regent George W. Littlefield (1842–1920) as a challenge to students to go out and do as well as he did. His widow, Alice, continued to live in the house until her own death in 1935, apparently too crazy to be let out—or to know that she died. She is still occasionally seen playing the piano or strolling the upstairs.

- College Station: Texas A&M University's Animal Industries Building used to be a slaughterhouse, with meat-carving classes offered in the basement. In 1965 an instructor was working one night with an electric saw, slipped, severed his femoral artery, and bled to death before help could reach him. Although too recent in some minds to be a classic haunting, the A&M Library maintains a vertical file of reports of creepy occurrences, cold spots in the lab, blood that suddenly appears on the

317

The Littlefield House, which can be found at the University of Texas at Austin campus, is said to be haunted by Alice Littlefield, wife of the university's former regent.

floor, and psychic "investigations" that reached positive conclusions. Today, some students scoff and others avoid the place.

- El Paso: El Paso High School was built in 1916 and was a wonder of its time and place, with roof gardens, massive Greco-Roman architecture, an elegant apartment for the headmaster, and is now on the National Register of Historic Places. Most notable are its basement and sub-basements, now known as the catacombs, which are a center of the building's long history of spooky happenings, but curiously, no specific instances are cited.

- Fort Worth: Miss Molly's Hotel, a former bordello from Cowtown days, is still frequented by ladies and cowboys who are sometimes seen playing cards.

- Galveston: The Hotel Galvez was once the queen of the beach and now is the survivor of that age of elegant resorts before they were challenged by cookie-cutter chain operations. Originally planned in 1898 to replace the grand and gaudy Beach Hotel that burned down, plans were stalled by the Great Storm of 1900 and then accelerated to bring tourists back to the island. It opened on the same spot as the Beach Hotel in 1911 at a cost of over $1 million. The hotel has changed hands several times, unknown to Audra, who hanged herself in her room upon hearing (erroneously) that her fiancé had been lost at sea. She still manifests her dismay in disquieting ways. The fifth floor is particularly notorious for paranormal phenomena.

- Goliad: Mission Presidio la Bahía was the scene of the Goliad Massacre, about four hundred Texas revolutionary volunteers executed on the orders of Antonio López de Santa Anna after having been given treatment as POWs by General José de Urrea. Forty wounded were shot in the courtyard, including the commander, Colonel James Fannin, shot in the face after having requested to be shot in the heart. The rest were murdered in the surrounding landscape. That is a lot of angry spirits to have roaming around, and tourists not infrequently report unexplained screams, bells, and gunfire.

- Houston: The Spaghetti Warehouse began its life as a grocery and pharmacy, and it opened its history of tragedy when a young druggist fell to his death in an elevator shaft. His distraught widow died a year later, and her continuing search for her husband is said to be one of the strongest hauntings in the state.

- Jefferson: Erected as a cotton warehouse in 1851 and later converted into a hotel, The Jefferson Hotel was the melancholy location of a nineteen-year-old bride hanging herself on her wedding night. Hers is said to be a strong haunting, complete with chills, touches, and dramatic demonstrations of objects that move by themselves and appliances that turn on and off.

- Mineral Wells: When it opened in 1929, the sumptuous $1.2 million hotel built by Theodore Brasher Baker was meant to attract more tourists to bathe in the town's supposedly curative waters. This it did, drawing celebrities from Lyndon Johnson to Bonnie and Clyde, but the concept of a 14-story, 450-room hotel on a scale of the grand European spas was just too grandiose for a Texas town of barely 6,000, nor did it help that it opened barely a week after the stock market crash plummeted the country into the Great Depression. Baker provided his mistress with a gaily painted suite, but that did not prevent her from flinging herself from a seventh-story window, and the woman's restless spirit famously disturbed many guests on that floor until the Baker Hotel closed in 1972. Now listed on the National Register of Historic Places, the Baker has been the subject of various schemes to bring it back, but until one of them succeeds, its peeling paint, echoing corridors, graffiti-covered chambers, and silent steam machinery make it prime ghost habitat.

- Saratoga: Bragg Road is an old logging road through this thickest part of the Big Thicket, and there, an ephemeral light marks where a railroad worker from years past is searching for his head, lost in a train accident.

- Wichita Falls: The Old Insane Asylum on the south side of town was the project of a Dr. White, who opened it in 1926 and treated his patients with rest and therapy instead of the harsher regimens such as electroshocks. For years after it closed, it was a favored spot for youthful ghost-telling stories, but its apparitions—laughing children, a young woman calling out "Hello!"—have not been of the threatening variety. The building is now a private residence.

- Yorktown: Yorktown Memorial Hospital is an abandoned hospital that was open from 1948 to 1988 and recorded a surprising two thousand deaths, then saw a second use as a drug rehabilitation facility. This seems to have given it a whole variety of restless spirits to walk the halls.

Why is Terlingua called a ghost town when people live there?

The origins of mercury mining in this area are not well documented, but at their height in the early 1900s, the mines brought upward of three thousand workers to Terlingua. It is not technically a ghost town but just seems like it by comparison. In addition to local ranches, the economy now is anchored by tourism and outfitting for rafters, mountain bikers, and rock climbers.

TEXAN NOTABLES

WRITERS

What was the first book written about Texas?

In November 1528, survivors of the Pánfilo de Narváez expedition were shipwrecked on what was probably Galveston Island. They numbered about eighty. At first, they were welcomed by the native Karankawa Indians, but as their European diseases decimated the tribe, they were enslaved and threatened with execution. Seven years later, the last four survivors reached New Spain, including the expedition's second-in-command, Álvar Núñez Cabeza de Vaca. His *Relacion* of their odyssey, first published in 1542, was remarkable for its sympathetic account of the Indians, and once he reached Mexico and observed conditions there, his condemnation of the Spaniards' cruelty toward them made him enemies who poisoned the rest of his life.

Did any books help spur or contribute to Anglo-American settlement in Texas?

After Stephen F. Austin led the first Americans to their colony in Mexico, his older cousin, Mary Austin Holley (1784–1846), visited Texas with a view to settling there. Her book *Texas: Observations, Historical, Geographical, and Descriptive* was published in 1833, followed by a history of Texas written during the revolution. Her combination of literate wit and practical advice on what immigrants needed to bring, or not bother with, made the books the equivalent of best-sellers in the United States.

What are the best memoirs of the frontier Texas experience?

No doubt, the founding of the Texas State Historical Association in 1897 spurred the literary output chronicling what life was like on the frontier. Noah Smithwick (1808–1899) was a blacksmith who arrived in 1825, witnessed much of colonial life, fought in the revolution, and observed Texas conditions until, being a Unionist, vigilantes murdered his nephew and burned down his mill; he left the state on the eve of the Civil War. Blind in his old age, he dictated *The Evolution of a State*, published in 1900, to his daughter. It is as memorable for its wry humor as for its breathtaking racism. Of the voluminous political memoirs, Francis Richard Lubbock (1815–1905) was a young trader who brought a boatload of merchandise up the Buffalo Bayou to the new town of Houston in 1837; twenty-five years later, he was governor of Texas. He had seen a great deal by the time he published *Six Decades in Texas* in 1900. Quality memoirs of less than book length were published in the early numbers of the association's *Quarterly*, many of them by women. They included Dilue Rose Harris (1825–1914), who two days before her eleventh birthday saw her father drag dead Mexican soldiers out of the San Jacinto road so they could return home, and Rosa von Röder (1813–1907), who survived the horrors of privation among the first German immigrants to marry into the King Ranch. The most astute social observer of antebellum Texas was not a Texan but an abolitionist reporter traveling through the state to write about conditions—Frederick Law Olmsted 1822–1903), whose *A Journey through Texas* of 1857 is as funny as it is trenchant.

What Texas short-story master went to prison and changed his name before becoming famous?

William Sydney Porter (1862–1910) was born in North Carolina but moved to Texas and its drier climate for his health. He worked for a time on a sheep ranch but really wanted to be a writer. In Austin, he founded a small literary magazine called *The Rolling Stone*, which failed, and he worked at various jobs, including draftsman in the Texas Land Office, where he grew so bored that he drew cartoons on his maps. As a new husband and father,

as well as being a bank teller and poor, he sometimes "borrowed" money from his bank drawer. It was a common practice and no one thought much of it as long as the money was repaid, but one day, the federal authorities cracked down and decided to make an example of him. Faced with arrest, he fled to Honduras, which made him look more guilty, returned to see his dying wife, and was sentenced to four years in prison. Having once studied to be a druggist, he saw many articles in the pharmacology text signed "O. Henry." In prison, he practiced his craft and when released, he moved to New York and became O. Henry. Some of his stories became icons of early 1900s America, including "The Gift of the Magi" and "The Ransom of Red Chief."

Better known as O. Henry, famed short-story author William Sydney Porter adopted Texas as his home.

What Texas author had her novel turned into a Lillian Gish silent film classic?

While Texas authorship is often thought of as being dominated by men, Dorothy Scarborough (1878–1935) created a sensation. Born near Tyler in east Texas, her family moved briefly to Sweetwater for her mother's health. Drawing on that experience, Scarborough wrote her novel, *The Wind* (1925), about a timid eastern girl driven mad by the relentless, arid wind of west Texas. The 1928 Lillian Gish film of the same name was a huge hit. Although Scarborough gained her greatest notice for a Texas subject, she was far more erudite than that, having studied at the University of Chicago and Oxford, before teaching creative writing at Columbia, where one of her students was Carson McCullers.

What famous Texas writer abandoned the state after being snubbed by the University of Texas?

Katherine Anne Porter (1890–1980), whose birth name was actually Callie Porter, was born in Indian Creek near Brownwood and was raised for a time by her grandmother in Kyle, between Austin and San Marcos. After four unhappy marriages, Porter perfected her writing craft in many different occupations, gaining such a reputation that, although she had never been to college, she was invited to lecture at such places as Stanford and Washington and Lee before coming home to the University of Texas. During the 1950s, Porter heard a rumor that the University of Texas planned to name a new library after her, and she commissioned a large photo portrait of herself to grace it. When the story proved untrue, Porter severed her ties to the university and moved to the Washington, D.C., area. She subsequently became wealthy from *Ship of Fools* (1962), won the Pulitzer Prize and Gold Medal for Fiction, and was inducted into the American Academy of Arts and Letters. Vindicated from her insults in Texas, she left her large literary archive to the University of Maryland.

What Texas author boldly went where no men had gone before?

Gene Roddenberry (1921–1991) was born in El Paso and served in World War II, flying eighty-nine combat missions before working as a commercial pilot after the war. He moved to California and found work as a screenwriter, authoring episodes of such 1950s series as *Have Gun, Will Travel* and *Highway Patrol*. His interest in writing an epic television series about space travel gained no traction until he was advised of a better "pitch," keying on a popular Western series, that it was *Wagon Train* in outer space. Thus was born *Star Trek*, which ran for three seasons before becoming a film franchise in which he remained involved. Roddenberry died of cardiac arrest on October 24, 1991. A small amount of his ashes were sent into space the following year on the space shuttle *Columbia*, but the goal of sending him into permanent orbit or deep space has not been realized.

What Texas fantasy author committed suicide rather than face the death of his mother?

Robert Ervin Howard of Cross Plains (near Brownwood), creator of the Conan the Barbarian series of stories, shot himself on June 11, 1936, aged thirty, in distress at his mother's approaching mortality.

Who was the Texas writer who infuriated Lyndon Johnson with his novel about Texas politics?

Dallas native Billy Lee Brammer (1929–1978) was a multiple-award-winning journalist in his mid twenties at the *Texas Observer* when Senate Majority Leader Johnson recruited him onto his staff. In Washington, Brammer began work on three interrelated novellas about seamy Southern (never identified as Texan) politicians, sold together as *The Gay Place* to Houghton Mifflin in 1958. Brammer was crestfallen at LBJ's rejection of the book, was banished from Johnson's circle, and was later employed by *Time.* The book won serious critical praise, but sales were poor. Despite denials that the novel's manipulative central character, Arthur Fenstermaker, was modeled on Johnson, other

There would be no Conan the Barbarian stories or movies without Texas author Robert E. Howard.

versions of events traced the enmity to Johnson's wife, Lady Bird, who was said to have perceived herself in the character's wife, Sweet Mama. Brammer entered a long decline before dying of a meth overdose at forty-eight.

What Texas writer rose from the most rural of origins to become dean of the school of creative writing at Columbia University?

William A. Owens (1905–1990) was born into poverty in Pin Hook, Texas, in Lamar County in the northeast. His father died immediately thereafter, and William grew up working on the family farm and trying to learn to read and write, although the Pin Hook school was open only three months each year. After struggling to attain an advanced education, Owens traveled through rural areas as a folklorist, gaining a PhD from the University of Iowa in 1941 before joining the Army intelligence service. He taught creative writing at Columbia for thirty years, starting in 1947. His most celebrated book, *Slave Mutiny*, was an account of the takeover of the slaving schooner *La Amistad*, published in 1953 and later the source material for a Steven Spielberg film.

What novel about a Texas ranching family annoyed Texans who felt they had been portrayed unfairly?

Giant was published in 1952, written near the end of her career by Edna Ferber (1885–1968), who was raised in Michigan and lived in New York. Many of her stories featured a motif of ethnic tension, as in *Show Boat* (1926), and *Giant* was no exception. Since she had little connection to Texas, it was easier for Texans to discount her unflattering portrayal of them, but it was hardly the last time they would feel scalded by a literary depiction of them.

Wasn't there a Texas writer who lost his job at the University of Texas for obscenely insulting its president?

J. Frank Dobie (1888–1964) was born in rural Live Oak County and grew up under the dual influences of his father, who read him and his siblings the Bible, and his mother, who read them classical literature such as *Ivanhoe* and *Pilgrim's Progress*. Fascinated by Texas folklore, Dobie became a journalist and teacher, joining the University of Texas faculty in 1914. His books, from *A Vaquero of the Brush Country* (1929) to *Coronado's Children* (1931), made his a leading voice in Southwestern literature. The university, however, was a highly politicized environment in which he did not thrive. When it was announced that the school's acknowledgment of the Texas Centennial would be to build a 307-foot (94-meter) tower to house the library, Dobie protested that the money would be better spent on faculty and programs. Although the Texas Constitution mandates that the university's oil revenues can only be spent on building construction, Dobie believed that some way could be found around that restriction. Work proceeded on the tower, which Dobie referred to as the final erection of an impotent administration, and that was the end of him at the university. Dobie went on to publish such masterworks as *Apache Gold and Yaqui Silver* (1939). Ironically, the university that ousted him now administers his Paisano Ranch on Barton Creek above Austin as an artist's retreat.

What is meant by the Golden Age of Texas Letters?

This is usually meant as a reference to the long-standing relationship of three Texas writers: historian Walter Prescott Webb (1888–1963), author of the influential *The Great Plains*; folklorist J. Frank Dobie; and naturalist Roy Bedichek. They largely became known to the world through William Owens's book *Three Friends*. Those three would frequently gather at "Philosopher's Rock" on Dobie's ranch and wax literary over whiskey.

What exactly is cowboy poetry, and is there any place in Texas where one can celebrate it?

"Cowboy" poetry is a tradition of extemporaneous oral composition, often around a

One of the many examples of cowboy poets is Red Steagall (1938–), who is also a musician. Born in Gainesville, he performed for President Ronald Reagan at the White House in 1983.

325

campfire after a day's work. Usually, it is built on simple rhymes and meter, and it extols Western or ranch life and traditional, conservative values. Today, the term rests on the genre itself more than on a requirement that it be actually written by a cowboy. Although nationally, Cowboy Poetry Week occurs in April, Alpine celebrates an annual fest of cowboy poetry usually in February.

Who was the Texas veterinarian who wrote popular short stories drawn, he claimed, from his own experiences?

Ben K. Green (1912–1974) was born in Cumby, Texas, in the northeast dairying region of Hopkins County. He was a gifted raconteur but a bit of a charlatan, having never studied at Cornell nor been a licensed veterinarian, as he claimed. His popular collections of stories about sharp dealing in a hard life began with *Horse Tradin'* in 1967, followed by *Some More Horse Tradin'*, *The Village Horse Doctor: West of the Pecos*, and *Wild Cow Tales*. His early books were published by Alfred A. Knopf, where his editor was the widely respected Angus Cameron, before he switched to Northland Press in Arizona.

What Texas practitioner of the western novel was honored with a record eight Spur Awards by the Western Writers of America?

Elmer Kelton (1926–2009) was literally born to cowboy life at Horse Camp on the Five Wells Ranch in Andrews County in the Panhandle. He grew up near Midland, where his father was a long time employee of the McElroy Ranch. His education at the University of Texas was interrupted by war action in Italy, but he finished school in 1948, after which he went to work for the San Angelo newspaper as the farm and ranch editor. While he always "kept the day job" as a journalist, Kelton's novels won eight Spur Awards between 1957 and 2009; he also won three Western Heritage Awards and an Owen Wister Award, among others. Some of his best-known novels were *The Day the Cowboys Quit* (1971), *The Time It Never Rained* (1973), and *The Good Old Boys* (1979), which became a film starring Tommy Lee Jones, Sissy Spacek, and Frances McDormand.

The author of over forty popular novels and nonfiction books, James Michener was known for his epic stories based on history, including 1985's *Texas*.

What literary giant moved to Austin to write a novel about Texas and endowed the university with a school of creative writing

Throughout his career, James Michener (1907–1997), who was the United States's leading practitioner of the sprawling historical fiction epic, made a habit of researching or even living in the locale he was re-searching. Texas's Governor Bill Clements invited Michener to Texas to write that book for the state's 150th anniversary of independence. Michener and his wife settled in Austin, where they remained for the rest of their lives. Michener donated his extensive art collection to the University of Texas, where he also endowed the Michener Center for Writers.

Who would be considered Texas's leading writer today?

Such a subjective question will find no unanimous answer, but based on a lifetime of output, a strong case could be made for Larry McMurtry (1936–), whose early novels included *Horseman, Pass By*, which was adapted into the film *Hud*, and *The Last Picture Show*, which also became a phenomenally successful movie. Among these and his other book-film tandems, such as *Terms of Endearment*, he has been nominated for and won scores of Oscar and Emmy awards. McMurtry won a Pulitzer Prize for his 1985 novel *Lonesome Dove* and, with coauthor Diana Ossana, an Academy Award for best adapted screenplay for 2005's *Brokeback Mountain*. Transcending his Texas base, McMurtry once served as president of PEN, and he contributes to the *New York Review of Books*. It was said that after his harsh portrayal of local characters in *The Last Picture Show*, he was no longer welcome to live in his native Archer City, which was the template for the fictional Anarene, and he relocated to Alexandria, Virginia, for many years before returning to open a used bookstore. Anarene was not totally fictitious; there had once been a town called Anarene nearby, but it dried up when the railroad passed it by.

ACTORS, DIRECTORS, RADIO PERSONALITIES

What silent-film megastar from Texas fled pictures altogether rather than make talkies?

Florence Arto (1895–1977) was born in Houston in 1895 and graduated from an exclusive finishing school. She had no ambition to act, and it was purely happenstance that she met Galveston filmmaker King Vidor, whom she married and moved with to Los Angeles. A famous beauty, she appeared in more than fifty silent films, often directed by her husband but also under her own contract with Vitagraph Studios, and with other notable directors such as Cecil B. DeMille and Ernst Lubitsch. After her divorce from Vidor in 1925, she married the great concert violinist Jascha Heifetz the next year and continued to make films. Her first effort at a talkie, however, *Chinatown Nights*, was such a scarifying disaster that she retired to family life and never returned. She passed away at age eighty-two.

What pioneering Texas stage and film figure is now confused with a more famous cousin, who was destroyed by a false rape accusation?

Macklyn Arbuckle was born in San Antonio on July 9, 1866, and did not begin acting until he was in his thirties. He debuted on Broadway in the hit *The County Chairman* in

1899 and had another great success with *The Roundup* in 1907. He starred in silent film versions of each after joining the Adolph Zukor film company. He came home in 1914 and with financial backing from Dallas started the San Antonio Moving Pictures Corporation. During the 1920s, he often appeared on-screen with Marion Davies, the protégé of yellow journalist William Randolph Hearst. Hearst, ironically, played a large role in ruining Arbuckle's younger and more famous cousin Roscoe, widely known as "Fatty" Arbuckle. Falsely accused of rape and manslaughter in the 1916 death of a party girl groupie, he defended his name through three trials, on whose lurid details Hearst bragged that he had made more money than on any other story since the *Lusitania* sank.

What Texas vaudeville and silent-film star became famous for her saucy greeting, "Hello, suckers"?

Born to Irish immigrants in Waco on January 12, 1884, Mary Louise Cecilia "Texas" Guinan led a very ordinary life—educated in Catholic schools before marriage at twenty. She threw all this over, divorcing in less than two years and starting a career as a singer and raconteur. She found success in vaudeville as "That Two-Gun Texas Gal" or, alternatively, "The Queen of the West." She was the first silent-screen cowgirl and in 1920 opened a speakeasy, the 300 Club on West 54th Street in New York City, that was frequented by such luminaries as George Gershwin, Mae West, John Barrymore, Gloria Swanson, and numerous others. Ruby Keeler was discovered in her chorus line. As

emcee, apart from her famous opening, she delighted audiences by thumping tennis balls at them and by repeatedly beating prosecutions for selling liquor. She made scores of silent "two reelers" in her Western guise and became enormously wealthy. She died at age forty-nine of amoebic dysentery on November 5, 1933.

What Texan had the longest career of any American film director?

King Vidor was born in Galveston on February 8, 1894, and survived the Great Storm of 1900, which became the subject of the first film he directed in 1913. Early declaring his commitment to films that promoted humanitarian aspirations, he made the first all-African American musical, *Hallelujah!*, in 1929. Five years later, his *Our Daily Bread* won a humanitarian award from the League of Nations. More commercially, he went on to direct Bar-

Actress Mary "Texas" Guinan performed in vaudeville acts and in silent movies but later in life garnered a reputation for running speakeasies during the Prohibition Era.

bara Stanwyck in the acclaimed *Stella Dallas* in 1937, and without screen credit, he directed the Kansas sequences of *The Wizard of Oz*. Later, he directed Gregory Peck and a steamy Jennifer Jones in *Duel in the Sun* in 1946, followed by Gary Cooper and Patricia Neal in *The Fountainhead* in 1949. During the period of Hollywood blacklisting in the 1950s, he was prominently anticommunist. Between 1913 and 1980, he directed seventy-eight motion pictures, longevity matched by no other American director, and he produced twenty-three more and wrote twenty-eight. He was nominated for Academy awards as best director five times without winning but was accorded an honorary Oscar in 1979. He was eighty-eight when he died on November 1, 1982.

What film shot in Texas won the very first Academy Award for best picture?

Between September 1926 and April 1927, the spectacular drama about America's World War I flying aces, *Wings*, was shot in and around San Antonio's Kelly Field. In the film, "It Girl" Clara Bow played the center of a love triangle between Richard Arlen and Buddy Rogers. It was directed by Richard Wellman, who chose the location for the same reason that made San Antonio the center of military flight training during the war: abundant fair weather and good flying conditions—plus, it had the best prospect of rounding up three hundred pilots as extras. Wellman himself had experience as a combat pilot during the war, which gave the action sequences breathtaking realism, although he was often at odds with the army officers who were supposed to be cooperating with him.

What Texas actress became as great an icon for her ruthless ambition as for her acting skill?

Joan Crawford (born Lucille LeSueur; c. 1904–1977) was born in San Antonio (other sources provide varying dates). She endured a difficult childhood; her father abandoned the family, and "Billie," as she preferred to be called, was molested by her stepfather, a stage entrepreneur who began casting her in plays in Lawton, Oklahoma. It was a life from which she was keen to escape, becoming a dancer and chorus girl, acting in silent films, working her way up through the ranks with roles in which she showcased a kind of heartbroken toughness. Her career peaked with the Academy Award for *Mildred Pierce* in 1945. Later, her battling stint on the Pepsi-Cola board of directors, and an unflatter-

The 1927 film *Wings*, which was shot in Texas, won the first Oscar for best picture.

ing portrayal in her daughter Christina's memoir *Mommy Dearest*, cemented her hard reputation.

What Texas actress first left the stage at forty-two to try her hand in films and went on to more than a hundred appearances?

Louise Latham was born to a ranching family in Hamilton on September 23, 1922, and attended high school in Dallas. Active primarily on the stage, she appeared on Broadway in a revival of *Major Barbara* in 1956 and toured with *Cat on a Hot Tin Roof*. At forty-two, she broke into film with a chilling turn as Tippi Hedren's emotionally maimed mother in *Marnie*. Over the next thirty-five years, she appeared in more than a hundred productions, often typecast in hard-bitten character roles at which she excelled, holding her own opposite such legends as Jimmy Stewart in *Firecreek*. Her television work spanned from such golden-era staples as *Gunsmoke* and *Bonanza* to *Murder, She Wrote* and *The X-Files*.

What Texas actors—mother and son—each enjoyed major careers?

Mary Martin grew up a carefree tomboy in the Parker County seat of Weatherford, where she was born in 1913, and where she, her sister, and a friend sang to entertain people outside the courthouse where her father practiced law. Forced to leave her Tennessee finishing school because she married and got pregnant, she returned to Texas and opened a dance studio. Freed from her marriage, she moved to California to study dance, also blossoming as a singer and actor, noted for her pitch-perfect impersonations of such leading entertainers as Fanny Brice and Ruby Keeler. Martin began a productive collaboration with the team of Rodgers and Hammerstein, winning fame playing Nellie Forbush in *South Pacific* and Maria von Trapp in *The Sound of Music*. She won Tony awards for both roles and also for the one that brought her lasting fame, in *Peter Pan*. She received a career accolade at the Kennedy Center Honors in 1989, the year before her death. The son produced by her first marriage, Larry Hagman, was born in Fort Worth in 1931, and he grew up largely with his grandmother and in boarding schools. Equally bitten by the urge to perform, he had several supporting film roles but found his great success on television, first costarring with Barbara Eden in *I Dream of Jeannie* (1965–1970) and later as the iconic oil tycoon and bad guy J. R. Ewing in *Dallas* (1978–1991; reprised in 2012–2013). Hagman was eighty-one when he died of leukemia late in 2012.

Who was the Texas war hero who became a major film star?

Born into sharecropper poverty in Hunt County in 1925, Audie Murphy had to help support his mother and eleven siblings after their father deserted them. Underage and slight of size, he sneaked his way into the U.S. Army in June 1942 and became the most decorated soldier of the conflict, receiving every combat decoration there is, including the Congressional Medal of Honor. After portraying himself in the biopic *To Hell and Back*, other acting jobs followed, but his life and career were hampered by severe post-traumatic stress syndrome. Murphy actively, and successfully, lobbied the government to

What Texas radio personality broke the grip of the Hollywood blacklist?

Although he grew up with money (his sister Mary Faulk Koock turned their Austin family mansion into a high-end restaurant called Green Pastures), John Henry Faulk's (1913–1990) Methodist parents also instilled a passion for civil rights in their children—a dangerous gift in Jim Crow's Texas. Faulk studied folklore at the University of Texas under J. Frank Dobie, wrote his master's thesis on "Ten Negro Sermons," and joined the American Civil Liberties Union. A gifted mimic and storyteller, he rose in the radio business to enjoy a thriving New York career and became the vice president of the American Federation of Television and Radio Artists. This post made him a target of AWARE, a McCarthyite, anticommunist protection racket that studios could pay to clear their artists of any communist association that had sought control of that union. Faulk was blacklisted and ruined, but with financial aid from Edward R. Murrow of CBS, he sued for vindication and damages. AWARE's attorney was Roy Cohn, counsel for the McCarthy Committee. Probably realizing they had no leg to stand on, Cohn won five years of continuances before a famous 1962 trial in which the deliberating jury came into court and asked the judge if they could award Faulk more damages than he had asked to get. He was awarded $3.5 million, which was later reduced on appeal to $500,000, but after paying legal fees and debts accrued during his years as a pariah, he actually won only $75,000. However, his book *Fear on Trial* became one of the signal epitaphs of the McCarthy era.

recognize and begin caring for veterans with mental and emotional combat wounds, but he was only forty-five when he was killed in a plane crash in the Georgia Appalachians. He was buried in Arlington National Cemetery.

What Texas actor started a national craze for coonskin caps?

Fess Parker (1924–2010) was born in Fort Worth and raised on a farm near San Angelo but almost never had a film (or any other) career, as he was stabbed by an enraged motorist after an auto accident in Abilene. Parker was a history major at the University of Texas, which he followed with study in film history at the University of Southern California. Walt Disney was impressed with Parker's minor role as a railroaded pilot in the sci-fi classic *Them!* and cast him in what has been called television's first miniseries, *Davy Crockett*. The 6-foot, 6-inch (2-meter) "King of the Wild Frontier" found himself the center of a marketing blitz. The shows were a sensation when they aired in 1954–1955, and America's sprawling, post-war suburbs came alive with cap guns and coonskin caps. Parker, however, found Disney's famous fetish for control limiting, and he left the studio. By then, he had been hopelessly typecast, successfully playing Daniel Boone in another popular series before retiring to become a winemaker.

What El Paso native became one of the most celebrated entertainers of her generation?

Born Mary Frances Reynolds in El Paso on April Fool's Day in 1932, her family knew grinding poverty, living in a shanty, her mother taking in laundry, and her father sometimes hunting jackrabbits in the desert. They moved to Burbank, California, where Mary Frances won a beauty contest and was signed to a film contract by mogul Jack Warner, who renamed her Debbie Reynolds. She rocketed to fame in 1952's *Singin' in the Rain* opposite Gene Kelly, even though she was learning to dance even as she performed those hugely complex numbers. After a luminous career in film, television, stage, and nightclubs (and equally dramatic private life), Reynolds died of a stroke on December 28, 2016, the day after the sudden death of her daughter, Carrie Fisher.

What San Antonio native rose to become one of America's superstars of television comedy?

Carol Burnett was born to alcoholic parents in San Antonio in 1933 and was largely raised by her grandmother in Hollywood, California. She entered UCLA to study writ-

One of the films El Paso native Debbie Reynolds will be best remembered for is *Singin' in the Rain* (1952). In this still, she is flanked by costars Gene Kelly (left) and Donald O'Connor (the inset is a photo of Reynolds in 2006).

ing but wound up in a play and was transformed by the warmth of the audience. Burnett was famously and anonymously gifted with $1,000 to go to New York and try to break into show business. It was a hard go, but she succeeded, enchanting the country with her hilarious performance of the song "I Made a Fool of Myself over John Foster Dulles." Best known for her 1967–1978 musical variety *The Carol Burnett Show* on CBS, Burnett also proved in other projects to have deep dramatic range, and three volumes of memoirs demonstrated her writing talent.

What Oscar-winning Texas actor never took an acting lesson, graduated with a degree in English literature from Harvard, and still actively works his Texas ranch?

Tommy Lee Jones was born in San Sabá in 1946. Attending Harvard on a scholarship, he was future vice president Al Gore's roommate. He graduated in 1969, the same year he debuted on Broadway, starting a New York career of several plays and four seasons in daytime soap opera before moving to Los Angeles and film distinction. He is known for roles that display an impatient and often sarcastic intelligence, whether in police drama such as *The Fugitive*, for which he won the Academy Award for Best Supporting Actor, or droll comedy such as *Men in Black*. He has a reputation for rewriting—and improving—his scenes in scripts, and he also directed, beginning with a film based on the Elmer Kelton novel *The Good Old Boys*. He raises polo ponies on his Texas ranch.

What brooding Texas character actor was best known for his portrayal of a cult leader?

Powers Boothe was born to a sharecropping family in Snyder in 1948. The first college graduate in his family, he took a B.A. from Southwest Texas State University (now Texas State) and an M.F.A. degree from Southern Methodist University, and he paid his dues in regional repertory theater before making it on Broadway. He won an Emmy for his chilling portrayal of Jim Jones in *Guyana Tragedy*, a role that launched him on a distinguished film and television career. He brought a hard edge to a variety of characters from the Roman general Flavius Aëtius in *Attila* to Raymond Chandler's *Philip Marlowe*. He was only sixty-eight when he died in 2017 of heart failure brought on by pancreatic cancer and was buried in Deadwood, Texas, in Panola County on the Louisiana border.

What other great actors have hailed from Texas?

Texas has produced a startling roll of front-rank actors, which has included Dabney Coleman (born in Austin in 1932); Gary Busey (Baytown, 1944); Jaclyn Smith (Houston, 1945); Farrah Fawcett (Corpus Christi, 1947–2009); Phylicia Rashad (Houston, 1948); Sissy Spacek (Quitman, 1949); Randy and Dennis Quaid (Houston, 1950 and 1954); Debbie Allen (Houston, 1950); Bruce McGill (San Antonio, 1950); Morgan Fairchild (Dallas, 1950); Patrick Swayze (Houston, 1952–2009); Bill Paxton (Fort Worth, 1955–2017); Woody Harrelson (Midland, 1961); Forest Whitaker (Longview, 1961); Lou Diamond Phillips (born 1962, raised in Corpus Christi); Robin Wright (Dallas, 1966); Jamie Foxx (Terrell, 1967); Owen and Luke Wilson (Dallas, 1968 and 1971); Matthew McConaughey (Uvalde, 1969); Chandra Wil-   333 son (Houston, 1969); Renée Zellweger (Katy, 1969); Ethan Hawke (Austin, 1970); Jennifer Garner (Houston, 1972); Angie Harmon (Highland Park, 1972); Eva Longoria (Corpus Christi, 1975); Beyoncé (Houston, 1981); and Selena Gomez (Grand Prairie, 1992).

MUSICAL TALENTS

What Texas musician's gift for syncopated rhythm swept America as "ragtime" and earned him a posthumous Pulitzer Prize?

Scott Joplin (1868–1917) of Texarkana was born into a musical family, growing up to be a guitar teacher even as he labored on a railroad for a day job. At about twenty, he left to earn a living as a musician wherever he could. By the time he performed at the Chicago World's Fair, he had written several ragtime songs, most famously "The Maple Leaf Rag," which gained great popularity. In all, he wrote over forty rags, plus more serious music including an opera, but he lost his manuscripts when his assets were seized for debt. Joplin was forty-eight when he died of syphilitic dementia, but his work was rediscovered in the 1970s with the production of a second Joplin opera, *Treemonisha*, which earned the Pulitzer Prize, and the popular film *The Sting*, which was scored with Joplin rags. Contrary to Joplin's intentions, ragtime quickly came to be played too fast; according to ragtime legend Eubie Blake, it was meant to be graceful and whimsical.

What Waco singer helped break the color barrier on Broadway?

African American Jules Bledsoe (1897–1943) was born into the most humble circumstances in Waco but grew up to attain a formidable education, including at Bishop College, Virginia Union College, and medical school at Columbia. He also studied his first love, singing, very seriously, performing in major productions of *Aïda*, *Boris Godunov*, and others, touring throughout the United States and Europe. His 1927 performance of "Old Man River" in *Show Boat* on Broadway made him one of the first African Americans to find regular work on Broadway, and he toured Europe again in Eugene O'Neill's *The Emperor Jones*.

Who was the "Father of Texas Blues"?

Lemon Henry Jefferson (1893–1929) was blind from birth, born into a family of African American sharecroppers in Freestone County, Texas, so he was fated to have to work out an original way to make it in the world. After learning guitar in his teens, he became a street musician, and if anyone's life was fodder for the blues, his was. Still, in Dallas, his own style cross-pollinated with T-Bone Walker, Huddie Ledbetter (Lead Belly), and others. Between the novelty that "Blind Lemon" Jefferson could play and perform at all and his unique sound, he moved into a successful career that took him to Chicago, where he recorded gospel songs and the grittiest of blues informed by his own life. He died there in uncertain circumstances—probably a heart attack, possibly lost in a snowstorm, maybe while being attacked by a dog. His body was returned to Freestone County, but his grave in Wortham was not marked for nearly forty years.

What happened to Bob Wills after Pappy O'Daniel left the flour business?

Wills's (1905–1975) relationship with O'Daniel was more or less one of mutual usage. At first, the only way O'Daniel would let the band play on the radio was if they all worked full days in the flour mill as well, which left their hands so sore and swollen they could barely play at all. Wills manipulated O'Daniel's vanity, encouraging his homespun homilies as a way to keep the Light Crust Doughboys on the air. O'Daniel fired Wills a final time for his playing at dances and for drinking. Wills put together a new band that he called the Texas Playboys in Waco, playing as far away

The brief life of Lemon Henry Jefferson didn't prevent his musical gifts from being recognized so that he is now remembered as the "Father of Texas Blues."

as Oklahoma City, but O'Daniel pursued a vendetta, getting them fired from gigs, until Wills found a protector in KVOO in Tulsa. To get even, Wills made a bargain with General Mills to produce a brand called Play Boy Flour, which he publicized as "formerly the Light Crust Doughboys." O'Daniel was apoplectic and brought suit but lost at every turn. Before Wills cut his band's first record in 1935, he had expanded his band to include horns, reeds, drums, and a steel guitar, which gave them a revolutionary sound. In a way, Wills's success was foresworn, as he was the son of Texas fiddle champion John T. Wills, who was content as Bob grew up to let him play with black children in the cotton fields, dancing jigs with them and absorbing their music, which later had its influence on Texas Swing.

Did any other Texas musical acts benefit from the success of the Texas Playboys?

"Texas Swing," also known as Western Swing, became hugely popular. Gene Autry (1907–1998) of Tioga was discovered by Will Rogers and started a radio career in 1928. He parlayed his singing cowboy shtick into a multimedia empire. Tex Ritter of Panola County came on the airwaves in 1934, followed by Ernest Tubb and the Texas Troubadors some years later.

What Texas dancer was eventually named a cultural ambassador of the United States?

Born in Rogers, Texas, southeast of Temple, Alvin Ailey (1931–1989) grew up under the twin threats of being black in rural Texas and being gay. At age eleven, he joined his mother in Los Angeles, where she had moved to find war work. Through high school, working odd jobs, he kept his keen interest in dance hidden from his mother, but he began taking lessons from dance teacher Lester Horton. Moving to San Francisco, he formed a nightclub act with a gifted poet and performer named Marguerite Johnson, later better known as Maya Angelou. By 1954 Ailey was in New York, appearing on Broadway with such luminaries as Pearl Bailey, Lena Horne, and Harry Belafonte. Dissatisfied with American choreography, Ailey formed his own dance studio, where he devised nearly eighty different performances for his company. Only gradually did he let his mother know what he was doing, when he had the fame behind him. Though he was suspicious of government notice, the U.S. Department of State sent the Alvin Ailey American Dance Theater on a foreign tour in 1962, which in reality was an unprecedented honor for a black dance company. Though he was accorded the Kennedy Center Honors the year before he died, in some ways, he could never escape the smallness of the culture he came from; when he died of AIDS, he arranged with his doctor to announce his cause of death as a blood disorder. Posthumously, Alvin Ailey received the Presidential Medal of Freedom.

Is there any place in Lubbock that commemorates "The Day the Music Died"?

Rock music legend Buddy Holly (1936–1959) was a Lubbock native from a musical family whose name was correctly spelled "Holley." His parents lived modestly and bought Buddy his first guitar from a pawn shop; by fifteen, he was partnering with high school friends and appearing on local radio. In 1955 he was opening for Elvis Presley and on his way to becoming a major star. Holly and two fellow musicians—Ritchie Valens and J. P. ("The Big Bopper") Richardson—per-ished together when the small plane they were sharing crashed into an Iowa cornfield on February 3, 1959, an event commemorated in the Don McLean song "American Pie." His life is commemorated at the Buddy Holly Center, which also gives directions to other sites, such as his grave, and the J. I. Allison House where he and his drummer, Jerry Allison, wrote many songs.

How did Willie Nelson get his start?

Born in Abbott, Texas, near Hillsboro, Willie Hugh Nelson (1933–) was raised partly by his grandparents, who were music teachers, so he was learning guitar by six and writing songs by seven. As the family moved to find employment, Nelson rose

Buddy Holly (center) with The Crickets (Jerry Allison at top and Joe Mauldin at bottom). Born in Lubbock, Holly's brief music career changed the course of American music.

through the musical ranks, singing in churches, with a family band, and eventually striking out on his own to different areas, including the Pacific Northwest. Writing as Hugh Nelson, he wrote hit songs such as "Crazy" for Patsy Cline. He himself settled in Nashville in 1960 and in four years had joined the Grand Ole Opry and signed with RCA Victor Records, a rapid rise by Nashville standards. In 1972 he changed direction, returning to Texas and, as Willie Nelson, helped to foster the outlaw country music movement in Austin. He quickly became, and remains, its most visible (and talented) exponent. Interestingly, Nelson's later brushes with the law—losing his assets to the IRS, trouble over his fondness for marijuana—which might have damaged or destroyed lesser careers, only seemed to burnish that outlaw image, and he emerged more popular than ever before.

Musician and songwriting legend Willie Nelson was born in Abbott.

What was the outlaw country movement?

Like most subgenres, it has complicated roots. It began as a reaction against the rhinestone country music of Nashville, which at times seemed in danger of becoming a caricature of itself. Earthier and influenced by rockabilly and honky-tonk with a little infusion of rock and roll, especially Texas's own Buddy Holly and Elvis Presley, it launched into a sound all its own. Some music historians date the advent of outlaw country from the time that Willie Nelson gained artistic control over his own output rather than pleasing the more commercial taste of producers. Just as important, he did this in tandem with a group of confederates such as fellow Texans Waylon Jennings, Kris Kristofferson, and others, such as Jerry Jeff Walker (a New Yorker by birth but a confederate spirit), who centered in Austin. There, that sound reigned virtually supreme from the early seventies through the early eighties, before the city's rapid growth and diversifying musical taste expanded the local scene into greater inclusion.

Where can one go to pay respects to Selena?

Latina singing legend Selena Quintanilla-Pérez (1971–1995) was a native of Corpus Christi and in her brief life rose to the pinnacle of the recording industry. She was a groundbreaker, recording Tejano music when that was considered a male endeavor, designed many of her own costumes, and started her own line of cosmetics. She won the

Tejano Music Awards Female Vocalist of the Year nine times in a row, but she was only twenty-three when she was shot and killed by the president of her fan club. The Tejano music community was devastated, and places in Corpus Christi associated with her remain heavily visited. The Selena Museum displays much of her memorabilia, and visitors can obtain maps to other Selena sites in the city.

ARTISTS

What celebrated European artist came to Texas to run a plantation?

Elisabet Ney, the niece of one of Napoleon's field marshals, was one of the most famous sculptors in Europe, having executed marble busts of the kings of Saxony and Bavaria, Italian patriot Giuseppe Garibaldi, and many others. The controversy of her private life, including living with her paramour and then declining to change her name when they married, prompted the couple to flee to Majorca and then Texas. Ney retired from art for nearly twenty years to run Liendo Plantation near Hempstead; there, she made a project of trying to educate her servants and plantation laborers and was mocked for it. She resumed sculpting after moving to Austin and accomplished some of her best work there. She commissioned life-sized standing marbles of Stephen F. Austin and Sam Houston for the Chicago World's Fair in 1893, and they are now Texas's two entries in National Statuary Hall at the U.S. Capitol.

How did Marfa become an arts center?

Donald Judd (1928–1994) was a large-scale sculptor who is usually associated with minimalism, which he denied. He moved from New York to Marfa in 1973, a time when he turned his attention to making furniture. Enamored of the desert environs, he formed a foundation to administer 40,000 acres (162 square kilometers) of his Ayala de Chinati ranch as a conservation easement. In 1979 he bought 340 acres (1.4 square kilometers) of the defunct Fort D. A. Russell of the U.S. Army Air Corps, which is still maintained as a museum and creative facility.

INVENTORS

What Houston photographer revolutionized taking pictures?

English-born J. H. S. Stanley (1799–?), formerly of the Daguerreian Sky-Light Studio in Galveston, set up shop in Houston and announced his invention of glass plate photography on May 27, 1852. He was in business there until 1870, when he disappeared from history. The exposure of light onto chemically treated, large-format glass plates created images of a clarity never before seen and left an indelible record of America in the latter 1800s.

What was the "Miracle Microbe Cure"?

German immigrant William Radam (1844–1902) was employed as a humble gardener in Austin in 1887. One day, he found himself in need of weed killer, and he concocted some from readily available household chemicals. It did the job admirably, which made Radam wonder if it might also work on the stomach ailment that was bothering him. He tried it and felt better. Thus was born Radam's Miracle Microbe Cure: water, to which he added some red wine, a little hydrochloric acid, sulfuric acid, and food coloring. It cost him a nickel to make a gallon, which he sold for a dollar. In 1890, he published a book to publicize his discovery that all diseases were one and needed only one treatment. Business took off, and by the time he was done, Radam owned seventeen bottling plants around the United States. He left Austin and moved into a brownstone on Fifth Avenue in New York—where he died of liver failure. The bottles are now highly sought on the collectors' market.

Is it true that a Texan built an early flying machine?

Immigrant Jacob Brodbeck (1821–1910) was a schoolteacher in the town of Luckenbach, one of the predominantly German settlements near Fredericksburg. An inveterate tinkerer, he worked on an ice machine and a self-winding clock before losing himself for twenty years in the design of an "air-ship." His spring-powered model proved successful, and he raised the funds to build a full-scale version with a rudder and compartment for the pilot. He staged a demonstration for his shareholders on September 20, 1865, in a field 3 miles (5 kilometers) east of Luckenbach. Brodbeck wound the springs tightly, and the contraption gained speed and lifted into the air, reaching 10 feet (3 meters). It then occurred to him, too late, that there was no way to rewind the springs while airborne. He descended gradually until he crashed into a chicken coop. He was not seriously hurt, but he was unable to raise more money to build a second machine, and his blueprints were stolen while he was in the North seeking funding.

Were there other Texas flying machines that predate the Wright Brothers?

At least two other flying machines appeared in Texas just on the eve of the Wright Brothers' success at Kitty Hawk. William Browning Custead of Elm Mott, near Waco, a cousin of Western showman Buffalo Bill Cody, was one of those who conceived of flying machines with wings that flapped like a bird's. The particular innovation in his craft was that its 60-foot (18-meter) wing-span consisted of slats that opened on the upstroke and snapped shut on the downstroke, which provided a lurching kind of lift. Witnesses claimed that Custead lifted the craft into a tethered flight, but then the Wright Brothers' success with the airfoil prompted him to abandon the enterprise. It was believed that he moved to Hawaii, where he lived as a nudist.

What Texans pioneered the making of operational model airplanes?

While the Wright Brothers transformed their dream of flying into reality, the brothers Victor and Joe Stanzel of Schulenburg shared the wonder of flight with thousands by pioneering the manufacture of model airplanes. Victor began the enterprise, selling his first models in 1929 and setting up shop in a bedroom of the family home. He brought his brother into the business and began offering models that were powered by electric motors. Marketing at county fairs and trade shows, their model planes became industry stars. In 1989 the aging brothers formed a family foundation, which converted the house into the Stanzel Model Aircraft Museum.

What was the Ezekiel Airship?

As opposed to Custead, Reverend Burrell Cannon (1848–1922) of Pittsburg, Texas, took his inspiration from the first chapter of the Book of Ezekiel, of the prophet's vision of creatures lifted up into the air on a mechanism powered by wheels. Like Brodbeck, he sold stock in his enterprise and built the craft in the Pittsburg Machine Shop, with billowing, fabric-covered, parachute like "wings" and an engine that powered four large paddlewheels. Like both his Texas predecessors, he managed to get the craft airborne at a demonstration in 1902, but it vibrated so hard that the pilot shut off the engine, and it was allowed to coast into what today would be called a hard landing. As did others, he surrendered the field to the Wright Brothers.

A replica of the Ezekiel Airship created by Reverend Burrell Cannon can be viewed at the Northeast Texas Rural Heritage Center in Pittsburg, Texas.

Where did Dr Pepper come from?

Charles Alderton (1857–1941) was a New York-born pharmacist working at Morrison's Old Corner Drug Store in Waco. He also tended the soda fountain, where he experimented with various sweeteners and syrup concentrates to produce new flavors. One became a sensation, first served to the public on December 1, 1885. The concoction became popularly known as a "Waco" until Alderton's employer, Wade Morrison, named it Dr. Pepper for a Virginia pharmacist for whom he had worked (the period after "Dr." was dropped in the 1950s). The drink made its national debut at the St. Louis World's Fair in 1904. It did not, contrary to the rumor started by a jealous competitor, contain prune juice. Much of its history is now preserved in the Dr Pepper Museum in Waco.

Did the electric typewriter really originate in Texas?

No, but it was invented by a Texan. Before hundreds of thousands of young American men marched away to fight in World War I, being a secretary was considered a man's job. James Field Smathers (1888–1967) was born in Llano County, Texas, and he graduated from Add-Ran College in Fort Worth (the forerunner of Texas Christian University) in 1904. He taught stenography and typing before moving to Kansas City to work as a typist. Unhappy with the finger-breaking manual machines of the time, Smathers tinkered with the notion of attaching an electric motor to one and obtained a patent for an electric typewriter in 1913. Fixation on the Great War killed any commercial interest in his invention, but he later sold the patent, which ended up with, and he went to work for, a company that evolved into International Business Machines—IBM!

What was "X-Gas"?

World War I generated enormous interest in the element helium. This gas, while it is the second most abundant element in the universe, was virtually unknown on earth. Its existence was theorized in 1868 but was not isolated until 1895; it comprises five ten-thousandths of 1 percent of the atmosphere, originating in uranium decay, and it is continuously lost to space. Then it was discovered that natural gas from wells in the Texas Panhandle contained as much as 1.5 percent helium. Under heavy pressure from the British, whose hydrogen-filled barrage balloons could explode with no warning, the U.S. government established a top-secret plant in Fort Worth, guarded by troops from nearby Camp Bowie, to extract the helium from Panhandle gas. Lest German agents discover what was afoot, the product was strictly referred to as "X-Gas."

How did Fritos originate?

Elmer Doolin (1903–1959), a San Antonio confectioner, is often credited with the idea for Fritos, but as with many other icons of American invention from sewing machines to television, a share of the credit belongs elsewhere. In 1932 Doolin purchased a small home-kitchen enterprise for $100 from Gustavo Olguin consisting of a modified potato ricer and a recipe for fried corn snacks. A blend of masa, salt, and water was extruded from the ricer into hot oil. Olguin had already garnered five retail outlets for his product. Doolin's genius lay in marketing. Within two months, he had tinkered with the recipe, named the product "Fritos" (fried things), and started the Frito Company. He patented a process for mass production, and by 1947, he had five bakeries of his own, plus franchises, had expanded his line to include crackers and roasted nuts, began selling Aus-Tex canned chili in 1952, and opened a concession in Disneyland when it opened in 1955. Despite his success, Doolin gained a reputation as a generous employer of his more than three thousand workers and a conscientious steward of his six "Frito farms," on which he experimented with improved corn breeds.

Enjoy a tasty corn chip? Thank Texan Elmer Doolin for bringing us Fritos™.

Is it true that the modern computer chip began in Texas?

Yes, the whole modern age of silicon chips and integrated circuits has its deepest roots in Texas. The medium was Texas Instruments, a company founded in 1951, which had evolved from previous identities in oil exploration and electronic warfare. The concern leapt to prominence with the manufacture of the first portable transistor radio in 1954. Mass production was made possible by making transistors of silicon instead of, as before, its heavier and much rarer relative, germanium. In 1958 Jack St. Clair Kilby (1923–2005), an electrical engineer at TI, developed a way to create a whole circuit from silicon. Once another engineer found a way for Kilby's tiny components to communicate with each other, the patent for the microprocessor followed in 1971, along with the first hand held calculator, and then the avalanche of digital products that revolutionized consumer life. Kilby was awarded the National Science Medal in 1969 and the Nobel Prize in Physics in 2000.

RANCHERS

Who was Texas's first "Cattle Queen"?

Under the law of Spanish Texas, women could own property and go into business the same as men, which was far ahead of the female lot in the English-speaking world. In the Spanish world, however, more so than in the emerging United States, being well-born was more important to position on the social ladder than ability. Rosa María Hinojosa de Ballí (1752–1803) had both advantages. She was noble on both sides of her family, and her father was the *alcalde* of Reynosa, Mexico, whose status as a "primitive settler" gave him preference to official consideration, including the assignment of land grants. She married equally well, and her father and husband applied for a large land grant in south Texas. The grant was approved but both men died, and under Spanish law, Rosa inherited an empire, although it was heavily in debt. In fifteen years of shrewd and active management both politically and in the saddle, she made it profitable, came to control 1 million acres (4,047 square kilometers), and enjoyed the awe of her *vaqueros*, who referred to her as *la patrona*.

Did any Anglo women ever attain an equal station in the ranching business?

No, but not many men did, either. Since Texas kept Spanish law allowing female inheritance, it was common enough for Anglo women in Texas to gain ownership of family ranches. Most remarried as soon as they could; few relished the work and responsibility as much as Margaret Borland or Lizzie Johnson. Borland (1824–1873) was five when her Irish parents immigrated and settled in the Irish colony of San Patricio (Spanish for St. Patrick). Margaret herself went the common route; she had one child with her first husband, who died, two with her second husband who died, and four with her third husband, who died. Widowed at forty-three and then bereft at losing several children and grandchildren to yellow fever, she threw herself into managing her ranch, and she had a shrewd eye for stock trading. In 1873, she became the only woman to lead a trail drive, from Victoria in south Texas to Wichita, Kansas, with twenty-five hundred cattle and three surviving minor children.

Lizzie Johnson (1840–1924) was more designing in her pursuit of a ranching empire. She was four when her schoolteacher parents moved from Missouri to the Republic of Texas, moving frequently until settling near San Marcos in 1852. Lizzie graduated from Chappell Hill Female College and undertook her own teaching career, working for others until more profitably opening her own school in Austin. Her additional employment keeping books for area ranchers, including land baron George W. Littlefield, alerted her to the money to be made in cattle. She registered her own brand in 1871, bought land, amassed a herd, drove it north on the Chisholm Trail, and assumed the station of a tough, independent, capable rancher. She did not marry until she was thirty-nine and then required her husband, Hezekiah Williams, to sign a prenuptial agreement guaranteeing her separate property even beyond Texas's generous legal protection of wives. She was also rather a miser; only after her death in 1924 was it discovered that she left an estate of a quarter of a million dollars.

How did rancher Charles Goodnight's wife survive the isolation of the Panhandle?

It was not easy, but she already knew the rigors of frontier life. Mary Ann (Molly) Dyer (1839–1926) was fourteen when her parents moved the family from Tennessee to Fort Belknap on the still dangerous fringe of Comanche and Kiowa territory. Soon afterward, both parents died, and Molly was left to care for her five brothers. In addition to chores, she became a schoolteacher to make ends meet. When she married Goodnight in 1870, 343 their first seven years together were in Colorado before Goodnight opened operations at Palo Duro Canyon. She set up housekeeping in a dugout; the rafters of her first house were discarded Comanche lodge poles. For years her only female neighbor was Molly Bugbee 75 miles (121 kilometers) away. For companionship she turned to three chickens that a hand brought her in a gunny sack. "No one can ever know," she wrote, "how much company they were to me. They would run to me when I called them and followed me everywhere I went. They knew me and tried to talk to me in their own language." It was she who cared for orphaned buffalo calves and sparked her husband's interest in preserving the species. She and Goodnight had no children, but she became mother, sister, and nurse to the JA Ranch hands. Eventually, Goodnight built them a nineteen-room house on the edge of the

The "Father of the Texas Panhandle," Charles Goodnight was the most well-known of the Texas ranchers of the Old West.

canyon, the city of Amarillo was born and grew, and Molly Goodnight lived to be honored as the "Mother of the Panhandle."

Did Charles Goodnight have any rivals as leader of the ranching industry in Texas?

Indeed he did, for Goodnight, although he had formidable frontier credibility, spent many years before the opening of the Panhandle in Colorado, and then he merely managed the JA Ranch for years before becoming part owner. Claiming deeper Texas roots was Christopher Columbus (better known as C. C.) Slaughter (1837–1919). Born in Sabine County, he began handling cattle at twelve and demonstrated a penchant for entrepreneurship in agricultural processing and freighting. When he was twenty, the family moved to the edge of the Comanche frontier, accepting the risk in exchange for the opportunity to begin a large cattle operation.

He and Goodnight were acquainted with each other, both having participated in raiding the Comanche camp that resulted in the recapture of Cynthia Ann Parker, but they had very different styles. Because he more than anyone opened the Panhandle, Goodnight's JA Ranch was largely contiguous; Slaughter came from the east side, and while his land holdings and cattle operation were comparable in size, they were scattered among several moderately large ranches instead of one colossal bloc. Where Goodnight was active in Panhandle affairs, Slaughter became more widely engaged. A preacher's son and lifelong Baptist, he helped lead the Southwestern Baptist Theological Seminary and the Southern Baptist Convention, and he supported the forerunner of the Baylor University Medical Center in Dallas as well as serving a stint as president of the United Confederate Veterans. Where Goodnight seemed forever engaged in legal disputes with the state over land titles, Slaughter prided himself on being "the largest taxpayer in Texas." He was also one of the ranchers who sponsored African American cowboy Daniel Webster Wallace to get a start in the business.

How did a Yankee ship captain become a kingpin cattleman?

It was not such an astonishing transition as it seems, considering the poverty of his youth and the fire of ambition to escape it. Richard King (1825–1885) was born in New York to Irish immigrants (long before the influx of the potato famine). When he was nine, his parents apprenticed him to a Manhattan jeweler; two years later, he ran away and sneaked onto a ship bound for Alabama. When he was discovered, the crew took him in rather than put him ashore. He learned navigation and river boat piloting, and the captain even took him home to Connecticut for eight months of formal schooling. During service in Florida during the Seminole War, King met and was befriended by Mifflin Kenedy, a Pennsylvania Quaker six years his senior and a more experienced seaman. They formed a partnership to run riverboats on the Rio Grande, underpinning their investment by continuing army service during the Mexican–American War. The river trade there proved enormously lucrative and they came to virtually monopolize it, investing their profits in south Texas land. Both men became enamored of the rank grasslands south of Corpus Christi and began buying and consolidating ranches. During the Civil War, their Rio Grande fleet was active in promoting trade between Mexico and rebel Texas, but they were careful to place the craft under Mexican registry to keep them out of Union hands. In retribution, a Union force looted King's Santa Gertrudis ranch, and after the Confederacy fell, King fled to Mexico until he won a pardon and returned. His last twenty years were devoted to cultivating his empire, which at the time of his death totaled some 625,000 acres (2,529 square kilometers), and expanded even more under his heirs.

In the Texas oil business, is anyone recognized as the greatest practitioner?

For a man who as a child learned to read and write at home, with a copy of the Bible as his only resource, it's remarkable that C. M. (Columbus Marion) Joiner (1860–1947) so finely honed his larcenous instincts. He was born in Alabama, moved to Tennessee where he served a term in the state House, then at thirty-seven settled in southwestern Oklahoma to be a farmer. The colossal Texas oil discoveries that began with Spindletop reached north Texas, just across the Red River from him, a decade later. He learned well the hard lessons of wildcatting, making and losing two separate fortunes in Oklahoma oil before moving to Texas in 1926. It was another oilman, A. D. "Doc" Lloyd, who persuaded Joiner that there must be oil near the town of Henderson in east Texas. Joiner kept at it for three years, using antiquated and worn-out equipment, raising more money by hook and crook, persevering after capping two dry holes, enduring the mockery of men who knew more about that than he did, including a Texaco man who looked at

Joiner's operation and said he would drink every barrel of oil to come out of that hole. On October 3, 1930, however, a gusher boomed out of Joiner's Daisy Bradford #3, and the East Texas Oil Field emerged. (It was Joiner's persistence that paid off, for while the pool of oil underlies five counties, it is long and narrow; many were the wildcatters who drilled ever so close to it but missed.) Joiner gained the nickname of "Dad" because it was he who discovered the East Texas Oil Field, but he had oversold stock and resorted to other sleight of hand to creditors who now came after him. Joiner volunteered to place his business in receivership and felt lucky to sell out his interest to a young oil tycoon from Dallas named Haroldson Lafayette (H. L.) Hunt Jr. for $1 million. In the end, Dad Joiner is considered the archetypical wildcatter not for his ultimate success (he died poor) but for the equanimity with which he accepted both the staggering success and the loss of everything that characterized the life of the independent driller.

How did H. L. Hunt fare in the business?

H. L. Hunt (1889–1974) was probably better suited to the oil business even than Joiner because he had a keener awareness of his abilities. Joiner could bet on a well, but Hunt always knew what the odds were. He was a skilled gambler. It was said that as a young manager of an Arkansas cotton plantation that suffered a flood, he turned his last $100 into $100,000 gambling in New Orleans. Back in Arkansas, he learned about the risks of wildcatting, as he made, ostentatiously squandered, and lost a fortune in oil around El Dorado. Acting on a tip, he investigated the stories of east Texas oil; to him, the geography was not just the oil and where it lay but who owned it and what his financial vulnerabilities were. In Dallas's Adolphus Hotel, Hunt met Dad Joiner over crackers and cheese and bought him out for $1 million.

Many people and some historians have felt that Hunt drove a cruelly hard bargain with Joiner, since the latter wound up in poverty and Hunt parlayed the East Texas field into billions. In fact, Hunt asked Joiner repeatedly whether he was sure he wished to unload his company (quite the opposite of the boiler room atmosphere of oil deals in that day). No doubt it was his offer to assume Joiner's liabilities that made the offer too good to refuse.

Hunt also enjoyed a vivid private life. He was a benefactor of fundamentalist education and a member of First Baptist Church in Dallas, but he also fathered at least fifteen children by three wives; he was also known to be bigamous. In the predatory environment of the petroleum

Oil tycoon H. L. Hunt managed to obtain ownership over most of the oil deposits in east Texas.

business, it seems inevitable that the politics of people involved in it should be as carnivorous as their eye toward competitors. Through the 1950s, Hunt sponsored two radio shows, through which he supported the anticommunist baiting of Senator Joseph McCarthy, and it was Hunt who placed the full-page advertisement in the *Dallas Morning News* excoriating President John F. Kennedy on the day before he was assassinated.

OUTLAWS AND LAWMEN

What turned Sam Bass into a train robber?

The early life of Sam Bass (1851–1878) was a perfect storm of circumstances that could lead a young man into a life of crime. Orphaned as a youth in Indiana, he ran away from the uncle who was raising him. Dissatisfied with labor at a Mississippi sawmill, he went to Texas with dreams of becoming a cowboy. Countless thousands did the same and, like most of them, he was quickly disillusioned by the realities of cow punching. He became a stable hand and freighter, developed an eye for horseflesh, and saw a ticket to easy and fun money in racing the fast horse he acquired. That worked for a while but proved to be self-limiting. He backed into crime by becoming a drover, collecting cattle from numerous others into one herd and taking them north to market. Instead of returning to pay off the owners, he and a partner lost the money gambling. He and a gang he fell in with practiced by robbing stagecoaches before they got lucky, hitting a Union Pacific train and making off with $60,000 in newly minted California gold coins. Bass got even luckier by making it back to Texas with his share as accomplices were killed and then mistook his luck for skill. He formed a new gang, which robbed four trains and two stages—all in the Dallas area—which made him a special target of both the Texas Rangers and Pinkertons. One member of Bass's gang was Jim Murphy, who had a sickly father, whom the Rangers seized and withheld medical treatment until Murphy agreed to act as an informant. When Bass planned to graduate to a bank robbery in Round Rock, Ranger John B. Jones was waiting with an ambush. Bass was wounded in the shootout on July 20, 1878, and died the following day, his twenty-seventh birthday.

When was west Texas's last train robbery?

On February 3, 1912, Ben Kilpatrick (the former Tall Texan of Butch Cassidy's Hole-in-the-Wall Gang), fresh out of ten years in prison, and an accomplice named Ole Hobek attempted to hold up the Southern Pacific near Sanderson. Express messenger David Trousdale managed to get hold of an ice mallet from a shipment of oysters, and when they were alone together in the express car, he whacked Hobek in the head and killed him. With Hobek's guns, Trousdale armed himself and two crewmen, who waited on Kilpatrick, who was holding the engineer hostage up front. In an hour, he came back to investigate and was sent on to the next world. Trousdale was showered with multiple rewards, while Kilpatrick and Hobek were buried together in one coffin. The grave of west Texas's last train robbers is in Sanderson.

Who were the most successful Texas outlaws?

Likely the strongest candidates are the Newton Boys, four brothers from and around Uvalde: Jess, Doc, Joe, and their leader, Willis. While bank and train robberies are usually thought of in a frontier setting, Willis Newton was first arrested in 1909 and robbed his first train in 1914, near Uvalde, getting away with some $4,700, which gave him an appetite for more. Willis robbed banks and stores through Texas and into Oklahoma and Kansas. In 1920 his brother Joe joined the gang, followed by Jess and Doc the following year, and they staged robberies as far away as Toronto, Ontario. In 1924 they took $3 million off a mail train they held up in Illinois, but it was one robbery too many. Although the Newton Boys were reckoned to have stolen more money than all other Texas outlaws put together, all four went to prison. They never killed anyone, so none were executed; all survived their prison terms and lived out their lives, mostly in the Uvalde area.

Who was the most prolific murderer in Texas history?

William Preston "Wild Bill" Longley (1851–1878) claimed that honor for himself. He was born in south-central Texas, too young to fight in the Civil War, and he came of age during Reconstruction in and around the town of Brenham, which was a focal point of hatred of occupation troops, freedmen, and the state police. Longley was seventeen when he began killing; he and two friends waylaid three black men near the Longley family farm in Lee County. They killed one named Green Evans and let the others escape as they emptied his pockets. Longley killed two more freed slaves—a man and a woman—the next year in Bastrop County. Longley's penchant for exaggerating his exploits began early, but he was bad enough that the occupying army placed a $1,000 bounty on his head, and he left Texas for Wyoming and South Dakota—far enough distant that he could claim all kinds of killing there, although records indicate only his joining the army and being imprisoned for desertion. He was back in Texas early in 1873, killed another freedman, and then committed the murder that brought him down. Longley's uncle blamed his son's death on Bill's childhood friend Wilson Anderson and asked Bill to kill him. On March 31, 1875, Anderson was plowing a field when Longley shotgunned him to death and fled the area. Two years and three murders later, Longley was arrested in Louisiana, returned to Texas, and convicted of Anderson's murder. Longley's boast that he had killed thirty-two men, if true, would place him at the top of the list as Texas's most productive killer. The true figure, however, as he is said to have once confessed, was a quarter of that number. Longley was hanged in Giddings on October 11, 1878, five days after his twenty-seventh birthday, before a crowd of thousands whom he addressed sensibly if not exactly contritely that he was not suited for life in the new and more civilized West.

Who was the meanest outlaw in Texas history?

If Wild Bill Longley lacked the truly black heart to be Texas's champion killer, one man who did possess the requisite narcissism and sociopathy was John Wesley Hardin (1853–1895). He was born in Bonham, in the northeast of the state, his father a Methodist circuit preacher. At fourteen, he stabbed a fellow student at his father's school; the following year, he shot and killed his uncle's former slave and then killed the three Union soldiers who came to his hideout to arrest him. Now a confirmed fugitive, Hardin left the state for the Indian Territory and Kansas, where his reputation as a quick-tempered killer was cemented. Most famously, he shot a man dead for snoring but in that instance, he fired through a wall at the sound of the snoring, so that death was reckless but accidental. Hardin returned to Texas in the fall of 1871, aged eighteen, as a hardened killer. He dispatched two state policemen sent to arrest him, then he killed widely despised Jack Helm, captain of the state police. Public opinion generally approved of those killings but turned against Hardin on May 26, 1874, when he murdered a popular deputy sheriff in Comanche who was not involved in any of the racial politics of Reconstruction. As Hardin's brother and two cousins were lynched for the killing, he fled with friends and other family to the border area be-

Gunfighter John Wesley Hardin was a sociopathic murderer whose victims included a man he killed just for snoring.

tween Florida and Alabama. It took more than three years, but in August 1877 ,Texas Rangers seized Hardin on a Florida train, returned him to Texas, and he served seventeen years of a twenty-five-year sentence for the killing. No doubt trading on his past as a preacher's kid, Hardin transformed himself into a model prisoner, even leading inmates in Sunday school, until he won a pardon and was set loose on the public once more. He set up a law practice in El Paso, far removed from his earlier haunts. There, he allegedly hired a shady lawman named Selman to kill his lover's husband; the deed being done, Hardin declined to pay up, for which Selman assassinated Hardin in a saloon on August 19, 1895. Estimates of Hardin's true body count vary from twenty-seven to forty-two, but whatever the figure, he was probably Texas's leading psychopath.

Is it true that Longley and Hardin once met?

Wild Bill Longley and John Wesley Hardin both came from fervently religious families and both were accomplished killers in their teens. According to a local newspaper, Hardin was about seventeen and Longley nineteen when they met by chance at a social gathering near Giddings. The two sat down for some gambling, and Hardin demonstrated a presage of his later skills by winning big. Longley took it in good part and the two went on together to a horse race, but Longley always kept an eye on Hardin and regarded him as something of a rival. His own claim was that he killed thirty-two men, two more than Hardin was popularly credited with, although there was sparse evidence to support Longley's figure, and he complained in widely read letters to newspapers that he was being put to death when Hardin only got twenty-five years and was pardoned.

Who was the Texas Ranger who actually captured John Wesley Hardin?

John B. Armstrong (1850–1913) came to Austin at twenty-one and entered Texas Ranger service in the Special Force, a unit commanded by Captain Leander McNelly and tasked with ending banditry and cattle rustling in south Texas. Ranger—soon Sergeant—Armstrong went about his duties in such a way as to become known as "McNelly's Bulldog." The Rangers stayed on Hardin's trail for three years, quietly collecting information. Armstrong had almost recovered from a gunshot wound when he was sent to Florida to bag him. In an incident that became Ranger legend, Armstrong boarded a train in Pensacola that contained Hardin and three attendants. Hardin saw him at once and had time only to say, "Texas, by God!" before Armstrong shot one of his accomplices, pistol-whipped Hardin senseless, and arrested the other two. (If Hardin's pistol had not become fouled in his suspenders, the story might have had a different outcome.) Although notable for Armstrong's personal bravery, the historical importance of capturing Hardin lies in a different area. Even as John B. Jones ushered the Rangers from Indian defense to civilian law enforcement, tracking down Hardin marked the Rangers' incorporation of modern detective techniques in getting their man.

What is the origin of the Texas Rangers' saying, "One riot, one Ranger"?

This is the most well-known motto attributed to the Rangers, but it is mostly apocryphal. In 1896, the Dallas sheriff sent for the Rangers to stop the impending but illegal prize fight between Pete Maher and Bob Fitzsimmons. When he met the train, he was alarmed that Captain Bill McDonald (1852–1918) was the only one to get off. When he asked where the others were, McDonald reportedly responded in astonishment, "Hell, ain't I enough? You only got one prize fight."

William Jesse McDonald's walleyed approach to enforcing the law shaped public perception of the Texas Rangers for decades. He was born in Mississippi, but his family was one of thousands who fled the ruined South for the opportunities in relatively unscathed Texas. His adult life began in a small way, as a grocer and an instructor of penmanship, but he found himself once he began chasing bad guys. Reckless of his personal safety in shootouts, he captured train robbers and cleaned out outlaw nests, and he rewarded himself by not being shy about a little self-promotion when he thought he deserved it. Governor Big Jim Hogg appointed him captain of Company B, Frontier Battalion in 1891, a position that he held for sixteen years. McDonald is also the likely source of the Rangers' other motto, almost as well known: "No man who is in the wrong can stand up against a fellow who is in the right and keeps on a'comin'." No wonder it was said of Captain Bill McDonald that he would charge hell with a bucket of water. He still had three bullets in him when he died in 1918.

What legendary Western con artist got his start in San Antonio?

In San Antonio, the neighborhood around South Flores Street is still known to long-time residents as Beantown, which is not a reference to Boston but to a late nineteenth-century shyster named Roy Bean. He made a dubious living butchering meat from cows of unknown origin and operating a dairy, and his reputation probably declined when one customer found a minnow in his milk. Eventually, Bean took advantage of the western railroad, leaving his wife and four children behind. He settled in a desolate Rio Grande Valley village called Vinegaroon (after a particularly large and nasty species of scorpion). He renamed it Langtry, after Lillie Langtry, the legendary beauty, actress, and mistress of the Prince of Wales. Bean was never able to entice her to visit his town, but she did offer to provide a decorative drinking fountain. Bean had to decline because, he said, water was the one drink that citizens of Langtry did not imbibe. Bean built a saloon, got himself elected county judge, and became Roy Bean, the Law West of the Pecos.

Bean held office until 1896. He was defeated in the 1886 election but held court anyway, explaining, "Once a justice, always a justice." The Texas Rangers gave Bean's regime further legitimacy, bringing prisoners to him for dispositions, as the nearest competent jurisdiction was 200 miles (322 kilometers) away. Bean ruled in cases beyond his authority. For instance, he granted divorces, which was the province of district courts. His reasoning was that since he was empowered to marry people, he must necessarily have the power to correct his errors.

Today, his Jersey Lilly saloon and court are found at the Judge Roy Bean Visitor Center, an essential tourist stop in San Antonio.

What is meant by "the town that was too mean for Bean"?

When he left San Antonio to establish himself as a rail line barkeeper on the route to El Paso, Roy Bean thought that Sanderson seemed a likely market. The town was started in 1881; it was halfway between San Antonio and El Paso and would not just be a whistle-stop, so they were building maintenance facilities and a roundhouse. Bean was too late, however. Already in possession of nearly all the town's lots was Uncle Charlie Wilson, owner of a saloon called the Cottage Bar. Unwilling to brook competition, Wilson

How many men did Roy Bean actually hang?

None. A lot of people confuse Roy Bean with the real "hanging judge," Isaac Parker of Fort Smith, Arkansas. Bean had larcenous instincts: once a corpse was found in town, whose pockets held forty dollars and a revolver, and Bean fined him forty dollars for carrying a concealed weapon. Bean famously classified cheating at cards to be "a hanging offense, if ketched," but condemned men were allowed to escape on the next train.

351

found a way to pour kerosene into Bean's stock of whiskey. That was too ruthless even for Bean's larcenous nature, and he retreated 60 miles (97 kilometers) back up the tracks to Vinegaroon and became the "Law West of the Pecos."

Who was the last man to be publicly hanged in Texas?

A crowd variously estimated at from four to ten thousand people gathered in Waco on July 30, 1923, to watch mass murderer Roy Mitchell be hanged. He was African American, and doubts have been raised about the justice of his trials. He had been arrested for gambling in his home, where police found evidence that they believed linked him to five murders in Cameron Park. Before the trial, Mitchell confessed to three assaults, four rapes, and six murders, but at the trial he recanted, alleging that the confessions had been tortured out of him. Although given an alibi by his wife in each case, his convictions were swift—including a sixth murder for which two other black men had already confessed. Mitchell confessed again on the gallows, and his last words were, "Good-bye, everybody." Waco had been in an unfavorable glare of national publicity over savage lynchings in 1916 and 1921 (one black victim and one white), and despite any legal irregularities, Waco considered the Mitchell case to be an advance for the city's black community, as the police were able to protect him from being lynched before he was hanged. Mitchell was not the last convict to swing in Texas. A month later, one Nathan Lee was executed in Angleton, but that was carried out in the privacy of the Brazoria County Courthouse. After this, the condemned were dispatched by electrocution.

What attracted Bonnie and Clyde to each other?

Clyde Barrow was from Teleco in the Valley. A small-time hoodlum and fifth-grade dropout, he was not much of a physical specimen; he was short, skinny, and dish-chested. When he met Bonnie Parker of Dallas in 1930, she was four feet, ten inches (1.47 meters) tall and weighed 85 pounds (38.5 kilograms), making him seem beefy in comparison. Although they reveled in the Robin Hoodish legend they created, they were united simply by their wild streak and their hatred for "John Law," and they knew that their liaison would end fatally. Evidence never made public by the Rangers made it certain that she was even more pathologically violent than he was. Their celebrity was vouchsafed as their dead bodies created a crush

Both native Texans, Bonnie Parker was born in Rowena, and Clyde Barrow was born in Ellis County. The story of the two murderous robbers has been romanticized in books and film.

of the curious in the Louisiana funeral home where they were taken, and their bullet-riddled car was picked clean for souvenirs. They were both buried in Dallas, but Bonnie's once expressed wish to be buried with Clyde was not honored.

Were Bonnie and Clyde really as cold-blooded as they were characterized by the authorities, or were they more like the folk heroes depicted in the 1968 movie?

Both, actually, for the capriciousness of their violence was part of their legend. Clyde Barrow, Bonnie Parker, and the others in their gang were essentially small-time hoods capable of occasional cold-blooded murder. There was nothing admirable about them. However, banks who foreclosed on the farms and homesteads of hapless citizens became viscerally hated by millions. Many people felt precious little sympathy for the institutions that had ruined so many lives, and indeed they felt a little vicarious thrill when they read about bank robberies. The world was better off when they died in a hail of bullets on May 23, 1934.

Was Texas Ranger Captain Frank Hamer really as sneaky and dishonorable as he was portrayed by Denver Pyle in the film *Bonnie and Clyde*?

In Texas, unlike most states, it is possible to libel the dead, and the family of Frank Hamer won a sizeable judgment against the producers of the film for their unflattering (and untrue) depiction of him. He had resigned from the Rangers over Ma Ferguson's corruption of the service but agreed to be recalled to track the duo.

Why did Frank Hamer come out of retirement to hunt down Bonnie and Clyde?

Frank Hamer (1884–1955) had an early exposure to Texas crime, being employed in his youth on a ranch owned by the brother of notorious outlaw Black Jack Ketchum. Oddly enough, law enforcement found Hamer rather than the other way around. He was still doing ranch work when he tracked down and captured a horse thief; the local sheriff noticed and pointed Hamer to the Texas Rangers, which he joined in 1906. At six foot three (1.9 meters) and maybe 230 pounds (104 kilograms), he was an intimidating figure, but his loyalty was to law and order more than to the Rangers themselves. He lasted only two years before resigning to become city marshal of Navasota for five years before becoming a private investigator and then deputy sheriff in Kimble County in the Hill Country.

He was back in the Rangers and heavily involved on the border during the troubles in 1915 before resigning again for special service with the Cattle Raisers Association, then became a U.S. government prohibition officer. On January 7, 1922, Hamer led eleven agents and Rangers in shooting their way into the Winter Garden, a notorious bootlegging nest in the lawless boomtown of Mexia. He turned the complex into a prison camp, into which he plugged some six hundred people he arrested; during a similar tear in the Panhandle boomtown of Border in 1926, he tied prisoners to a "trot-line" for area law officers to visit and pick out whomever they had charges on.

Texas's squeaky-clean governor, Pat Neff, who had sponsored the Mexia raid, was replaced by the helplessly corrupt Ma Ferguson, with her husband's desk abutting hers.   **353**

Protecting bootleggers was a substantial slice of their income. Their method was to award special Ranger commissions to hundreds of shady characters, who undertook not so much the suppression of bootlegging as, in several cases, getting control of the operations. Senior Captain Hamer was among the real Rangers who resigned from the force in disgust. When it became clear that apprehending Bonnie and Clyde would take a major effort, it was Lee Simmons, director of the state prison system, who suggested to Ma Ferguson that Hamer was the only man for the job and asked if she objected. When the governor said she had "nothing against him" for his quitting, Simmons talked Hamer back into special service. What was remarkable about his pursuit of Bonnie and Clyde was his adaptation of frontier trailing—sifting through their still-warm campsites, learning their brand of cigarettes and her color of lipstick—to modern police techniques.

OTHER NOTABLES

What famous Texans are remembered in Uvalde?

Uvalde was home to a U.S. vice president and a governor of Texas. When he ran for his first political office, Uvalde County judge John Nance Garner defeated a bold female suffragist, Ettie Rheiner. He was impressed, and he married her. He went on to serve fifteen terms in Congress, rising steadily until he became Speaker of the House in 1931, gaining fame for deals he could strike over poker and whiskey. He stepped down from power only two years later to be Franklin Roosevelt's running mate; the vice presidency was a job that he famously loathed, and FDR dismissed him after two terms of Garner's increasingly reluctant support. Although much of his story is preserved in his museum, his notes and memoranda would be more interesting if Ettie had not bowdlerized them after his death. (Nance famously said that the vice presidency "is not worth a bucket of warm piss," though for a long time, "spit" was the word used in the quote.) Later, the museum also took on the job of showing the life of Texas governor Dolph Briscoe, morphing the facility into the Briscoe-Garner Museum.

Who was La Porte's most famous resident?

Aside from the historic battleship USS *Texas*, La Porte's most famous resident was Sam Houston's second son, Andrew Jackson Houston (1854–1941), who for many years served as superintendent of the San Jacinto battleground. He was an avid amateur historian and spent tremendous effort in collecting the papers of his famous father, eventually amassing nearly five thousand of them, which he housed in his properties in La Porte. In 1941 at the age of eighty-six, Houston was appointed U.S. senator to replace Morris Sheppard, who died in office after serving just over twenty-eight years. Governor W. Lee "Pappy" O'Daniel really desired the post for himself and knew that Houston would not run in the special election to follow. Houston died just over two months later, and O'Daniel easily won election over Lyndon Johnson and the rest of a fractured ballot. After Houston's death, his daughters Ariadne and Marguerite took care of the Sam Houston papers until former governor Price Daniel and his wife (and their cousin), Jean Houston Daniel, convinced them to give the collection to the Texas State Archives. The Andrew Jackson Houston Collection is now one of the most important troves of Sam Houston papers in existence, although in the confusion after an earlier fire, a few hundred of the papers wound up in the Catholic Archives of Texas.

Governors and Presidents of Texas

Under Spain

Name	Years in Office
Domingo Terán de los Ríos	1691–1692
Gregorio de Salinas Varona	1692–1697
Francisco Cuerbo y Valdez	1698–1702
Mathías de Aguirre	1703–1705
Martín de Alarcón	1716–1719
Simón Padilla y Córdova	1708–1712
Pedro Fermín de Echevérs y Subisa	1712–1714
Juan Valdez	1714–1716
Martín de Alarcón	1716–1719
José de Azlor y, Marqués de Aguayo	1719–1722
Fernando Pérez de Almazán	1722–1727
Melchor de Media Villa y Azcona	1727–1730
Juan Antonio Bustillo y Ceballos	1730–1734
Manuel de Sandoval	1734–1736
Carlos Benitez Franquis de Lugo	1736–1737
Prudencio de Orobio y Basterra	1737–1741
Tomás Felipe de Winthuisen	1741–1743
Justo Boneo y Morales	1743–1744
Francisco García Larios	1744–1748
Pedro del Barrio Junco y Espriella	1748–1751
Jacinto de Barrios y Jáuregui	1751–1759
Angel Martos y Navarrete	1759–1766
Hugo Oconor	1767–1770
Juan Maria Vicencio, Barón de Ripperdá	1770–1778
Domingo Cabello y Robles	1778–1786
Bernardo Bonavia y Zapata	1786
Rafael Martinez Pacheco	1786–1790

Under Spain (continued)

Name	Years in Office
Manuel Muñoz	1790–c. 1798
José Irigoyen	1798–1800
Juan Bautista Elguézabal	1800–1805
Antonio Cordero y Bustamante	1805–1808
Manuel María de Salcedo	1808–1813
Juan Bautista Casas	1811
Cristóbal Domínguez	1814–1817 (1813–1814?)
Ignacio Pérez	1817 (1816–1817?)
Manuel Pardo	1817
Antonio Martínez	1817–1821

Under Mexico

Name	Years in Office
Antonio Martínez	1821–1822
José Félix Trespalacios	1822–1823
Luciano Garcia	1823–1824
Rafael Gonzales	1824–1826
José Ignacio de Arizpe	1826
Victor Blanco	1826–1827
José Ignacio de Arizpe	1827
José María Viesca y Montes	1827–1830
José María Letona	1831–1832
Rafael Eca y Músquiz	1832–1833
Juan Martín de Veramendi	1833
Juan José de Vidaurri y Villaseñor	1833–1834
Juan José Elguézabal	1834–1835
José María Cantú	1835
Marciél Borrego	1835
Augustín Viesca	1835
Miguel Falcón	1835
Bartolomé de Cardenas	1835
Rafael Eca y Músquiz	1835

Revolutionary Period

Name	Years in Office
Henry Smith	1835–1836

Presidents of the Republic of Texas

Name	Years in Office
David G. Burnet (ad-Interim)	1836
Sam Houston	1836–1838

Presidents of the Republic of Texas (continued)

Name	Years in Office
Mirabeau B. Lamar	1838–1841
Sam Houston	1841–1844
Anson Jones	1844–1846

Governors of the State of Texas

Name	Political Party	Years in Office
J. Pinckney Henderson		1846–1847
George T. Wood		1847–1849
Peter Hansbrough Bell		1849–1853
James Wilson Henderson		1853
Elisha Marshall Pease		1853–1857
Hardin Runnels	Democrat	1857–1859
Sam Houston	Independent	1859–1861
Edward Clark	Democrat	1861
Francis Richard Lubbock	Democrat	1861–1863
Pendleton Murrah	Democrat	1863–1865
Andrew Jackson Hamilton	(under military occupation)	1865–1866
James W. Throckmorton	(under military occupation)	1866–1867
Elisha Marshall Pease	(under military occupation)	1867–1869
Edmund J. Davis	(under military occupation, Republican)	1870–1874
Richard Coke	Democrat	1874–1876
Richard B. Hubbard	Democrat	1876–1879
Oran Milo Roberts	Democrat	1879–1883
John Ireland	Democrat	1883–1887
Lawrence Sullivan Ross	Democrat	1887–1891
James Stephen Hogg	Democrat	1891–1895
Charles A. Culberson	Democrat	1895–1899
Joseph Draper Sayers	Democrat	1899–1903
Samuel W. T. Lanham	Democrat	1903–1907
Thomas Mitchell Campbell	Democrat	1907–1911
Oscar Branch Colquitt	Democrat	1911–1915
James E. Ferguson	Democrat	1915–1917
William Pettus Hobby	Democrat	1917–1921
Pat Morris Neff	Democrat	1921–1925
Miriam Amanda (Ma) Ferguson	Democrat	1925–1927
Dan Moody	Democrat	1927–1931
Ross S. Sterling	Democrat	1931–1933
Miriam Amanda (Ma) Ferguson	Democrat	1933–1935
James V. Allred	Democrat	1935–1939
W. Lee (Pappy) O'Daniel	Democrat	1939–1941
Coke R. Stevenson	Democrat	1941–1947
Beauford H. Jester	Democrat	1947–1949
Allan Shivers	Democrat	1949–1957
Price Daniel	Democrat	1957–1963

Governors of the State of Texas (continued)

Name	Political Party	Years in Office
John Connally	Democrat	1963–1969
Preston Smith	Democrat	1969–1973
Dolph Briscoe	Democrat	1973–1979
William P. Clements	Republican	1979–1983
Mark White	Democrat	1983–1987
William P. Clements	Republican	1987–1991
Ann W. Richards	Democrat	1991–1995
George W. Bush	Republican	1995–2000
Rick Perry	Republican	2000–2015
Greg Abbott	Republican	2015–

Further Reading

GENERAL HISTORY

Calvert, Robert A., and Arnoldo de Leon. *The History of Texas*. 2nd edition. Wheeling, IL: Harlan Davidson, Inc.: 1996.

Campbell, Randolph B., et. al.: *Gone to Texas: A History of the Lone Star State*. New York: Oxford University Press, 2003.

Fehrenbach, T. R. *Lone Star: A History of Texas and the Texans*. New York: Macmillan, 1968.

Frantz, Joe B. *Texas: A History*. New York: W. W. Norton, 1984.

Glasrud, Bruce A., et. al., eds. *Discovering Texas History*. Norman: University of Oklahoma Press, 2014.

Haley, James L. *Passionate Nation: The Epic History of Texas*. New York: Free Press, 2006.

McComb, David G. *Texas: A Modern History*. Revised edition. Austin: University of Texas Press, 2010.

Richardson, Rupert N. *Texas: The Lone Star State*. 7th edition. Saddle River, NJ: Prentice Hall, 1997.

Tyler, Ron, Jesús F. de la Teja, and Paula Mitchell Marks. *Texas: Crossroads of North America*. Belmont, CA: Wadsworth Publishing, 2003.

OMNIBUS RESOURCES

Handbook of Texas On Line. https://tshaonline.org/handbook/search.

Portal to Texas History. https://texashistory.unt.edu.

Southwestern *Historical Quarterly*. https://texashistory.unt.edu/explore/collections/SWHQ/.

Texas Almanac. Dallas: Dallas Morning News, annual editions 1857–2017.

Texas Beyond History. https://www.texasbeyondhistory.net.

Natural History

Ajilvsgi, Geyata. *Wildflowers of Texas*. Bryan, TX: Shearer Publishing, 1984.

Bomar, George W. *Texas Weather*. Austin: University of Texas Press, 1983.

Cox, Mike. *Texas Disasters: True Stories of Tragedy and Survival*. Guilford, CT: Insiders Guide, 2006.

Niehaus, Theodore F. *A Field Guide to Southwestern and Texas Wildflowers*. Boston: Houghton Mifflin, 1984.

Spanish Period

Alamo de Parras. *The Second Flying Company of Alamo de Parras*. http://www.sonsof dewittcolony.org//adp/.

Chipman, Don. *Spanish Texas, 1519–1821*. 2nd edition. Austin: University of Texas Press, 2010.

Jackson, Jack. *Los Mesteños: Spanish Ranching in Texas, 1721–1821*. College Station: Texas A&M University Press, 1997.

John, Elizabeth A. H. *Storms Brewed in Other Men's Worlds: The Confrontation of Indians, Spanish, and French in the Southwest, 1540–1795*. College Station: Texas A&M University Press, 1975.

Austin and the Anglo Colonies

Cantrell, Gregg. *Stephen F. Austin: Empresario of Texas*. New Haven, CT: Yale University Press, 1999.

Jackson, Jack, and John Wheat, trans. *Almonte's Texas: Juan N. Almonte's 1834 Inspection, Secret Report & Role in the 1836 Campaign*. Austin: Texas State Historical Association, 2003.

Ramsay, Jack C. *Texas Sinners and Revolutionaries: Jane Long and Her Fellow Conspirators*. Plano, TX: Republic of Texas Press, 2001.

Texas Revolution

Brands, H. W. *Lone Star Nation: How A Ragged Army of Volunteers Won the Battle for Texas Independence—and Changed America*. New York: Doubleday, 2004.

Davis, William C. *Three Roads to the Alamo: The Lives and Fortunes of David Crockett, James Bowie, and William Barret Travis*. New York: HarperCollins, 1998.

Dimmick, Gregg J. *Sea of Mud: The Retreat of the Mexican Army after San Jacinto, an Archeological Investigation*. Austin: Texas State Historical Association, 2004.

Hardin, Stephen. *Texian Iliad: A Military History of the Texas Revolution, 1835–1836*. Austin: University of Texas Press, 1994.

Jordan, Jonathan. *Lone Star Navy: Texas, the Fight for the Gulf of Mexico, and the Shaping of the American West*. Washington: Potomac Books, 2006.

Lack, Paul W. *The Texas Revolutionary Experience: A Political and Social History, 1835–1836*. College Station: Texas A&M University Press, 1992.

Moore, Stephen L. *Eighteen Minutes: The Battle of San Jacinto and the Texas Independence Campaign*. Dallas: Republic of Texas Press, 2004.

Scheer, Mary L., ed. *Women and the Texas Revolution*. Denton: University of North Texas Press, 2012.

SAM HOUSTON

Friend, Llerena. *Sam Houston: The Great Designer*. Austin: University of Texas Press, 1954.

Haley, James L. *Sam Houston*. Norman: University of Oklahoma Press, 2002.

James, Marquis. *The Raven: A Biography of Sam Houston*. New York: Bobbs-Merrill, 1929.

THE ALAMO

Crisp, James E. *Sleuthing the Alamo: Davy Crockett's Last Stand and Other Mysteries of the Texas Revolution*. New York: Oxford University Press, 2005.

Donovan, James. *The Blood of Heroes: The 13-Day Struggle for the Alamo—and the Sacrifice that Forged a Nation*. New York: Little, Brown, 2012.

Groneman, Bill. *Eyewitness to the Alamo*. Revised edition. Plano, TX: Republic of Texas Press, 2001.

Matovina, Timothy M. *The Alamo Remembered: Tejano Accounts and Perspectives*. Austin: University of Texas Press, 1995.

Tinkle, Lon. *Thirteen Days to Glory: The Siege of the Alamo*. New York: McGraw Hill, 1958.

Wallis, Michael. *David Crockett: The Lion of the West*. New York: W. W. Norton, 2012.

THE REPUBLIC OF TEXAS

Hogan, William Ransom. *The Texas Republic: A Social and Economic History*. Norman: University of Oklahoma Press, 1946.

Kemp, Louis Wiltz. *The Signers of the Texas Declaration of Independence*. Houston: Anson Jones Press, 1944.

Nance, Joseph Milton. *After San Jacinto: The Texas-Mexican Frontier, 1836–1841*. Austin: University of Texas Press, 1963.

Weems, John Edward. *Dream of Empire: A Human History of the Republic of Texas, 1836–1846*. New York: Simon & Schuster, 1976.

FRONTIER TEXAS

Carlson, Paul H., and Tom Crum. *Myth, Memory, and Massacre: The Pease River Capture of Cynthia Ann Parker*. Lubbock: Texas Tech University Press, 2010

Graham, Don. *Kings of Texas: The 150-Year Saga of an American Ranching Empire*. New York: Wiley, 2004.

Haley, J. Evetts. *The XIT Ranch of Texas and the Early Days of the Llano Estacado*. New edition. Norman: University of Oklahoma Press, 1953.

Leckie, William H. *The Military Conquest of the Southern Plains*. Norman: University of Oklahoma Press, 1963.

Lich, Glen E. *The German Texans*. San Antonio: Institute of Texan Cultures, 1981.

McCoy, Dorothy Abbott. *Texas Ranchmen: Twenty Texans Who Help Build Today's Cattle Industry*. Austin: Eakin Press, 1987.

Pearce, W. M. *The Matador Land and Cattle Company*. Norman: University of Oklahoma Press, 1964.

Robinson, Charles M., III. *Frontier Forts of Texas*. Houston: Gulf Publishing, 1986.

Utley, Robert M. *Lone Star Justice: The First Century of the Texas Rangers*. New York: Oxford University Press, 2002.

TEXAS AND THE CIVIL WAR

Cantrell, Gregg. *An Empire for Slavery: The Peculiar Institution in Texas, 1821–1865*. Baton Rouge: Louisiana State University Press, 1989.

Clark, James Lemuel, and L. D. Clark, ed. *Civil War Recollections of James Lemuel Clark*. College Station: Texas A&M University Press, 1984.

Fornell, Earl Wesley. *The Galveston Era: The Texas Crescent on the Eve of Secession*. Austin: University of Texas Press, 1961.

Pickering, David, and Judy Falls. *Brush Men and Vigilantes: Civil War Dissent in Texas*. College Station: Texas A&M University Press, 2000.

INDIAN WARS

Gwynne, S. C. *Empire of the Summer Moon: Quanah Parker and the Rise and Fall of the Comanches*. New York: Simon & Schuster, 2010.

Haley, James L. *The Buffalo War: The History of the Red River Indian Uprising of 1874–1875*. New York: Doubleday, 1976.

Leckie, William H. *The Buffalo Soldiers: A Narrative of Negro Cavalry in the West*. Norman: University of Oklahoma Press, 1967.

———. *The Military Conquest of the South Plains*. Norman: University of Oklahoma Press, 1963.

Nye, Wilbur Sturtevant. *Carbine and Lance: The Story of Old Fort Sill*. Norman, University of Oklahoma Press, 1937.

MODERN TEXAS

Green, George Norris. *The Establishment in Texas Politics: The Primitive Years, 1938–1957*. Norman: University of Oklahoma Press, 1979.

Haley, James L. *Texas: From Spindletop Through World War II*. New York: St. Martin's, 1994.

Martin, Roscoe. *The People's Party in Texas: A Study in Third-Party Politics*. Austin: University of Texas Press, 1933.

Olien, Roger. *Black Gold: The Story of Texas Oil & Gas*. San Antonio: Historical Publishing Network, 2004.

———. *From Token to Triumph: The Texas Republicans since 1920*. Dallas: Southern Methodist University Press, 1982.

———., and Diana Davids Olien. *Wildcatters: Texas Independent Oilmen*. Austin: Texas Monthly Press, 1984.

Spratt, John Stricklin. *The Road to Spindletop: Economic Change in Texas 1875–1901*. Austin: University of Texas Press, 1955.

HERITAGE, LIFE, AND CULTURE

Atwood, E. Bagby. *The Regional Vocabulary of Texas*. 2nd edition. Austin: University of Texas Press, 1969.

Awbrey, Betty Dooley, and Claude Dooley. *Why Stop? A Guide to Texas Historical Roadside Markers*. 3rd edition. Houston: Gulf Publishing, 1978.

Baker, T. Lindsay, *Ghost Towns of Texas*. Revised edition. Norman: University of Oklahoma Press, 1991.

Blevins, Don. *A Priest, A Prostitute, and Some Other Early Texans: The Lives of Fourteen Lone Star State Pioneers*. Guilford, CT: Twodot, 2008.

Dingus, Anne. *The Dictionary of Texas Misinformation*. Austin: Texas Monthly Press, 1987.

Elliott, Alan C. *Texas Ingenuity: Lone Star Inventions, Inventors & Innovators*. Charleston, SC: The History Press, 2010.

Hood, R. Maurice, M.D., ed. *Early Texas Physicians, 1830–1915*. Austin: State House Press, 1999.

Hubbard, George U. *The Humor and Drama of Early Texas*. Plano, TX: Republic of Texas Press, 2003.

Jordan, Terry G. *Texas Log Buildings: A Folk Architecture*. Austin: University of Texas Press, 1978.

Marks, Paula Mitchell, and Walle Conoly. *Hands to the Spindle: Texas Women and Home Textile Production, 1822–1880*. College Station: Texas A&M University Press, 1996.

McComb, David G. *Spare Time in Texas: Recreation and History in the Lone Star State*. Austin: University of Texas Press, 2008.

McQueary, Carl R. *Dining at the Governor's Mansion*. College Station: Texas A&M University Press, 2003.

Porterfield, Bill. *The Greatest Honky-Tonks in Texas*. Dallas: Taylor Publishing, 1983.

Reusch, Ed, ed., et. al. *Texas on Ice: Early Strides to Pro Hockey*. Dallas: Brown Books, 2016.

Teague, Wells. *Calling Texas Home: A Lively Look at What It Means to Be a Texan*. Berkeley, CA: Wildcat Canyon Press, 2000.

Tolbert, Frank X. *A Bowl of Red, Being a Natural History of Chili con Carne*. New York: Doubleday, 1953.

———. *Tolbert's Texas* Garden City, NY: Doubleday, 1983.

Vernon, Walter N., et. al. *The Methodist Excitement in Texas: A History*. Dallas: Texas United Methodist Historical Society, 1984.

Waters, Michael R., et. al. *Lone Star Stalag: German Prisoners of War at Camp Hearne*. College Station: Texas A&M University Press, 2004.

Index

Note: (ill.) indicates photos and illustrations.

369

382